INTERNET MARKETING FOR INFORMATION TECHNOLOGY COMPANIES

Second Edition

Other Titles of Interest From Maximum Press

Internet Marketing for Your Tourism Business: Sweeney, 1-885068-47-6

Marketing With E-Mail, Second Edition: Kinnard, 1-885068-51-4

Business-to-Business Internet Marketing, Fourth Edition: Silverstein, 1-885068-72-7

Marketing on the Internet, Fifth Edition: Zimmerman, 1-885068-49-2

101 Internet Businesses You Can Start From Home: Sweeney, 1-885068-59-X

The e-Business Formula for Success: Sweeney, 1-885068-60-3

101 Ways to Promote Your Web Site, Third Edition: Sweeney, 1-885068-57-3

Internet Marketing for Less Than $500/Year, Second Edition: Yudkin, 1-885068-69-7

The Business Guide to Selling Through Internet Auctions: Hix, 1-885068-73-5

Exploring IBM Technology, Products & Services, Fourth Edition: Hoskins, 1-885068-62-X

Exploring IBM RS/6000 Computers, Tenth Edition: Davies, 1-885068-42-5

Exploring IBM @server iSeries and AS/400 Computers, Tenth Edition: Hoskins, Dimmick, 1-885068-43-3

Exploring IBM @server xSeries and PCs, Eleventh Edition: Hoskins, Wilson, 1-885068-39-5

Exploring IBM @server zSeries and S/390 Computers, Seventh Edition: Hoskins, Frank, 1-885068-70-0

Building Intranets With Lotus Notes and Domino 5.0: Krantz, 1-885068-41-7

Exploring IBM Network Stations: Ho, Lloyd, & Heracleous, 1-885068-32-8

Exploring IBM e-Business Software: Young, 1-885068-58-1

For more information, visit our Web site at *www.maxpress.com* or e-mail us at *moreinfo@maxpress.com*

INTERNET MARKETING FOR INFORMATION TECHNOLOGY COMPANIES

Second Edition

Proven Online Techniques to Increase Sales and Profits for Hardware, Software and Networking Companies

Barry Silverstein

MAXIMUM PRESS
605 Silverthorn Road
Gulf Breeze, FL 32561
(850) 934-0819
www.maxpress.com

Publisher: Jim Hoskins

Manager of Finance/Administration: Joyce Reedy

Production Manager: ReNae Grant

Cover Design: Lauren Smith Designs

Compositor: PageCrafters Inc.

Copyeditor: Ellen Faulk

Proofreader: Jacquie Wallace

Indexer: Susan Olason

Printer: P.A. Hutchinson

This publication is designed to provide accurate and authoritative information in regard to the subject matter covered. It is sold with the understanding that the publisher is not engaged in rendering professional services. If legal, accounting, medical, psychological, or any other expert assistance is required, the services of a competent professional person should be sought. ADAPTED FROM A DECLARATION OF PRINCIPLES OF A JOINT COMMITTEE OF THE AMERICAN BAR ASSOCIATION AND PUBLISHERS.

Recognizing the importance of preserving what has been written, it is a policy of Maximum Press to have books of enduring value published in the United States printed on acid-free paper, and we exert our best efforts to that end.

Library of Congress Cataloging-in-Publication Data

Silverstein, Barry, 1948-

  Internet marketing for information technology companies: proven online techniques to increase sales and profits for hardware, software and networking companies / Barry Silverstein. -- 2nd ed.

      cm.

  ISBN 1-885068-67-0 (alk. paper)

  1. Internet marketing. 2. Information technology--Marketing--Computer network resources. 3. Computers--Marketing--Computer network resources. 4. Computer software--Marketing--Computer network resources. 5. Computer engineering--Marketing--Computer network resources. I. Title.

  HF5415.1265 .S5353 2001

  658.8'4—dc21

                          2001003632

To IT Marketers Everywhere

Praise for *Internet Marketing for Information Technology Companies*

"The examples in this book are extremely telling—and the history and description of the Internet surge is a perfect backdrop to motivate marketing managers to move faster. . . if they want to stay in business. Barry Silverstein will convince you that direct marketing will never be the same, and that's a good thing. There are tons of tips and techniques that will slightly change your approach—and greatly change your results."

Ann Schuster
Former Director, Americas Marketing
GE Global eXchange Services

"This book is relevant to a much wider audience than just the high technology companies it uses as examples. What I particularly liked is the realization that the Internet doesn't stand alone—rather it is part of a larger direct marketing solution. Barry Silverstein supports my belief that the context is larger than the Internet. He uses such compelling phrases as 'intersecting points' and 'combining the best of traditional media with the Internet' in a way that will surely help marketers make it to the next level less painfully than they might otherwise."

Richard Hochhauser
President
Harte-Hanks, Inc.

"Straightforward and powerful, this book is a must read whether you're a novice or seasoned veteran. Real life examples and practical applications illustrate the keys to marketing success for all technology companies. Barry Silverstein takes direct marketing techniques and cleverly migrates many of the proven success factors, mapping these to the Internet. This is one resource that should be used by all members in your marketing department."

Maureen Daniell
Director of Marketing
Siebel Systems, Inc.

Acknowledgments

Thanks go to:

- my agency's clients, who have provided me with the ability to continuously learn and to hone my craft

- my agency's employees, who make Directech | eMerge a very special place to work

- my professional associates, who have offered me valued guidance and counsel

- Anne Holland, publisher of MarketingSherpa.com, for allowing me to use material from the excellent case studies and other information provided by the e-newsletter, B2BMarketingBiz

- Josh Silverstein, for his invaluable research and editorial assistance

- and my family, especially Sharon, for their on-going support and love.

Disclaimer

The purchase of computer software or hardware is an important and costly business decision. Although the author and publisher of this book have made reasonable efforts to ensure the accuracy and timeliness of the information contained herein, the author and publisher assume no liability with respect to loss or damage caused or alleged to be caused by reliance on any information contained herein and disclaim any and all warranties, expressed or implied, as to the accuracy or reliability of said information.

This book is not intended to replace the manufacturer's product documentation or personnel in determining the specifications and capabilities of the products mentioned in this book. The manufacturer's product documentation should always be consulted, as the specifications and capabilities of computer hardware and software products are subject to frequent modification. The reader is solely responsible for the choice of computer hardware and software. All configurations and applications of computer hardware and software should be reviewed with the manufacturer's representatives prior to choosing or using any computer hardware and software.

Trademarks

The words contained in this text that are believed to be trademarked, service marked, or otherwise to hold proprietary rights have been designated as such by use of initial capitalization. No attempt has been made to designate as trademarked or service marked any personal computer words or terms in which proprietary rights might exist. Inclusion, exclusion, or definition of a word or term is not intended to affect, or to express judgement upon, the validity of legal status of any proprietary right that may be claimed for a specific word or term.

Foreword

The last few years bear witness to many changes wrought by the Internet and new Web-centric business processes, and evidence of that dramatic growth can be seen from Wall Street to mainstream media. Although the Internet's growth so far has been impressive, we have yet to see the true impact of this new channel on big business. To date, much of the Internet market has focused on the business-to-consumer market. It is true that the Internet is shaking the foundations of traditional retail, yet it is the business-to-business Internet market that represents the largest opportunity yet. Specifically, the B-to-B Internet market is expected to grow to at least five times the size of the Internet retail market over the next five years.

This fact is of great significance to information technology (IT) companies, which increasingly are focusing their marketing efforts on the business buyer. It is a common misconception that traditional IT companies are often the first to embrace new technologies such as the Internet for use in their marketing strategies. Indeed, many IT marketers struggle to understand how to best use the Internet as a marketing, communication, and selling channel. But today's IT marketers must understand how to leverage the power of the Web to attract and retain customers. This channel is invaluable to building and maintaining strong business relationships and communicating corporate branding messages. Those IT companies that are not already using the Web to communicate with customers will struggle to gain back that customer attention from competitors that have moved faster toward the Web.

But the Internet offers much more than just increased customer commerce and communication opportunities. In fact, the Internet provides an opportunity for significant cost savings in marketing and business processes. Our research shows that Internet marketing can cost up to 65 percent less than traditional direct marketing. Additionally, the flexibility of the Web allows for real-time control over marketing messages, as well as feedback from customers. Migrating customer services processes over to the Web through new Web-based Customer Relationship Management (CRM) systems is yet another way the Internet provides cost savings and increased business efficiencies.

The cost benefit of Internet marketing is particularly relevant to information technology marketers. Many IT companies have already significantly reduced the marketing cost of software and technical documentation distribution via CD-ROM. Now they are even more dramatically cutting that marketing expense by distributing information and products via the Internet. Many software companies are offering "try-before-you-buy" promotions through their Web sites, allowing customers to experience the product before the sale. The use of e-mail as a promotional channel is providing double-digit response rates throughout the e-business world. This low-cost, high-return promotional channel is proving very popular with leading Internet marketers.

Perhaps the most compelling benefit for IT companies, however, is e-commerce. The Web provides a much more streamlined environment for selling products. IT companies can both sell and deliver software, and potentially services, online. In the business-to-business market in particular, buyer–seller marketplaces are already reshaping the way business is conducted. Smaller companies now have access to formerly out-of-reach large potential partners. Market incumbents, such as the yellow pages companies, now face serious competition for the first time online.

However, as today's business market moves full-speed ahead into embracing the e-business phenomenon, there still are many challenges. Online marketers will have to navigate privacy issues very carefully, as more and more personal information becomes available through the Web environment. E-commerce systems will need to be integrated seamlessly with back-end legacy systems to provide customers a consistent message across all marketing and sales channels. This process requires not only Web-based integration, but often an overhaul of the overall marketing process to help integrate the real-time nature of the Internet with existing stores, customer service centers, and traditional marketing messages. And finally, online marketers will need to pay close attention to the security of both public and privately accessed sites.

Despite these near-term challenges, the opportunities in Internet marketing cannot be overlooked. The Internet is the holy grail of direct marketers, and any IT marketer who wants to achieve success must view the Web as a *central marketing channel*. The arsenal of any top marketer is incomplete without a true understanding of how to leverage the Web as a customer channel. Those IT marketers who today understand the strategic value of Internet marketing will own the future.

Melissa Bane
Director, Internet Market Strategies
The Yankee Group

Table of Contents

Introduction xxv
    About This Book xxix
    Your "Members-Only" Web Site xxx

Chapter 1:
How IT Marketers Can Put the Internet to Work   1

    The Internet Business Imperative 2
        The Wired World 4
        Intranets and Extranets 7
        The True Impact of the Internet on the IT Company 8
            Hardware 9
            Software 11
            Networking 11
            Service Companies and Resellers 12
            The Dot Coms 13
        Why All the Marketing Excitement about the Internet? 14
            The Internet Is Boundless 14
            The Internet Makes Global Marketing a Reality 15
            The Internet Reaches People with
                Intellect, Power, and Money 16
            The Internet Offers Increased Business Penetration 17
            The Internet Provides a Unique Form
                of Communications Intimacy 19
            The Internet Changes the Economics of Marketing 20
            The Internet Establishes a Brand New Sales Channel 20
    The Key Areas of Internet Marketing for IT Companies 22

Chapter 2:
How IT Marketers Can Benefit
from the New Direct Marketing   23

    How Direct Marketing Is Being Transformed 24
        The Internet Address Is the New 800 Number 26
        The Internet Is the Future of IT Marketing 26

Moving into the Future Means Transitioning Now *28*
Where Are IT Marketers Really Headed? *30*
Going Global: How Internet Marketing Can Create
a Worldwide Business for IT Companies 31
The Worldwide Impact of the Internet *33*
Expanding Markets and Territories 36
Developing Global Marketing Partnerships 37
Providing Worldwide Customer Service 37
Approach Global Marketing with Caution *37*
The New Response Model: "Intersponding" 39
The Web Defies Logic *39*
Call It "Intersponding" *41*

Chapter 3:
Making the Most of Your Web Site   46

Using Your Web Site for Lead
Generation and Qualification 47
How an IT Company Built a "Cool"
Web Site That Didn't Work *48*
A Word about ".com" *49*
Seize the Opportunity to Set Your Web Site Apart *49*
Incorporate Direct Marketing Techniques into Your Web Site. *50*
Characteristics of Effective Marketing Web Sites *52*
Compelling, Well-Designed Home Page 52
Timely Updating 52
Intuitive Navigational Flow 53
High-Value Information Content 54
Fast Response Time 54
Response Orientation 54
Respect for Privacy 55
What You'll Get When You "Follow the Rules" *56*
A Baker's Dozen of IT Web Sites to Explore *56*
Apple (*www.apple.com*) 56
Beyond.com (*www.beyond.com*) 57
Cisco Systems (*www.cisco.com*) 57
Dell Computer *(www.dell.com)* 57
Hewlett-Packard (*www.hp.com*) 58
IBM (*www.ibm.com*) 58
Macromedia (*www.macromedia.com*) 58
McAfee Associates (*www.mcafee.com*) 59

Microsoft (*www.microsoft.com*) and Microsoft
Network (*www.msn.com*) 59
Oracle Corporation (*www.oracle.com*) 59
Siebel Systems (*www.siebel.com*) 60
Sun Microsystems (*www.sun.com*) 60
WorldCom (*www.worldcom.com*) 60
How Do You Get Repeat Visitors to Your Web Site? 60
Automated E-mail Response 61
Cookies 61
Databases and Personalization 62
Interactivity and Multimedia 63
A Technology Trick for Blocking Web Site Access 64
How Do You Measure the Direct Marketing
Effectiveness of Your Web Site? 64
Creating "Mini-Sites" 65
Mini-Site Helps Launch a New Product 66
Mini-site Promotes Special Offers 66
Mini-Site Transitions Customers 67
The Sponsored Site 67
Using Web Response Forms 69
*Web Response Forms Tighten the
Lead Capture and Qualification Process* 71
The Basics of Constructing Web Response Forms 72
Employing Web Site Links to Generate Leads 75
Free Links 75
Paid Links 77

Chapter 4:
Using Search Engines and Newsgroups   78

How to Gain Visibility on the Internet 79
Using Search Engines 79
Image Maps 80
Don't Try to Trick the Search Engines 80
Meta Refresh 81
How to Get Found with Directories 82
Keywords Are of Key Importance 82
Submitting Your Site to Spiders and Crawlers 85
Learn from Competitor Sites 86
Marketing Implications of Page Titles 87
Meta-Tags 88

Using Submission Services 88
Top Search Engines and Directories 89
   www.about.com 89
   www.altavista.com 90
   www.ask.com 91
   www.directhit.com 92
   www.excite.com 92
   www.google.com 92
   www.hotbot.com 92
   www.lycos.com 92
   www.northernlight.com 93
   www.yahoo.com 93
Using Newsgroups for Internet Marketing 93
   Basic Rules 96
      Keep to the Newsgroup Topic 96
      Stay on the Thread 96
      Make a Contribution 97
      Do Not Post Commercials 97
      You Don't Have to Have the Last Word 97
      Use a Signature File if Appropriate 97
   Start Your Own Newsgroup 97
      Request for Discussion 97
      Vote 98
      Result 98

Chapter 5:
The Ins and Outs of E-mail   99

Why E-mail Is So Attractive 100
Integrating E-mail into Your Marketing Programs 102
   Inbound E-mail 102
   Outbound E-mail 103
   Limit Your Risk 105
      Always Ask Permission to Send E-mail 105
      Always Provide the Recipient with
         the Ability to "Opt Out" 106
      Be Very Cautious if You Choose to Share, Sell, or
         Rent a List of Your Own E-mail Addresses 106
   Building Your Own E-mail List 107
   Opt-in E-mail 107
   Effective Use of Outbound E-mail 109

Customer Communications 110
Follow-ups 110
Major Announcements or Alerts 111
Serial E-mail 111
E-mail Newsletters 111
E-mail and Online Surveys 115
E-mail Discussion Groups 116
Making E-mail Work Harder 117
The Rise of HTML E-mail 118
E-mail Innovations are on the Way 118
What about Viral Marketing? 120
Automated E-mail Response 121
Other Important Facts about E-mail 122

Chapter 6:
Internet Advertising and Public Relations   124

Creating and Placing Online Advertising 125
How Effective Is Banner Advertising? 127
Will Rich Media "Save" Banner Advertising? 130
Best Practices in Online Advertising 131
Online Ad Placement Is Critically Important 136
Other Important Facts about Online Advertising 139
Newsletter Sponsorships: For IT Marketers,
    It Could Be the Better Way to Advertise 140
Advertising Tip: Don't Forget Those
    Search Engines and Directories 142
Incentive Programs: Another Form of Online Advertising 142
ClickRewards *(www.clickrewards.com)* 143
Flooz *(www.flooz.com)* 143
MyPoints *(www.mypoints.com)* 143
Online Advertising Is Undergoing
    Continuous Innovation 144
Public Relations on the Internet 145
PR Opportunities on IT Sites 147
CMPnet *(www.cmpnet.com)* 147
C|Net *(www.cnet.com)* 147
Internet.com *(www.internet.com)* 147
IDG.net *(www.idg.net)* 147
ZDnet (www.zdnet.com) 147
Using the Internet for PR Campaigns 148

Chapter 7:
Internet Events and Meetings 149

Are Live Events Good Marketing Investments? 149
   The Typical Seminar Series 151
The Net Event 153
      Analysis of Live Seminar Program versus
      Online Seminar Program 155
   Replacement or Enhancement? 156
   An Online Seminar Success Story 157
   Who Is Using Online Seminars Effectively? 159
      AXENT (*www.symantec.com*) 159
      Centra BCN (Business Collaboration Network)
      (*www.centranow.com*) 161
      Cisco Systems (*www.cisco.com*) 161
      ITWorld (*www.itworld.com/webcasts*) 162
      Oracle Internet Seminars (*www.oracle.com/iseminars/*)
      and Oracle eBusiness Network (*www.oracle.com/*
      ebusinessnetwork) 162
      Placeware Seminars (*www.placeware.com/seminar*) 162
      Microsoft Multimedia Central
      (*www.microsoft.com/seminar*) 163
   The Net Event Is Not Without Technological Challenges 163
   Types of Internet Events 167
      The Online Trade Show 167
      The Online Seminar or Presentation 167
      The Online "Webcast" 168
      The Online Meeting 168
      The Online Chat 168
   "Crossing Over" with Online Events 169
   Developing and Hosting the Internet Event 169
   Guidelines for Developing and Hosting
   Your Own Internet Event 170
      Plan Your Event 170
      Develop the Event 171
      Critical Success Factors 171
      Establish a Structure for the Event 172
      Create the Content for the Event 173
      Research and Add Appropriate Technologies 173
      Determine How the Event Will Be Hosted 174

Program and Test the Event 175
Promote the Event.. 175
Evaluate the Results 176
Promoting Events Using the Internet 176
Promoting the Net Event 180
Holding Online Marketing Meetings 181
Using Distance Learning for Marketing 182

Chapter 8:
Internet Fulfillment   185

Traditional Fulfillment: An Aging Process 185
The Transformation of Traditional Fulfillment 187
Direct Mail 188
Fax 188
Telephone 189
The Electronic Fulfillment Difference 189
Means of Electronic Fulfillment 193
"Pulling" the Prospect to You 193
The Web Response Area 193
The Web Site 194
E-mail 194
"Pushing" Information to the Prospect 195
Some Interesting Variations on Pushing Information 198
The Unique Benefits of Fulfillment on the Internet 200
Acknowledgment 200
Confirmation 200
"Instant" Fulfillment 201
Instant Online Help 203
Moving to Web-based Information Dissemination 204
HTML Pages 205
XML 206
PDFs 206
The CD/Web Connection 209
The Kiosk/Web Connection 210
Future Information Dissemination Channels 211
Creating Online Demos and Trials 212
Order E-Fulfillment and Distributing
Live Products over the Internet 214
E-Fulfillment Resources and Services 216

DHL (www.dhlmasterclass.com) 216
FedEx (www.fedex.com) 216
MarketFirst (www.marketfirst.com) 216
MarketSoft (www.marketsoft.com) 216
NetQuartz (www.netquartz.com) 217
Netship (www.netship.com) 217
SubmitOrder (www.submitorder.com) 217
UPS (www.ups.com) 218

Chapter 9:
Internet Customer Service   219

Building Better Customer Relationships 220
Using the Internet to Learn What Customers Want 222
   Maintaining Ongoing Relationships
   with Your Most Valued Customers 222
   Moving Your Customers Up the "Marketing Pyramid" 224
   Internet-Based Customer Service 227
      Aspect *(www.aspect.com)* 227
      ATG *(www.atg.com)* 228
      BEA *(www.beasys.com)* 228
      Bowstreet *(www.bowstreet.com)* 229
      Brightware *(www.brightware.com)* 229
      Broadvision *(www.broadvision.com)* 229
      ePage *(www.epage.com)* 229
      E.piphany *(www.epiphany.com)* 229
      eShare Technologies *(www.eshare.com)* 230
      Kana *(www.kana.com)* 230
      LivePerson *(www.liveperson.com)* 230
      NativeMinds *(www.nativeminds.com)* 231
      Net Effect *(www.neteffect.com)* 231
      Net Perceptions *(www.netperceptions.com)* 232
      PeopleSupport *(www.peoplesupport.com)* 232
      Revenio *(www.revenio.com)* 232
      Teradata CRM *(www.teradata.com)* 232
   Internet Telephony and Customer Service 232
Moving to the One-to-One Customer Relationship 234
   The Personalization Phenomenon 236
Five Ideas for Building a One-to-One
Customer Relationship Program 238

Treat Customers Like Prospects 238
Ask Customers What They Want—and Give It to Them 239
Explore New and Innovative Ways
    to Encourage and Reward Customers 240
Recognize the Differences between Classes of Customers—
    and Treat Customer Classes Differently 241
Make One-to-One Fun 241
Building Customer-Driven Extranets 242
A Checklist for Developing Customer Extranets 245
Note 246

Chapter 10:
Internet Communities and Exchanges   247

What Is an Internet Community? 248
Types of Communities 249
Online Service Providers 249
Portals and "Vortals" 251
Auctions 253
    eBay (*www.ebay.com*) 253
    DoveBid (*www.dovebid.com*) 254
    Egghead (*www.egghead.com*) 254
    FairMarket (*www.fairmarket.com*) 254
    FreeMarkets (*www.freemarkets.com*) 255
    Online Asset Exchange
        (*www.onlineassetexchange.com*) 255
    Priceline (*www.priceline.com*) 255
    TradeOut (*www.tradeout.com*) 255
Information Technology Supersites 256
    CMPnet (*www.cmpnet.com*) 256
    C|Net (*www.cnet.com*) 258
    IDG.net (*www.idg.net*) 258
    Internet.com (*www.internet.com*) 258
    TechTarget (*www.techtarget.com*) 259
    ZDnet (*www.zdnet.com*) 259
Other Business Communities 259
Business Communities and Exchanges 260
    BizProLink (*www.bizprolink.com*) 260
    CommunityB2B (*www.communityb2b.com*) 260
    ConcertGlobalMarket (*www.concertglobalmarket.net*) . 260

Converge (*www.converge.com*) 260
Covisint (*www.covisint.com*) 261
e2open.com (*www.e2open.com*) 261
Exportall (*www.exportall.com*) 261
GE Industrial Systems EliteNet (*www.geindustrial.com*) 261
Manufacturing.net (*www.manufacturing.net*) 262
Office.com (*www.office.com*) 262
Oracle Exchange (*www.oracle.com*) 262
PeopleSoft Marketplace
   (*www.peoplesoftmarketplace.com*) 262
VerticalNet (www.verticalnet.com) 262
Yahoo! Industry Marketplaces
   (*industrymarketplaces.yahoo.com*) 264
Becoming Part of a Community 264
Find the Right Communities 264
Narrow Your Options 265
Which Free Services Are Offered? 265
What Opportunities for Free Publicity Exist? 265
What Opportunities for Paid Advertising
   and Promotion Are Available? 266
Should You Build a Sponsored Community? 267
The Use of Sponsored Communities by
   IT Companies Is Growing 268
Tools to Help You Build a Community or Exchange 269
Ariba (*www.ariba.com*) 269
Comercis (*www.comercis.com*) 269
Commerce One (*www.commerceone.com*) 269
Delphi (*www.delphi.com*) 270
Excite (*www.excite.com*) 270
Involv (*www.involv.net*) 270
Participate.com (*www.participate.com*) 270
PurchasePro (*www.purchasepro.com*) 270
What to Build into Your Community 270
Determine the Type of Community You Need 271
*Set Objectives for Your Community
and Establish an Operating Budget* 271
Establish a Community Structure 271
Information Center 271
Community Services 272
Interactive Areas 272

Conducting Business or Using e-Commerce 272
Involving Partners 272
Set Up the Back-End 272
Launch and Publicize Your Community 273
Maintain and Grow Your Community 273

Chapter 11:
Internet Partnering   274

Partnering—The Traditional Way 275
Cooperate But Do Not Capitulate 275
Accentuate Your Compatibility 276
Centralize Lead Processing 276
Offer Resellers Turnkey Programs—
and Make It Easy to Participate 276
Support Partners with Traditional Direct Marketing 277
The Starting Point for Internet Partnering:
Affiliate Marketing 279
Making Affiliate Marketing Programs Meet Your Needs 280
Tips on Becoming an Affiliate 281
Choose Affiliate Programs Carefully 281
Verify the Legitimacy of the Programs
You are Considering 282
Select Programs That Meet Your
Web Site Visitors' Needs 282
Test One Program 282
Continuously Evaluate the Program and
Add Other Programs Selectively 283
Guidelines for Creating Your Own Affiliate Program 283
Establish an e-Commerce Operation First 283
BeFree (www.befree.com) 283
ClickTrade (www.clicktrade.com) 284
Commission Junction (www.cj.com) 284
LinkShare (www.linkshare.com) 284
Performics (www.performics.com) 284
Construct an Affiliate Program That
Benefits Everyone 284
Work Out All the Details 285
Protect Yourself with a Legal Agreement 285
Service Your Affiliates 286

Make a Long-term Commitment to Affiliate Marketing 286
Examples of IT-Related Affiliate Programs 286
Build My PC.com (*www.buildmypc.com*) 286
BuyTELCO (*www.buytelco.com*) 287
Dell (*www.dell.com; www.linkshare.com*) 288
GE Express (*www.geexpress.com*) 288
HP Garage Affiliate Network
(*www.hp.com/solutions1/garage/affiliates/index.html*) .. 288
iGo (*www.igo.com*) 288
Outpost (*www.outpost.com*) 288
Sundial.com (*www.sundial.com*) 288
VeriSign (*www.verisign.com*) and Network Solutions
(*www.networksolutions.com*) 289
Using the Internet to Support Channel Partners 289
Building an Internet-based Channel Partner Program 290
"Web-ize" the Partner Relationship 291
Link Your Communications Electronically 292
Promote Your Partners in a Special
Area of Your Web Site 292
Establish a Partner Service Extranet 292
Examples of IT Internet Partner Programs 293
Cisco (*www.cisco.com*) 293
IBM (*www.ibm.com/partnerworld*) 293
Intel (*channel.intel.com*) 293
Microsoft (*www.microsoft.com/directaccess/partnering/
microsoft/*) 294
Novell (*partnerweb.novell.com*) 294
Oracle (*www.oracle.com/partners/*) 295
Partnering, Internet Style: What the Future Holds 295

Chapter 12:
Selling on the Internet   299

Putting the e-commerce Explosion into Perspective 300
Dell: An IT Online Success Story 303
Dell Premier Web Pages 306
DellHost 307
Dell Software and Accessories 307
Dell Exchange 308
Dell Learning Center 308

How e-commerce Works with Your Selling Model 308
   The Retail or Mail-Order Model 308
   The Reseller Model 310
   The Sales Force Model 312
A New Twist to e-commerce: The Shopping Bot 313
   www.mysimon.com 313
   www.rusure.com 314
   www.dash.com 314
   www.respond.com 314
How to Get an e-commerce Order Generation
  System Up and Running 314
   Transitioning from an Existing Order Generation System 315
   Starting a New Order Generation System on the Internet 318
Should You Use a Web Hosting Service for e-Commerce? 320
Taking Orders Electronically 322
Driving Traffic from the Internet to a
  Traditional Order Generation Channel 324
The Business of Order Fulfillment 325
Where to See IT e-commerce in Action 326
Notes 327

Chapter 13:
Integrating Online and Offline Marketing   **328**

Online and Offline: The Reality
  of a Changing Marketing World 329
   Your Market and Your Audiences Will Determine
    How You Integrate Online and Offline Marketing 331
   How to Integrate Online and Offline Media
    in the Internet Marketing Era 332
   An Example of How to Execute Online-Offline Marketing .. 336
The Impact of Internet Marketing on the
  Marketing Organizations of IT Companies 339
   The Impact on Marketing 340
   The Impact on the Marketing/IT Departments 342
   The Impact on Sales 342
Presenting the Case for Internet Marketing 344
   Focus on the Quantifiable Business
    Benefits of Internet Marketing 344
The Internet Marketing Audit 349

The Internet Marketing Action Plan 350
  Developing the Action Plan 351
  Implementing the Action Plan 353
  In-House or Outside? 354
  Staff Requirements for Internet Marketing 355
The Internet Is Part of a Changing Marketing World 358
A Final Word 360
Note 363

Appendix A: Other Resources 364
Appendix B: Glossary of Direct and Internet Marketing Terms 384

Introduction

In October 1998, my book, *Business-to-Business Internet Marketing,* was published. It was the first combination book/Web site to show how to apply proven direct marketing principles to business-to-business Internet marketing. Every year a new edition of this book has been published, because a year in Internet time is a lifetime.

But Internet marketing is now mainstream marketing, so its application by individual industry segments is not only appropriate, but essential. The original edition of *Internet Marketing for Information Technology Companies* was the first title in a series of industry-specific Internet marketing books published by Maximum Press. This second edition is completely revised and updated to keep pace with industry change.

Internet usage in general continues to grow at a blistering rate, and Internet marketing is now widely adopted by information technology (IT) companies. Yet one of the biggest changes since the publication of the original edition of this book has been the Dot Com Crash of 2000–2001. This shakeout continues to cause tremors in the e-conomy as technology companies are battered by layoffs and falling stock prices. Although not all technology companies are Dot Coms, most have aggressively moved to the Internet as a way of doing business. It is important to distinguish becoming an e-business, or using the Internet to improve business functionality, from being a Dot Com.

In this context, the Dot Com Crash may in the long term be a good thing. Why? Because as in Darwinism, it represents the survival of the fittest. Many of the Dot Com disasters may be occurring for the right reasons: These failures are companies in search of a mass market, or with an undifferentiated offering, or with inadequate infrastructure, or with a poor business plan. These may be companies looking for high growth and high profits, but with little intention of truly growing a business of lasting value. Nonetheless, it is a wake-up call to technology companies in particular to have as sound an Internet strategy as a business strategy. And that thinking transfers to an Internet marketing strategy.

There is some irony in the fact that there is even a need to instruct IT companies how to use the Internet for marketing. After all, if IT companies are the primary creators and innovators of the Internet, shouldn't they know how to market with it?

Well here is a dirty little secret: Understanding the technology of the Internet does not make one an Internet marketing expert. On the contrary, sometimes the technology itself is so stunning that its glare obscures the basic principles of marketing. It turns out that many technology companies are pretty lousy marketers. It is not entirely their fault. Their roots are in product engineering, not marketing. Even if they rise above this and recognize that they must sell products to survive, chances are these companies pour their dollars into a hard-driving sales force. The popular belief has been that "street on the feet" sells products, not marketing.

I have watched this phenomenon repeat itself over and over again in my 25-plus years of dealing with IT companies. I started my direct marketing career at Epsilon, a company that pioneered database-driven direct marketing before most people knew what it was. When I launched my own agency in 1983, I focused on the IT niche. At that time, companies like Apollo Computer, Digital Equipment Corporation, and Wang Laboratories (Remember them?) were the daring darlings of industry, makers of the "Massachusetts Miracle." They could not throw money at marketing fast enough.

Of course, everything changed dramatically with the stock market crash of 1987. I never saw the marketing muscle of the early 1980s being flexed by IT companies again—until the late 1990s. That is when the Age of the Dot Com arrived. And what better evidence of this rebirth than the spectacular January 10, 2000, announcement that America Online would merge with Time Warner—with a younger and smaller AOL actually in the role of acquirer because of its market capitalization. Compaq's buying Digital in the 1990s was inconceivable enough, but the AOL–Time Warner deal gave testimony to the fact that absolutely nothing was to be impossible in the Internet Era.

But late in the year, Dot Com optimism turned to pessimism. Despite this market softening, however, I believe that IT companies that keep their eye on sound marketing principles, and pragmatically apply them to the Internet, will be among the survivors.

I must admit that, over the years, I have seen some of the largest and fastest-growing IT companies mismanage opportunities when it comes to basic marketing. The good news is that many of them are learning from their mistakes. Today there are IT companies (among them Dot Coms) that are not only smart, but in fact are brilliant marketers. Many of them are mentioned in this book. These are the companies that are driving marketing to new heights, setting examples for others, and intelligently applying the power of the Internet to achieve remarkable marketing success.

Internet marketing is now very much an integral component of the overall marketing program for every marketer. In *Business-to-Business Internet Marketing*, I predicted that Internet marketing would ultimately dominate the marketing world, with all other forms of marketing becoming subordinate to it. The time frame is still in doubt, but I believe this will eventually be the case.

The question is, although IT companies are Internet innovators in every other way, will they become the Internet marketing leaders of the future? That is what this book is all about.

Before they can become Internet marketing leaders, IT companies must become *direct marketing* leaders. That is because Internet marketing is direct marketing—at its most developed potential. It is the logical extension of a measurability mentality that is already inbred in direct marketers. Direct marketers recognize the importance of the brand, and they understand the need for awareness, but they also know that marketing must go well beyond brand image and awareness advertising. They need marketing that makes an impression and produces results.

Their challenge in business-to-business especially is to target a variety of audiences (people with different job titles, in different functional areas, in different companies, in different industries), all with very different needs. They use targeted techniques involving audience, offers and creative formats to generate response, qualify leads, identify good prospects, shorten the sales cycle, and sell products through different channels.

For the direct marketer, generating and qualifying leads is a never-ending battle. The marketer's arsenal includes direct response advertising, direct mail, telemarketing, events such as trade shows and seminars, and sometimes even radio and television. Direct marketers measure and analyze everything. They establish response management systems to qualify, prioritize, and move the prospect closer to becoming a customer. They strategize about ways to keep customers loyal and happy, and they make intelligent use of marketing databases to track it all—and learn how to do it better. All of these fundamental underlying strategies of measurable, accountable direct marketing will remain, but built on top of them will be a new marketing infrastructure as the "Age of the e" continues.

The reality is that everything is moving to the Internet. Businesses of every type are creating Internet-driven intranets and extranets that connect all types of computers inside and outside the enterprise. The Internet has become, in a sense, the universal operating system everybody was searching for.

Businesses large and small are moving their entire IT infrastructures to the Internet. New Internet-based businesses are forming at a dizzying rate. There is talk of a new world economy dependent on digital cash and desktop diplomacy.

So it is with marketing, whose current condition bears a striking resemblance to the point at which information technology finds itself. Direct mail is the mainframe (and mainstay) of direct marketing. Will it go away? No, but, as with the mainframe computer, direct mail will be a legacy system that will feed the new media instead of itself remaining in the limelight. In fact, every indication points to the inevitability that direct mail and other traditional direct marketing media are to become supporting players to the Internet.

The good news is that everything direct marketers believe about direct marketing transfers almost point by point to the Internet. The underlying principles are the same; the marketing methodology is the same. What is radically different is the electronic medium—because it is not just a new direct marketing channel, it is a whole new way of communicating. It is no longer direct marketing it is now Internet marketing—a form of direct marketing that is immediate, instantaneous, full of impact, and downright cheap.

What this means for you and your company's management is the following: You will need to adopt a transitional strategy that protects your investment in traditional marketing and direct marketing methodology and media—while leveraging it to take full advantage of Internet marketing. You will need to straddle the traditional marketing world of today and the rapidly emerging Internet marketing world.

It is all about using information technology to market more effectively. That is why the goal of this book is to turn IT companies into Internet marketing leaders. To survive in this new marketing world, they cannot follow. They will have no choice but to lead.

About This Book

You can consider this book an Internet marketing sandwich: The real meat is in the middle (Chapters 3–12) held together by the bread on the outside (Chapters 1, 2, and 13). Although it is recommended that you consume the entire thing bite by bite, you could skip around from chapter to chapter, depending on your appetite.

Chapter 1 explores the impact of the Internet on IT companies in general and on marketing in particular, and Chapter 2 suggests that a new response model called "intersponding" will emerge as a result of the Internet's vast influence.

Chapters 3 through 12 cover each aspect of Internet marketing in considerable detail. Throughout these chapters are screen captures of Web pages to illustrate some of the examples used. These screen captures are the copyrighted property of the Web site owners.

Chapter 3 focuses on the heart of any Internet marketing program, the Web site, and Chapter 4 details the use of search tools and newsgroups. Chapter 5 is about e-mail marketing, and Chapter 6 covers Internet advertising and public relations. Chapter 7 explores how you can enhance or replace traditional marketing events with Internet events.

Chapter 8 covers Internet fulfillment; Chapter 9 is a comprehensive examination of customer service, one of the most important aspects of Internet marketing. Chapter 10 addresses the growing use of communities, and Chapter 11 covers affiliate programs and other forms of Internet partnering. Chapter 12 addresses the explosive growth of e-commerce and shows you how to take advantage of selling on the Internet.

Finally, Chapter 13 is that bottom piece of bread. It supports the rest of the book, pulling together what you have learned, showing you how to integrate online and offline marketing, and guiding you through the inevitable transition you will need to make to Internet marketing.

The book concludes with a section on resources. Appendix A provides a complete list of every Web site referenced in this book, in order of appearance. It also contains a specially selected list, by category, of particularly useful Web sites of interest to marketers. In addition, you will find a selected list of books of special relevance to direct and Internet marketers.

Appendix B is the glossary, a comprehensive listing of direct marketing and Internet marketing terms.

Your "Members-Only" Web Site

Internet marketing is in a state of constant change. That is why there is a companion Web site associated with this book. On this site, you will find the latest Internet marketing news, book updates, expanded information, and other pertinent Internet marketing resources. You will also find links to every Web site mentioned in this book. Although the book uses printed screen captures, Web pages change so frequently that it is a good idea to supplement your reading by viewing these pages on the companion Web site. The best way to view and interact with Web pages is to be on the Internet.

To access the companion Web site, go to the Maximum Press Web site located at *www.maxpress.com* and follow the links to the "Internet Marketing for Information Technology Companies" companion Web site. When you try to enter the companion Web site, you will be prompted for a user ID and password. Type in the following:

- For User ID enter: imtech2e

- For Password enter: sharks

You will then be granted full access to the "Members Only" area. After you arrive, bookmark the page in your browser and you will never have to enter the user ID and password again. Visit the site often and enjoy the Internet marketing news and information with our compliments—and thanks for buying the book. We ask that you not share the user ID and password for this site with anyone else.

1

How IT Marketers Can
Put the Internet to Work

The Internet has fundamentally changed the way the world works. Internet technology (IT) companies are at the heart of this change, creating the tools to enable it. In many cases, these companies have become Internet marketing leaders, but not always. It is the fact that IT companies are technological innovators that sometimes acts as an impediment to marketing their products or services. That is because many IT companies are engineering- rather than marketing-driven. They may have fabulous technology but not the slightest idea how to market it. They also may not see a need to make an investment in something as "soft" as marketing. These are the companies whose "not invented here" arrogance pervades their marketing organizations and sometimes paralyzes their marketing efforts. Still other IT companies successfully built their businesses with a direct sales force that basically kicked down doors and sold products face-to-face. Companies with this type of heritage often relegate marketing to stepchild status, believing that it is little more than literature production for sales support purposes.

This chapter helps break down some of these barriers to effective Internet marketing. We look at the reason for all the marketing excitement about the Internet, and we explore how IT companies can develop their own special brand of Internet marketing.

The Internet Business Imperative

As an observer of the IT industry for more than 20 years, I can recall only a few times when the industry has truly moved in a single, unified direction. Yet, there is no hesitation today to embrace the Internet as the definitive way to re-engineer network infrastructures and extend the enterprise. Entirely new businesses are being built around it. The Internet has reached such ubiquity that the world's largest technology companies are waging nothing less than war to take control of it.

As evidence, you only have to look at the antitrust case against Microsoft by the U.S. government. In November 1999, a federal judge declared that Microsoft's actions were predatory and represented a monopoly. Although the case focused on the software company's competitive practices, it started with Microsoft's embedding its Web browser into its Windows operating system.

Computer technology has stretched across physical boundaries, and we have created a virtual world no less real than our physical one via networked communications. The Internet has caused networking, telecommunications, hardware, and software companies to completely re-engineer themselves. Practically all other businesses are following suit by reorienting their business operations and information systems for the electronic future. Organizations are feverishly building intranets and extranets ("private-use" Web sites), depending more and more on the Internet for entire networking infrastructures.

As a testament to this fundamental change and the influence of the Internet, *Communications Week*, long a major computer industry publication, was renamed *Internet Week* (*www.internetwk.com*) in late 1997. In early 1998, one of the computer industry's flagship magazines, *DATAMATION*, announced that it would cease print publication after 40 years and reinvent itself as a Web-only magazine (*www.datamation.com*). In 2000, *PCWEEK* was renamed *eWEEK*. That's just the beginning. Now there are more publications (both in print and in electronic versions) covering the Internet and the Web than in any other publishing category.

Statistics seem to support the fact that it is very much a permanent presence in daily and business life. Statistics regarding usage and business-to-business (B-to-B) e-commerce are changing so rapidly that they will be out of date by the time you read this sentence. Rely on such Web sources as eMarketer (*www.emarketer.com*), CyberAtlas (*www.cyberatlas.internet.com*), and Statmarket (*www.statmarket.com*) to gain access to the latest statistics.

But just to put things into perspective, let us examine a few significant facts. By year-end 2000, according to CyberAtlas, there were about 136 million Internet users in the United States, 27 million in Japan, 19 million in Germany, and 18 million in the United Kingdom. It is estimated that there could be 490 million people online by 2002.

According to International Data Corporation (*www.idc.com*), worldwide e-commerce revenue was about $350 billion in 2000 and will rise to about $3.14 trillion by 2004. Gartner, Inc. (*www.gartner.com*) says that worldwide B-to-B online sales will grow from $433 billion in 2000, to $919 billion in 2001, to $8.5 trillion by 2005. The Boston Consulting Group (*www.bcg.com*) estimates that B-to-B online revenue in Asia will be $430 billion by 2003.

The Internet's economic impact is reported in research conducted by the University of Texas's Center for Research in Electronic Commerce, commissioned by Cisco Systems (*www.internetindicators.com*). The results of the fourth study covering the first half of 2000 reveal some fascinating statistics:

- Although Dot Coms have been the center of media attention, they are not the center of the Internet economy. Only 9.6 percent of the firms in the study are true Dot Coms, with 95 percent or more of their revenue from the Internet.

- For Internet economy companies, Internet revenue is one-quarter the size of non-Internet revenue, but is growing three times as fast as corporate revenue as a whole. In the first half of 2000, Internet economy companies generated $1 of every $5 in revenue from the Internet. Internet economy revenue is growing twice as fast as Internet economy employment. The Internet economy was projected to produce $830 billion in revenues in 2000, a 58 percent increase over 1999, according to the study.

- The Internet economy directly supports more than 3.088 million workers. Total employment at Internet economy companies grew 10 percent between the first quarter of 1999 and the first quarter of 2000. The Internet economy is creating jobs in numerous areas. Interestingly, seven of every ten jobs created are traditional, not high-tech jobs. According to the study, the job function generating the most Internet-related employment is sales and marketing (33 percent), with IT jobs at only 28 percent.

According to the report, *2000 Economic Impact: U.S. Direct & Interactive Marketing Today* by the Direct Marketing Association (*www.the-dma.org*), U.S. consumers and businesses spent over $24 billion as a result of direct marketers' online media expenditures in 2000. Direct marketers spent $2.8 billion on interactive media marketing in 2000, up from over $1.6 billion in 1999—this, the report emphasizes, in spite of a weaker economy and Dot Com failures.

The Wired World

Today the Internet is already a mature medium, despite its newcomer status. It is certainly the technology area with the most significant and explosive growth ever. In 1998 and 1999, the Internet's economic impact on the U.S. economy was clearly proven just by the amount of venture capital invested in Internet companies, and by the number of successful Internet company IPOs launched. By early 1999, Internet IPOs had dominated the stock market, creating another round of young billionaires, not unlike the software boom decades earlier. By late 1999, it was the Dot Coms that moved "offline," dominating the airwaves, feverishly snapping up television time, and grabbing national magazine and newspaper space to launch their fledgling brands. By 2000, the success of the Dot Coms had started to dwindle. Many merged and many more failed. But not before the Internet had permanently become part of the fabric of American business.

The Internet is very serious business, and it is an unavoidable fact of business life. A recent study by IT research firm Forrester Research (*www.forrester.com*) said that 98 percent of large businesses (more than 1,000 employees) and 45 percent of small businesses (fewer than 100 employees) will do business online by 2002. The Internet is fast becoming the marketing medium of the present (and the future) as it stakes its claim to marketing dominance.

Arguably, the most fertile ground for IT media opportunities today is the Internet. A landmark study done by the NEC Research Institute (*www.neci.nec.com*) in early 1999 put the number of individual Web pages at some 800 million, with 3 million added each day. The predicted rate of Web page growth is phenomenal, perhaps 1,000 percent over the next few years, yet the NEC Research Institute study indicated that even the most comprehensive Web search engines combined covered no more than 42 percent of indexed pages. That is one good reason that Internet information access services are growing at such a rapid rate. Businesses that never would have existed before the Internet are now springing up to help online visitors find what they are *really* looking for on the Net.

The number of unique visits major Web sites receive on a daily basis is astounding. It can be in the tens or hundreds of thousands. E-mail newsletters are proliferating as well. Some of the major information technology newsletters spun off by such information supersites as *www.cmpnet.com, www.cnet.com, www.idg.net, www.internet.com,* and *www.zdnet.com* (now part of C|Net) report circulations approaching or exceeding 1 million readers.

There has never been a time when a mass medium has held such potential. For example, consider the national publications that span the general IT market. Circulations in the hundreds of thousands are considered large. The Internet has the potential to dwarf those kinds of numbers. The Internet is more accessible to more people globally than any other medium except television. Web sites and e-mail newsletters are for the most part free.

With all this, however, there are still significant challenges facing the Internet. One of its greatest challenges may be the privacy issue. With the mass adoption of external e-mail by consumers and businesses alike, this "private" one-to-one communication quickly became another promotional channel for IT marketers. It was not long before unsolicited e-mailings ("spamming") were commonplace.

Now, the heat is very much on those who do not respect an individual's privacy on the Internet. For example, the Direct Marketing Association (*www.the-dma.org*) launched an electronic media privacy program in 1998, encouraging organizations that use the Internet for direct marketing to post a privacy policy prominently on their Web sites. In February and March 2000, the Federal Trade Commission (*www.ftc.gov*) conducted a survey of commercial sites' information practices, using a random sample of 335 Web sites, in addition to "most popular sites"—91 of the 100 busiest U.S. commercial Web sites. The survey found the following:

- In the random sample, 88 percent post at least one privacy disclosure, and 100 percent of the most popular sites post at least one.

- In analyzing these disclosures in light of the fair information practice principles of Notice, Choice, Access, and Security, the percentage drops dramatically. Only 20 percent of the random sample sites that collect personal identifying information, and 42 percent of the most popular sites, implement (at least in part) all four fair information practice principles.

- The commission also looked at the number of companies enrolled in the primary industry self-regulatory initiative, online privacy seal programs. The survey found that 8 percent of the random sample, and 45 percent of the most popular sites, display a privacy seal.

The survey led the FTC to conclude that privacy self-regulation alone would not suffice and, as a result, the Commission recommended that Congress enact legislation that will help to ensure adequate protection of consumer privacy online.

This, of course, is only the federal perspective. There are states that have already adopted legislation that restricts unsolicited e-mail and protects consumer privacy. This increasingly strict regulatory environment should be taken into consideration by every IT marketer in planning and executing Internet marketing programs.

No less daunting is the technology of the Internet itself and access to it. On the service side, major telecommunications and cable companies have already entered the ISP market. AT&T, WorldCom, and Sprint provide Internet access services, as do all of the Regional Bell Operating Companies. Communications giants are lining up to compete in the massive Internet market. AT&T and cable leader TCI merged in 1998, and AT&T now offers cable modem service. WorldCom's former UUNET division makes WorldCom the world's largest business ISP. The Internet access alternatives available to businesses and consumers are proliferating, as are the ways access can be provided. Internet access over both telephone and cable connections is commonplace. It's only a matter of time before Internet access is bundled with electric service. The end result will be the same: the "massification" of the Internet.

One of the biggest concerns has been the bandwidth associated with delivering Internet service. As more people sign up for Internet access and actively use the Internet to conduct business, networked portions of the Internet can become choked with traffic. The demand for bandwidth rises exponentially, but even the bandwidth problem is on the way to being alleviated. Massive technological improvements are being made to the Internet infrastructure by leading networking companies.

Innovations are coming from all sides. Most cable companies are becoming broadband-enabled. Broadband is basically Internet access over cable, and it is feeding hungry Internet users with electronic information at blazingly fast speeds. Broadband is one significant advance, but it is not the only way that consumers and businesses are getting high-speed Internet feeds. Through faster ISDN (Integrated Services Digital Network) connections running over ordinary phone lines, and with the new higher-speed modems that are hitting the market every day, fast access will be a diminishing problem for even the smallest businesses. ISDN is fast being replaced by ADSL (Asymmetric Digital Subscriber Line). Telecommunications and cable companies alike are introducing DSL rapidly throughout the United States, targeting both business and home use with the hope that DSL will be the killer Internet access application. That is because DSL can share phone lines, using modems that are 50 times faster than conventional modems.

DSL and other technologies mean that Internet access soon will be a utility. People will not even need to think about turning it on and off, because it will be more like the telephone, cable television, and electricity.

Lately, talk is about the "second Internet," an industrial-strength Net that may be only a few years away. Infrastructures are being built today that are expected to solidify the "Internet economy" and make it a global reality. And those infrastructures may not even be underground. Cisco Systems, the leading manufacturer of networking devices, announced that it would introduce a wireless Internet in the year 2000. The company is beginning to offer Internet connections up to ten times faster than DSL via low-frequency microwave transmission.

Even today, wireless connections to the Internet via cellular phones and PDAs are possible, and this market is expected to grow rapidly.

Intranets and Extranets

IT companies are not just driving electronic commerce. They quickly go beyond Internet marketing usage alone, creating intranets and extranets, perhaps two of the most-used words in the trade press in their reporting of the Internet.

Both intranets and extranets are now becoming populated with marketing initiatives. Technically an Internet-enabled internal network intended primarily for employee usage, an intranet is a media channel in and of itself—a very targeted one, in fact. Imagine if a Fortune 500 company were to allow advertising on its intranet—so that its employees would receive promotional messages from selected providers of products and services. What if that same company were to actively promote its own products and services, and those of its divisions, to the employee base? Through an intranet, large companies can market themselves very effectively and provide highly valued service to a very targeted audience—their employees.

An extranet is really a private-label Web site, offering access to a selected group of customers, prospects, partners, or suppliers outside the sponsoring organization's network. It is the extranet, and all its variations, that companies started using in earnest in 1997 to help solidify existing business relationships and form new ones.

These extranets have proliferated rapidly and now take on numerous life forms. Some extranets service only customers; others are targeted specifically to business partners. Some are designed as private consortiums where members share resources and do business with each other. Still other extranets provide private-access seminars, courses, and conferences, either free or paid, to prospects, customers, partners, or students. The extranet is both a useful marketing channel itself and, like an intranet, a place to potentially reach targeted audiences.

This is an aspect of the Internet that is not quite the same as any other medium. You can create intranets, extranets, Web sites, Web communities, and newsgroups—tangible places where business can be conducted, marketing information can be exchanged, and dialogue can occur. Then, you can use these newly created media vehicles to place promotional advertising that takes further advantage of Internet marketing.

Even at the beginning of the Internet marketing curve, there was a remarkable richness to the medium. There can be little doubt that the Internet is having a permanent impact and a lasting effect, not just on marketing, but on the manner in which businesses conduct business.

The True Impact of the Internet on the IT Company

The third annual America Online/Roper Starch Cyberstudy, conducted in August 2000 among a random sample of over 1,000 adult online users, suggested significant positive shifts in Internet acceptance. For the first time ever, more than half of the survey respondents indicated that they shop online, nearly double the percentage who did so two years earlier. More than half the respondents would be interested in using a small Internet device to go online from any room in their house. Close to half log on to their home accounts even when they are away from home. And two-thirds of the respondents would be interested in checking out a Web site they'd seen on TV without leaving their TV to find it.

The business impact of the Internet on IT companies cannot be underestimated. According to Internet statistics source eMarketer (*www.emarketer.com*), a survey conducted by Knowledge Systems and Research on behalf of Arthur Andersen showed that in 2001, 25 percent of technology company business activity is conducted online. That percentage is expected to rise to 48 percent in two years.

In November 1999, "The Internet 500" list was first published by *Interactive Week* magazine (*www.interactiveweek.com*), and IT companies dominated the list. This first-ever ranking of the top 500 businesses by revenue generated only from online sales is a fascinating look at who is getting the biggest boost from e-commerce. The ranking shows that the top Internet-revenue producers are actually traditional companies, not Dot Coms. It also shows that, of the top 200 companies, those losing money outnumber companies making money by almost two to one. Eight of the top ten companies are true IT companies, with only FedEx and UPS being outside the IT industry. Intel, with $10.5 billion in online revenue out of its total $27 billion, ranked number one. Numbers two, three, and four were Cisco at $9.5 billion, IBM at $8.8 billion, and Dell at $6 billion, respectively. FedEx was number five with $5.6 billion in online sales.

Among all of this, the IT company must evaluate the true impact of the Internet on its business and its business model. There probably is not an IT company in existence today, whether large or small, that is not re-engineering its business, its products, and its service to fit the wired world. But the Internet has its unique impact on each type IT company.

Hardware

The glory days of selling iron are long gone. The hardware manufacturer is, today, just as dependent on the necessary operating systems and available applications as on getting chips for the computer. For the manufacturer, the Internet is forcing a business refocus: If the hardware is not "e-enabled" it will be history. Open systems are mandatory, as is any-to-any networking capabilities.

Beyond the box, however, is the business impact of the Internet on the hardware company. Hardware manufacturers are now expected to be e-businesses themselves, and the end user will accept nothing less. This means that every system the manufacturer has needs to be Internet-enabled. The reality of such business change is likely to make the Y2K problem look minuscule. Entire business processes will need to move to the Internet—human resources, customer service, inventory control, order processing, and fulfillment. Business partner relationships will be e-based. Everyone will want everything instantly and electronically. Internet marketing is just part of the story.

Of those reinventing themselves, two worthy of note are IBM and Sun. IBM coined the term "e-business" and has put it into play with a vengeance. In fact, one could say IBM's e-business marketing campaign has been as much as anything responsible for the feverish pitch associated with products and services that begin with "e." Now there are few promotions from any company touting the Internet that do not have a reference to "e." IBM has not only talked about e-business, but it has become an e-business, in countless ways. And that is not easy for a computer giant to do.

Sun appropriated "Dot Com" in much the same way, even if not with the same marketing muscle as IBM. With its strong track record as the Internet's server of choice among leading ISPs and Web sites, Sun keeps bombarding the marketplace with Java and Jini technologies. In addition, Sun made at least two significant moves in 1999 to further its Internet position.

First, Sun formed the "Sun–Netscape Alliance" with America Online. The goal of the Alliance, according to its Web site, is to "help companies realize their Net Economy vision—putting the power of the Internet in their hands with the broadest and best Internet infrastructure and e-commerce software and professional services." Second, Sun acquired StarOffice, an office-productivity software suite, later that year. The most important aspect of this acquisition was Sun's launch of the suite as a free set of tools available for download from the Internet. Sun announced its intention to eventually offer "StarPortal" at no charge to end users.

This was clearly designed to put applications formerly on Windows desktops onto the Internet. You could look at this as a crazy move or a crazy-like-a-fox move, depending on where your allegiances might be.

And Sun was not the only company to speculate that the days of desktop OS were waning. In December 1999, WebOS (*www.webos.com*) launched a free service that makes it possible to run a virtual desktop from a Web server. The company calls it "the world's first Web operating system."

And let's not forget the hardware vendors who have taken an early stake in e-commerce and have been rewarded handsomely as a result. One that comes to mind is Dell Computer. Dell pioneered the use of the Internet for truly customized PCs and became the acknowledged IT leader in hard-good sales by 1999. Now half the company's revenue is generated online.

Software

Is there a software company in existence today that is not working on, if not offering, an e-enabled version of its flagship product? The demand, from a software perspective, is for everything Internet, and it is likely to be increasingly intense. Those software publishers who did not move quickly enough are now scrambling to catch up—if their Internet-savvy competitors do not put them out of business first. It is no accident that the software giants have "discovered" the Internet, now touting online customer service, developing their own portals, and crafting cooperative deals with other companies to offer a more complete e-suite of products. You will find the traditional standard bearers of the industry—such companies as Microsoft, Computer Associates, Lotus, Oracle, and SAP—enthusiastically embracing and pitching the Internet and e-everything. Although software companies can move faster than the hardware companies, their challenge is no less significant. If their products are not e-enabled, they are dinosaurs.

Networking

Networking companies, ISPs, and, to a certain extent, all IT-based communications companies have been the unique beneficiaries of Internet mania. These are the companies that build the equipment and the infrastructure, and provide the service, that run the Internet. What a great time it is for them. For others, however, it is not such a great time. Why? Because this is a time of weeding out the weaker ones and consolidating the bigger ones. And that can mean that some businesses will not exist anymore, and some people will not be employed anymore. On the positive side, however, shakeouts often result in better technological offerings. The competition is more visible, the battle lines more defined. This is where a lot of the action is, and will be, in the Internet-focused IT world.

Service Companies and Resellers

IT service companies that focus on networking could be in an enviable position. The need to interconnect LANs, WANs, and the Internet will grow exponentially, as will issues surrounding connectivity, compatibility, security, redundancy, and so on. Those service companies that can use the Internet itself as a conduit for servicing customers will be able to stay significantly ahead of their competition. Resellers of IT products and services who use the Internet as a new distribution and sales channel to supplement their own selling efforts will likely benefit as well, but they will also face new competition from Internet-based selling by the manufacturers they represent.

The ISPs themselves have obviously capitalized on the Internet in ways few others can. Although some are a strange mix of technology and telecommunications, the ISPs are IT leaders in their own right. The dominant player, America Online (*www.aol.com*), had 30 million users worldwide by mid-2001 with 24 million in the United States alone. But they have done more than that. On January 10, 2000, AOL announced the unthinkable—a plan to merge with Time Warner. Incredibly, the smaller but more highly valued AOL would own about 55 percent of the new company in a stock deal that would be valued at $350 billion, the largest to date in U.S. history.

Regulatory issues notwithstanding, the business and economic significance of such a combination cannot be minimized. If ever there was a question about the Internet's dominant influence, it was resoundingly answered with the AOL–Time Warner deal. Industry and financial analysts alike immediately recognized the implication: that the world of e-commerce and media would change forever. At its most basic level, it brings together the online prowess of AOL with the deep content and broadband access of Time Warner. But it means far more than that if you look at all of the properties each company holds, as well as the far-reaching influence such a mega-corporation will have. This one merger is as telling of the future as any. The good news for IT companies is that it speaks to the dominance of information technology in the greater scheme of things.

The deal dwarfed the 1999 merger of EarthLink and Mindspring, an effort to play catch-up to AOL's rising star. Together, these ISPs would serve over 3 million users. Growth across consumer- and business-focused ISPs has been brisk, even as the traditional telecommunications and cable firms enter the ISP space.

In late 1999, Prodigy (*www.prodigy.com*) and SBC, the nation's largest local telephone company, announced that they would combine their Internet operations, with SBC taking 43 percent ownership of Prodigy. This deal turns Prodigy, a once-failing ISP, into a powerhouse with more than 2 million customers. But more importantly, Prodigy now has broadband access to the 100 million people served by SBC. This could help reshape the ISP landscape fairly significantly.

Also in 1999, the economics of the ISP began to dramatically shift as free Internet access became a popular phenomenon in the United States. By November 1999, for example, free access provider NetZero (*www.netzero.com*) had acquired more than 2 million users. Alta Vista (*www.altavista.com*), the search engine that reinvented itself as a portal offering free access, announced that month that it had acquired 800,000 users in its first three months of service. Of course, users agree to view plenty of advertising in exchange for free Internet access. With companies such as Gateway and Compaq bundling in Internet access, and creative telcos using access as a new business hook, sometimes offering it free as part of a total service package, ISPs had to reevaluate their business model. A November 1999 report published by The Yankee Group (*www.yankeegroup.com*) predicted that free Internet access would have a significant impact on numerous businesses, including ISPs, communications providers, and PC manufacturers.

The Dot Coms

This special breed of company is a category that obviously did not even exist in the pre-Internet world. Some would not consider the Dot Com an IT company as much as a business that happens to use IT to succeed. Unlike companies in the preceding categories that have moved to e-business, the Dot Com company started as an Internet-only business. As such, it can uniquely leverage the Internet, of course, but it can just as easily be vulnerable to category killers and look-alikes. Ironically, being a Dot Com is not necessarily equivalent to being an effective marketing or even Internet marketing company. It is the unknown Dot Coms in particular that must create much-needed awareness for their brands, build traffic for their sites, and ultimately find ways to generate revenue. One of the interesting aspects of this in late 1999 was the way Dot Coms snapped up "offline" media in an attempt to legitimize their businesses. Obviously, the Dot Coms acknowledged that it took traditional media marketing, in combination with Internet-based marketing, to launch their brands.

The legendary Dot Com, Amazon.com (*www.amazon.com*), was single-handedly responsible for establishing many of the e-commerce practices companies live by today. Among other things, Amazon broadly introduced the community concept of customer reviews, e-mail notification of new products, personalized purchase recommendations, affiliate programs, and one-click ordering. *Time* magazine did not miss its significance when it declared Amazon's founder, Jeff Bezos, 1999's Person of the Year. This despite Amazon's chronic money-losing financials.

The Dot Com phenomenon has certainly changed the business world. The impact of the Dot Com on the economy in terms of venture capital, IPOs, and job creation was notable by late 2000. Admittedly, Dot Coms were in disfavor by mid-2001. Many of these companies had failed to build the critical mass necessary to survive. Still others had run out of capital trying to create successful businesses on the Internet. Nonetheless, Dot Com failures did not dampen interest in the Internet among IT companies. If anything, the Internet became more integrated into the business strategies of traditional companies, whose movement to e-business continued to increase.

Why All the Marketing Excitement about the Internet?

The Internet Is Boundless
According to CyberAtlas (*www.cyberatlas.internet.com*), there were almost 136 million Internet users in the United States by the end of 2000. Japan ranked second in the world with some 27 million users, Germany was third with about 19 million, and the United Kingdom was fourth with about 18 million. And China was a surprising fifth with almost 16 million online users. The Computer Industry Almanac projected that 490 million people worldwide would have Internet access by the year 2002.

The economic impact is staggering. Research firm International Data Corporation (*www.idc.com*) predicted in March 2001 that e-commerce revenue will rise from about $350 billion in 2000 to more than $3 trillion by 2004. Growth in the rest of the world will actually outpace the United States, which will capture 38 percent of the global market by 2004. Gartner, Inc. (*www.gartner.com*) forecasted that B-to-B e-commerce sales alone will reach $8.53 trillion by 2005.

Imagine the impact on IT marketing if, with this kind of future, marketers begin to significantly shift their promotional dollars from traditional media to Internet-related advertising and marketing activities. Surely, that is inevitable. Although television has long been accepted as the world's greatest marketing medium for reach, at some point in the not-too-distant future, the Internet could possibly overtake television or converge with it.

Actually, convergence is already here. WebTV (*www.webtv.com*), now owned by Microsoft (*www.microsoft.com*), provides easy television access to the Web via a set-top "terminal." WebTV also provides Internet access at a variety of price points, similar to Internet service providers. It is part of Microsoft's strategy to own emerging Internet channels of distribution. In June 1999, Microsoft invested $30 million in Wink Communications, an interactive TV data service that could enable TV-based e-commerce. Other entries in this emerging market take a different approach. WorldGate Communications (*www.wgate.com*) feeds Web pages directly through a cable system's set-top boxes.

The legitimate question of whether or not the consumer will *want* to view the Web in this fashion remains, but the Internet/TV technologies and services mentioned here and others now in development will continue to blur the lines between television and the Internet. The consumer convergence market may not directly affect the IT marketer, but next on the horizon for business is convergence in a different form. Now every type of portable communications device, from laptop to organizer to cell phone to pager, will move into the Internet realm as wireless communications technology advances.

The Internet Makes Global Marketing a Reality
The Internet continues to grow as rapidly worldwide as it has in the United States. Europe and Asia are already seeing extraordinary increases in Internet usage. For example, Boston Consulting Group (*www.bcg.com*) predicts that B-to-B e-commerce in Asia will reach $430 billion by 2003.

The Internet has already become the first truly cost-effective, widespread global-marketing medium. With the Internet's roots in worldwide networking and its technology enabled via simple telephone line or television cable access, any marketer theoretically could reach any online consumer anywhere in the world at any time. Information can be transmitted via e-mail or over the Web and be received instantly, without regard to time zones or geographic location. No technical skills are necessary to receive it.

Very little on the Internet is currently regulated in terms of international markets. As such, the Internet represents a kind of worldwide electronic free-trade zone. Nations are just now trying to determine what regulations and taxes, if any, should be imposed. The U.S. Congress in 1998 enacted the Internet Tax Freedom Act, which placed a three-year moratorium on new and discriminatory taxes on Internet commerce and created a commission to develop a uniform system for the application of existing taxation of remote sales. The moratorium was expected to be extended as of 2001. The World Trade Organization in 1998 reached agreement among its 132 member countries not to impose customs duties on electronic commerce transmissions.

Also in 1998, the U.S. and Japanese governments agreed to keep electronic commerce essentially free from regulation and agreed to cooperate at an international level to remove barriers to electronic commerce. A nonprofit organization was established by the U.S. government to take over the technical management of the Internet Domain Name System (DNS). The Digital Millennium Copyright Act was passed to ratify and implement the World Intellectual Property Organization (WIPO) Copyright Treaty and the WIPO Performances and Phonograms Treaty, protecting copyrighted material online.

As for the Internet's continuing worldwide reach, international acceptance is growing rapidly. Although the Internet is still predominantly an English-language medium and the largest area of Internet activity is in the United States, European mirror sites of U.S. multinational companies are commonplace. Worldwide organizations now acknowledge that maintaining a Web site is a mandatory business practice. Multiple-language versions and country-specific editions of Web sites are becoming more common.

This growth promises to continue as global e-commerce becomes a reality. The introduction of the "Euro" as Europe's consolidated currency will help fuel the Internet economy. With the acceptance of digital certificates, which will both verify a sender's identity and make sure the recipient is authorized, digital "cash" transactions could become common the world over.

The Internet Reaches People with Intellect, Power, and Money

Despite the ubiquitous nature of the Internet, early Internet users were somewhat elite—educated, influential, and upscale. In the case of businesses, this often means key decision makers.

The core audience of the Internet is still there, even as the Internet becomes more of a reflection of the U.S. and global population. It is likely that these affluent individuals will still be primary users of e-commerce and thus continue to form the core of the Internet's true buying public. The Internet is home to these desirable and discerning consumers and business people. They are predominantly individuals who may watch television only occasionally but are avid Internet surfers and in many cases Internet buyers. And by the way, the Internet has shaken its early reputation as a predominantly male haven. The earlier-referenced 1999 Internet study by Commerce.net indicates that 46 percent of Internet users in North America are women.

As the Internet marches into consumer homes via DSL over ordinary phone lines, or modem connections via television cable, ISPs will continue to compete on price. This will drop the bar even further, so that the Internet expands well beyond the upscale demographic group and becomes more a reflection of society. Yet IT marketers will still be able to find and target the upscale, influential buyers they are looking for, both on the consumer and the business-to-business side—those who started the stampede in the first place.

The Internet Offers Increased Business Penetration

As a business tool, the Internet is unprecedented in its penetration of the business community. The Internet's historic roots are implanted in science and business, and B-to-B usage has continued to lead the growth of the Internet. With the emphasis on intranets and extranets, B-to-B usage is virtually exploding, even as consumers "sign on" at a dizzying rate. The Internet will continue to be an accepted place, potentially the preferred place, for businesses to do business and for marketers to reach consumers and business people. In fact, the opportunities for segmentation and targeting proliferate dramatically with the Internet's growth.

One of the very real differentiators of the Internet's power is that it has a remarkable *leveling effect* on business. It can make a very small company look larger than it is. That means that even a tiny company can compete, at least electronically, with organizations many times its size. That company can extend its marketing efforts through the Internet to any part of the globe and take advantage of the same Internet channel used by industry giants. Internet technology is inexpensive and widely available, and can be completely outsourced. A company does not have to make a major investment to get on the Net and use it as a powerful means of marketing.

An encouraging statistic is that Internet business penetration is finally reaching down into the small-business market. A study of small-business Web presence, commissioned by Prodigy Biz, the third-largest small-business Web-hosting company in the United States, was conducted by International Communications Research in late 1999. The study reported that one-third of businesses with fewer than 100 employees had a Web presence in 1999, up from 19 percent a year earlier. Ninety percent of respondents felt they would benefit from the Internet, with the top three anticipated benefits being promoting to prospects, e-commerce, and better customer service.

Even if a company does not aggressively use the Internet to market itself, that organization can benefit greatly from using the Internet as a competitive research and business learning tool. This is one of the sometimes-hidden benefits of the Internet. It is amazing how much information companies post about themselves on their Web sites. Sometimes you have to wonder if they are so enamored with the technology that they will put even the most sensitive company documents out there for anyone to see. This is a goldmine for all of us who consider some form of marketing as our livelihoods. What used to take weeks of work now takes minutes, because competitive research can be accomplished with a few clicks of the mouse. The value of this aspect of the Internet extends far beyond marketing alone. With the amount of information resident on the Web, virtually any research in any discipline can be conducted online and at no cost for the information itself.

On the downside, however, the Internet is certainly seductive. A number of studies have suggested that unrestricted employee Internet usage can seriously reduce company productivity. As a result, an entire business centered on "site blocking" has developed, as software companies pitch products that cut down on unauthorized Web visits.

Another hidden benefit of the Internet for marketers is the way in which it improves overall business efficiency. Beyond marketing, using the Internet to do business is both efficient and competitively wise. My company, Directech | eMerge *(www.directechemerge.com)*, is a direct marketing agency whose business efficiency has dramatically increased because of the Internet. Of course, we routinely use e-mail to communicate with clients and prospects, many of which are IT companies. We also present conceptual creative work over our own secure "WorkWeb." Some of our clients prefer to view work on the Web, and as a result, it has replaced paper layouts. This way of doing business is particularly advantageous when we need to present creative work to a local client contact on the East Coast or in the Midwest, along with contacts on the West Coast or in Europe who need to review the work simultaneously.

At other times, we have posted direct mail work on a client's intranet or extranet so its sales force, distributors, or resellers could see the work prior to distribution to customers and prospects. Not only does this facilitate communications, it also eliminates the cost of printing an overage of the mailing and sending it to these internal audiences.

One of the fastest-growing applications in this area is Internet conferencing. Through such technologies as Internet telephony and audiovisual streaming, communicating in real time over the Web is becoming commonplace, dramatically increasing business efficiency as cybermeetings replace face-to-face meetings.

The Internet Provides a Unique Form of Communications Intimacy
If marketing is about building relationships, then Internet marketing is about building *lasting* relationships. With the medium's maturation and the increasing integration of database marketing practices, targeting and one-to-one marketing on the Internet will be the norm, and that means marketers will be able to address the individualized needs of constituents.

Targeting on the Internet, as you will see in subsequent chapters, is not only feasible, but can be just as efficient as direct mail in reaching particular audiences. There are as many specialized Web sites as there are specialized consumer or trade publications—primarily because virtually every specialized publication has established a sister Web site. That means you can be as selective with Web-based media as you can with print-based media.

The same is true of lead-generation and order-generation programs. You can select the most appropriate Web sites for banner ad placement and reach a targeted audience, as you would with traditional print media.

Outbound unsolicited e-mail certainly does not have the acceptance of traditional direct mail, but the use of e-mail is another option that should be considered, if cautiously. Legitimate opt-in lists of individuals who are willing to receive promotional e-mail are increasingly available for rental. Customers and prospects who are receptive to promotional e-mail could form the basis for an e-mail list that is potentially one of your best-performing lists. E-mail lists will continue to come onto the market, and the selection criteria will continue to improve as promotional e-mail gains acceptance.

E-mail newsletters are enormously popular because they put valuable information into subscribers' e-mail boxes, usually free of charge.

E-mail is one-to-one correspondence, quite like traditional direct mail. Today, e-mail is private and personal and is read more attentively than any other medium.

The World Wide Web is truly an intimate and personal "playspace" for adults. Used effectively, the Web can deliver personalized content to each and every visitor, or even automatically to a visitor's computer desktop via push technologies. As a result, a marketer can initiate a one-to-one relationship via e-mail and the Web with a prospect, customer, or business partner. The marketer can also learn from that relationship via database marketing and can grow the relationship over time.

The Internet Changes the Economics of Marketing

The stunning cost implications of electronic marketing in part fuel the Internet's unprecedented growth. The Internet is not only cost-effective, it is also cheap in comparison to other media. The Yankee Group estimates that Internet direct marketing is 60 to 65 percent cheaper than traditional direct mail marketing.

A marketer can build and host a Web site and reach a worldwide audience at a cost that is far less than the cost of one national television commercial. Electronic communication has a whole different cost structure from traditional print, direct mail, telemarketing, or television media. There are no media placement costs associated with launching a corporate Web site or employing e-mail as a marketing medium. You may have to rent e-mail address lists, but you do not have to engage printers or mailhouses, or pay postage, when you disseminate e-mail. There are no hotel, travel, or on-site material costs for virtual seminars and events. There are no printing and mailing costs for electronic fulfillment. Even order taking is cheaper with the Internet, especially if electronic catalogs are used in place of traditional paper catalogs.

The Internet Establishes a Brand New Sales Channel

The Internet completely transforms the selling process for marketers. Even early successful electronic commerce users have found that they can dramatically reduce the cost of sales via the Internet. The story of Amazon.com, a company that defied the standard practice of opening retail store locations and instead chose to sell books exclusively on the Internet, is legendary.

Amazon.com became one of the most successful Internet business launches ever and forged the way for other hard-goods marketers (including many competitors) to stake their claim on the electronic frontier. With the advent of secure online ordering, electronic commerce will undoubtedly reach its full potential as more marketers use the Internet to sell their goods and services.

A review of both specialized and general media sources suggests that 1997 was the year the Internet found its legs as a tool for selling. Although electronic commerce was still in its infancy, 1997 saw the Internet's first $1 billion in advertising revenue, according to Reuters, up from $267 million in 1996. As proof positive of the future, consumer-goods giants took to the Internet in 1997, not just by establishing top-shelf Web sites, but by aggressively integrating Internet advertising and electronic commerce initiatives into their promotional marketing strategies. In 1998, consumer giant Procter and Gamble organized an unusual Internet marketing summit to elicit ideas for future initiatives.

In 1998 and 1999, e-commerce really hit its stride. There was greatly increased activity on the consumer side, but the majority of Internet-based sales have still been generated by businesses selling to other businesses. The successes of the past few years have been amazing.

Dell Computer (*www.dell.com*) is testament to that. By the end of 1997, it was widely reported that Dell had logged $4 million a day from online sales. By early 1999, however, *The Wall Street Journal* was reporting that Dell had reached $14 million a day in online sales and 2.5 million visitors a week in site traffic. According to the company, online sales accounted for 25 percent of Dell's business by early 1999, and it accounted for half its business by the end of 2000.

Dell was not the only company achieving such spectacular business-to-business success. Networking giant Cisco Systems (*www.cisco.com*) had already established an industry-leading e-commerce benchmark by the end of 1997, averaging $9 million per day of online sales. That translated into 40 percent of the company's total annual revenue being generated via the Web even in those "early days" of e-commerce. Cisco's numbers by early 1999 reached $21 million a day. Intel (*www.intel.com*) was pulling in $2.5 billion of online income by the end of the first quarter of 1999.

It is this final element of Internet marketing that has generated the most excitement among IT companies, as well as throughout the business world. If the Internet can help companies sell products and services more efficiently, it will become the new dominant sales channel that lives up to every marketer's dream.

The Key Areas of Internet Marketing for IT Companies

In the following chapters, we will explore in detail the areas of Internet marketing you will need to leverage:

- How IT Marketers Can Benefit from the New Direct Marketing

- Making the Most of Your Web Site

- Using Search Tools and Newsgroups

- The Ins and Outs of E-mail

- Internet Advertising and Public Relations

- Internet Events and Meetings

- Internet Fulfillment

- Internet Customer Service

- Internet Communities

- Internet Partnering

- Selling on the Internet

- How IT Marketers Can Integrate Online and Offline Marketing

Internet marketing may require a new set of practices and a new way of thinking, but it is, at its heart, good, solid direct marketing. Read on and see for yourself.

2

How IT Marketers Can Benefit from the New Direct Marketing

Internet marketing has already been heralded as "the new direct marketing" by many. Although Internet marketing has not completely replaced traditional direct marketing, it is fast becoming the preferred direct marketing channel. IT companies have already shifted promotional dollars into traditional measurable media, recognizing that brand awareness goes only so far. Direct marketing is the "direct" beneficiary of this shift, and the result has been strong, consistent growth in direct marketing over the past several years.

Now, with the Internet's broad acceptance as a direct marketing medium, IT marketers are making the next logical move: They are investing more heavily in Internet marketing. The issue facing them, however, especially in light of a more uncertain economic future, is proving that there is an acceptable return on their investment (referred to as ROI) with interactive media. In this context, Internet marketing must prove to be as measurable as traditional direct marketing. In this chapter, we'll explore that need ... and see if the Internet can meet it.

How Direct Marketing Is Being Transformed

Direct marketing in the United States had its roots in direct response advertising in early newspapers and, later, in national magazines. That was just the beginning of direct marketing's rising popularity. With the advent of direct mail, the direct marketing business went through its own paradigm shift. Cut-out coupons that appeared in early direct marketing advertising did not go away—they still exist in newspaper circulars and in some print advertising—but the new format for the coupon became the business reply card and order form in direct mail. Generating leads and orders quickly became the staple of consumer and business-to-business direct marketers alike.

Database marketing was another direct marketing breakthrough of historic proportions, yet a small technological innovation that truly changed the direct marketing business forever was something far simpler. The innovation that opened the door for personal direct marketing is interactivity: the toll-free 800 telephone number.

The 800 number has been in existence since 1967, yet it has been so thoroughly embraced by the world in recent years that the supply of 800 numbers has already been exhausted. In 1996, 888 numbers were introduced, and in 1998, 877 numbers were added to supplement 800 numbers.

The impact of the 800 number on direct marketing cannot be underestimated. It created a whole new form of "we pay for the call" marketing and changed the dynamics of the inquiry and order process forever. The toll-free number functionally reverses telephone charges so that the caller does not pay, but it does something more important than that: The toll-free number *extends a marketer's reach*. It removes a physical, costly barrier to eliciting a response from a prospect or customer. Now, the individual can make a quick, easy call to any location without paying for it, and if the telemarketer is so staffed, that person can call on any day and at any time.

Think about what the 800 number really does. It means that a marketer can effectively open up the entire North American market and serve customers from anywhere, still maintaining the brand and product awareness so important to the marketer. In many cases, a marketer can even select a toll-free number that supports and enhances the brand. (Some examples: 1-800-CALL-ATT, 1-800-THE-CARD [American Express], 1-800-FLOWERS.)

The 800 number is now universally recognized and accepted by all marketers, but it revolutionized mail order marketing. Mail order marketers learned that by offering an 800 number, two things happened:

1. Their number of orders via the 800 number surpassed other response paths.

2. In addition, the total number of orders from all sources generally increased as well. In other words, adding the 800 number had a residual effect: *It increased the overall volume of orders coming in from all response paths.*

This is a principle that applies well to direct marketing in general. *By offering multiple response paths, you tend to increase overall response.* That is because individuals tend to respond individually, and by offering them many response options, you respect each individual's desired way of responding. Some people are comfortable picking up the phone; others prefer responding via mail or fax. Still others would much rather respond over the Internet.

Let us return to that 800 number. You would be hard pressed to find any serious mail order marketer who does not offer an 800 number. Of course, you still may chuckle when you see and hear them repeated over and over again on those television commercials, but they work—or you would not see them repeatedly used. Mail order success with the 800 number led to general business success. Now the 800 number has reached mass acceptance.

The 800 number has become so commonplace in business communications that any business interested in getting responses considers using one. There is a toll-free telephone book and a toll-free number to call for toll-free directory assistance. Toll-free numbers are in use by local plumbers and electricians. You can even get your own personal toll-free number, so friends and family can reverse the charges on you!

With mass acceptance comes the "put it everywhere" syndrome. It was not long before you began to see 800 numbers appearing frequently in print ads and television commercials. You even began to see them as customer service enhancements on consumer goods products—cereal boxes, potato chips, detergents, and the like.

In effect, the 800 number has now become not only an accepted part of marketing, but an accepted part of life—part of the fabric of America, a commodity that is no longer just a marketing gimmick, but rather a necessary business tool.

The Internet Address Is the New 800 Number

Have you noticed that there is something new at the bottom of magazine ads and at the end of television commercials? It is not an 800 number anymore; it is the URL of a Web site. Look for the "www" on ads and on TV. It is everywhere, the way the 800 number used to be. The Web address seems to be gaining rapid acceptance as the new 800 number—at least in the minds of advertisers and their advertising agencies—and that is just one basic reason that the Internet will transform direct marketing. It is a transformation that is destined to reach far beyond what the 800 number had to offer.

Suppose Internet usage continues to grow at its current rate. That means the Internet will be the medium with the most extensive reach—perhaps even topping television. As indicated earlier, widespread acceptance and dropping access prices will dramatically accelerate this growth.

What will this growth mean to IT direct marketers? The use of direct marketing itself continues to grow in its own right. A Direct Marketing Association study indicates that direct marketing is expected to outpace total U.S. growth through 2002, growing at a rate of almost 7 percent annually.

This same report projects that interactive marketing will grow by 54 percent annually through 2002, and that electronic commerce will grow by nearly 61 percent annually. These statistics are supported by similar projections from numerous respected research firms. You will find many of them referenced elsewhere in this book. All of the forecasts point to the same conclusion: It will not be long before the Internet will be the undisputed king of the media world.

What we have going forward, then, is an interesting phenomenon. From a marketing perspective, use of the Internet is growing at such a rate that it will soon overshadow and surpass traditional media.

This suggests an intriguing scenario on the near horizon that B-to-B marketers must take into consideration:

> *If the Internet takes over the lead, and other media flatten out, then other media will be subordinate to the Internet and, therefore, they will primarily be used to support the Internet.*

The Internet Is the Future of IT Marketing

I believe that, even now, we have reached a point of intersection between usage of the Internet and usage of traditional direct marketing media

(Figure 2.1). At this intersection point, the Internet and other media cross. After the intersection point, the Internet trajectory continues upward and traditional media begin to flatten out. As the next few years progress, usage of the Internet goes up steeply, so the gap widens. That's why you will likely see a very different marketing world emerging.

Every fact in this book supports the inevitability of the Internet. All the conditions are right. It appears from every perspective that the planets are aligned for the Internet to ascend, unchallenged, into marketing dominance.

As a long-time direct marketer, I was a little frightened by this new marketing world at first, but now I am excited and invigorated by the potential of Internet marketing. I have personally witnessed in my own business, and working with leading IT companies, how the Internet increases the yield from traditional direct-marketing media, and I have seen the power of the Internet in generating interest in products, capturing qualified leads, servicing customers, and making sales.

The significance of Internet marketing is even greater with a more clouded economic picture. When you consider the potential to reach

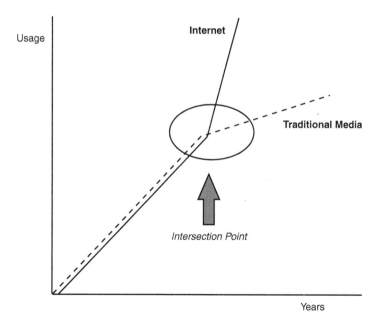

Figure 2.1. The Internet and traditional direct marketing media are now at an intersection point. Over the next few years, the Internet trajectory continues upward, while traditional media begin to flatten out.

large audiences very economically via e-mail, online advertising, affiliate marketing, and your own Web site promotions, Internet marketing can look like a media bargain. Of course, you need to balance that factor against the reality that Internet marketing is still not nearly as targetable as direct mail. With direct-mail lists, you have a much greater ability to segment and target audiences with pinpoint accuracy. But that is changing as Internet marketing matures and online targeting opportunities increase.

Moving into the Future Means Transitioning Now

As traditional media become subordinate to the Internet, IT marketers will face a new media world—one that has different kinds of challenges. With the upward spiral of the Internet trajectory, you will need to adjust your marketing and media strategies. What this really means is that you will need to redefine your use of direct marketing in the context of the Internet and ready yourself for a future that looks very different from the past.

You can begin by taking advantage of the intersecting point where the Internet and traditional media cross now. You can continue to use advertising, mail, phone, and other traditional media. You would be wise, however, to increasingly enhance them by adding Internet response paths, offering Internet fulfillment, using e-mail for follow-ups, driving individuals to your Web site, and inviting prospects and customers to virtual events that occur on the Internet.

> *Now is the time to take a new look at what you are doing and build a transitional marketing strategy that will combine the best of traditional media usage with the emerging world of Internet media usage.*

Chapter 13 of this book offers additional discussion on the move from "offline" to "online" marketing. For now, here is an overview of the basic steps you will need to take:

1. *Assess your Internet marketing readiness.* Now is the time to evaluate your organization's Internet marketing capabilities. Will you be ready to transition to largely Internet-based marketing in a year?

What about in two years? Evaluate your company's current use of Internet technology, and your current use of Internet marketing.

– Do you already take inquiries over the Web? Are you doing electronic fulfillment? Are these things in your future plans?

– Is your Web site capable of order entry, processing, and tracking?

– Do you have a marketing database that can be integrated with the Internet? Have you started to use database-driven Internet marketing?

– Is your organization planning investments to make all of this happen?

2. *Begin the move to Internet direct marketing now.* Do not let the assessment process deter you. The fact is that most of the B-to-B marketing world is at the beginning of the Internet trajectory, just as you are. The important thing is to understand your current state of readiness and recognize where you are today—and where you will need to be soon. Start the move to Internet direct marketing now. Capitalize on the Internet trajectory by integrating the Internet with your use of traditional media and conventional direct marketing.

3. *Prepare your management for the Internet-dominated future.* The Internet has already captured top-of-mind awareness among senior management at many companies. Make sure your company is one of them. Help your management prepare for the electronic future by sharing Internet direct marketing information from authoritative sources.

4. *Develop an Internet marketing action plan.* If you are in a position to do so, participate in or chair a committee in your organization that is charged with developing an implementation plan for using the Internet as a strategic marketing tool. You may find that there is an even larger issue—using the Internet as a strategic business tool. If management is already on that course, so much the better. Then Internet marketing and electronic commerce can be positioned as a logical subset of your organization's Internet business plan.

Where Are IT Marketers Really Headed?

Let us take a look ahead and envision what the Internet marketing future might look like for a company that markets its software to businesses.

Company
A maker of personal productivity business software.

How the Company Markets and Sells Its Product
The company has no direct sales force. It sells directly to the end user via the Internet and also through a consortium of value-added resellers. The company offers all product information, including technical specifications, user testimonials and case histories, and analysts' reports, on its Web site. The company promotes the Web site at trade shows, in targeted trade journal advertising, and by using high-impact direct mail postcards to drive prospects to the Web. The company also promotes the Web site via electronic public relations activities, Web banner advertising on select sites, and reciprocal links with its partners' sites.

The company hosts an ongoing series of invitation-only virtual seminars, featuring a product demo and a chat room with guest speakers, on the Web. Individuals are selected from targeted outside lists and from the company's in-house qualified prospect and customer list. Individuals receive direct mail or e-mail invitations to the seminar. Each invitation carries a personal access code so that the individual can be identified and greeted when he or she logs on to the seminar. Top prospects receive follow-up e-mails and faxes to encourage attendance at the seminar.

The company uses an area of its Web site to offer a try-and-buy downloadable demo to prospective buyers. Prospects can fill out a Web response form, provide electronic credit authorization, and unlock a demo for 30 days. After 30 days, they are electronically billed unless the company is otherwise notified. All products and services offered by the company can be purchased online. Customers have the option of downloading products and printing out necessary documentation from the company's Web site at a lower price or receiving physical product with packaging at a higher price.

The company maintains an extranet that is accessible by customers and partner suppliers. Customers are asked how they wish to receive communications from the company—via e-mail, Web content pushed to their desktop, automated fax, mail, or phone. Each customer's preference is stored in a database.

Users can access a support area that features 24-hour-a-day support via an intelligent agent system that answers most questions online. Some questions are referred to live representatives, who are automatically notified during business hours and respond via e-mail or phone within 12 hours.

Suppliers can access a special area of the extranet that allows them to conduct business electronically with the company, including issuing purchase orders, acknowledging orders, handling inventory control, shipping, and billing.

Media Usage for Direct Marketing

The company invests 70 percent of its marketing budget on Internet-related marketing and 30 percent on a combination of trade shows, limited advertising, direct mail, telemarketing, and fax communications.

Effectiveness

The company carefully tracks all inquiries and orders via a Web-connected marketing database. Updates to the database can be made in real time over the Web. The database is scrupulously maintained. Because the company knows what is and isn't working well, it can modify its program rapidly. In fact, the company's Webmaster can make changes to the Web site on the fly. The company's small fulfillment staff can handle a large volume of electronic inquiries and orders.

Going Global: How Internet Marketing Can Create a Worldwide Business for IT Companies

As a marketing medium, the Internet is well on its way to becoming the easiest, most cost-effective route to global marketing. There has never been a single medium that, even at its inception, offered this promise. The Internet is a medium that already has the infrastructure necessary to serve international markets from the United States, and to encourage businesses from outside the United States to market their products and services here.

To see why, we will briefly examine how the Internet works. Basically, the Internet is a network of networks that, through a sometimes puzzling assortment of communications links, allows anyone with a computer and a means of access (such as a modem) to get on an information highway. Although there are gatekeepers (such as Internet Service Providers, or ISPs), Internet access is relatively easy and inexpensive for businesses and consumers alike. The structure of the Internet is such that ISPs can "plug in" directly via the Internet's backbone. Smaller ISPs buy access from larger ISPs, which are closer to the backbone. The market is so huge that most of them can coexist, at least currently. In total, ISPs efficiently provide access to large numbers of end users.

Competition among online services and ISPs keeps prices relatively low and service quality relatively high. The impact on the pricing structure of giant online services such as America Online and CompuServe, and of large and small ISPs alike, is significant. The pricing model has been unlimited Internet access for a reasonable monthly fee, on average around $20. Some ISPs offer variants of the model that reduce the price and put a cap on the number of monthly hours. That is quite different from earlier pricing models, which sold access by the hour. In many cases, basic Internet access is now equivalent to or cheaper than basic telephone service in many areas of the United States. Price is no longer a major barrier to widespread Internet access. As mentioned in the previous chapter, free Internet access became a phenomenon in the United States in 1999, with similar services coming onto the worldwide market shortly thereafter. In the United States, Gateway announced that it would offer one year of free Internet access with the purchase of a computer. Search engine Alta Vista announced free Internet access in late 1999. Internationally, more than a million people had signed up with Freeserve, a British Internet access service that vaulted past America Online in less than a year. How do the free services do it? Typically, by connecting the access to another purchase, or by exposing the subscribers to plenty of mandatory advertising.

Communications technology is continuously improving. Consumers increasingly will have access to DSL, which allows Internet access using phone lines already installed in the consumer's home. The phone line can be partitioned so that it can actually carry voice and data simultaneously. Most importantly, the service is always on, just like a dial tone. That means that a consumer could use one phone line to access the Internet without tying up the line for other family members.

Modems are dropping in price and are becoming more technologically sophisticated. The emerging 56K standard will bring universal uniformity to modems, much as Windows has done for PCs. As a result, vendors will fight less over conforming to standards and more over modem features. Modems are easy to use and inexpensive. Many PCs offer the option of internal modems, and external modems are available that connect several PCs at once or provide pooled access to the Internet.

The end user reaps huge benefits from all of this. We get all the Internet has to offer—worldwide e-mail (which is often offered free by

ISPs, search engines, and other service providers), newsgroups, the Web, and more—at a reasonable cost. In most cases, consumers can get dial-up access to the Internet by making local phone calls, and with Internet access at our place of business, it may not even cost us that.

Internet technology is moving at such a breathtaking pace that some of the developments seem almost unbelievable. In July 1999, for example, *The Boston Globe* reported that a Boston-based company, SpeechWorks International (*www.speechworks.com*), would be introducing a product by the end of the year that would allow people to browse the Internet via the telephone. The company's SpeechSite software now makes it possible for Web sites to recognize voice commands. In November 1999, a company called DigiScents (*www.digiscents.com*) launched a technology that promised to digitize scents and send them across cyberspace. Maybe the "Smell-o-vision" that failed in the glory days of television will work over the Internet.

Meanwhile, business use of the Internet is soaring. Businesses look at Internet access as a necessity. Industrial-strength Internet access is provided through ISPs that offer high-speed 56K, T1, and T3 connections. The Internet will soon be regarded to be the "always-on" equivalent of the telephone.

More and more, companies throughout the world increasingly depend on the Internet. They are furiously forming intranets, the internal networks that run off the Internet, and extranets, corporate networks that permit select outsiders in. Intranets seem to be growing faster than the rate of PC growth.

As businesses actually run their networks across the Internet, they will need to deliver Internet access directly to the computer desktops of their employees. Internet browsers are already built-in features of today's computers, similar to any operating system or application. Employees will view it as an application, expecting that Internet access will always be there, just like an electric light. They will not even think twice about it.

The Worldwide Impact of the Internet

We have just set the stage for Internet usage on a massive global scale. Now, how does all of this impact IT marketers?

If your company has any kind of substantial sales revenue, chances are there already is an international marketing component to your business. As a matter of course, most U.S.-based companies extend their marketing activities into Canada without hesitation. Various sources report that over half the Canadian population now has Internet access.

(An interesting aside: Time and again, Canada proves to be fertile ground for marketers of computers and other information technology products. My experience has been that direct mail response rates from mailings directed to Canadian prospects beat out U.S. response rates, sometimes by as much as two to one.)

After Canada, the next market many U.S. companies seem to pursue is the United Kingdom. Logic tells us that it is because of the commonality of the English language that England, Scotland, and Ireland are prime targets, with Australia and New Zealand close behind. These markets are also exhibiting burgeoning Internet usage.

Depending on the geographical distribution of a company's sales offices or distributors, the rest of the world may change in marketing priority. Certain European countries may be next in line. Latin America may show the most promise for some companies. IDC projects e-commerce to hit $8 billion in Latin America by 2003, with 19 million users. The Pacific Rim may also be a likely target. Japan, Hong Kong, and China are certain to be tantalizing markets for larger U.S. companies. The point is that U.S. companies have already established a strong foothold beyond the boundaries of the United States. Taking full advantage of the global economy is nothing new for them.

What is new, however, is the global marketing impact of the Internet. The Internet truly flattens the world. The rate of growth in Europe is impressive, but even more so in the Asia Pacific region. IDC's 2001 projections indicate that the Asia Pacific region, excluding Japan, will see Internet usage grow to more than 240 million users in 2005 from just 64 million users in 2000. That means that Internet usage in that region could be greater than in the United States by 2005. The number of Japanese Internet domain names (those with .jp) grew 84 percent just from 1998 to 1999 (Japan Network Information Center).

Even if the IT marketer wants to make use of e-mail alone, global marketing becomes an inexpensive reality. With an e-mail address in hand, a marketer can reach anyone, anywhere. E-mail is delivered in most cases to an individual's PC private mailbox. Sending e-mail from the United States to Hong Kong is no more expensive than sending it from one town in Massachusetts to another. The Internet simply does not recognize physical distance. What could be more attractive for a global marketer?

The primary place for business to be done on the Internet is, of course, the World Wide Web. There are currently some 1 million Web sites on the Web, and the growth is not letting up. All of those URLs (Uniform Resource Locators) start with *http://www,* representing the

World Wide Web. Most of us simply call it the Web, but we should not overlook the significance of those first two Ws.

Surf the Web and you quickly realize that you can happen upon non-U.S. sites very easily. (They typically are identified by a country abbreviation at the end of the URL, such as *.uk* for the United Kingdom.) It is just as easy to get to a site in any state as it is to get to a site in any country of the world. It is no less complicated to get to a U.S. site from outside this country. It is all quite transparent and instantaneous.

It is not difficult to understand why this phenomenon occurs. You can search, find, and link to any Web site in the world, simply by entering its URL. Your computer does not care where the host computer is— and at this stage of the Internet's life, *you pay no premium or penalty for accessing a site on the other side of the globe.* Probably all you do is make a local phone call and, magically, you are connected.

That is one extremely compelling reason that global Internet marketing—and the electronic commerce associated with it—is predicted to escalate so dramatically in the next several years. Today, nothing flattens the world, or brings it closer at a lower price, than the Internet. IT marketers with global goals are now establishing mirror sites and multiple-language versions of their Web sites; Internet translation tools are available that make this easy to do. It is only a matter of time until these same marketers use their Web sites to accept and fulfill orders online from customers worldwide.

In fact, they do not even have to learn how to process the orders. Today, there is a whole class of Web sites that "insulate" the marketer from the entire order-taking and fulfillment process. These "electronic malls," or Web communities, are really Web storefronts, established by an electronic commerce "reseller" who "rents" space to marketers on a multi-advertiser Web site. Some malls are set up so that the marketer still handles inquiries and orders. Others overlay an order-processing front end onto the site so that the marketer becomes one of many who take advantage of a system already in place—at a cost that may be far lower than doing it in-house.

Another option is outsourcing Internet services to ASPs (Application Service Providers). ASPs offer sophisticated e-business and e-commerce offerings on a subscription-type basis, so companies do not have to invest in the technology and infrastructure.

There are, of course, both advantages and disadvantages to such approaches. On the positive side, the marketer gets someone else to do all the promotional, technical, and operational work. On the negative side, the marketer shares resources and customers with others and therefore relies on the site owner's capabilities to bring in and support the business, or relies on the ASP's resources, which may be limited. Nonetheless, these are fascinating business models that can potentially launch a marketer's worldwide business effort quickly and cost-effectively.

For some marketers with a large international component to their businesses, the Internet is nothing short of a marketing miracle. Imagine the small IT company with international marketing goals. With the Internet, this business owner can communicate 24 hours a day, 7 days a week, with points worldwide via inexpensive e-mail. The savings on international phone calls, faxes, delivery services, and travel can be astonishing. Similarly, if this same business establishes a Web site, a literal world of opportunities opens up:

- The company can promote its Web site to prospects and customers simply by including the URL on business cards and letterhead, and in literature and other promotional materials.

- The Web site can be a repository of information, in multiple languages if necessary, that can be accessed by anyone, from any place at any time.

- The Web site could become an order-processing channel so that the company could accept orders from its worldwide customers and acknowledge these orders electronically.

- The company can set up an extranet, using the Web as a place where business can be privately conducted between the company and worldwide customers and suppliers.

- The company principal could even hold special events or conduct live videoconferencing via the Web.

The IT marketer can take full advantage of the Internet's global reach in numerous ways. Following are just a few of the possibilities.

Expanding Markets and Territories

Marketing no longer has to artificially stop at a country's borders. An Internet marketing program can make a global initiative not only possible, but also practical. A company's Web site can be mirrored in several languages, and it can address country-specific issues. An intranet can be established to provide low-cost, instant communications with every sales office, sales representative, distributor, reseller, or retailer worldwide. An extranet can be used to admit partners, suppliers, and customers into select portions of the intranet. The Web site can be promoted inexpensively throughout the world with links on other Web pages and in e-mail newsletters. Simple, inexpensive mailings can be executed in each target country to drive prospects to the corporate Web site.

Developing Global Marketing Partnerships

Internet marketing makes joint ventures attractive and easy to implement. An IT marketer can join together with one or more partners whose products or services complement the marketer's products or services. Then this consortium can pool their resources. They can execute cooperative e-mail campaigns by sharing each other's lists or can form a collaborative Web site that features their solution set. They can also use their own extranet to speed communication with sales and marketing personnel from all participating companies throughout the world.

Providing Worldwide Customer Service

In an era of emphasized customer service, the IT marketer can now use the Internet as the foundation for 24-hour-a-day, 7-day-a-week, 365-day-a-year customer support. The way a company services its business customers differentiates it from its competitors. The Internet can facilitate online customer service centers and provide customer-only information, service, support, and, in the case of software and information, live product. With the advent of Internet telephony, companies will be able to interconnect the Internet and voice response, so customer service will take on a new level of quality.

Approach Global Marketing with Caution

Despite all the apparent benefits of global Internet marketing, it should be pointed out that marketers cannot take other countries and their populations for granted. The European countries are a good example. Europeans live on a single continent, have open borders, trade freely, and are currently engaged in moving to a unified European currency, yet each country retains its very distinct personality, and in the case of marketing, individuals in each country may react differently to promotions.

Some countries are more advanced than others in adopting the Internet, and some people are more receptive to its use. Although English-speaking countries generally appear to be the fastest adopters, other countries are fast becoming huge Internet markets.

Additional issues may occur that could create barriers to Internet-related marketing activities. For example, Europeans generally are less likely to share personal profile information. In fact, some countries have regulations restricting the use of such information. Stringent privacy regulations covering all of Europe, effective October 2001, will make it illegal to solicit via e-mail without the express permission of the consumer. E-commerce may also be less desirable to Europeans because of such issues as individual country currencies, individual country taxes, shipping products across borders, and others. As a result, you cannot assume that an Internet marketing program that works successfully in the United States will automatically succeed globally.

If you are going to make a serious effort to market in Europe or anywhere else in the world, you would do well to learn about the likes and dislikes of the business population in each target country. You will need to know what kind of messaging works and does not work, and how much of what you routinely use in the United States will work in other countries. You will also have to recognize the fact that, to best appeal to a specific country's population, you will need to recognize cultural differences and communicate in that country's language. U.S. companies that have mailed English language material into the Quebec province of Canada have learned that lesson the hard way.

Generally, concentrating on any specific country means doing your marketing homework by enlisting the help of an outside resource within that country or by relying on your own local country representatives. People who live in the target country, or at least have intimate knowledge of that country, are the best sources of marketing information.

Global marketing can cause numerous problems for the U.S. IT marketer. In many cases, U.S. direct mail campaigns use colloquial expressions and "American humor" that may not translate well into other languages. Several languages, most notably German, take up considerably more physical space than English, and mailing sizes, specifications, and postage vary from country to country. The European size for mailing packages, for example, is different from standard U.S. sizes. Advertising specifications are publication-specific, and, depending on the publication, the primary language may not be English. Even English is not English—at least in the rest of the world, which tends to use the British conventions for spelling (e.g., colour, not color; organisation, not organization) and grammar. Even the meanings of words can change.

The Internet generally makes global marketing less complicated, but marketers with a sizable stake outside the United States should take advantage of the medium's ability to tailor messages for different prospects based on where they reside—respecting their individuality and catering to it. With that in mind, the Internet clearly has the potential to escalate global marketing in a way no medium before it has done—providing business marketers with a potential for worldwide business they previously could only dream about.

The New Response Model: "Intersponding"

We have been talking about how the Internet will transform direct marketing and drive the globalization of marketing. Now it is time to address the most intriguing aspect of Internet direct marketing: *how the Internet will fundamentally change the way people interact with marketers and respond to them.*

Unlike any other medium, the computer delivers Internet-based Web content in an entirely new form: *nonlinear information.* All other media are linear: They have a beginning, middle, and end. Direct response print advertising has a headline at the beginning, body copy in the middle, and a call to action at the end. A direct mail package typically is organized in a very logical, linear fashion: The outside envelope is first, followed by the letter, brochures and any other inserts, and the reply device with a call to action; each individual element of the package is linear, with a beginning, middle, and end.

Each element in a good direct mail package reinforces the offer and call to action, so even if two different people read the package elements in a different order, all of the elements relate and ultimately lead to the call to action. This is true, by the way, of other direct mail formats as well, such as self-mailing pieces and catalogs. Direct mail is logical, linear, and integrated. Even telemarketing calls and direct response television commercials are logical and linear, with a beginning, middle, and end. But then we come to the Web. It defies logic.

The Web Defies Logic

Admittedly, many Web sites are logically designed to lead you through from beginning to end, yet the Web site is faced with a technical limitation that paradoxically is its most unique strength. Web sites need to be *nonlinear* so that each visitor can have immediate access to the majority of the information on a site. This is essential because the Web site visitor sees one "page" at a time on the computer screen, yet the Web site has many pages that must be served up to the visitor. How do visitors find out what is on those pages?

The functional way most Web sites deliver this nonlinear information is through a home page. On that home page, visitors typically will see almost every area or section of the site's contents at the same time. It is more like a book's table of contents than anything else, but not quite, because the sections on the home page are nonlinear and modular. You could flip through the sections of a book and move from page to page, but most readers still tackle a book from beginning to end.

The Web site, on the other hand, invites nonlinear reading. The home page encourages movement and flexibility, even though each section has its own purpose and its own content. It is a very different look and feel, is it not?

Actually, the difference is startling. With every other direct response medium, the direct marketer makes a concerted effort to *progressively disclose information* to the prospect or customer in a logical pattern. The AIDA formula—Awareness, Interest, Desire, Action—emphasizes this. It is intentionally broken into stages or steps.

With the Web, however, the visitor is exposed to everything simultaneously. He or she has the ability to see it all, at least on the surface, at one time, from this giant control panel called the home page, and here is the important point:

The visitor is no longer directed by the marketer—instead, the visitor does the directing.

You could make a case that a direct mail catalog provides the same flexibility. In some respects, it does. The reader can thumb through the pages of a catalog randomly, and its contents page is kind of like a Web site's home page. However, when the visitor to a Web site browses pages, he or she is exposed to far more "eye candy" and interactivity than with a printed catalog. A Web site is not physically bound, as a catalog is, so the nonlinear nature is more evident—a benefit as well as a feature.

With a Web site, visitors have a new level of control over the manner in which information is delivered. They can randomly move around the Web site, starting anywhere, going anywhere, finishing anywhere or not finishing at all. In fact, a visitor can leave a page or an entire site very quickly, go to other pages at numerous other sites, and return just as quickly.

Web pages become almost separately interconnected elements, functioning as tiny bits of marketing information in a much greater scheme of things, sometimes melding from one marketer's site to another. This presents a challenge for Internet marketers—to keep visitors on their site and to remind those visitors of exactly where they are: on *their* site.

It also means that there is a whole new dynamic in Internet marketing. With the power in the hands of the prospect or customer, the marketer needs to be mindful of that individual's wants, needs, likes, and dislikes. Instead of randomly receiving promotional messages from you, as might be the case with direct mail or advertising, the Internet prospect or customer expects you *either to ask permission to communicate or to know when to make a contact.*

The Internet promotes one-to-one communications intimacy and encourages a correspondence relationship between the marketer and the end user—the kind of relationship that demands something of one another. This is conceptually different from traditional marketing, and marketers need to deal with the implication.

With the Web, it is almost as if the visitor is a bumblebee, moving from flower to flower, creating his or her own unique formula for consuming marketing information—a formula designed to meet his or her uniquely individual needs. It is truly random, because things just do not happen when you expect them to, and that visitor may want to interact with you at any time during the process.

Call It "Intersponding"

In fact, I believe the Internet creates an entirely new response model, which you might call "intersponding"—a new kind of *interactive, instant, interspersed* pattern of responding. To see what this means from a marketing perspective, let us go back to the Web site visitor. There he or she is, navigating through a Web site, uniquely and freely. Perhaps no two visitors move through a Web site in exactly the same way.

The visitor goes from place to place, consuming bits and pieces of information as the need arises, sometimes at random, sometimes in logical order. Because Web browser software makes it so easy to go from page to page with "Back" and "Forward" buttons, the pattern may be quite complex. That is a good reason for your Web site to provide navigation elements that remain on pages appearing after the home page, so that the visitor can continue to move with total freedom from section to section, yet recall the section for reference. It is just as easy for the visitor to print an occasional page when the need arises.

The Web makes it easy to select and copy text and graphics from other Web sites—and even to obtain the HTML (Hyper Text Markup Language) source code for each Web page with a simple click of the mouse. This is unheard of, and unthinkable, in any other medium! It provides a level of insider access to a Web site visitor (who could just as easily be your competitor as your customer). It puts the power of not just easy information access, but easy information duplication, in the hands of the individual.

In sum, the Web offers a single unique individual a very unique, personal way of interacting with information on your Web site or through one-to-one e-mail communication. In a very real sense, the information this person receives is being individualized, because the visitor is requesting and receiving it in just the way he or she wants it to be delivered.

The level of individualized information will intensify even further as databases are used to power Web sites. With database marketing, marketers will be able to capture information about how visitors are using the Web site and use that information to structure and refine the information flow to the visitors. When a visitor returns to the Web site, the Web site will "know" the individual's likes and dislikes and will feed personalized information to him or her by creating Web pages on the fly that include uniquely personalized content.

This is already a built-in aspect of some advanced sites on the Web, which allow you to individualize or personalize pages by providing profile data. A database engine analyzes the data, and Web pages are then created just for you. You can "pick them up" at the Web site, or have them "pushed" to your computer in some cases. Try it yourself. Go to any of the larger commercial sites or portals and find the "My Page" feature for a completely personalized experience on each site.

Now, what about the *responding* part of "intersponding"? Well, this is truly interesting: If a Web site is set up correctly, the visitor can instantly respond at any time along the way—whether it seems logical or not to respond at that point. Some Web sites embed e-mail response areas so that visitors can click an underlined address, type in an inquiry or response, and send it immediately. Many Web sites go beyond that, however, by using interactive forms. These forms collect basic information about the visitor—name, address, phone number, and so on—and sometimes ask qualifying questions of the visitor. Well-constructed Web sites prominently show a link to this form on the home page and provide multiple links to the form throughout the site.

Even better, the visitor is offered something special (good direct marketing!) for completing and sending the form. It can be sent with a simple click of the mouse.

But wait, there is something wrong. So far, all of this does not sound very different from the traditional way of responding, does it? The Web site has a form that a visitor fills out and sends—the same as with a direct mail reply form or order form, the same as with a call to an 800 number. What is the big deal? Remember this is not responding, this is *intersponding* (Figure 2.2). There is another facet of intersponding that makes it completely unique.

> *Not only can the visitor interactively respond via the Internet, he or she can also instantly be fulfilled via the Internet.*

Once the visitor sends the Web response form, he or she can *instantly* and *automatically*:

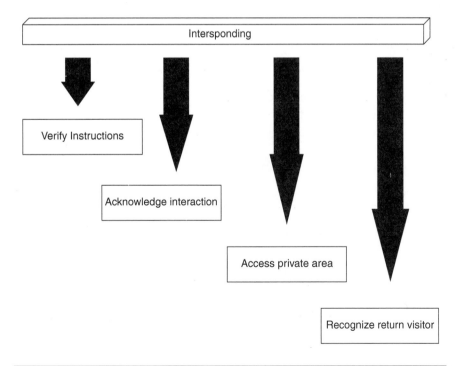

Figure 2.2. Intersponding is a new response model that includes interactive, instant, interspersed fulfillment of a Web visitor's interest.

- Receive an answer that verifies the visitor's instructions or acknowledges an order

- Receive a more detailed acknowledgment of ordering information via return e-mail

- Unlock or receive documents or special Web pages, personalized to his or her specific needs

- Download a demonstration, trial, or full version of a software product onto his or her computer for immediate use

- Gain access to a private event or virtual seminar that offers the visitor a free interactive learning experience

- Be acknowledged as a *returning* visitor or customer, and therefore be given special treatment. For example, the visitor's name, address, and previous ordering information can be stored by the marketer and recalled for use by the visitor when a new order is placed.

Each of these potential responses is an "intersponse"—an interactive, instant fulfillment of the visitor's inquiry—an immediate payback for the visitor's time and trouble.

Intersponding feeds the need for so many things on the part of the prospect or customer:

- Instant gratification

- Total and immediate responsiveness

- One-to-one communication

- Personal correspondence

- The ease and convenience of an automated response

Intersponding *completely changes the relationship* the prospect or customer has with the computer, the Internet, and the marketer. Even though the prospect or customer is sitting in front of a machine and is typing on a keyboard, the response he or she receives is warm, personal, and intimate—because it is intended just for him or her and it is delivered instantly, a direct response to an immediate need. Properly executed, it is the ultimate in fulfillment—what everyone expects when they think of personalized customer service and responsiveness. Ironically, it is what good old-fashioned commerce used to be.

You may not remember this, but there was a time when you could visit a friendly neighborhood store and the proprietor recognized your face and knew your name. He or she knew your family and what you liked to buy, how much you needed, and when you probably would be back. In short, the proprietor had a relationship with you.

The proprietor was not just a store clerk. He or she was a person. He or she chatted with you about the weather, ordered products for you, held them for you when they came in, and sent you on your way with a smile when you were done shopping.

For the most part, we have relegated these kinds of personal business relationships to the past. We have few experiences in our consumer or business lives that replicate them. It is sad, but people just do not seem to know whom they are doing business with anymore.

Maybe that is one more reason for the Internet's popularity. The Internet can, in a business relationship sense, be that proprietor. It may be sobering to think that individuals need to go to a computer to get the same kind of personalized attention they received from a real-live store owner years ago, but the reality is that businesses cannot always provide that kind of face-to-face contact anymore. Customers are all over the world, retail establishments are depersonalized and automated, and the cost of maintaining intense personalized relationships is high.

With the Internet, it's likely that this will not be a problem anymore. With the Internet, maybe intersponding can be the new response model that will make marketing personal once again.

3

Making the Most of Your Web Site

At the core of a successful Internet marketing strategy is the Web site. For most IT companies, the Web site is now an essential part of the marketing mix. In many cases, the Web site has become not only the central repository of marketing and sales information, but also a primary order and even delivery vehicle for software. There are good reasons this is happening so rapidly. In addition to the obvious customer service benefits, the money-saving potential is enormous. According to 1999 statistics from the Organisation for Economic Cooperation and Development, it costs about 50 cents to distribute a software product electronically versus $15 by traditional methods.

Although your company is probably investing a good sum of money in its Web site, the key issue is whether or not you are getting a true *return on that investment*. To obtain a marketing ROI from your Web site, you need to be able to prove to yourself and to your management that it is achieving *measurable results*. This means that your Web site must be structured to capture and qualify leads, accept online orders, provide e-service to customers, and become a distribution center for patches and upgrades.

With these assumptions in mind, this chapter discusses how to ensure that your Web site is a good *direct marketing* tool for you.

Using Your Web Site for Lead Generation and Qualification

Many books are available that cover how to build Web sites. Some of these go into the necessary detail you will need to execute such a project. That is not the purpose of this chapter. Instead, our focus here is on how to use your Web site in the context of direct marketing—to *generate and qualify leads, get response,* and *achieve measurable results.*

The fact is that the majority of sites on the Web today may be marketing sites, but not as many as you might think are *direct* marketing sites. You can prove this to yourself by visiting your favorite sites, or by going to any of the Web's best sites (*www.hot100.com*), as reported by various trade publications and Web sources.

In particular, check out the sites that are *not* directly involved in electronic commerce (that is, directly selling products through the site). E-commerce sites have to be doing a good direct marketing job to generate orders, but what about those other marketing sites. Apply these questions to each site:

- How many of the non e-commerce sites make a special offer that leads to a Web response form that further qualifies your interest?

- How many of these Web sites have a prominent response area (not just a passive "sign-in" or "guestbook") and repeat a call to action throughout the site?

- How many of them have a promotional area that reinforces campaigns the company may be running in other media?

- How many of these sites do you suspect might have the capability to count more than hits, analyzing not meaningless numbers but rather responses and leads generated, qualified, prioritized, and converted to sales?

From a direct marketing perspective, a lot may be lacking in many Web sites. That is because some marketers are still using the old advertising model to create their Web sites. They look at the Web as an awareness medium. The result is that too often the sites have lots of cool technology, lush graphic design, and "eye candy"—but little marketing depth, solid content, and response-oriented techniques. In many cases, they may be nothing more than brochureware.

How an IT Company Built a "Cool" Web Site That Didn't Work

This is a true story. A start-up IT company had decided to rely heavily on its Web site for the launch of both the company and its product. The company selected an award-winning design firm to execute the site from the ground up. The site looked terrific from a design perspective, so management was happy. But the president realized that the company needed to beef up its marketing, so he hired an experienced professional to spearhead the effort as vice-president of marketing. When the vice-president arrived on the scene, one of his first tasks was to analyze the effectiveness of the Web site. Although it appeared that the site was generating a good number of hits, it seemed that people were spending very little time on the site.

The VP wondered why, so he took a close look at the site from every angle. It did not take him long to figure out the problem: The site was crowded with graphic images. Large, sophisticated graphics took a long time to load. Also, the site was difficult to navigate. The worst part of it was when the VP saw what the company had paid for the Web site. He nearly fainted.

The VP made the obvious but painful decision: He trashed the whole site and started over again, this time with marketing objectives and usability in mind. He directed a freelancer to design a clean and simple site with modular graphics that would load quickly. Graphic links were kept to a minimum, with text links predominating. Offers and response paths were very prominent on the home page. He bought electronic rights to articles and product reviews so that he could post them on the company's site instead of sending visitors elsewhere to read them.

The impact was enormous. Not only did traffic increase, but visitors were staying on the site an average of six to nine times longer than before. The Web site quickly became a major lead generator for the company, with lead quality improving monthly, and the redesign of the site cost a mere fraction of what the fancy design firm had charged.

This marketing tale had a happy ending, but the price for success was steep. Let that be a lesson to all those who design a Web site first and ask tough marketing questions later. You need to be ready when senior management asks the dreaded question about *your* Web site: How do we know it is *working*?

A Word about ".com"

It used to be that every IT company's Web site had to have a ".com" on the end. In a few cases, ".net" was adopted as an alternative, primarily by ISPs and other networking companies. Until recently, there were few other options for commercial organizations.

Well, all that is changing, and changing rapidly. New suffixes, such as .biz, .tv, .md, and .info are becoming available as the Web expands to keep up with the demand for domain names. Although ".com" has become a standard for U.S.-based commercial organizations, it may lose its luster (much the way Dot Coms did) as time goes on. Keep an eye on this changing environment to determine if there are marketing opportunities for you hidden behind the dots.

Seize the Opportunity to Set Your Web Site Apart

For a Web site to be used as a tool to generate and qualify leads, it must follow the basic principles of good direct marketing.

Begin with the design of your Web site and its home page. In the previous chapter, you read about the nonlinear nature of the Web. You saw how a site visitor could jump from place to place, freely and randomly. This is true, but it is also true that a Web site can be designed to *highlight or emphasize certain areas* so that the visitor is drawn to them. The design of a page can assist the visitor in locating offers and finding a Web response form.

One possible way to influence your visitors' navigational path is to make the most prominent part of your home page a special offer, highlighted by an animated graphic. If it stands out from the rest of the page and leads to a Web response form, the offer could potentially draw a majority of visitors to that area. Another way is to feature a promotional area that makes the same offer to visitors as a current direct mail or direct response advertising campaign. Leveraging the direct marketing offer potentially could enhance response.

The Web provides the distinct marketing advantage of speed. An offer can easily be posted on a Web site in time to coordinate with any direct marketing campaign—before the campaign even appears in print. If the offer is prominently featured on the home page, perhaps through an on-site banner ad that ties in creatively with the direct mail or advertising, you would gain from the power of integrated media.

Good direct marketing copywriting can also improve the effectiveness of a Web site. Direct marketing copy tends to be written in a friendly, me-to-you style with a heavy emphasis on benefits. It uses short sentences and an informal structure that makes it easier to read and follow. It makes liberal use of "graphic signals" and eye rests, such as indented paragraphs and bulleted lists.

As you explore Web sites, read the words carefully and evaluate the structure and quality of the writing. Notice how tedious it is reading lengthy copy on a computer screen? A good site will take that into account by keeping sentences and paragraphs short; using frequent subheads in bold or in color; breaking copy into sections; using bulleted lists, tables, and indents; and bolding or italicizing appropriate words and phrases.

Incorporate Direct Marketing Techniques into Your Web Site

Here are a few ways you can use direct marketing to improve the efficiency of your Web site in generating and qualifying leads:

1. *Make it easy for a prospect to locate and gain access to a Web response area.* Many Web sites either bury the response area or do not even have one. A prominent response area on a Web site, even a simple Web response form, will encourage prospects to identify and potentially qualify themselves. Reinforcing that response area throughout the Web site by providing links across many of your site's pages will remind prospects of the offer and give them multiple opportunities to respond.

2. *Create a promotional area with special offers.* Change your response area into a promotional area, featuring special offers that change from time to time. Tie these offers in with direct marketing campaigns by leveraging the copy and graphics used in other media and "Web-izing" the creative for use on your site.

   Netscape (*www.netscape.com*) consistently places among the Web's busiest Web sites, largely because so many people come to the site to download Netscape's browser software, but Netscape knows it needs to capture leads from this potentially anonymous legion of prospects and customers. To get visitors to identify themselves, Netscape offers them the opportunity to "join" the Netcenter site instead of just visiting the site.

One of the advantages of joining Netcenter is the fact that Netscape uses the information you provide to "recognize your preferences." Once you tell Netscape your interests, every time you return, Netcenter "remembers" all of your preferences and offers you personalized information and choices just for you. This is an excellent example of using database-driven technology in a nonthreatening way to enhance the Web experience for site visitors.

3. *Place an "on-site" banner ad.* A banner ad is a promotional technique most often used as advertising on other Web sites to draw people to your Web site, but you can also create and place a self-promotional banner ad on your *own* site—to draw attention to a response area on your site. The banner ad could reinforce a campaign in other media or promote a free offer independently and could link to an on-site Web response form.

4. *Offer a free subscription to an e-mail newsletter on your site.* An e-mail newsletter is really an electronic continuity program that gives you the ability to communicate periodically with prospects and customers. You can offer an e-mail newsletter to prospects who provide you with contact information and answer questions on a Web subscriber form. Then build a list of subscribers and send them an e-mail newsletter regularly. Use the e-mail newsletter to convey valuable information, as well as to make offers and further qualify prospects.

5. *Drive traffic to your Web site via traditional media.* Once you invest in a Web site, be sure to capitalize on its existence. Promote the Web site aggressively, especially if it has informational or educational value. Include your Web site address in all promotions and on business cards. Drive traffic to your Web site using other media. For example, numerous IT marketers are achieving significant success generating Web site traffic by mailing an oversized postcard promoting the site to prospects and customers. If you have a special offer of any kind, make that offer on your Web site and promote it in order to drive individuals to the site.

Characteristics of Effective Marketing Web Sites

Use the following as a checklist to determine if your own Web site includes some of the more common characteristics of effective marketing sites.

Compelling, Well-Designed Home Page

An effective marketing Web site starts with a well-designed home page. The home page is not unlike the cover of a magazine. It should be interesting, attractive, and intriguing to your target audience. Key content areas should be highlighted so that visitors can find what they need quickly and easily. The home page itself serves as a gateway into the entire site. From a marketing perspective, it should embody the personality of your company and immediately convey a distinct message. It is generally a good idea for the home page to have a look and feel that complements your corporate or promotional identity.

Timely Updating

The Web is a dynamic medium that demands freshness. Some marketers take advantage of this by prominently posting the date each day on their Web sites. Others include daily updates to give the impression of immediacy. Although daily updating may be too ambitious a goal for some, you should at least set a periodic update schedule, perhaps monthly, and adhere to it.

Frequent updating is becoming one of the differentiators of a Web site. More sites now post "today's date" on the page and include news that is updated frequently. Some sites make use of streamed content from other sources to keep their sites current. Others use content-management systems to automatically update pages.

Consider establishing a prominent "What's New" area so you can localize the information that needs frequent updating. Change this area on a periodic basis. Review the remainder of your site for periodic updating. Consider refreshing the look of the home page every six months.

One clever technique for keeping your home page "fresh" is to employ rotating images or copy that changes within the page. You can set up your home page so that it actually has several different versions, or specified areas, that continuously change as visitors hit the page. In this way, each hit generates a page with a different image, providing the impression of a new page with every visit.

Be vigilant about reviewing your Web site for outdated content, broken links, and coding errors. All of these problems lead to unhappy, frustrated visitors. There may be some small comfort, however, in the fact that you will not be the only IT company that may have Web site problems. In late 1999, ParaSoft, a maker of error-detection technology, conducted a survey of Fortune 100 companies. According to *InformationWeek* magazine, the survey found more than 35,000 dead links and more than 2 million HTML coding errors on the Web sites of the largest leading hardware vendors, namely, Compaq, Dell, Hewlett-Packard, IBM, and Xerox. In fact, the computers and office equipment industry segment ranked second in the "most HTML errors per page" category.

Intuitive Navigational Flow

The nonlinear nature of the Web requires a navigational system that is structured to offer visitors maximum flexibility and freedom to move around. Most navigational systems use several "buttons," icons, or images, accompanied with words or phrases, to identify major areas of a Web site. Often these buttons run across the top or down the left side of the home page, sometimes in frames that remain visible on subsequent pages. Once inside a particular section, additional navigational buttons or text links may be necessary to help the visitor move from page to page.

Continuously improving Web technology is making navigational systems more useful. It is becoming increasingly common for the navigation buttons to "respond" or appear highlighted when visitors roll over them with the mouse. Some buttons or icons "respond" when clicked on by moving or changing color, or even producing a sound (although that generally requires a plug-in). These techniques bring enhanced CD game-like interactivity to the Web and help visitors feel like they are making something happen when they roll around the site or click on their mouse.

The increasing use of "dynamic HTML," JavaScript, and Java applets will make navigational systems even better, as long as a visitor's browser supports these technologies. With dynamic HTML, for example, visitors can see subtopics in drop-down menus when they roll over navigational buttons on the home page. This is especially useful for sites with a lot of depth beneath the home page.

Regardless of the technologies employed, the key point is to make navigating a Web site easy, intuitive, and "idiot-proof." As more people become Web-adept, they will move through Web sites and pages skillfully and quickly. Web sites with well-founded navigational structures will ensure that visitors have a good experience—and stay awhile.

High-Value Information Content

An effective marketing Web site offers visitors reasons for spending time at the site *and* for coming back. Snappy graphics and technological tricks attract attention, but they soon lose their impact if there is no substance to the site. Most Web experts agree that "content is king." Good sites go beyond simply providing product details—they also include product benefits and, more than that, offer high-value information that visitors can use, *whether or not they purchase the product.* The rationale for this is simple: If prospects or customers learn something from a Web site, they will come back for more. Many times, they will also "pledge allegiance" to the site's sponsor by considering that company's product for purchase when the need arises. You lose nothing by posting high-value information that relates to your products or services on your Web site—by doing so, you help to position your company as a knowledge-able leader in your field and gain the respect and potential buying interest of visitors to your site.

It is content that keeps your site "sticky"—which means that visitors come back frequently. Your goal should be to have a visitor bookmark your site and use it as a primary informational resource.

Fast Response Time

Do not underestimate the "hang time" problem with the Internet. The Web has not so jokingly been referred to in the industry as the "World Wide Wait" because the continuous growth of Internet traffic, combined with increasingly sophisticated technology, can sometimes make getting onto the Web—and navigating Web sites—a painfully slow experience.

You can do a lot on your end to help ease the problem by designing your Web site for the fastest response time so that pages load quickly. In general, that means containing graphic images to small files, being careful of full-page background graphics, and ensuring that any advanced technologies, such as integrated databases, multimedia, Internet telephony, or live chat, are supported by adequate Web servers.

Response Orientation

A good lead-generation and qualification Web site should provide prospects and customers with opportunities to interact and respond. Response paths should stand out and be clearly defined on the home page and be referenced throughout the site. Offers should be prominent and lead directly to qualifying Web response forms. Downloads should be easy to execute. Customer service areas should include e-mail links, online forms, and, if possible, 24-hour auto-responders.

Games and contests can help to draw attention to response areas, but they can also generate a large number of unqualified responses—so use them with caution. Make your Web site active, not passive. Make calls to action prominent, and make it easy for visitors to find response areas by instructing them where to go and what to do.

Respect for Privacy
This is listed as a characteristic for effective Web sites because it is increasingly important with the Internet's growth as an influential advertising medium. It is recommended that you post a privacy policy on your Web site. You can create your own privacy policy simply by "filling in the blanks" of a free form provided by the Direct Marketing Association at *www.the-dma.org*. The form leads you through a series of questions to help you determine what to tell your site visitors about the way in which the information they provide will be protected and used.

The Internet privacy issue looms as states, the federal government, and other countries scrutinize cyberspace. It is far too easy to abuse someone's right to privacy electronically, and good marketing use of the Web should include ethical practices. Post a privacy policy on your Web site now, refuse to send unsolicited e-mail unless you are certain it is acceptable to the recipient, and protect the privacy of any e-mail marketing lists you have in your possession.

Despite the need for caution, the news is not all bad from consumers regarding privacy issues. Greenfield Online (*www.greenfieldonline.com*), a leading market research firm, conducted a survey of about 2,000 consumers in October 1999 who were regular Internet users and buyers. Seventy-six percent said they thought Web sites were tracking information about them, but only 8 percent said this practice had an effect on their usage or choice of sites. Sixty-six percent said they were "accurate and truthful" in providing Web sites with information about themselves. Seventy-six percent of the respondents said they would offer additional personal information for participation in incentive programs, and 59 percent said they thought the government did NOT need to regulate data collection.

What You'll Get When You "Follow the Rules"

Follow some of the "rules" listed above and you'll get more visitors, as well as visitors who come more often and stay longer.

A study released in early 2001 by Booz-Allen & Hamilton and Nielsen/NetRatings (*www.netratings.com*) found that online users behave differently based on their informational needs. The study provides some insight into different levels of interactivity and interest. Of the seven categories described in the study, a few have special relevance to the IT marketer.

One category, titled "Do It Again," consists of users who engage in sessions of about 14 minutes in length, with page views of as much as 2 minutes in length. Users in this category spend 95 percent of their time at sites visited at least four times before. Another category, called "Loitering," consists of users similar to those in the "Do It Again" category, but these individuals spend 33 minutes in a session, again with 2-minute page views. Loiterers spend a substantial amount of time at sites that are familiar to them, and they come back for more. If you can attract users in one of these two categories, you are achieving success with your Web site.

A Baker's Dozen of IT Web Sites to Explore

The following sites are a representative sample demonstrating how IT companies use the Web for marketing purposes. Because Web sites are updated frequently, the descriptions here may not be based on the most current version of the Web site. It is therefore recommended that you check out the Web site for yourself using the URLs listed, or by linking to each site through this book's companion site.

Apple (*www.apple.com*)

Apple's Web site is a fitting one for a company reborn. It is as clean and neat as any on the Web, completely in keeping with its brand image. The site appropriately features photography of the striking new iMac and G4 products, but just as important, it leads the visitor to the prominent Apple Store. This, too, is so neat and clean and easy to use, you'd want to order a product just to try it. Apple does a nice job of serving its key markets, too: There are separate Web site sections for Education, Creative, SmallBiz, and Developers.

Beyond.com (*www.beyond.com*)

Acknowledged by many to be one of the Internet's software e-commerce leaders, Beyond.com has taken a new turn on their Web site, featuring "e-Stores," a suite of services that enables companies to market and sell online. This end-to-end solution allows Beyond to build and operate stores for client companies. Beyond also offers government agencies such services as digital software distribution through "gov.beyond.com." Quite a switch in strategy for a company that was the Amazon.com of software and hardware. Beyond still offers these products at its online store, but the store has now taken a subordinate position to the other services.

Cisco Systems (*www.cisco.com*)

Cisco is widely known as one of the first IT companies to make a big push into e-commerce—one that has paid off handsomely. Cisco reportedly grew its online sales from some $10 million daily in 1998 to nearly $23 million per day in 1999. But Cisco's Internet success is not about e-commerce alone. This is a networking company that has made a total corporate commitment to e-business by substantially moving its operations, both external and internal, to the Internet to reduce costs and increase productivity and efficiency. As their Web site demonstrates, Cisco has done it from start to finish: Internet-based learning, ordering, information fulfillment, customer service, employee relations, partner programs, and more. Despite its depth, "Cisco Connection Online" is a clean, easy-to-navigate site that is current, useful, and top-notch . . . and has won numerous awards to prove it.

Dell Computer (*www.dell.com*)

The Dell Computer Web site is all marketing, and the centerpiece is The Dell Store—a place where you can literally build your own computer system online. Actually, The Dell Store is segmented into "specialty stores" such as Home and Home Office, Small Business, Federal Government, Healthcare, and Education, where a shopper's unique needs can be met. The Dell Store features an uncomplicated but remarkably sophisticated ordering process that lets you build and custom-configure a computer and get it delivered in less than 30 days.

Although online ordering is the cornerstone of Dell's online success, the company has innovated in other areas of Internet marketing. For example, Dell provides its key business customers with "Premier Pages"—extranets that display only the Dell products approved for purchase by the customers, along with the special pricing to which those customers are entitled. Dell is facilitating the integration of these customized online order areas with its customers' own accounting systems.

Dell is already legendary as a company that has migrated its traditional direct marketing to Internet direct marketing with phenomenal success. More than 70 percent of Dell's online revenue comes from business customers. In 1999, Dell was averaging $14 million a day in online sales, 30 percent of its total revenue. By 2000, Dell was up to $50 million a day in online sales, with more than 50 percent of its sales from the Internet. (More about Dell in Chapter 12.)

Hewlett-Packard (*www.hp.com*)

The HP home page has a friendly uncomplicated look, albeit somewhat sparse. The "HP Store" leads to an area separated into home/home office and business. The prominent "Drivers" section on the home page was clearly the result of market research that must have told HP that this is what many visitors are looking for. Solutions areas feature a lot of good information; for example, the Small and Medium Business area includes business services, industry-specific solutions, productivity tools, and advice/consulting. The "Support" area offers customers the ability to solve problems themselves and get help when they need it.

IBM (*www.ibm.com*)

IBM.com is one of the largest and busiest sites on the Internet, with 70 different country versions and available in 16 languages. It provides a single point of access to information, commerce, and support resources across 125 IBM divisions and includes a shopping area where customers can purchase over 14,000 products direct from the company. Despite its sheer volume, the IBM home page features a simple and clean design. The company is not afraid to highlight products and special offers, and the site provides easy access to software trials and purchasing opportunities from the home page. And, of course, IBM never misses an opportunity to promote its "e-business" initiatives.

Macromedia (*www.macromedia.com*)

Macromedia, creator of such pervasive Web tools as Dreamweaver, Flash, and Shockwave, has a site that stays on top of technology. In late 1999, the site was recognized as one of the "Ten Best Web Support Sites of 1999" by the Association of Support Professionals (ASP). Macromedia's site is divided into individual Support Centers for each of its products. Customers can quickly find information through TechNotes, "Show Me" movies, and 40 discussion groups.

McAfee Associates (*www.mcafee.com*)

McAfee has become the undisputed leader in the anti-virus field, and their site takes advantage of this reputation. For example, the "McAfee.com Clinic" features total online PC care. Positioned as "the Internet's first online PC manager," the clinic is a subscription-based area that features complete online VirusScan protection, PC maintenance and optimization tools, and more. McAfee's site also features stand-alone anti-virus, PC checkup, shopping, download, and support centers, as well as a free virus e-mail newsletter. McAfee recently launched "McAfee.com Kids," which it describes as a Web site designed to act as a vehicle for parents, teachers, guardians, and students to learn Internet safety, practice responsible Web surfing, and identify age- and content-appropriate Web sites for children.

Microsoft (*www.microsoft.com*) and Microsoft Network (*www.msn.com*)

The Microsoft corporate site is rich and deep in product information and online resources. The site is divided into customized "customer sites" for home and personal, business, developer, education, IT professional, and partner/reseller. Microsoft Network, better known as MSN, is one of the leading ISPs in its own right. The MSN site also includes access to HotMail, a free e-mail service.

Oracle Corporation (*www.oracle.com*)

Oracle has made a big push into everything "e." Interestingly, Oracle.com is one of the most underdesigned sites of any IT company. Take a look at the home page and you'll see a two-color treatment that's virtually all type, with just a few icons at the top to take you to such places as products and the store. Not that Oracle.com isn't loaded with content: It offers news, features, communities, resources, and more. Oracle has also made extensive use of online seminars, which are accessible through its "iSeminars" home page. *Inter@ctive Week* reported that by late 1999, Oracle had already led the market in Internet-based procurement software, and that the company had over 400 customers using its CRM application. In fact, Oracle expected its Business OnLine division to account for almost half the company's sales within five years.

Siebel Systems (*www.siebel.com*)

Siebel is a company that managed to connect itself with e-business early on . . . and succeeded admirably. In fact, Siebel was named by *Business Week* as the most influential software company. Siebel provides a range of e-business solutions, with sales force automation and CRM as its primary focus. On Siebel's Web site, you can browse through 100 case studies, log on to Web-based training through Siebel University, register for free online seminars, access the Siebel Alliance Partner and Reseller portals, and more. The site also features "Siebel.com Passport," a "single login" service that makes navigating all Siebel sites easier.

Sun Microsystems (*www.sun.com*)

The company with the reputation for putting "the dot in dot.com" uses the Web as a primary communications tool to address customers and developers. The site is a somewhat odd mix of funky and corporate (as you might expect from Sun). Perhaps its most distinguishing attribute is "My Sun," one of the early entries into personalized corporate Web pages, which have now become commonplace. My Sun allows you to change the look and feel of the page; link to the SunStore, the Product Configurator, the Spares Buying Guide, and an Online Order Status Report; customize your own stock portfolio; get customized Reuters news feeds; use your own quick links, and more.

WorldCom (*www.worldcom.com*)

This site is included primarily to demonstrate just how much telecommunications companies have embraced the Internet. WorldCom is a major provider of local, long-distance, international, and Internet services. One look at their Web site tells you they are going about as far away from analog, the older telephone technology, as they can get. The theme of the site is the theme of the company's advertising: "generation d," for digital, of course. The Web site is heavily people-oriented, representing primarily their "gen d" employees. Contemporary graphics and bright colors complement the theme.

How Do You Get Repeat Visitors to Your Web Site?

The most successful Web sites enjoy heavy repeat traffic because there is something new for the prospect to experience each time he or she visits. The most common way to achieve this on a Web site is through a What's New or a News area, which is updated as frequently as possible, but even these areas are passive and will not by themselves turn visitors into leads.

The key is to find ways to encourage a dialogue and build a relationship with visitors so that your site will be tops on their list of bookmarks. A frequent browser today could be a buyer tomorrow. Following are a few technology-driven techniques you can use to engage visitors and turn a Web site monologue into a dialogue.

Automated E-mail Response

It is easy to build in a "mail to" e-mail link so that visitors can instantly inquire about your products or services, but it is just as important to respond promptly, if not instantly. There are a variety of auto-responder ("autobot") tools available that can respond automatically to such requests. On good electronic commerce sites, for example, your order is instantly acknowledged as soon as you place it. An e-mail message is sent to your mailbox verifying your order and providing you with an order number and shipping information. This is also a good way to prevent fraud, because if the recipient did not place the order, he or she can immediately inform the sender of the e-mail.

One effective way of encouraging a dialogue with prospects is to encourage them to sign up for a free "alert service" or e-mail newsletter. As soon as prospects enter their e-mail addresses, they should receive an instant e-mail acknowledgment letting them know they have been added to your list and also giving them the option of unsubscribing. This is not just a courtesy; it also prevents your sending unwanted e-mail to someone whose e-mail address may have been added to your list without his or her knowledge.

Cookies

Cookies are not quite as controversial as unsolicited e-mail, but they do cause some concern in the Web community. Cookies are basically little files that a computer stores when the user pays a visit to a particular Web site. A cookie allows the Web site to identify the user's computer when he or she returns to the site. Although the Web browser can be set to alert users to the use of cookies and "turn them off," most users are not even aware they can do this.

On the positive side, a cookie can be very useful in identifying a returning visitor so that the Web site can provide customized Web pages on the fly, if the appropriate database technology is in place. The ultimate value is that a visitor can have a very personalized experience and see pages intended just for him or her. This is a strong motivation for the visitor to return to that particular Web site. E-commerce Web sites routinely use cookies to identify returning customers and help facilitate the ordering process.

Some online advertising resources are using advanced technology that goes beyond the basic cookie. This technology can not only identify the user's address, but also the country and organization of the user. This information is then used to serve up advertising targeted to the user.

Although personalization and customization on the Internet are increasingly common and even desirable, this kind of information intimacy could spook some users if they are not prepared for it. It is a good idea to mention, somewhere on your site, that you use cookies or other such tools for relationship marketing to benefit the visitor; visitors can be encouraged to inform you if that is objectionable.

Databases and Personalization

Perhaps the most significant advance in marketing-oriented Web sites has been the adoption of database-driven personalization. Basic personalization, such as having a Web page greet you by name, is relatively easy to implement, but industrial-strength personalization needs to be powered by database technology.

Internet database and communication technology has advanced to the extent that entire books are being written about it. Suffice it to say that such technologies are revolutionizing marketing on the Internet. Tools are now available that permit mass customization of e-mail and Web pages, offering completely personalized communications to unlimited numbers of users.

Some of the best examples of such personalization are resident in the "My" pages that are now prevalent on the Web. "MySun" was mentioned earlier as one example. "My" pages allow the user to customize preferences on a Web page. Then, on return visits, the page "remembers" what the user selected and provides the information formatted to those preferences.

Another well-known example that pushes personalization into the one-to-one marketing world is Amazon.com's ability to make purchase suggestions. This functions in two important ways: Amazon analyzes each customer's purchase history and makes suggestions based on past purchases. The company personalizes a "New for You" page and notifies the customer periodically that it has been updated. In addition, Amazon makes suggestions on the fly when the customer is engaged in the buying process. For example, as you are selecting a computer printer for purchase from Amazon (yes, they now sell computer printers, too), you will be informed that "customers who purchased this item also purchased . . ." Then you'll see a printer cable, or a cartridge, or other items relevant to your planned purchase.

Obviously, for this to function day in and day out with millions of customers, a massive data-warehousing capability must be in place. Whereas this might be justifiable for e-commerce, it may be less attractive for nonpurchase marketing applications. Nevertheless, the move to personalized, customized Web pages, and one-to-one e-mail marketing campaigns, is significant. It must of course be balanced against growing concerns about privacy and the undisclosed use of customer data, but personalization is fast becoming a requirement for successful Internet marketing.

Interactivity and Multimedia

Java, Sun's Web programming language, is a platform for building interactivity that is not simply cute, but very useful. There are a wide variety of Java-based interactive tools that can really benefit visitors to the extent that they will come back and use them repeatedly. JavaScript, developed by Netscape, extends Java's capabilities. For example, you can build an automatic calculator into a worksheet so that a visitor can do a personalized ROI analysis online. You can offer a survey form that, when completed and sent, triggers exactly the right personalized information to be delivered to the visitor. You can build a database of products or solutions and let visitors select their own criteria to locate just the right ones. Since Java is built into current versions of Web browsers, the Web visitor can automatically take advantage of these enhancements.

Online query tools and search engines are so powerful that requests for information can be pinpointed with remarkable precision. Internet interactivity has advanced to the point at which chat sessions are now commonplace, and online events, discussed later in the book, can include real-time audio and video.

You can provide visitors with a wide variety of multimedia experiences—and the technologies to do so are getting better every day. To hear sound and view extended-time graphic motion or video, visitors often will need to download special software or use a "plug-in" browser accessory, but Web technology is advancing so rapidly that multimedia tools that do not require plug-ins are already available. Even videoconferencing can be accomplished online with inexpensive digital cameras and the appropriate software. Multimedia opens up all sorts of possibilities for attracting repeat visitors, especially if you combine it with interactivity and personalization.

A Technology Trick for Blocking Web Site Access

Afraid a competitor will get hold of a good idea? Want to feed customized information through your Web site that only certain visitors can see? There are technologies available that actually block Web site access on a selective basis by using domain-name identification. This practice was discussed in detail in a *Wall Street Journal* article ("A Secret Cat-and-Mouse Game Online," October 13, 1999). According to the report, Web site marketers can use a very simple process to look up a visitor's Internet address and then program the Web site to "block, steer or misdirect the visitor in a matter of milliseconds." The article reported that Cisco Systems used this technique to send competitors to their hiring page. The company also used reverse blocking to protect itself against a competitor that referred its prospects to an outdated Cisco Web page. Cisco reportedly redirected those referred visitors from the old page to an updated site.

How Do You Measure the Direct Marketing Effectiveness of Your Web Site?

In the early days of the Internet, counting Web site hits may have been acceptable. But today, direct marketers realize that hits are irrelevant to the measurement of overall results. The gross number of hits a Web page gets simply represents the physical interactions performed by one or several individuals. Hits do not tell you anything about the level or quality of response, or the leads generated or qualified.

There are numerous Web analysis tools and service providers at both the low end and high end that now go beyond counting hits. You can use these tools and services to track and analyze a visitor's *interactions* with your Web pages—sometimes right down to how long someone stays on a certain page or even a certain item on the page. This kind of information can be very useful in improving your Web site and making general judgments about marketing efforts. There are second-generation tools and services that improve analysis considerably. Now you can learn even more about the way a visitor interacts with your Web pages.

Such vendors as NetGenesis (*www.netgen.com*) and WebTrends (*www.webtrends.com*) provide measurement tools that help marketers know how well their Web sites are working. In January 2001, it was announced that WebTrends would be acquired by NetIQ (*www.netiq.com*), a software company with e-business interests. Other vendors, such as OpinionLab (*www.o-pinion.com*), offer automated page-by-page feedback systems for the Web. Its "OnlineOpinion" product allows site users to provide their input on the usability of Web pages.

Some measurement tools are even free, such as HitBox (*www.hitbox.com*). By linking to the HitBox server, you can count how many times your page is viewed. There is more than just data on hits, though; you can also gain access to log file analysis information, so you will know things like common paths through your site, search words used to find your site, visitor domains, browser type, and more.

From a direct-marketing perspective, however, nothing beats obtaining hard, quantifiable data about and from visitors—and determining if those visitors are qualified prospects. That is what you get when you collect leads through Web response forms, asking questions so that you can qualify and prioritize your leads into prospect groups. Then you have the data you need to analyze true *responder* activity, not just visitor activity. That is the true measurement of a Web site's success, and this is not unlike the everyday demand for marketing accountability put on the traditional direct marketer.

Creating "Mini-Sites"

A "mini-site" or micro-site is a smaller, self-contained Web site that can stand on its own or be part of a larger Web site. Mini-sites are an effective way to launch a promotion, highlight a product, or drive response to a special offer. Because they are set up as discrete Web areas, they can be used to generate and qualify leads for specific campaigns. Following are three examples.

Mini-Site Helps Launch a New Product

An IT company wanted to launch a new software product with a target audience of technical professionals and senior executives. A high-impact direct-mail package was created. It included a personalized letter, a die-cut color brochure, and a personalized reply form, mailed in an unusual-sized outer envelope. The offer: an interactive tour of the software product. To encourage response, the offer was enhanced with a free downloadable white paper, plus a special discount on the product if purchased. Prospects were instructed to visit a special URL of a mini-site created especially for the product promotion.

Upon visiting the mini-site, the prospect was asked to provide a code from the mailing piece for tracking purposes, in addition to name, title, and basic contact information. Then the prospect could gain access to the mini-site, which included the product tour, along with benefits targeted to each specific audience who received the mailing. Also included was a special-offer section. After the direct-mail promotion was complete, the mini-site was attached to the corporate Web site as a special area featuring the new product.

Mini-site Promotes Special Offers

A leading telecommunications company wanted to make several specific service offers to small businesses in a particular region. The offers were to be promoted via television, print, radio, direct mail, and Internet advertising. A mini-site was created to promote and consolidate the special offers, and its URL was used in all of the advertising. Prospects who visited the mini-site saw graphics from the television commercials and print ads, reinforcing the campaign. They could go to the specific offer that interested them from the home page of the mini-site. Once in the individual offer area, prospects were asked to select their state so the state-specific offer Web pages could be served up to individuals. Although prospects may have been responding to one of the service offers, they could see the other offers on the mini-site. This meant the company had the opportunity to cross-sell other services. The mini-site was also accessible through the company's corporate Web site via an on-site banner that promoted the special offers.

Mini-Site Transitions Customers

A major technology company was merging a division into the parent company. Customers of the division were used to doing business through that division, but now the division's name and identity would be phased out. A mini-site was created to address the transition, and a direct-mail campaign was launched to drive customers to the new site.

Customers were provided with a special access code to make them feel special. The code also tracked the results of the campaign. The site provided customers with the rationale behind the company's name change and reassured them that their primary business contacts would remain the same and that service would be unaffected. The site also reinforced the fact that new, even better products would now be available directly to the customer. Customers had the ability to interact with the company, ask questions, and express any concerns via Web-based forms.

The Sponsored Site

Some IT companies have achieved success with Web-marketing initiatives that run counter to a corporate Web site. They create sites that serve a marketing purpose without openly promoting the sponsoring company. These sites are sometimes spun off as truly separate entities, as was the case with Siebel Systems' Sales.com (*www.sales.com*), a community targeting sales professionals.

A good example of the sponsored-site strategy in action comes from BMC Software (*www.bmcsoftware.com*), as reported in the e-newsletter and Web site, B2B Marketing Biz (*www.b2bmarketingbiz.com*). In order to educate different corporate audiences, particularly in large companies, BMC launched four different individually branded sites. Although each site is sponsored by BMC Software (in some cases, as a co-sponsor with other organizations), the company's brand is intentionally underplayed. There are, of course, links to BMC Software's corporate site when appropriate.

AgileBrain (*www.agilebrain.com*) (Figure 3.1) talks to marketers and e-business directors in nontechnical terms. DBAzine (*www.dbazine.com*) addresses database issues for technical types. NextSLM (*www.nextslm.org*) focuses on service-level management. And QualityofExperience (*www.qualityofexperience.org*) (Figure 3.2), targeting senior executives, is positioned as "a learning center for op-

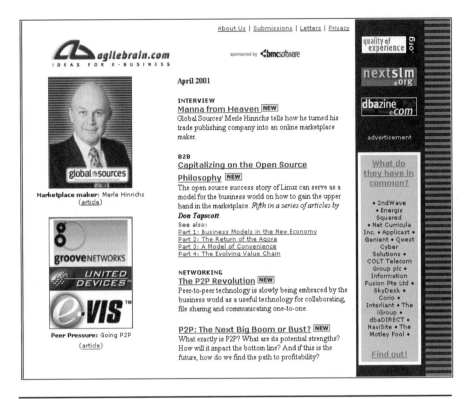

Figure 3.1.   One of several sites sponsored by BMC Software, AgileBrain speaks to marketers and e-business directors in non-technical terms. In keeping with the educational nature of the site, BMC's presence is subtle.

timizing the e-business experience." This last site counts Patricia Seybold Group, PricewaterhouseCoopers, Sun Microsystems, and SummitStrategies as its sponsors, along with BMC.

The results of this marketing effort have been impressive. Visitors stay at AgileBrain for an average of 12 minutes, and at DBAzine for 44 minutes. Fifty percent of the editorial site visitors also visit the BMC corporate site, according to BMC. And 85 percent of visitors who saw an editorial article about BMC's free assessment tool went to the BMC corporate site to follow up. Even the simple link that reads "sponsored by BMC" is getting a 5 to 6 percent return, says BMC.

Figure 3.2. "Quality of Experience," targeting senior executives, is another BMC Software-sponsored site. It is positioned as "a learning center for optimizing the e-business experience."

Using Web Response Forms

The Web Response Form (WRF) may seem like just another response technique, but for many direct marketers, it is nothing short of a breakthrough. A WRF is a "landing page" or termination point of a specialized URL designed to funnel response not just from a Web site, but from traditional direct-marketing media. Unlike the passive e-mail address, the WRF is active. In fact, it is *interactive*. And Internet marketers are using it with great success.

Here is how it works: You place a direct-response ad or you send out a piece of direct mail. In the call to action, you include the following response paths:

- An address or fax number for the respondent to return a coupon (if it is an ad), or to mail in or fax back a reply card or form, if it is direct mail

- A phone number (preferably a toll-free 800 or 888 number) to take inquiries or orders

- A special Web URL, set up as a *unique identifier* for the specific campaign, if possible

The special Web URL can "hang off" of your existing Web site. Simply create a URL address, such as *www.*[your Web site name].*com/* [promotional identifying word]. Alternatively, the URL can be attached to someone else's Web site.

Or you can apply for a *completely unique* URL that relates specifically to the product promotion—although there is an additional cost associated with this. Completely unique URLs could be beneficial because they lead the prospect *away* from a general Web site's home page. That is important if you are truly trying to track the lead back to a specific campaign. Another way to accomplish this is to use a URL that is an extension of the home page—but to make sure that the home page itself has a strong direct-response orientation. In this case, the home page should direct the respondent to a special area to take advantage of an offer.

Why? For the same reason you include a reply card in direct mail and say "Respond today for this free offer by returning the reply card" instead of simply saying "Contact us for more information." In direct marketing, you need to facilitate response by telling the respondent specifically what to do and where to go. Making a specific offer instead of offering general information is a proven response generator. Asking for a specific response to that offer facilitates and potentially increases response.

Directing a prospect to a corporate Web site in a lead-generation campaign simply opens up a multitude of options that could actually get in the way of generating a response. When prospects go to a Web site's home page instead of a Web response form, they may not be able to easily find the response path. That is because many home pages are busy and are filled with links, and most Web marketers do not give a lot of thought to including a WRF that stands out from all the home page clutter.

There is another nasty side effect to not using a WRF. Prospects are becoming far more accustomed to the Web as a means of learning about companies and their products. That means they may go to a company's general Web site when they see an ad or receive a piece of direct mail—even if a special URL is included in the promotion. Prospects visit the general Web site, look around, find the information they want, and then leave. As a result, the campaign generates responses, maybe even good leads, but they cannot be attributed to that specific campaign. As a result, the campaign is really "leaking leads," because the marketer never captures any identifying information about the prospects. When the marketer analyzes the campaign, it may look as if it did not do so well, when leads were actually coming in—but through a response path that was not being measured as part of the campaign.

That is why it is essential to tie a compelling and unique offer to your WRF—preferably something a prospect can receive *only* by going to that specific WRF. If the offer is unique, prospects will be more likely to go to a special place to get it. A common mistake is making a direct-marketing offer that is already on your Web site. If anyone can gain access to the offer through your corporate Web site and it is not necessary to provide identifying and qualifying information to read it, you may get a visitor—but you will not get a lead.

Web Response Forms Tighten the Lead Capture and Qualification Process

The WRF is designed to tighten the entire lead-generation process. When the respondent goes to your special URL, he or she finds the WRF—a page or a series of pages, along with an interactive form, reinforcing that individual's interest immediately. The WRF potentially turns that preliminary interest into *an action*. A WRF can also capture valuable marketing information about the respondent and ask qualifying questions.

WRFs can be especially effective as the termination point of Web banner advertising. The Web banner ad can be linked directly to the WRF. The prospect clicks on the ad and is routed instantly to the WRF.

In this case, since the banner ad is just a teaser, the WRF can be a Web response area, perhaps even a Web "mini-site." The purpose of the Web response area is to share information so that the prospect can make a more informed inquiry and possibly even a purchase.

WRFs are also an essential part of online seminar campaigns. Directing a prospective attendee to an online registration form is the most expedient way to capture a response. An added benefit is that the WRF can fully describe the event, including an agenda, photos of the speakers, and other information that reinforces the value of the event. If you are using newsletter sponsorships, banners, or Web site buttons to promote attendance at such events, your promotional space is limited, so the WRF performs a vital function in fully describing the event and encouraging online registration.

A Web response area can be thought of as "electronic fulfillment." (More about that later.) Electronic fulfillment is something that is likely to become standard practice in the future world of Internet direct marketing. As the cost of printed materials goes up, electronic fulfillment becomes all the more attractive.

There may be a time when all that is needed in a direct-mail lead-generation campaign is a cost-effective postcard that alerts a prospect to an informational offer that can be obtained by visiting a special URL. There, the prospect arrives at a Web response area and finds complete information about the offer and the product being promoted. The prospect can then "pay" for the offer with "marketing currency" by typing in his or her contact information and answering some qualifying questions. The prospect sends the form, the marketer gets the lead, and the prospect instantly receives the offer online via electronic fulfillment.

The Basics of Constructing Web Response Forms

Web response areas and WRFs can be constructed in a number of ways, but here are some of the basic things to include:

- A headline at the top of the WRF welcomes respondents or thanks them for visiting. The headline acknowledges the fact that the respondents came to this special page to get or do something. The headline should tie in directly with the promotion itself in terms of graphic look and feel and copy.

- The WRF reinforces the promotion and summarizes the offer. It is a good idea to use some of the same copy from the original promotion to integrate and leverage the messaging.

- If necessary, one or more pages provide product information.

- Instructional copy tells respondent *what they will receive* if the WRF is completed and sent. The offer can be handled in a variety of ways:

  - Instant fulfillment: The respondent sends the form and instantly receives the desired information in return.

  - Unlock and download: The respondent sends the form and receives instructions for how to unlock and download a document or software, typically a trial or demonstration version of the product.

  - Private access: The respondent sends the form and receives an acknowledgment, either instantly or via return e-mail, that includes a special URL or a password that allows access to a separate, private Web area or virtual event.

  - Traditional fulfillment: The respondent sends the form and receives the information requested via fax or traditional mail, or receives an item ordered via traditional mail or delivery service.

- The form itself allows the respondent to interactively fill in basic data: name, title, company name, address, city, state, zip code, phone number, fax number, and e-mail address. The form should also ask several qualifying questions, including whether or not the prospect grants permission to use e-mail for correspondence. Some marketers make certain questions required (i.e., the form cannot be sent unless the required fields are completed).

- It is generally a good idea to offer a link to the corporate Web site only at the *end* of the WRF, or on the acknowledgment page the respondent receives once the WRF is sent. This funnels the respondent's actions and does not let him or her "escape" from the WRF, but it gives the person the ability to learn more by visiting the corporate Web site after responding.

The WRF is an excellent way to capture responses electronically. Including a Web URL typically helps increase overall response to a direct-marketing campaign. If the target audience is composed of technical professionals or individuals who frequent the Web, they may in fact prefer the Web response path to more traditional response methods. Individuals who "live" on their networks and use the Web extensively for research and information are far more likely to respond over the Web than they are to return a reply card or make a phone call.

Finally, there is growing evidence that individuals who respond via WRFs are highly qualified prospects. I was involved in one print advertising campaign for a software company in which a special Web URL was used in addition to the traditional mail, fax, and phone response paths. A tear-out business reply card accompanied the ad. The advertising ran in national trade publications targeted to IT professionals.

Twenty percent of the total responses came in via the Web. Of those responses, over 50 percent were considered high-quality leads. This is two to three times greater than the norm for qualified leads generated by traditional print advertising or direct-mail lead generation.

There is some logic to this if you consider the fact that a Web respondent has to "work harder" to respond. Finding the URL may be easy, but typing in all the requested information and answering questions on a computer screen takes some time and effort. There is no easy way around this. WRFs can be simplified by using drop-down menus for multiple choices (to indicate your state, for example) or radio buttons and check boxes, but individuals still need to type in certain basic contact information, which can be tedious. Doing so suggests that the prospect wants to obtain the offer or get more information and is willing to do a little bit of work to get it. In today's high-pressure, compressed-time business environment, that says something.

Despite the WRF's advantages as a response mechanism, it is not entirely foolproof. Even if you use a special URL, potential prospects could fill in false information, or go to your regular Web site instead. That is why, if you are doing a promotion that features a special URL, you might want to mention that promotion *and* have a link to a version of the WRF on your Web site home page for prospects who show up there instead of coming to the special URL.

Another potential problem is the interactive form itself. Be sure it is constructed properly (most forms use CGI or JavaScript) and that you test it with several different computers and browsers. It is also a good idea to try it out on several different people to see if the form is easy to understand and easy to use. You need to ensure that the respondent can easily send the WRF—and that you receive the information you need.

Employing Web Site Links to Generate Leads

One of the unusual technological aspects of the Web is the ability visitors have to seamlessly link from not just one page to another within a single Web site, but from one Web site to another just as easily. As a result, a visitor to your site can instantly visit any other site with a quick click of the mouse, if you provide a live link. Similarly, a visitor on any other site can visit your site if a link to your site is present on that other site. That is why employing Web site links is a separate, uniquely Web, way of generating response and, potentially, leads. There are both free and paid links available to Web direct marketers, and each kind of link has its trade-offs.

Free Links

Free links are typically provided either on a limited-time promotional basis or in return for a reciprocal link. The most obvious free link, one that you should certainly take advantage of, is the search engine link. Getting your site and pages listed by major search engines such as AltaVista, Excite, HotBot, Infoseek, Lycos, WebCrawler, Yahoo!, and others is a prerequisite for any Web marketer.

The easiest way to do this is through a variety of free or paid Web listing services, which can automatically send your URL to numerous sources (*www.addme.com* for example). You could also do it yourself by going to each search engine's home page—a considerably more time-consuming task. Getting listed on such engines will not guarantee leads, but it will certainly increase traffic to your Web site, some of which may well turn into leads.

You should also be aware of "meta-tags," which help search engines identify key words for each of your Web pages. Using the appropriate tags will make your Web pages come up when prospects search on the particular keywords. But meta-tags are becoming less effective in securing top rankings in search engines. That is because some site owners who load up their pages with them in the hope of "fooling" the search engines have abused them. Filtering technologies are now being used to prevent this, so evaluate the use of meta-tags carefully. Another technique is using a "gateway" page, which is designed to improve the ranking of the page with particular search engines. (More about this method in the next chapter.)

A second avenue for free links is an informational Web site. Not all informational sites accept free links, but some do. Some informational sites represent a number of sources, such as magazines or newspapers. Others are Internet-based directories or "yellow pages." Still others are special-interest, affinity groups or "Web communities" established as loose affiliations of a number of organizations. The best way to find these sites is to do some searching of your own using keywords that may lead to business interests similar to yours.

A third place to look for free links is on Web sites that share similar or complementary characteristics to yours. An example might be a company that markets to the same kind of audience you do, but does not sell a competitive product or service. Such sites may already have free links to other sites, but if they do not, it does not hurt to inquire. Simply contact the Webmaster and ask if the site will accept a link. Be aware, however, that the site will almost always want a reciprocal link—which means you will have to provide a link to that site from your Web site.

That may sound harmless, but there are some risks involved. For one thing, you want to be sure to provide links only to legitimate, "clean" sites to which you would feel comfortable sending visitors. (It is probably wise to have some general disclaimer copy on your site so that you do not become liable for another site's content.)

A bigger issue, from a marketing point of view, may be whether or not you want external links to appear on your site. By providing an external link, you provide a "side door" for a prospect to easily exit your site—and perhaps not come back. Some Web experts believe that external links only serve to encourage the fickleness of a Web site visitor and that such links should be used sparingly.

Paid Links

An increasing number of Web site owners are trying to build traffic and create credibility for their sites—as well as generate income. A paid link is one way to do that, and they are common on the Web. Basically, the Web site owner offers a link to your Web site for a fee, usually based on a set period of time, although it could also be based on the number of "impressions."

You pay the fee and the Web site owner posts your link. For an additional fee, you may be able to get a more detailed listing or description of your Web site; for an even higher fee, you may be able to purchase advertising space on the Web site. Some or all of this could be available at special promotional pricing, or even free for a limited time, so that the Web site owner can build up the site with lots of links.

It is not always easy to decide whether or not to pay for a link. In considering paid links, look for Web sites that can:

1. Target an audience of likely prospects for your business

2. Offer you something of marketing value in terms of the site's reach, its reputation, or your association with other well-regarded companies

3. Provide you with specific reports or other evidence that allows you to measure the effectiveness of your link on that site

Links are also available on a paid and sometimes free basis within some e-mail newsletters. If an e-mail newsletter serves your market or you suspect that it reaches your target audience, you should look into this opportunity. As mentioned earlier, e-mail newsletters are requested by subscribers and are closely read by them—which means they are also seeing your link.

4

Using Search Engines
and Newsgroups

If you build it, will they come? That question is a legitimate one when discussing Web sites. For the IT company, as for others who launch Web sites, it quickly becomes apparent that you cannot sit back and wait for people to come to your Web site—you have to drive them to it. As a result, IT marketers are employing a variety of strategies and tactics to build Web site traffic. This chapter, as well as the next two chapters about using e-mail and online advertising, addresses the very real need to actively promote your Web site and turn it into a true marketing destination.

This chapter begins where Chapter 3 ended, with a more in-depth look at search tools. In addition, we also discuss the use of newsgroups. Although newsgroups are not specifically Web site-related, they are another important Internet-based way IT companies can leverage the power of Internet marketing.

Much of the information in this chapter has been adapted with permission of the author from the book *101 Ways to Promote Your Web Site*, 2nd edition, by Susan Sweeney (Maximum Press, 2000).

How to Gain Visibility on the Internet

Once you have built a Web site, you want it to be found easily by customers, prospects, investors, prospective employees, journalists, and other audiences.

Using Search Engines

One of the most popular ways people find Web sites is via Internet searches. According to a Georgia Tech survey, 87 percent of people find Web sites via search engines. However, people rarely go beyond the first few pages of results, so you need to get your Web site to appear in the top 20 search results to be noticed. A Roper Starch survey of Internet users conducted in early 2001 indicated that more than 70 percent of users experience frustration when searching.

Even more remarkable is a 1999 study conducted by Steve Lawrence and Lee Giles of the NEC Institute. The study indicated that no engine will index more than about 16 percent of the estimated size of the publicly indexable Web (*www.metrics.com*).

The most common search tool is the search engine. Search engines use programs ("intelligent agents"), called bots, to actually search the Internet for pages, which they index using specific parameters as they read the content. The agent will read the information on every page of your site and then follow the links. For example, AltaVista's spider continually crawls the Web looking for sites to index and, of course, indexes sites upon their submission. Infoseek uses a spider as well, but their spider does not scour the Web for sites to index. You must submit your site to Infoseek or it will never be listed. Inktomi also uses a spider; however, users cannot access Inktomi's information directly to search. Instead, a user will use other search engines and directories that use Inktomi's search engine technology, such as HotBot, Lycos, and Yahoo!. Inktomi is very important in the search engine community, so be sure your site is easily accessible to its spider.

To register with search engines, you simply submit your URL on their submission form. (This will be discussed in greater detail later in the chapter.) Even if your URL is not registered with search engines, most of the major search engines will eventually find you because these bots are continually roaming the Internet looking for new sites to index. There are millions of sites out there, so we suggest you be proactive and register your site to ensure a speedier listing. Once you are registered, the bots will periodically visit your site looking for changes and updates. The following sections discuss what to do and what not to do during Web site design and development to best accommodate the search engines.

Image Maps

An image map is a single graphic or image that has multiple hot links to different pages or resources. Image maps prevent search engines from getting inside your site—so you're basically locking the door on many of the search engines if you use image maps. This may result in some of the pages on your site not being indexed, or none of your site being indexed at all.

For example, similar to an individual using an old browser, many search engines cannot follow image maps. If you do use image maps, make sure that your site is easy to navigate with **hyperlinks**. This will ensure that search engines will find all of your pages and index them. Another tip you should be aware of is to create a **site map** that has text links to all relevant pages within your Web site. Once you have created your site map, submit it to the major search engines. This will help the search engines to index the pages within your site.

Don't Try to Trick the Search Engines

Some Internet marketers try various techniques to trick the search engines into positioning their sites higher in search results. These techniques are considered cheating by many Internet users. It is up to you whether you want to risk discovery by the search engines or **flames** from other marketers by implementing them. These tricks do not work with every search engine, and if it is discovered that you are trying to dupe the search engines, some may not list you at all. They have been programmed to detect some of these techniques, and you will be penalized in some way if you are discovered. A few of the search engine tricks pertaining to Web site design are as follows:

- Repeating keywords over and over again hidden in your HTML and Meta tags. For example,

!games, games, games, games, games, . . .>

- Repeating keywords over and over again by displaying them at the bottom of your document after a number of line breaks

- Hiding keywords by displaying them in your document using a very small font

- Repeating keywords in your document by making the text color the same as the background color

- Making frequent and regular title changes so that the bots think your site is a new site and they list you again and again

- Changing the name of your site to have a space, exclamation mark (!), or A as the first character so that you come up first in alphabetical lists

- Any time you make significant changes to your site, you should resubmit your site to the search engines. Search engines normally revisit on a regular schedule. However, these search engines are growing smarter every day—some monitor how often the site is updated and adjust their "revisit" schedule accordingly.

Meta Refresh

Have you ever visited a site and then automatically been transported to another page within the site? This is the result of a **meta refresh tag.** A meta refresh tag is an HTML document that is designed to automatically replace itself with another HTML document, after a certain period of time, as defined by the document author. Now that we've mentioned this, don't use them. Search engines generally do not like meta refresh tags. Infoseek will not add sites that use a fast meta refresh. If you do use a meta refresh tag to redirect users, you should set a delay of at least seven seconds and provide a link on the new page back to the page they were originally taken from.

How to Get Found with Directories

Directories are often referred to as search engines. Unlike search engines, directories will not find your site if you do not tell them about it. Directories do not use bots or other intelligent agents to scour the Internet for new pages. Web sites must be submitted, and the submissions are monitored by human administrators. Some of the more popular directories are LookSmart, Yahoo! (the most popular of all search engines and directories), and the DMOZ Open Directory Project. In general, directories do not index nearly the amount of sites the search engines do; however, the sites that are indexed typically are more appropriate content-wise.

In order to be listed in a directory, you need to submit or register your site information and URL address. This is best accomplished by visiting all the directories in which you want to be listed and filling out the required form. The registration forms are all quite similar and generally require information such as your URL, the name of your site, a description of your site, a list of keywords, your contact information, and other information depending on the particular directory. You must complete the form and click on the Submit button to complete the registration process. More detail on submitting your site to a directory is covered later in the chapter.

Know your search engines and directories. Each one is different, using different criteria or algorithms to determine which sites rank highly. They also use different mechanisms to provide a description of your site and allow different lengths for a description. Search engines and directories are constantly changing, so to stay current you should follow up with a visit to the search engine and directory Web sites and read their instructions and **FAQs.**

Some directories automatically include the information you have submitted, whereas others review and approve your site for inclusion. The latter can take up to a month.

Keywords Are of Key Importance

Keywords are an important aspect of every Web page because the search engines use keywords in determining your site's ranking, and these are the words people are most likely to use when they're searching for your site. When creating your keyword list, don't just use nouns. Think of descriptive words that may be associated with benefits of your products or services.

When determining what your keywords will be, always keep the customer or your target visitor in mind. Try to think as they would if they were to do a search for information on your topic. Don't just think about what people would do to find *your* site, but what they would do if they didn't know your company existed and were looking for the types of products and services you provide. If you find this a difficult exercise, then ask around. Talk to both people that know about your business and people that don't. Ask what keywords they would use to find a site like yours.

Start by taking the company's brochures and other corporate marketing materials, as well as the site itself, and indiscriminately highlight any words that individuals might search on if they are looking for the products or services the company has to offer. Record these words in a text document in your word-processing program.

Next, edit the list by deleting words that either are too broad (for example, "business") or are not appropriate for keyword purposes. Review each word and ask yourself if someone would search using that word if he or she was looking for your products and services.

Always use the plural when forming your keywords (adding an "s" usually forms the plural). If you list "game" as your keyword and someone uses "games" to do a search, then your site will not be found. If you include the word "games" in your keywords and someone requests information on the word "game," then your site will be found because "game" is part of the word "games." Never use both versions because you're then running the risk of spamming the search engines, and you want to be able to use other keywords to increase your chances of achieving high rankings. The only time it is acceptable to use both the singular and the plural is if the plural does not include the singular in its entirety—for example, if the word and its plural are something like "dairy" and "dairies," you should list both as part of your keyword list. It is also important to note that when most people perform their searches, they will use the plural version. You're more likely to search for "computers" than you are to search for "computer."

Now, reorganize the remaining keywords in order of importance. By having the most important words first, no matter how many keywords the particular directory will allow, you are ready to submit—simply copy and paste the keywords into their form.

Now you have a good master keyword list. Different directories allow for different numbers of keywords to be submitted. Because you have organized your list with the most important words first, you simply include as many of your keywords as the directory will allow. When a directory will allow multiple submissions for the same URL, you might consider submitting as many times as it takes to include all your keywords. You won't have to change your description or other information every time, just the keywords.

If you plan to submit every page of your site, your master list provides a valuable document. For each page that you are indexing, take a photocopy of the comprehensive list and delete words that are not appropriate for that particular page. Then re-prioritize the remaining keywords based on the content of the page you are indexing. This is then the keyword list for that page. Repeat this procedure for every page you will be indexing.

If you make changes to your Web pages, change the title and keywords contained in the title as well. This will allow you to be re-indexed by search engines.

There is often the question as to whether to include your competitors' names in your keywords. This follows the premise that if someone searches for them they will find you as well. There is, however, an ongoing debate as to whether this is ethical. My position on this issue is NO. Due to the fact that several of the search engines allow only 200 or less characters for keywords, you would be losing vital space to include keywords that describe or even name a competitor's products or services. In addition, there have been recent legal battles regarding the use of competitors' keywords within one's own keywords.

Your keyword list should be included in your submissions to directories and in a keyword meta-tag. However, to be listed in a higher position in search results, you should include your most important keywords in other places as well, such as

- Your page title

- Your description

- The first 200–250 characters of your page

- Beginning, middle, and end of your page text

- If frames are used, between the <noframes> tags

- In Alt tags

- Keywords meta-tag

- Descriptions meta-tag

- Comments tags

Include a comments tag that has your keywords and your description in it. You can repeat this a couple of times if you wish. It is used by the Excite spider, and if repeated may yield a higher placement in search results.

Some search engines rank sites by how early the keyword appears on the site. The earlier a keyword is mentioned on your site, the higher your site may be positioned in search results. And remember the points made earlier: Though you don't want to repeat a keyword hundreds of times (some search engines are on to this), you do want to repeat keywords a number of times on each page of your site. AltaVista, Infoseek, and Webcrawler all like it when different keywords appear relatively close together in the page content.

You can check the effectiveness of your keyword placement and utilization by using Web traffic analysis techniques. You can use these techniques to look at what sites are referring people to you. You can strip down this information further to view only search engine referrals. By looking at this information, you can see exactly what keywords people are using to find you, and you can alter your keywords based on this information. Keep the keywords that prove to be effective; those that provide little or no traffic you can change to something else and see if that's more effective. Refining your keywords is one of the key elements to success—you're letting the search engines tell you what you're doing right and what you could be doing better.

Submitting Your Site to Spiders and Crawlers

Although **spiders** and **crawlers** can find your site whether or not you actually submitted it, you should be proactive with them. Check to see if they have already found your site; if they haven't, submit your URL.

When a spider adds your page to its database, it uses the title found in the <TITLE> tag as the title of your page; hence, using good descriptive titles is very important. Different spiders use different methods to index a site. A spider will index a portion of the page or the entire page. Numerous keywords should be used on your home page to ensure that people who are looking for your type of company will find you. For example, Lycos uses the first 200 characters in the description, yet it indexes the 100 most important words on each page. Infoseek takes the first 250 characters of a site for its description.

For your site to be listed higher in search results, you must do a fair bit of research on ranking criteria and adjust your submission accordingly. WebCrawler, for example, will give your site a higher ranking if the word the user is employing as the keyword of the search (vacation, graphics, boats, whatever) appears many times in the first paragraph or so of the page. Print your home page to get an idea of what may be listed for your site after you submit and your site is indexed. Check to ensure that this is an accurate portrayal of your site.

Because spiders will index pages other than your home page, you should go through this process for your entire site. Remember to have good navigational tools on every page of your site—you never know where your prospective customer is going to enter the site! With a good navigation bar, users can get where they want to go on your site quickly and easily.

Learn from Competitor Sites

Check out your competition . . . not just your direct competition, but also industry leaders (whether or not you compete directly) and companies that sell noncompeting products to your target market. Search their names and see what they are using for descriptions and keywords. Next, search using some of your keywords and see what sites receive top ranking. This research will illustrate why they have received such a high ranking—and you can incorporate what you've learned into your Web site or doorway page for that search engine or directory.

Check to see what your competitors have for meta-tag. Not only can you learn from the sites that catch your eye, you can also learn from your competitors' mistakes. After you have done a thorough job of this market research, you will be in a good position to develop a description that is catchy and adequately describes your site.

To check your competition's meta-tag in Microsoft Internet Explorer, you simply go to their site, click on "View" from your menu bar, and in the drop-down menu select "Source." This will bring up the source code for that page in whatever your default text browser is.

Looking for the same information in Netscape is just as easy. From the menu bar select "View" and then select "Page Source" from the drop-down menu.

Another technique you should apply when checking out competing sites is to reverse-search the links to their sites. Many search engines now use link popularity in deciding which sites achieve the highest rankings. By looking at who links to your competitors, you may be able to get some more links that point toward you, ultimately increasing your site's popularity. If you want to check out who's linking to one of your competitor's sites in AltaVista or Infoseek, you simply go to the respective search engine and then enter "*link:competitordomain.com*" in the search field. You can also use one of the many link-popularity checkers found on the Web.

Marketing Implications of Page Titles

The <TITLE> tag is the first item a search agent reads and many believe that next to site content, the title tag is the most important element used in determining your site's relevancy. Make sure every page on your site is titled properly for marketing purposes.

Don't use just your company name—use a descriptive title and make sure you include some keywords. Search engines will retrieve your page, look at your title, and then look at the rest of your page for keywords that match those found in the title. Many search engines use title tags in determining your ranking. Among the search engines that use pages titles in their ranking criteria are AltaVista, Excite, Google, HotBot, Infoseek, NorthernLight, WebCrawler, and Yahoo!. Pages that have keywords in the title are seen as more relevant than similar pages on the same subject that don't, and thus may be ranked in a higher position by the search engines.

Keep in mind that when someone bookmarks your site or adds it to their favorites, it is the page title that appears as the description. It is important that you keep your page titles under 50 characters in length if possible. Most search engines will not read past 50 characters; therefore, you should concentrate on two or maybe three keywords in your title tag.

Meta-Tags

Meta-tags are an important part of reaching your search engine goals online. AltaVista, Excite, Inktomi (e.g., Hotbot), Infoseek, Lycos, WebCrawler, NorthernLight, and Google are all examples of search engines that use meta-tags in one form or another. Some search engines use your keyword meta-tag and description meta-tag in determining your ranking in their results. Some search engines also use this information as the source of the description displayed to searchers looking for information.

As a general rule of thumb, keep your description and keyword meta-tag under 200 characters in length. When you use too many keywords, you end up diluting the importance of each keyword, meaning potentially lower rankings in the search engines. Another rule of thumb is to use lowercase letters when formulating your keyword meta-tag because most search engines are not case-sensitive.

It is important not to repeat a keyword more than five times within your keyword meta-tags. Doing so may result in spamming the search engine, which means they'll likely ignore your submission. Not something you want. Another tactic to prevent keyword spamming is to formulate keyword phrases. Instead of using the word "Marketing" over and over again, mix it up by creating phrases like "Internet Marketing, Internet Marketing Consulting, Internet Marketing Research." When you do this, be sure to separate the phrases with commas or it will simply look like "Marketing Internet Marketing"—often spam to some of the search engines.

As always with keywords, place the most important words first in your description and keyword meta-tags. This will help you in achieving higher rankings because most search engines consider the first few keywords the most important in their ranking criteria.

Using Submission Services

Although submission services save a lot of time, it is essential that you are registered accurately in search engines and directories. For the best results, register individually in as many of the top search engines as you can before you resort to multiple submission sites. There are not that many search engines or directories that have long submission forms, so submit manually to the top sites to ensure the best results.

Many multiple search engine submission services are available on the Internet, some free and some paid. They will register your URL, description, and keywords, and then submit your site to varying numbers of indexes, directories, and search engines. Check them to see how comprehensive they are before using these services, and do not duplicate your effort if it appears that the services are essentially the same.

Top Search Engines and Directories

Submitting to the search engines and directories is a very time-consuming but extremely important task. Take your time, do your research, know the ranking strategy employed, and prepare your submission for optimal results. It is very difficult to change your entry after it has been submitted, and the last thing you want is a typo. If the time available for indexing is limited, start by focusing on the major search engines and directories for individual submissions, and use multiple submission services for the others.

Search engines and directories themselves are undergoing some fairly significant market shifts, as more of them become portals. The portal is a Web destination or gateway—a site where visitors start at, and come back to often. In this respect, some would consider America Online and other major Internet service providers to be portals. Portals are part search engine, part community, and part something else.

Portals are designed to engage visitors, provide them with attractive free services (such as free e-mail and free home pages), expose their eyes to online advertising, and create loyalty and repeat usage. Some of these portals have started to consolidate and make strategic moves in preparation for the future.

Whatever they are called, search engines are extremely important. Some of the newer search engines or directories combine judgment with search—they actually evaluate your questions and answer them accordingly.

For more information about search engines, check out Internet.com's site, *www.searchenginewatch.com* (Figure 4.1). The following is a list of some of the key search engines and directories currently available:

www.about.com
About.com (Figure 4.2) is a combination search tool/collection of online communities that positions itself against Internet search engines and directories. About calls itself "the human Internet" because it is a net-

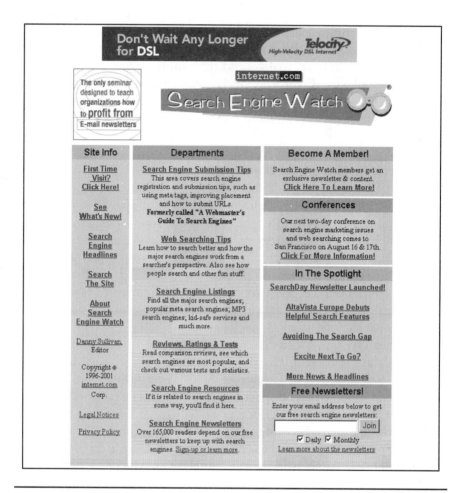

Figure 4.1. Keep your eye on all the search engine developments with Searchenginewatch.com.

work of over 700 sites, each run by a human guide, organized into 36 channels, each with separate URLs so that the user can go directly to the topic if desired, instead of wading through a single home page. About claims to cover more than 50,000 subjects with over 1 million links and an archive of original content.

www.altavista.com

This search engine was re-launched in late 1999 and remains one of the more important major search engines, despite going through a change

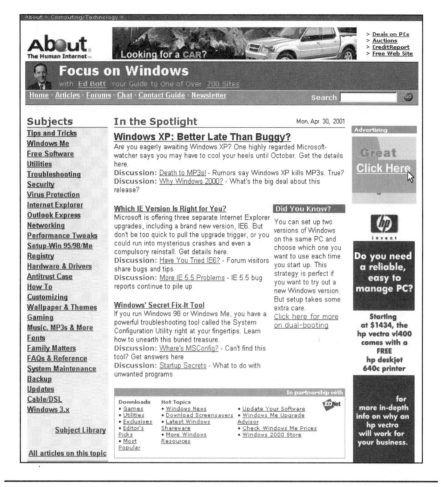

Figure 4.2. About.com features "Guides," experts who help users navigate over 700 subject areas. This is the home page for Windows.

of ownership and management upheaval. One of its interesting capabilities is AltaVista's free page-translation service: You can enter the URL of a Web page that appears in one of several different languages and then ask AltaVista to provide a translation into English.

www.ask.com

Ask Jeeves, also known as Ask.com, uses a butler cartoon character to represent its "at your service" positioning. You can ask Jeeves any question and "he" will suggest places to find the answer. Ask Jeeves is based on a proprietary technology that has now been extended to its "Ask Jeeves Business Solutions" service that has 100 corporate customers. One of the more engaging search engines, Ask Jeeves acquired Direct Hit (see below) in 2000.

www.directhit.com

Direct Hit assumes that others have already searched for what you want. So it uses that intelligence, along with other metrics, to provide you "the most relevant sites" for your search. Since the engine analyzes hits in aggregate, not IP addresses, it does not invade anyone's privacy. Direct Hit actually services other search engines, including HotBot, InfoSeek Express, Lycos, and Microsoft Network.

www.excite.com

Excite is one of the Internet's leading search and directory companies whose technology is licensed to other sites. Excite now includes WebCrawler *(www.webcrawler.com)* as part of its network. This spider/crawler has existed since 1994, so it has had a lot of time to scour the Internet. The number of links you have to your site affects your position here. If other sites have more links to them, they may be ranked more highly in WebCrawler's search results. Excite is part of Excite@Home, a leader in broadband, with close to 3 million cable modem subscribers across North America.

www.google.com

Google has quickly become one of the Web's more popular search engines. Its technology is used in more than 30 countries by clients including Yahoo!, Virgin.net, and Netscape's Netcenter. Google also provides commercial products for use by companies that don't want to manage their own search software and resources.

www.hotbot.com

A search engine spun off by Wired, Hot Bot has been known to be at the top of the list in terms of numbers of indexed pages. It uses Inktomi, one of the leaders in search engine technology.

www.lycos.com

With its signature phrase "Go get it!" Lycos has positioned itself as a "retriever" of any information on the Internet. It consistently ranks as a top spider and has often been in a fierce battle with Yahoo! for the leadership position. In October 2000, Lycos combined with Terra Networks to create Terra Lycos, a global Internet company that is now one of the most popular Internet networks in the United States, Canada, Europe, and Asia, and is the leading portal to Spanish- and Portuguese-speaking markets.

www.northernlight.com

Northern Light is a search engine with a twist in that it combines Web results with information from "premium material" in one search, giving users access to books, magazines, databases, and newswires not available from other search engines. The Northern Light research engine uses patented classification intelligence and precision relevancy ranking to deliver results from the Web and their "Special Collection" of over 7,100 full-text publications not otherwise available to Web searchers.

www.yahoo.com

Yahoo! is the behemoth of the search engines/portals, the largest of its kind on the Internet. It is really a directory, but it does not read pages like the other search engines. You must fill out a form on the site to have your site added to Yahoo!, and it is checked by Yahoo! to make sure it matches the correct category on the site. Some of Yahoo's statistics are staggering: For example, the company reported that its traffic increased to more than 1.1 billion page views per day on average during March 2001. Yahoo! owns 24 properties worldwide and reaches some 192 million individuals each month worldwide. Yahoo! offers a broad range of services, including value-added premium services, business and enterprise services, and interactive marketing and merchant services. Yahoo! and SAP announced an agreement in early 2001 to develop a joint-enterprise portal.

Using Newsgroups for Internet Marketing

Newsgroups predate the Web and, in many respects, represent the first real Internet communities. Newsgroups are found in an area of the Internet called "Usenet," a kind of public forum. They are really discussion groups on the Internet focusing on specific subjects, and with over 100,000 topics, they attract more than 10 million people.

Since each newsgroup's readers are interested in that newsgroup's specific topic, you can reach a very targeted audience with a very specific interest. Although some newsgroups enjoy participation by hundreds of thousands of readers a day, others may see very little traffic. Large is not always better. A smaller group may provide you with a better chance of having your message read by your ideal market, even though a larger group offers better exposure by sheer volume. Obviously, the way to choose a newsgroup for participation is more related to the subject matter than to the newsgroup size.

Newsgroups also exist within online services. CompuServe (*www.compuserve.com*), a heavily business-focused online service, has forums and special-interest groups (or "SIGs"), and America Online has forums and clubs. Other ISPs may have similar groups available, as do an increasing number of Internet communities. Newsgroups are valuable for a number of reasons:

- *Reaching prospective customers:* You can immediately reach thousands of your targeted prospects with a single message.

- *Communicating with existing customers:* You can find newsgroups of customers and provide them with valuable information.

- *Market research:* You can use newsgroups to find out about the latest trends, customer needs, what people are looking for, and what they are talking about.

- *Reputation building:* By answering people's questions and helping to solve their problems, you will build your reputation as an expert in the field.

- *Increased traffic:* You can direct people to your commercial Web site, as long as you do it in an informative way.

Newsgroups are organized into different types of discussions or categories, which in turn have hundreds of individual newsgroups to participate in. Major newsgroup categories include:

- alt (alternative topics)

- biz (business topics)

- comp (computer-related topics)

- misc (topics that do not have their own categories)

- news (Usenet news and administration)

- rec (recreation topics)

- sci (science)

- soc (social issues)

- talk (conversation)

To most effectively use newsgroups for Internet marketing, you must first *look for a close fit* between a newsgroup and your product or service. For example, if your company sells software that aids genealogical work, then one appropriate newsgroup for your business might be *soc.genealogy.methods.*

Search for newsgroups using the newsgroup functions in Netscape Navigator and Microsoft Internet Explorer browsers. You can also use **specialized search engines** such as Liszt at *www.liszt.com* to find newsgroups. Liszt is the largest and best-known e-mail list directory. It includes a comprehensive directory of newsgroups, as well as a unique directory of chat channels. In April 1999, Liszt was acquired by Topica, a company that helps users find, manage, and participate in e-mail lists.

After you have compiled a list of what you think are the most appropriate newsgroups related to your target market, you can begin to *qualify your list.* Go to the Usenet Info Center Launch Pad at *www.ibiblio.org/usenet-i/home.html* and look up the FAQs for the newsgroups on your list. The FAQs will probably tell you whether or not each newsgroup accepts advertising. You will also be able to learn how many people participate in each newsgroup.

It makes sense to do some "lurking" on the newsgroup (spending some time browsing around without posting anything) just to determine if the participants of the newsgroup are, in fact, potential customers. Read through each newsgroup's rules about posting and advertising and, after you are convinced the newsgroup is a good fit, you can begin posting messages.

Be very cautious about messages that are advertising in disguise. If the newsgroup does not allow advertising, then do not blatantly post an ad. To take full advantage of the newsgroup, you have to gain the trust of its members. With one wrong message you could outrage all of the potential customers who participate in the newsgroup.

Newsgroups are real communities, so you should be willing to make a commitment to participate on a regular basis. You can position yourself as an expert, but it may be some time before you want to mention your company's Web site, and it should be mentioned only when there is an appropriate opportunity to do so. Much of the newsgroup is discussion between people interested in the subject, not salesmanship. Nonetheless, newsgroups can help promote your subject area, and ultimately your company's products or services.

When first starting out, keep all messages focused on the topic. Message length should be short—no more than 24 lines. Messages should briefly discuss main points and ask if readers would like to have more information. Once readers show an interest in learning more, you can tell them more.

When responding to a message in a newsgroup, you have the option of responding to the individual who posted the message privately, or responding through the newsgroup. If your message will be of value to the entire group, or will appropriately promote your company's capabilities, then post the response to the newsgroup for all to see. Prompt response is recommended.

Basic Rules

Following are some basic rules to help you post well-received messages:

Keep to the Newsgroup Topic
Make sure to always stay on the newsgroup topic of discussion. People participate in specific newsgroups because of that subject and don't appreciate off-topic postings.

Stay on the Thread
When responding to a message, use the reply option to stay on the same thread. For the benefit of the readers, summarize the parts of the original message that you are responding to; do not include the entire message.

Make a Contribution
Informed quality responses to people's questions will give you credibility with the group and will reflect well upon you and your company.

Do Not Post Commercials
Advertising is not welcome in most newsgroups, and many newsgroup charters specifically disallow the posting of ads. That does not mean you cannot mention your company or its products or services, but be respectful of each newsgroup's rules.

You Don't Have to Have the Last Word
Do not post gratuitous responses in newsgroups. If you respond with just a "Thanks" or "I like it," you are wasting people's time.

Use a Signature File if Appropriate
A signature file is an "e-business card" usually attached to the end of an e-mail. This can be a clever way to append promotional information to your newsgroup responses. Typical signature files include four to eight lines of basic information, such as your name, business name, URL, e-mail address, and perhaps a promotional copy line. A particular signature file may be appropriate for one newsgroup, but not for another, so change your signature file accordingly.

Start Your Own Newsgroup

In certain instances, it may be advisable to start your own newsgroup. For more information about starting newsgroups, visit *news.announce.newsgroups*, *news.announce.newusers*, and *news.answers* on the Internet. All group creation requests must of course follow the set guidelines for newsgroups. Here is the way it works:

Request for Discussion
You should post a request for discussion on creation of a new newsgroup to *news.announce.newsgroups*. The request can also be posted to other groups or mailing lists that are related to the proposed topic. The name and charter of the proposed group, and whether it will be moderated or unmoderated, should be determined during the discussion period.

Vote

The Usenet Volunteer Vote Takers (UVT) is a group of neutral third-party vote takers that currently handles vote gathering and counting for all newsgroup proposals. There should be a minimal delay between the end of discussion period and the issuing of a call for votes. The call for votes should include clear instructions on how to cast a vote. The voting period should last for at least 21 days and no more than 31 days. Only the votes that are mailed to the vote taker will be counted.

Result

At the completion of the voting period, the vote taker must post the vote tally to the applicable groups and mailing lists. The e-mail addresses and names (if available) of the voters are posted along with the tally. There will be a five-day waiting period, beginning when the voting results actually appear. During the waiting period there will be a chance to correct any errors in the voter list or the voting procedure. In order for a proposal to pass, 100 more YES/create votes must be received than NO/do not create votes. Also, two-thirds of the total number of votes must be in favor of creation. If a proposal fails to achieve two-thirds of the vote, then the matter cannot be brought up for discussion until at least six months has passed from the close of the vote.

5

The Ins and Outs of E-mail

E-mail has become an essential component of Internet marketing for IT companies; for some, it is the primary means of e-marketing. But it hasn't always been so. Early on, e-mail received negative attention because of spam—unsolicited e-mail not requested by the recipient.

Unsolicited e-mail became such an annoyance by late 1999 that numerous states had already enacted anti-spam legislation. During that year, however, the concept of "permission marketing" launched e-mail's rebirth, driven in part by the best-selling book of the same name by Seth Godin. The idea struck a chord with marketers everywhere, and it held special relevance to Internet marketers. Permission marketing is, basically, sending e-mail only to those people who give the marketer permission to send it. Such permission is granted when a prospect or customer subscribes to a newsletter mailing list or answers a specific question in the affirmative—for example, "May we communicate with you via e-mail?" It is recommended that individuals periodically be requalified.

This is the manner in which companies have built substantial e-mailing lists. Even so, the controversy over e-mail has continued, largely due to the growing availability of "opt-in" e-mail lists. The question is whether or not these lists are truly opt-in, legitimately including people who really want to receive promotional e-mail. It seems that some are and others are not. As a result, the more conservative Internet marketer might refrain from using any opt-in list, whereas the more aggressive marketer actively seeks out such lists. One way some marketers minimize the problem is with "double opt-in"—the marketer e-mails an individual on an opt-in list, asking again for permission to send e-mail.

This chapter offers you some strategies for succeeding with e-mail and guidance so you can make your own informed decisions about the most sensible use of e-mail marketing.

Why E-mail Is So Attractive

The Direct Marketing Association (*www.the-dma.org*) reports that in 1999, for the first time, more e-mail was sent in the United States than U.S. Postal Service mail. An August 2000 survey by Pitney Bowes confirmed that e-mail was the most common communication tool in U.S. and Canadian businesses. According to Messaging Online (*www.messagingonline.com*), 569 million active e-mail accounts existed in the world by the end of 1999, an 83 percent increase over the previous year. Every one of those accounts represents an individual who can be reached with a promotional e-mail message. Messaging Online suggested that it would be only two to three years before the number of e-mail accounts surpass the number of telephone lines and televisions. Roper Starch Worldwide said e-mail is preferred by 48.5 percent as the primary business communications vehicle, versus 39 percent for the telephone and 3.5 percent for traditional mail.

A report on e-mail marketing published by eMarketer (*www.emarketer.com*) in May 2001 said that U.S. e-mail marketing expenditures were a little over $1 billion in 2000 and were expected to more than double to just over $2 billion in 2001. eMarketer says there will be 227 billion permission e-mail messages sent by 2003. Opt-in News (*www.optinnews.com*) reported in a May 2001 study that 50 percent of media buyers think e-mail is the most effective marketing vehicle for generating response. Forrester Research says e-mail will be a $4.8 billion industry by 2004.

Because of the current economics of Internet usage, e-mail direct marketing can be even more cost-effective than traditional direct-mail lead generation. After all, there are no materials or postage costs. Jupiter Media Metrix (*www.jmm.com*) says e-mail costs from 1 cent to 25 cents each to distribute, versus $1 to $2 apiece for direct mail. It takes just two days to receive responses with e-mail versus six to eight weeks (the time it takes to produce and send a typical direct mail piece) for direct mail. eMarketer claims that permission e-mail response rates average 11.5 percent, with an average cost of 25 cents each. Forrester Research says rented e-mail lists achieve click-throughs of 3.5 percent and in-house e-mail lists can achieve click-throughs as high as 10 percent.

At an April 2000 e-mail conference, Rick Bruner of IMT Strategies (*www.imtstrategies.com*) presented some intriguing statistics attesting to the increasingly attractive marketing return on investment of e-mail. Bruner looked at the cost of acquiring customers via e-mail, traditional direct mail, and banner advertising. Using a 1 percent click-through and a 1 percent conversion, Bruner estimated that it would cost $100 to acquire a customer with banner advertising. Assuming 10 cents per name, 50 cents per mailing, and a 1 percent direct mail response, it would cost $50 to acquire a customer with traditional direct mail.

For e-mail, the numbers are very different. Bruner claimed that e-mail typically produces a 10 percent click-through and 10 percent conversion rate. With a cost of about 20 cents per name for e-mail, that translates into an acquisition cost of only $20 per customer.

There is an added bonus to Internet direct marketing in general and e-mail specifically. There is nothing to physically produce, so your production time line is compressed. Instead of waiting to print and mail something, you can distribute even thousands of e-mails very fast, and you can make modifications to programs just as fast. That means you can see the results of your efforts very quickly as well. In fact, responses to e-mail programs start to come in immediately and may be completed in just days, as compared to weeks with direct mail.

Although the Internet can be proven to enhance the traditional media used in your lead generation programs, it is probably premature to assume that e-mail can replace direct mail or telemarketing entirely. For one thing, the Internet is not yet a precision medium for targeting. It has not reached the level of maturity of direct mail in terms of your ability to hone a prospect list by using key criteria to select exactly the right individuals for a mailing program.

In addition, access to individual names and titles via the Internet is problematic. As you will see in the following discussion of e-mail, prospecting via the Internet presents a whole set of unique challenges to the IT marketer.

You must also consider the fact that Internet lead generation and qualification is still not entirely accepted by everyone. Some target audiences may be comfortable with it; others may not be. Generally, those in IT and technical professions are fairly accepting of e-mail and Internet marketing. But not all individuals in all areas of business are as accepting. For example, marketing professionals tend to be more accepting than financial professionals. With consumers, acceptance tends to vary. Consumers who are active users of the Internet will obviously be more accepting, but acceptance of the Internet as a means of self-qualification will vary from prospect to prospect. Nevertheless, now is the time to think about augmenting traditional lead generation media with e-mail.

As evidence of the increasing acceptance of marketing e-mail, consider the results of a market research study released by IMT Strategies in November 1999. The firm surveyed more than 400 consumer and business e-mail users in the United States and looked at performance data from 169 companies doing e-mail campaigns. Although 64 percent of those surveyed had very negative perceptions of spam, more than half of them felt positively about *permission* e-mail marketing, and three-quarters of them said they responded to permission e-mail frequently. In fact, over 80 percent of these e-mail users had granted marketers to send them e-mail promotions.

Integrating E-mail into Your Marketing Programs

One of the easiest ways to take advantage of the transition to Internet direct marketing is to integrate e-mail into your existing direct marketing lead generation, qualification, order generation, and customer relationship programs. E-mail can be an effective way to receive responses from prospects and to reach prospects and customers with promotional messages—*as long as they want to receive them via e-mail.*

Inbound E-mail

Inbound e-mail is e-mail that comes in from prospects or customers. You should consider offering an e-mail address as a response path in direct marketing programs. (Better yet, offer a URL leading to a Web response form. See Chapter 3 for more about Web response forms.) An e-mail address can be reached by virtually anyone with Internet access, because e-mail is still the most popular Internet application.

The mechanics are simple: You set up an e-mail address through your online service or your Internet Service Provider (ISP) and use it as one of the response paths in your direct marketing promotions. E-mail addresses used for marketing purposes often are labeled *info@[e-mail box location]* so that prospects and customers can respond electronically to a general post office box instead of an individual's e-mail address.

The downside, however, is that the e-mail response vehicle is relatively passive. Most e-mail boxes are just that—electronic repositories that have no greeting, no call to action, and no way to qualify the respondent. When prospects respond to an e-mail box, they have to know what information to leave and what to ask for. Although you will know which e-mail address the response came from, you will not know much else—including the source of the response (unless you set up an e-mail response path for a specific mailing or campaign).

If you are interested in capturing qualifying information, asking questions, conveying information, or making an offer—and measuring the results—inbound e-mail is the least desirable response path. If this were your only electronic option, it would probably be more effective to use traditional response paths—a mail or fax-back reply card or form, or a special telephone number, preferably a toll-free one. The better electronic response option is a Web response form.

Nonetheless, inbound e-mail has its purposes. It is an important vehicle for customer service and technical support and as a means of communication on a corporate Web site. Inbound e-mail used for such high-traffic applications as these should be backed by auto-response systems that immediately acknowledge receipt of the incoming e-mail. To permit general inquiries, an e-mail address should always be included on business cards, letterheads, and corporate literature.

Outbound E-mail

If you "follow the rules" of outbound e-mailing, this aspect of Internet marketing can have a substantial positive impact on your existing lead generation and qualification program. *But there are rules*. E-mail is one-to-one electronic communication—similar to a personal, private letter—but there are some distinct differences:

- *E-mail is delivered directly to a user's mailbox.* It contributes to "filling" that mailbox and always stays there, unless it is deleted or opened by the recipient. In that respect, it is more intrusive than direct mail, which can easily be discarded.

- *E-mail costs the end user money.* If the end user is an individual subscriber to an online service or buys Internet access from an ISP, e-mail is one of the items he or she buys. (More and more, e-mail is bundled in as a free service from Sips, Web search engines, and other Internet services. However, one way or the other, the end user pays for Internet access.)

  If the end user is at a business e-mail address, the business is "paying" for the e-mail address as part of its Internet access. Unlike the receipt of direct mail, which is free to the end user, the receipt of e-mail therefore has a cost associated with it.

- *E-mail was not designed for unsolicited promotions.* E-mail was first intended to be an electronic communications vehicle, not a marketing vehicle. You could say the same thing about early direct mail, but it took decaOdes before direct mail became an accepted form of advertising.

  Today, unsolicited e-mail already has a poor reputation. Known as "spamming," it can create nothing short of fury on the part of recipients. In fact, some recipients of unsolicited e-mail have been known to give spammers a taste of their own medicine by overloading senders with countless e-mail replies. A word of caution: If you choose to use unsolicited e-mail to promote something to someone, you should be aware that not all recipients will be favorably predisposed to the practice. If in doubt, *do not do it.*

Unsolicited e-mail and Internet privacy are hot issues. As early as 1999, California, Maryland, Nevada, and Washington had enacted anti-spam legislation. The California law in particular has national implications. It basically says that it is illegal to send unsolicited commercial e-mail to an individual in California without that person's consent. It goes further by saying that an ISP with an anti-spam policy can sue anyone, anywhere, if the ISP's equipment located in California is used to deliver that unsolicited e-mail. This effectively makes it illegal to send spam nationwide, because the sender is likely, one way or the other, to reach California names, or use an ISP with equipment in California.

By the first half of 2001, there were at least three different bills introduced in the U.S. House of Representatives and the U.S. Senate that would regulate unsolicited commercial e-mail. The Senate bill under consideration in May 2001 would levy harsh penalties against commercial spammers, including criminal penalties. The House bill, also under consideration at that time, would allow individuals to sue but wouldn't carry a criminal penalty. Fifteen states already have laws addressing unsolicited e-mail in some way, and additional laws are pending in numerous others. Check out *www.spamlaws.com* for the latest on such legislation. For an excellent overview of the situation, read "What B2B Marketers Need to Know about Spam," a special issue of the *B2B Marketing Biz* newsletter (*www.b2bmarketingbiz.com*).

Canada already has strong privacy principles in place. In addition, the "European Union Data Protection Directive," which effectively outlaws unsolicited e-mail throughout Europe, was scheduled to be implemented by October 2001. Given this regulatory environment, you would do well to stay away from unsolicited e-mail and be sure to use any form of e-mail appropriately.

Limit Your Risk

The real issue with outbound e-mail is limiting your risk when you use it for direct marketing. Following are some suggestions.

Always Ask Permission to Send E-mail

You have every right to ask for and collect e-mail addresses, just as you collect other pertinent information about prospects and customers, but when you ask for an e-mail address, it also is appropriate to ask the question, "May we communicate with you via e-mail?" If you receive a "Yes" response, then the individual has "opted in." If you receive a "No," take it seriously and code that individual on your database so you will not send him or her unwanted e-mail messages. There are some marketers who believe a "softer" opt-in strategy is acceptable: They turn opt-in into a negative option. A popular execution of this type of opt-in is asking individuals to "uncheck" a box on a Web response form to eliminate themselves from receiving e-mail. This practice may result in more opt-in e-mail records, but it could backfire in the long run. It is not equivalent to asking a direct permission question and, as such, may ultimately lead to complaints from e-mail recipients.

"Permission e-mail" and "permission marketing" have become popular phrases that associate e-mail with the concept of asking recipients to approve your use of e-mail for promotional purposes. Some marketing experts believe the concept of permission marketing will extend outward from the Internet to all media, becoming a standard marketing practice in the near future.

Always Provide the Recipient with the Ability to "Opt Out"

Even if you have received permission to send someone promotional e-mail, it is good practice to let the recipient opt out (tell you he or she does not want to receive future promotional e-mails from you). The most common way of doing this is to include some copy at the beginning or end of the e-mail that, in effect, asks the recipient to simply respond with a word, such as "unsubscribe," to prevent receiving future promotional e-mails from you. Some experts believe you should include a Web page link in your e-mail for opting out. At this link, you could offer the individual an opportunity to change his or her mind about opting out. You might want to test this approach yourself.

Be Very Cautious if You Choose to Share, Sell, or Rent a List of Your Own E-mail Addresses

Some organizations generate substantial revenue by renting name and address lists of prospects and customers to others for commercial usage. Other organizations share or swap lists to broaden their prospecting efforts. These practices are common in the direct marketing industry, but they have led to such a proliferation of mail and telephone calls that the industry's major trade organization, the Direct Marketing Association (*www.the-dma.org*), now offers mail preference and telephone preference services that allow consumers to elect *not* to receive solicitations.

The "P" word—privacy—is one of the largest looming issues in Internet marketing. Do not underestimate its importance when it comes to your Web site or your house list of e-mail addresses. You would be well advised at this stage to hold any e-mail list you may own "close to the vest" and treat it as the confidential and valuable marketing asset that it is. Keeping it private and for your use only is probably a wise decision at a time when privacy on the Internet is being scrutinized by the consumer and government alike.

Building Your Own E-mail List

If you plan to fully integrate e-mail into your marketing initiatives, it will make sense to build your own e-mail list. Ideally, it won't be a separate list at all, but rather a component of your marketing database. To the extent possible, it is best to acquire e-mail addresses as part of a marketing campaign that also acquires other basic contact information, such as name, title, company name, address, and phone number.

If you already have a database, one easy way to start building an e-mail list is to make an offer to the individuals on the database via direct mail and ask for an e-mail address in return. (Be sure to ask permission as well.)

There are numerous other ways to build an e-mail list, including making promotional offers on your Web site, offering an e-mail alert service or e-newsletter, asking for e-mail addresses in direct mail campaigns, collecting e-mail addresses at trade shows, adding e-mail addresses via online advertising and promotions, adding respondents from opt-in e-mail campaigns, and viral marketing. We discuss several of these in further detail later in this chapter. Whenever you add e-mail addresses to a database, always make sure to separate "permission to e-mail" addresses from "do not send e-mail" addresses.

Opt-in E-mail

As with direct mail, the rapidly increasing popularity of promotional e-mail has led to an entire business of providing e-mail names for rental. Although list availability is far more limited and also doesn't provide the selectability of direct-mail lists, e-mail lists may be attractive to IT marketers looking to aggressively market their products and services at a relatively low cost.

Rental e-mail lists are often referred to as "opt-in" lists, meaning that the individuals on them have indicated in some way that *they have given permission* to receive e-mail. Although opt-in e-mail lists may sound like the acceptable alternative to sending unsolicited e-mail, keep in mind that just because you are told these lists are opt-in, they may not always be opt-in. It is essential to verify with any e-mail list owner or service that any list being represented as opt-in is guaranteed to be just that.

Additionally, it is a good idea to verify the list owner or e-mail service's practices. The provider should have a written privacy policy and should also be committed to the earlier-referenced concept of permission e-mail. Individuals on e-mail lists should always have the ability to opt out of participation on any given list.

In many cases, e-mail list vendors do not release the actual e-mail addresses on a list to third parties. Instead, you write a promotional message (typically no more than 500 words) and give it to the e-mail list vendor along with your list selections, and the vendor delivers the e-mail to the recipients within two or three days. Depending on the list source, there may be selection criteria available, so you may be able to target a specific audience.

In the information technology marketplace, typical e-mail lists rent for $200 to $300 per thousand names, with an additional $150 per thousand names for e-mail delivery. This is typically referred to as CPM, or "cost per thousand." There may be minimums of 3,000 to 5,000 names per list order. The reply-to address is generally the service provider's, and responses are handled for an additional fee, typically $50 per thousand names. Your e-mail promotional copy could encourage a reply-to response, or you could mention a Web link as a response path.

You might be able to negotiate something called a "cost per action" (CPA) media purchase as a counter to the CPM purchase. The concept of CPA is based on your own experience as a marketer and the response rate you actually get with e-mail marketing. If the owner of the e-mail list is highly confident of its quality, CPA could be attractive because it could mean more revenue. You, as the marketer, pay on the basis of response, so it more like a revenue-sharing approach than a straight list rental. This is a relatively new idea, but it could potentially be a win–win for list owner and marketer alike.

Unlike direct mail, you will not be able to obtain a magnetic tape of the names and addresses—which means you generally will not be able to eliminate duplicates from multiple list sources. As a result, your e-mailing strategy may be different from direct mail—you may want to test one well-targeted e-mail list first and mail to another later, rather than to two similar lists at the same time. If, however, you are acquiring numerous e-mail lists from the same vendor, it always pays to ask about duplicate elimination (known as "merge purge" in the direct mail business).

Some of the better-known opt-in list owners, managers, or brokers serving the IT market include 21st az Marketing (*www.21staz.com*),

Direct Media (*www.directmedia.com*), ALC (*www.amlist.com*), IDG List Services (*www.idglist.com*), NetCreations' Postmaster Direct (*rentals.postmasterdirect.com*), Worldata's WebConnect (*www.webconnect.com*), and YesMail (*www.yesmail.com*). YesMail, a CMGi company, claims to top the industry with over 7 million people who have opted to receive information and offers via e-mail. In May 2001, YesMail introduced a service that allows marketers to send HTML e-mails with audio capabilities. The recipient of the e-mail can click a button and then speak with the sender's call center via telephone or directly over the computer.

Mass mailing to opt-in e-mail lists is often referred to as "blast" or "broadcast" e-mail. Typically, what seems to work best is e-mails with compelling subject lines, strong offers, short copy tending toward informational rather than promotional, and embedded links to Web response pages.

Expect responses to e-mail to begin immediately. You will start getting responses within 48 hours, and you could receive as much as 85 percent of the total response to your e-mail campaign within the first week. E-mail response in general tends to be considerably higher than traditional direct mail response. If you use an e-mail list that you obtained from another source, it is probably a good idea to acknowledge this fact in e-mail copy when you give the recipient the ability to opt out.

Does opt-in e-mail marketing really work for IT companies? Consider this case from the e-newsletter *B2B Marketing Biz*, reported in March 2001: Sento Corporation is a provider of IT training courses priced from $3,000 to $8,000. The company converted from fax marketing to e-mail marketing, first using relatively general e-mail lists. Click-throughs averaged about 3 to 5 percent. When the company switched to highly targeted e-mail opt-in lists to reach individuals with an interest in specific types of IT training, click-throughs more than doubled, averaging 10 to 12 percent. The company reported that almost 10 percent of the visitors convert to serious sales leads. To see a landing page Sento used for the campaign, go to *www.mcsetraining.com*.

Effective Use of Outbound E-mail

Following are some of the most effective ways to use outbound e-mail for direct marketing.

Customer Communications

Customers tend to be receptive to e-mail marketing, especially if the e-mail is used as an alert service to give them advance notice or an "inside track" on new product developments or late-breaking news. As such, e-mail can be a very effective way to pre-announce products or upgrades to customers, send a flash about a product update or a problem, inform customers about changes in service, announce important news about the company, invite them to a customer-only event, and so on. As with any good direct marketing, a call to action should be included, even if it simply states, "To take advantage of this offer, respond to this e-mail today." It is generally safe to assume that customers will find e-mail acceptable if they have given you their e-mail addresses. Even so, some of these customers may be upset by your use of promotional e-mail, so you should offer them the ability to "unsubscribe."

Follow-ups

Both customers and prospects will be more accepting of e-mail marketing if it is used to follow up on inquiries or orders, especially inquiries or orders that were electronically sent by them to your organization. If the e-mail message clearly states that it is in response to an inquiry or confirming an order, it is generally acceptable if that message also includes some marketing information and a call to action.

An increasingly common practice in direct marketing is using a direct mail, fax, or telemarketing follow-up to an original promotional contact. In direct mail, the follow-up can be as simple as a double post-card or a standard business letter. Direct mail testing supports the fact that such follow-ups usually generate an additional one-half of the original response rate. For example, if an original mailing generates a 3 percent response, the follow-up will typically generate another 1½ percent response. The added bonus is that most follow-ups can be executed at a very low incremental cost because you are reusing a list, and the physical piece itself is inexpensive to produce.

E-mail holds great promise as a replacement for or enhancement to the follow-up strategy. If you have a prospect's or customer's e-mail address, sending an e-mail that reiterates the offer and message of an original contact (whether it is by mail or phone) could be effective. E-mail may break through in a way that a follow-up mailing or phone call may not—and at a much lower cost than mail or phone contacts.

E-mail can also be very effective as a means to quickly follow up on a personal meeting, summarize what was discussed, and offer an opportunity to respond, and e-mail is a personal way to just say thank you when you cannot reach someone by phone.

Major Announcements or Alerts

It may be appropriate to do a broadcast e-mail to a large number of customers and prospects when you have something very important to say. Of course, "big news" may be a matter of interpretation, and not every e-mail recipient will react the same way, but if it really *is* big news (such as a merger, an acquisition, a new president, going public, or something similar), then nothing can beat the immediacy of e-mail. It is likely that customers and even prospects would subscribe to an "alert service" that keeps them in the know about such developments.

One interesting variation of the alert service is the "event-driven" e-mail. This type of e-mail is automatically sent when a certain key event occurs; for example, if a customer's service contract is about to expire, an e-mail encouraging renewal can be sent.

Serial E-mail

More and more IT marketers are using serial e-mail—e-mail that is sent in a series to work as a single campaign. An example of this is the "before, during, and after" approach: An e-mail is sent to pre-announce a forthcoming offer, followed several weeks later by an e-mail with the offer, followed several weeks after that with a reminder e-mail. As with direct mail, serial e-mail could be an effective way to build interest in a product or service because of the build-up effect of multiple contacts. This technique can be especially effective in converting warm prospects to hot prospects; however, it should be used only when truly appropriate because it can cause negative reactions from individuals who may feel overwhelmed by too many contacts.

E-mail Newsletters

Shrewd electronic marketers have figured out a way to implement e-mail in a nonobjectionable format that reaches target individuals on a regular basis. It is called the *e-mail newsletter.* The e-mail newsletter is basically a longer e-mail that is regularly and automatically sent to a customer or prospect "by subscription"—*upon request.* The best e-mail newsletters contain information of high-perceived value about a pertinent topic area, but they are, of course, marketing vehicles as well. Although most are free, some e-mail newsletters are sent on a paid subscription basis.

E-mail newsletters are hugely popular. They have become the acceptable method for using e-mail as an ongoing form of promotional communication. Every major high-tech information provider, including CMPnet (*www.cmpnet.com*), ClNet (*www.cnet.com)* and its property ZDnet (*www.zdnet.net*), and IDG (*www.idg.net*), publishes numerous free e-mail newsletters, some on a daily basis. Reportedly, some of the more popular e-mail newsletters have circulations as high as 1 million subscribers.

But that is only the tip of the e-mail newsletter iceberg. Now e-mail newsletters have pervaded every business and industry. E-mail newsletters have proliferated to the extent that there are likely to be many to choose from in even the narrowest of interest groups. And the majority of these newsletters are free. An increasing number of marketing Web sites offer free newsletters as part of their promotional strategy.

Why do organizations and individuals distribute these free e-mail newsletters so widely? For one thing, it keeps their names in front of a very large number of people, all of whom have given the information providers their e-mail addresses. As a result, *they are building their own opt-in e-mailing lists for free,* and the e-mail addresses they acquire will be available to them for ongoing use. The cost to e-mail these names is very low, and when compared with the cost of other promotional means of reaching prospects, e-mail is downright cheap. Newsletters are, in effect, one of the best ways to build your own house list of e-mail prospects and customers.

Publishing an e-mail newsletter and collecting subscriber names is a smart business strategy. As the regulatory environment changes, unsolicited e-mail has become either unethical or illegal. Even opt-in lists are not completely foolproof. As an e-mail newsletter publisher, however, you are building your own e-mail list. You can continue to use it to send e-mail ethically and legally, because the recipients *have asked for it.* Of course, it is still good practice to offer e-mail newsletter subscribers the option of deleting their names from your list.

There are other benefits to publishing e-mail newsletters. As an e-mail newsletter publisher, you are constantly promoting yourself. Many e-mail newsletters drive subscribers back to linked Web pages to learn more about a particular topic. E-mail newsletters can be distributed at a very low cost. Imagine the cost for printing and postage to send 1 million paper newsletters. Even if they were simple one-page documents sent by fax, the newsletter publisher would have to pay to call every recipient's fax machine.

E-mail, on the other hand, can be broadcast across the Internet via automated methods at a very low cost. As long as you have the proper e-mail addresses and the necessary software and systems support, you can send e-mail to hundreds, thousands, or even millions of individuals instantly. In fact, with advanced database-driven technology, you can *personalize and customize* e-mail newsletters. E-mail newsletters can include an individual's name, but more importantly, you can even tailor e-mail newsletters to the needs of individual target audiences. Some e-mail newsletters even customize information within the newsletter itself to specific audiences.

As e-mail newsletters have become popular, services have been introduced to help marketers with the publishing and distribution process. IMakeNews (*www.imakenews.com*) automates the e-newsletter publishing process. Topica (*www.topica.com*) provides an integrated suite of services to help marketers of high-volume newsletters create and distribute them.

Most e-mail newsletters are published in text, but a growing number are published as HTML newsletters so the graphic look and feel can be enhanced. HTML versions of e-mail newsletters might offer additional opportunities for advertising sponsorships. The HTML newsletter can be sent as an HTML e-mail or it can be posted on the Web and linked via a hyperlink in the text e-mail. If you send an HTML e-mail newsletter, prepare a default text version and use an e-mail distribution service that can detect whether recipients can receive HTML.

A common e-mail newsletter technique is to publish article summaries in newsletter form and then post the full articles on a Web site. The newsletter summaries then link the reader directly to the article pages. One such newsletter, ClickZ (*www.clickz.com*), part of the Internet.com network, is a combination e-mail newsletter and Web site that serves online marketers. ClickZ (Figure 5.1) provides online marketing information and uses e-mail notifications to its subscribers with links to each of its articles, which are then published as HTML pages. Advertisers sponsor several of the recurring columns. ClickZ cleverly ties in the column to the sponsor by utilizing the advertiser's logo and corporate color to "brand" the information. ClickZ publishes articles, hosts online discussion forums, offers marketing guides, and sponsors live conferences about online and e-mail marketing.

Although most e-mail newsletters are designed to drive traffic, they can be revenue generators in and of themselves. Many of the larger-

Figure 5.1. Internet.com's ClickZ is a combination e-newsletter/Web site for Internet marketers. Published daily, the e-mail newsletter describes the articles and links to each article on the Web site. An article on ClickZ by the author is shown here.

circulation e-mail newsletters are also important vehicles for Internet-based advertising. Some e-mail newsletter publishers accept paid advertising messages and append them to the newsletter text. The advertiser is often positioned as a "sponsor" of the newsletter and can embed a live link to a Web site in the promotional message. Most e-mail programs accept Web links, so this can be a very effective way of driving a target prospect directly to a specific URL.

Advertising in e-mail text newsletters may not be fancy, but industry sources say it is very effective. My direct and e-marketing agency has extensively tested e-mail newsletter ads against outbound e-mail and banner ads. The newsletter ads have almost always outpulled both e-mail and banner ads. I have seen numerous industry reports supporting this data. E-mail newsletter advertising is such a significant business that now Internet advertising networks and service providers are working them into their offerings.

There is a logical reason that advertising in e-mail newsletters works. Newsletter subscribers are looking for high-value content and they have requested the newsletter. Chances are the subscribers are reading each issue closely. Text-based ads are generally placed within the body of the newsletter. Although they are separated from the text itself, the reader can't miss them. If the ads embed Web page links, all the reader has to do is click to go to the advertiser's Web page. It's simple, effective direct marketing . . . and it works.

Before we leave the subject of newsletters, it's worth mentioning that customer e-mail newsletters can be quite effective in developing ongoing relationships. In the winter 2001 issue of *The DMA Insider*, published by the Direct Marketing Association, it was reported that Hewlett-Packard employed e-newsletters to reach three different customer audiences, each with targeted messages. HP integrated "Call Me Now" buttons within the newsletter and achieved a 12 percent click-through rate. What's more, they've achieved a click-through rate of from 25 to 40 percent when e-mails have been forwarded to colleagues of the recipients.

By the way, I consider e-mail marketing newsletters among my top sources for information about Internet marketing. I've listed several of my favorites in Appendix A.

E-mail and Online Surveys

Surveys that ask the opinions of customers or prospects, allowing them to respond by copying and answering the survey questions, can be as effective as surveys conducted via mail, phone, and fax—maybe more so. E-mail surveys are easier to respond to and less intrusive than phone surveys, so they may ultimately prove to generate a higher level of response. E-mail surveys can also contain a link that takes respondents to a Web response page to facilitate response. This is an increasingly popular way to execute online surveys, because a form-based survey is much easier to answer.

Customer surveys that use traditional media such as direct mail and the telephone are known to generate response rates as high as 20 percent or more, and online surveys are achieving results just as impressive.

There are several services that allow do-it-yourself online survey creation. Zoomerang (*www.zoomerang.com*) is a free service that allows small companies and individuals to create and send online surveys. Created by Web researcher MarketTools, Zoomerang uses professionally designed templates that make it easy to create and customize surveys on anything from customer satisfaction to new product testing to event planning.

My company used Zoomerang to create an online survey about online seminars. We sent an e-mail to a house e-mail list of customers and prospects and asked them to complete the survey by clicking on a link to the survey page. We offered to send the survey results to all respondents, and we also offered a drawing for several e-gift certificates. We asked 15 questions about the use of online seminars by these companies. We got a 23 percent response and some very valuable insight that guided us in the way we structure and sell our services. Online surveys should have the potential to do the same for you if they are used appropriately.

E-mail Discussion Groups

Discussion groups about virtually every subject exist on the Internet, so chances are that one or more of them relate to your product or service. Some of these groups allow free or paid "advertising" or sponsorships by appending some copy about your company, product, or service to discussion text. It must be done appropriately, in the proper context, and always with permission—but it does present you with another way of reaching a very targeted audience via e-mail.

A company called Keyva Technologies (*www.keyva.com*) had an interesting experience with e-mail discussion groups, according to an April 2001 report in *B2B Marketing Biz* (*www.b2bmarketingbiz.com*). The company wanted to target small and medium-sized ISPs and decided to use e-mail discussion groups instead of e-mails, because they felt this audience would respond poorly to opt-in e-mail. The company's strategy was to participate in e-mail discussion groups and only send notes when a useful contribution could be made to a technical discussion. It's only when an ISP responds to Jack Permison, Keyva's president, that he gets a return e-mail with sales information. The results? Keyva has acquired about 75 percent of its customers via e-mail discussion groups, says Permison. (Refer to Chapter 4 for more on discussion groups.)

Making E-mail Work Harder

Numerous technologies are being introduced regularly to make e-mail work harder. There are products and services available to enhance your ability to personalize and customize e-mail, and e-mail service bureaus that can provide you with start-to-finish services, including building and managing your own e-mail list.

Basically, you can decide to outsource your e-mail or manage e-mail lists and programs in-house. Two of the better-known firms in the outsourced e-mail business are MessageMedia (*www.messagemedia.com*) and Digital Impact (*www.digitalimpact.com*). MessageMedia makes available ten free "SmartMarketer" lessons in e-mail marketing on its Web site. These short lessons are a useful primer to direct e-mail marketing.

A number of products and services, from simple to extremely sophisticated, are available if you want to handle e-mail yourself. Interact from Responsys (*www.responsys.com*) is one of the more-sophisticated systems. Responsys's Interact provides support for dynamic personalization so marketers can personalize messages based on customer contact and profile data. It supports text and HTML e-mail, provides list and data management, and has a complete response management and tracking capability. TargetMessaging from Exactis.com (*www.exactis.com*) allows users to mine customer data and build targeted lists, create personalized offers or communications, use Exactis.com to build and send the offers, and analyze the tracking data provided to construct reports and improve later campaigns.

Personalized, targeted e-mail is on the rise. For example, an issue of the Peppers & Rogers Group e-mail newsletter, *INSIDE 1to1* *(www.m1to1.com)*, distributed in mid-2000, reported on a personalized e-mail system established by Onsale. Onsale, now part of Egghead (*www.egghead.com*), moved from standard, non-personalized e-mails sent to customers in 1998, to e-mails that targeted customers with specific product recommendations based on their purchase history. Information from the customer's registration record, transaction data, and click-throughs on the site was used to create a one-to-one e-mail strategy. According to *INSIDE 1to1*, Onsale improved its response rates by more than 40 percent—and 74 percent of the company's orders were from repeat buyers after Onsale began using the personalized e-mail system.

The Rise of HTML E-mail

More and more e-mail systems are moving to "visual" e-mail. Although the predominant form of e-mail is still text-based, e-mail is increasingly becoming HTML-based. The result is that messaging might soon resemble mini-Web pages, complete with formatting and graphics, rather than standard text-based communication.

The lingering issue with HTML e-mail is that not all e-mail systems can receive it. But as systems are upgraded, HTML e-mail is sure to become a far more common format. Some studies suggest that HTML e-mail outpulls text e-mail in terms of response. Today, the IT marketer would do well to consider creating e-mail in both text and HTML formats to accommodate this shifting market. Use an e-mail distribution service that can detect whether or not the recipient's e-mail system can receive HTML and then you can use text e-mail as the default version.

A more conservative alternative to HTML e-mail is to introduce HTML gradually by using Web page links in text-based e-mail to send readers to an HTML newsletter or promotional page. As mentioned earlier, e-mail newsletters are using this hybrid strategy to mix the advantages of traditional e-mail and HTML pages.

My agency, Directech | eMerge (*www.directechemerge.com*), uses this strategy in publishing our own direct and e-marketing newsletter. We send out an HTML- and text-based e-mail periodically to our house list of clients and prospects with a link to the latest issue of our HTML e-letter, "Direct Insight Online." In the e-mail is a hyperlink to the current newsletter, as well as a link to the "subscriber services" page. Subscribers can also access newsletter archives. You can subscribe to this newsletter free on our Web site.

E-mail Innovations are on the Way

Innovative e-mail tools and techniques are being introduced at Internet speed. Here are just a few examples:

- MessageMates are similar to banner ads, but they attach to e-mail. They are part of a product line of e-mail attachments and other multimedia innovations from a company called Indimi (*www.indimi.com*).

- Rich Media e-mail features sound and animation and is available through Media Synergy (*www.mediasynergy.com*) and its "Flo Network," which offers the ability to create, deliver, personalize, track, and report on e-mail campaigns. Rich-media advertising vendor Bluestreak (*www.bluestreak.com*) offers RichMail, which allows e-mail to include rich media and, interestingly, permits the advertiser to change the offer in real time, right until the recipient opens the e-mail. E-mail service provider Britemoon (*www.britemoon.com*) offers "talking e-mails" through a partnership with BYOBroadcast. MindArrow (*www.mindarrow.com*) delivers multi-media "eBrochures" as e-mail attachments. In May 2001, MindArrow announced an alliance with NetCreations to deliver rich-media e-mail to customers of PostMasterDirect.com.

- Zaplet (*www.zaplet.com)* resides on top of e-mail, arriving in the e-mailbox and acting like e-mail. Once opened, however, a Zaplet acts more like the Web, incorporating graphical and interactive capabilities. Zaplets can be created by anyone, updated as individuals respond, and analyzed as responses come in.

- LifeFX (*www.lifefx.com)* allows a 3D rendered face to appear in a person's e-mail box. An agreement with Kodak will lead to people being able to send images of their own faces via e-mail.

In March 2001, one of my agency's media analysts received quite an unusual HTML e-mail. It was a promotion for the 2001 Rich Media Road Show, sponsored by Emerging Interest and MediaPost Communications. The e-mail included the analyst's name, graphically spelled out in an animated portion of the e-mail (Figure 5.2). But the e-mail went one step further and also spoke the analyst's name! According to an April 16, 2001, report in *BtoB* magazine, this rich e-mail campaign was sent to 20,000 media professionals and achieved a 6 percent click-through rate.

Keep in mind, however, that any new e-mail technology should be pretested and verified prior to use. Also realize that not every recipient's e-mail system will be able to accept e-mails or attachments using newer technologies.

For serious e-mailers, e-mail management systems are becoming a necessity. These systems not only handle outbound e-mail, but process inbound e-mail in much the same way as a call center or direct mail lead

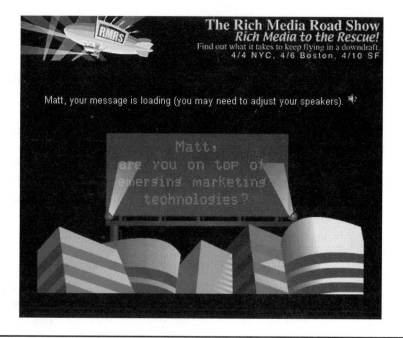

Figure 5.2. This unusual rich e-mail included the recipient's name in a graphic headline. But that's not all—the e-mail included a personalized audio file that spoke the person's name as well.

processing center would do. E-mail management systems identify, route, and sometimes automatically answer incoming e-mail. Many such systems also include full reporting capabilities and the ability to survey e-mail respondents on the quality of service received.

What about Viral Marketing?

There is even new terminology associated with the emerging importance of e-mail marketing: "viral marketing." This somewhat unfortunate moniker wrongly associates e-mail marketing with viruses. The intended meaning, however, is marketing that spreads rapidly via e-mail or other Internet communications.

Writing in *Red Herring* (May 2000), Steve Jurvetson says viral marketing got its start when Hotmail, a Web-based e-mail service, included a promotional message about its service with a URL in every message sent by a Hotmail user. The result, says Jurvetson, was that "every customer becomes an involuntary salesperson simply by using the product." He says that Hotmail's subscriber base reached 12 million users in only 18 months, with a meager advertising budget of just $50,000. It was all because of viral marketing.

Given the nature of the Internet and e-mail, it is easy to see how marketing messages can spread just as rapidly as can computer viruses themselves. By simply adding a promotional message to an e-mail, that e-mail becomes a promotion that can then be forwarded to one, or one hundred, or one thousand individuals in no time. For viral marketing to be most effective, there should be a valuable reason that someone should want to forward your e-mail. Maybe it is a discount or a freebie, a brief test or a free report, or maybe it is just something with sound or motion. Whatever it is, if you offer both the sender and the recipient something of perceived value, viral marketing will be that much more potent.

A common variation on the viral marketing theme is "tell a friend" or "forward to a colleague." Basically, this means the marketer suggests that the recipient of an e-mail pass it along to someone else, and provides an easy way to do this, perhaps with a "forward to a colleague" button within the body of the e-mail. There may or may not be a reward attached to this. Some e-mail distribution services can track pass-along back to the original recipient so marketers can find out how well the concept works for themselves.

Automated E-mail Response

It is easy to build in a "mail-to" e-mail link so that visitors can instantly inquire about your products or services, but it is just as important to respond promptly if not instantly. There are a variety of auto-responder or autobot tools available that can respond automatically to such requests. On good electronic commerce sites, for example, your order can instantly be acknowledged as soon as you place it. An e-mail message is sent to your mailbox verifying your order and providing you with an order number and shipping information. This is also a good way to prevent fraud, because if the recipient did not place the order, he or she can immediately inform the sender of the e-mail.

Other Important Facts about E-mail

Here are a few more facts you should know about e-mail:

- Various software tools are available to help you automate e-mailings. You can use these tools to build e-mail lists, do "e-mail blasts" and automatically respond to inbound e-mail. There are numerous firms that will rent e-mail lists to you or help you implement full-scale e-mail campaigns from start to finish.

- E-mail addresses change even more rapidly than business addresses, so expect at least 10 percent of an e-mail list to be undeliverable at any point in time. Obviously, starting with a clean list and scrupulously maintaining it will help.

- Response to e-mail campaigns can be fast, even immediate, so be prepared to handle the "back end"—acknowledgment, processing, and fulfillment—*before* you execute an outbound e-mail campaign.

- Expect e-mail to generate some *negative* responses. Even if you are e-mailing to customers, or to an opt-in prospect list, there may still be a few recipients who resent receiving promotional e-mail and will not hesitate to let you know about it. It is good business practice to send these people an apology and suppress their e-mail addresses from future promotions.

- E-mail can be—and should be—personalized and customized whenever possible. As with personalized direct mail, if you can use an individual's name, recognize any relationship the individual has with your organization, and incorporate pertinent information in an e-mail, it will potentially increase response. E-mail can also be customized to the needs of the recipient via database technologies now available; for example, different e-mail texts can automatically be generated to different audiences based on database criteria.

- Use the Subject line of an e-mail appropriately. The Subject line is like teaser copy on a direct-mail envelope, or the headline on a print ad—it could determine whether or not the recipient reads the e-mail. The Subject line should be a few words of intriguing copy, but it should not mislead the recipient or misrepresent the content of the e-mail.

- E-mail is "short form" communication, except for the e-mail newsletter format. Paragraphs and sentences in e-mail should be short and concise. E-mails should generally be no longer than 500 words.

- E-mail is still primarily an informational vehicle. Some readers may react negatively to overuse of very promotional language. You need to be careful with tone, because e-mail comes across as "flat" copy without graphic signals to emphasize certain words or phrases. For example, anything in CAPITAL LETTERS is usually seen as SHOUTING when used in e-mail. Avoid overuse of exclamation points. Don't oversell. Make use of good direct marketing copywriting techniques, such as incorporating a call to action into your e-mail, but be aware that all words may appear the same. So, using larger point sizes, bolding, underlining, or italicizing will not necessarily be seen.

- Send e-mails "raw"—do not format the text, change fonts, or use attachments, tables, graphics, or artwork. E-mail campaigns should be designed for the lowest common denominator, which today is plain text only.

- Use e-mail to drive recipients to specific Web pages with more information, or to reference your Web site. It is very likely that individuals with an e-mail address will also have Web access. You can embed a link to your Web site in an e-mail, but some readers may not be able to access the link directly through their e-mail programs, so be sure to spell it out also.

- Use good sense in executing e-mail direct marketing. Integrate e-mail appropriately with other techniques in your direct marketing lead generation programs. Be sure you use e-mail wisely. Build your own e-mail list and keep it current with the addresses of individuals who give you permission to communicate with them via e-mail. Do not use unsolicited e-mail. Test opt-in e-mail cautiously. Respect the privacy and needs of your target audience.

6

Internet Advertising and Public Relations

For IT Internet marketers and others, there has been some wariness about online advertising. Banner advertising in particular has been under attack because of dropping click-through rates. Nonetheless, Internet advertising continues to grow, even if at a slower pace than previously. The Interactive Advertising Bureau (*www.iab.net*) reported in April 2001 that online advertising in 2000 reached $8.2 billion, up from $4.6 billion the prior year. Although this was an increase of 78 percent, the IAB said it was lower than in past years. Banner advertising made up 47 percent of the year's ad revenue, with sponsorships accounting for 28 percent. AdRelevance (*www.adrelevance.com*) says about 63 percent of all online ads are branding, and the rest are direct response. Forrester Research (*www.forrester.com*) believes online advertising in the United States will reach over $25 billion by 2004, with online advertising in Europe expected to hit about $5.4 billion by 2005.

The real issue with online advertising for IT marketers, regardless of the growth of online advertising, is whether or not it is the most effective way to achieve a decent Internet marketing ROI. This chapter helps you answer that question by examining the various online advertising vehicles available to you. It also shows you how to take advantage of "free" advertising through online public relations.

Creating and Placing Online Advertising

The good news is that IT companies are more successful than others in using online advertising, according to a May 2001 study by Nielsen/NetRatings (*www.netratings.com*). Nevertheless, the study suggests that banner ads are run too frequently on sites with limited audiences, concluding that this causes click-through rates to plummet. Nielsen/NetRatings says that online advertising frequency rates are in the high teens versus 3–4 percent in offline advertising. The statistics in the 2001 eAdvertising Report published by eMarketer (*www.emarketer.com*) are even more sobering. The report says more than 99.7 percent of banner ads do not get clicked, and 74 percent of online advertising space is not sold.

An interesting benefit of such statistics, however, is that in a softer economy, advertisers willing to commit to even modest ongoing spending can get great deals and can even stretch the boundaries of what can be done. Web site owners hungry for advertising revenue will heavily discount. Sometimes they will also allow advertisers to go quite beyond the ordinary, permitting regular advertisers to even modify their sites' home pages. That means you may be able to do some breakthrough online advertising.

The banner ad celebrated its sixth birthday in October 2000, but industry experts continue to look beyond the banner for advertising effectiveness. For example, the number of vertical online ads increased by almost 70 percent in the fourth quarter of 2000, according to Jupiter Media Metrix (*www.jmm.com*). In early 2001, new online advertising specifications recommended by the Interactive Advertising Bureau included vertical banners as well as pop-up units.

Today's online advertising consists of much more than banners alone. For example, there are:

- *Advertorials* are a form of paid advertising created to take advantage of the look and feel of a particular Web site. They typically are integrated with the other copy and graphics on a Web page, offering the appearance of editorial matter even though the message is advertising.

- *Buttons* typically are small banners. They often run next to one another at the side or bottom of a page. They tend to look more like sponsorship ads than promotional ads. Some advertisers feel that their "less salesy" nature might improve the chances of higher click-throughs.

- *Interstitials (or pop-ups)* appear between Web site pages. The new page loads and an interstitial pops up to convey something about a company and its products or services. Because of their intrusive nature, there is a significant annoyance factor, yet a number of online advertising studies have shown interstitials to outpull banner click-through rates. One company, Unicast (*www.unicast.com*), has developed the Superstitial, a "polite" interstitial that only plays when it is completely loaded. It is now available on a number of Internet advertising networks, including Engage's AudienceNet, an online profile-driven ad network (*www.engage.com*). Recognizing the B-to-B ad surge, Engage launched a new division in May 2000: "Engage Business Media." The Superstitial occupies nearly the full screen and utilizes rich media. (More on that later.) There is also a variation to interstitials that some advertisers are testing—a "Webmercial" which essentially is an under-10-second commercial played over the Web. Growing evidence seems to indicate that interstitials are proving to be more effective than banner ads. Interstitials accounted for 4 percent of all advertising revenue in 2000, according to the Internet Advertising Bureau.

- *Skyscrapers and boxes.* One look at such IT-related sites as CMPnet (*www.cmpnet.com*), ZDnet (*www.zdnet.com*), and ClNet's News (*www.news.com*) will show you the changing face of Internet advertising. The first two sites run numerous "skyscrapers," long, narrow vertical ads that appear to the right or left of the editorial page. They're hard to miss, even as a site visitor scrolls up or down the page. Several of CMP's individual sites provide advertisers with "extramercials," vertical ads that run along the right side of the editorial space on the Web page. They are intermingled with editorial matter; visitors click on a bar that says "Expand Ad" to make the entire ad appear. "Messaging Plus" ads on News.com are placed in large squares near the center of each page. And they are far more than traditional ads: They embody rich media and interactivity that turns them into micro-sites. Despite their higher cost, these newer advertising vehicles seem to be resulting in higher click-throughs.

- *Web sponsorships.* Some Web sites allow advertisers to sponsor content on pages or within entire sections of the site. Such content sponsorships may be in the form of promotional buttons, mastheads, banner ads, or other promotional vehicles. Internet.com's ClickZ (*www.clickz.com*), mentioned in Chapter 5, allows advertisers to sponsor regular columns on such topics as e-mail marketing and affiliate marketing. The advertiser's corporate look and feel are integrated right into the header of the column. In addition, the advertiser gets exclusive visibility with a banner at the top and a skyscraper to the right of the column. Some sites offer a wide array of promotional opportunities to advertisers sold as advertising packages, ranging from Web page sponsorships to participation in online seminars to creation of promotional micro-sites.

- *Games, incentives, and online coupons.* Increasingly, e-mail sweepstakes and games are being used to advertise products on the Internet. Also on a growth curve are the use of incentive programs (rewards for providing information or buying on the Internet) and online coupons. These approaches are discussed in detail later in this chapter.

How Effective Is Banner Advertising?

Because banners are still the heaviest-used online advertising format, it is important to spend some time analyzing their effectiveness. Banners are like little electronic billboards or flashing neon signs on Web sites, appearing at the top, bottom, or sometimes within a Web page. The advertising area is restricted to a small horizontal or vertical space—hence the name "banner." Basic banners use several frames, the last frame of which leads to a Web response form or other Web page. Banners typically incorporate some form of graphic movement through simple "GIFs" (Graphic Interface Format). More and more, banner ads are relying on rich media (discussed later).

Although the banner ad may seem almost insignificant as an advertising medium, it can be used for both creating awareness and driving traffic to a Web site or a Web response form. You could read entire books about Web banner advertising, but the purpose here is to cover the basics of banners as they specifically apply to IT marketing.

The trend seems to be toward declining banner ad click-through rates. Along with this has come a general drop in banner advertising media costs, which is good news for advertisers. Of course, the more important statistic for direct marketers is what percentage of those "clicks" become responses, or real leads. Clicking on a banner is not a complete action; the prospect needs to go one step further and fill out the form on the other end to make an inquiry or a purchase. With a high conversion rate, banner ad campaigns with a low click-through rate might actually end up being successful. But if the conversion rate is unacceptably low, even the highest click-through rates won't make a difference.

Is there a secret to using banner ads effectively? A lot of it has to do with the marketing mentality of the advertiser. If the banner ad is designed as general advertising, then it will do what general advertising does best—generate awareness, not response. One 1999 study by Ipsos-ASI, a market research firm, in collaboration with America Online, indicated that online banner advertisements apparently matched television commercials in awareness. The study suggested that both banner ads and 30-second TV spots were recalled by survey respondents just about equally. On the other hand, if the banner ad utilizes solid direct marketing techniques—sound media selection to reach the right audience, a compelling offer, and response-oriented creativity—chances are it will generate responses and, potentially, qualified leads.

You should approach the creation and placement of banner advertising in much the same way you would implement a traditional direct response advertising campaign:

- Set advertising goals and measurable objectives

- Establish budget parameters

- Determine your target audience

- Research available media that will target that audience

- Develop a media schedule

- Create the advertising

- Place the advertising

- Measure the effectiveness

- Analyze the results

- Refine the advertising program

Of course, that is easier said than done. With traditional media, some IT marketers execute and place their own advertising; others would not think of it. In this case, you are probably better off using skilled outside resources, such as interactive agencies, for banner advertising. That is because it requires specialized expertise in media placement and creation.

There are several electronic media placement services, some of which might be useful for the IT marketer to investigate. Perhaps the most prominent of these services is DoubleClick (*www.doubleclick.net*). DoubleClick uses its network of Web sites to place advertising that you pay for *only* if you actually get click-throughs, responses, or sales. DoubleClick also offers extensive testing, and reporting services, but the company generally represents consumer-oriented Web sites with the highest traffic—and therefore the highest cost.

Engage (*www.engage.com*) focuses its approach on ROI by using sophisticated media-planning and behavioral-targeting models to pinpoint banner ad effectiveness. Engage has the ability to determine the geographic location of a user's computer and, as a result, has helped pioneer "local" advertising on the Internet.

The adVENTURE Internet Marketing Network (*www.adventure.com*) claims to be a true direct marketing network, offering advertisers targeting by site, affinity group, and network. The B2BWorks ad network (*www.b2bworks.net*) focuses on business-to-business and features leading Web sites from more than 70 industries. The advertising network 24/7 Media (*www.247media.com*), which markets advertising and sponsorship programs, may have been the first to signal a consolidation trend with its acquisition in early 1999 of an e-mail marketing service.

VentureDirect's B2BfreeNet (*www.b2bfreenet.com*) integrates direct mail, Web site advertising, and e-mail into a single media buy. An IT marketer with a B2B focus could run the same promotions across all media, reaching targeted audiences in 23 different industries.

There are also numerous Internet media buying services, such as Worldata's WebConnect (*www.webconnect.com*), as well as services that bring together Web site owners who want to exchange free banner ads, such as Microsoft's LinkExchange (*www.adnetwork.linkexchange.com*).

The online advertising environment is undergoing significant change. In some cases, Web users may view banner ads and online advertising in general as nothing more than an annoyance, since they can sometimes slow down a page from loading and be distracting. In a corporate environment, advertising can even consume precious bandwidth. As a result, a new industry is evolving: ad-blocking software. If filtering products that actually block ads from downloading gain in popularity, it could create new concerns for online advertisers.

There are also some interesting innovations in online advertising that could extend the life of banner ads. A unique innovation comes from Alexa (*www.alexa.com*), a service that sells ad space based on "smart links" and individual Web site statistics. The service is being used largely for competitive purposes, because it can place an advertiser's banner ad on a rival company's Web page. These ads can only be delivered to people who download Alexa's special free toolbar, but even by 1999, there were close to 1.5 million of them.

Will Rich Media "Save" Banner Advertising?

If anything will "save" banner advertising, it is likely to be rich media. Rich media—the ability to build sound, motion, and interactivity into online advertising—has proven, at least, that there is life left in that little old banner ad.

Jupiter Communications predicts that one-third of all ad spending will be in rich media by 2002. This growing popularity means that Web sites will increasingly need to accommodate the technology.

One leader in the field is Enliven (*www.enliven.com*), formerly Narrative Communications, which was acquired by and made part of the @Home Network in 1999. Enliven delivers banner ads using its special server over Web sites that will accept them. The banners do not require any plug-in, and they are not limited by file size as are ordinary banners. However, they are more expensive to produce, and not every user will have the bandwidth necessary to support them.

Enliven ads do some interesting and novel things. In addition to incorporating sound and motion, Enliven ads have the ability to offer heightened interactivity, directly from the banner. For example, an Enliven banner could offer a prospect the option to immediately print a data sheet by clicking a "Print" button in the banner. (Figure 6.1) Another feature is a banner that "expands" into a form that a prospect can fill out and send immediately. (Figure 6.2) Enliven banners even allow prospects to place an order for a product directly, thus enabling "instant" e-commerce.

Other ways to implement rich media include IBM's "HotMedia" technology and Macromedia's Shockwave and Flash technologies. The increasing use of Flash in particular is leading to advertising with animation and sound, sometimes even online movies. An Enliven competitor, Bluestreak *(www.bluestreak.com)*, offers On-The-Fly technology that allows advertisers to create, produce, and change rich media ads easily, on their desktop, so that campaigns can be modified in real time. Bluestreak's E*Banners expand when the consumer clicks on them, so more advertising content can be conveyed. IQ Commerce *(www.iq.com)* promises to energize ordinary banners with its Click & Stay feature, which allows prospects to make a purchase from a banner from within a pop-up window. iLOR *(www.ilor.com)* introduced a technology in 2001 that adds a "banner console" to any size online ad. The console allows ads to be duplicated and made available to viewers to "check later."

The advertising implications of rich media could be significant. A 1999 study sponsored by Wired Digital *(www.wired.com)* tracked the impact of rich media advertising for Barnes & Noble, Intel, and Novell. The three advertisers together reported a 340 percent increase in click-throughs with rich media ads.

Best Practices in Online Advertising

With the primary goal of generating leads or orders, online advertising is best used as a "feeder" medium. An online ad can incorporate a link to any Web page, so if a prospect clicks on your ad, he or she is instantly

Figure 6.1. This interactive rich media banner ad for HP allows the prospect to print specs directly from the banner.

Figure 6.2. This banner ad for Intel first appears in a traditional size, but it can expand to reveal much more when it is clicked.

transported to the page of your choice (preferably a landing page where an action can be taken). Using the appropriate technology, prospects can even take action right from within the ad, without leaving the page they are on.

The banner ad can combine the best attributes of advertising and direct marketing. Think of the banner ad as an electronic direct mail envelope with interactive teaser copy. It appears on a Web site page, usually at the top or the bottom, depending upon the nature of the site and the price you paid for placement. Just as your direct mail piece competes with others for the attention of the recipient, your banner ad competes for attention with other banner ads on that same site, as well as with the information resident on the site. In fact, your banner competes with anything else that crosses the visitor's path during a Web session—and that could be hundreds of Web pages.

Your first challenge, then, is to make your banner graphically stand out in some way. Most banners use a variety of colors, large type, and graphics—often animated graphics—to distinguish themselves. Most banners have several "frames" that change to attract attention. Rich media, as discussed, adds a whole new dimension to banner ads.

In direct marketing, of course, you need to go beyond standing out. You need to get response. So your banner ad should also *make an offer* and include a *call to action*. With a banner ad, you will not have the luxury of a lot of copy space, so you will have to be clever about it. If your objective is to generate a lead, your offer should have high-perceived value to the target audience. Ideally, the target prospect sees the offer in your banner and is intrigued enough to click on it ("click-through"), but it helps to *tell* the prospect what to do ("Click here for your free demo" or "To get your report, click now").

Click-throughs are nice, but they are a measure of advertising *awareness,* not advertising *responsiveness.* A click-through is not much of a commitment—a site visitor can click on a banner, take a quick look at your offer, and back up or move on in a few seconds. Converting that click-through to a "complete," or a response, is the direct marketer's primary objective. So the real issue is, *Where does that click-through lead?*

There are three basic options for the terminating point of a banner or any online ad:

1. *The on-page response.* As online advertising progresses, on-page, within-the-ad responses will become more common. That means someone who clicks on your banner or ad can take an action instantly—get an answer to a question, receive a piece of information, or actually place an order. At this stage, even if the visitor goes no further, the technology exists to capture not just the incident, but also the e-mail address of the respondent. This action does not provide you with any real qualification information if the visitor stops there. However, instant response with little or no qualification requires the least amount of commit-

ment on the part of the respondent—so you could generate a high number of responses, even if they are unqualified. Online ordering driven by advertising, with the order taken within the advertising, is growing in the consumer market. It is still somewhat early to tell how successful this will be as a direct-order channel for IT use.

2. *The Web response form.* If you make an offer of value that elicits a response from a qualified prospect, you obviously want to capture information about that prospect. Your second option, then, is to have your ad lead directly to a special Web response form (WRF). The WRF should continue to entice the prospect with the offer, encouraging him or her to complete the form and answer some qualifying questions to obtain the offer. If the offer can be fulfilled online (as with information that the respondent receives, or a demo that unlocks and can be downloaded once the form is sent), so much the better. Similarly, if you are using the banner ad to generate orders, the WRF or landing page should offer the prospect the opportunity to learn more about the featured product and provide the ability to order it online.

3. *The Web site.* Many online ads terminate at the advertiser's Web site home page. The objective is to tease the prospect with the ad and then engage him or her at the home page of the Web site. This is fine if you are measuring the success of your advertising campaign by the amount of Web site traffic it generates, but Web site traffic is meaningless to a direct marketer unless it can be converted into measurable results—identifiable responses and qualified leads.

   Of course, if your Web site home page does a solid job of highlighting a response area and making an offer to capture a prospect's interest, you could ultimately elicit a qualified inquiry. In that case, you could accomplish a lot by leading the prospect directly to your Web site. However, you may be better able to focus your prospect's attention by giving him or her a limited number of options, and that could make the WRF more suitable for direct marketing. Even if the WRF resides on your Web site, you can lead the ad respondent there by linking to the response form's specific URL.

Knowing where to send prospects from an online ad is the most important decision you need to make from a direct marketing perspective. But using the ad properly in the first place is also essential. Given the decline of advertising click-through rates, IT marketers should be extra careful about usage. Here are a few "best practices" for making the most effective use of online advertising.

1. *Test banners and other online ad spaces against e-mail newsletter sponsorships.* Find one or more e-mail newsletters with sizable circulations that appeal to your target audience. Compare the cost per thousand for the banner advertising on a comparably targeted Web site to the e-mail sponsorship. Test banners and sponsorships head-to-head and judge them in terms of lead quality rather than quantity. Include a link to a Web response form in the e-mail ad, and link the banner ad to a different Web response form so you can accurately measure response to each.

2. *Test rich media ads against animated GIF ads.* Rich media banners cost more to produce and place, and not all Web sites will accept them. If you find a Web site targeted to your audience that will accept rich media ads, test them head-to-head against a traditional, animated GIF ad. Determine if the increased cost is paying you back in terms of an increased click-through rate and qualified leads.

3. *Test media offers and creative approaches.* Pick Web sites that effectively target your audience and negotiate aggressively for the most attractive rates. Test Web sites one against the other. Also test at least two different creative approaches on the same site by asking the site to randomly rotate the banners or ads. Keep the offer consistent to test the creative (or alternatively, keep the creative consistent to test the offer). Different banners or ads should lead to different Web response forms so you can track responses to each.

4. *Use banners as precampaign teasers.* Banner advertising has shorter lead times than traditional print or direct mail campaigns. Use this to your advantage by placing banner ads strategically on sites that reach the same prospects as your forthcoming campaign, *before* the campaign runs, leveraging the creative work but using it to "tease" the audience. The banner will then act as an elec-

tronic "advance man," preparing the audience for the traditional media advertising to come.

5. *Promote an Internet event.* Banners, buttons, or other ads can be effective alone, or in conjunction with direct mail, e-mail, or e-mail newsletter sponsorships, in driving traffic to online seminars or events. The ad acts as a teaser invitation, pushing the prospect to an online promotion page with a registration form.

6. *Use banners to launch and support affiliate-marketing programs.* Affiliate marketing (see Chapter 11 on Internet partnering) is projected to grow beyond banner advertising. If you have products or services that can be resold by affiliates on the Internet, consider creating an affiliate program and providing your affiliates with free banners they can place on their sites so they sell more of what you have to offer.

7. *Extend banner effectiveness by extending your media buy.* Look for opportunities beyond the banner and you could dramatically improve your online advertising effectiveness. Increasingly, Web sites are moving away from banners and are providing larger ad spaces, such as skyscrapers and boxes. As mentioned earlier, some sites offer promotional opportunities such as contests, online seminar sponsorships, and micro-sites. In addition, many sites may offer subscription e-mail newsletters, yet another promotional opportunity, or opt-in e-mail lists. When you find the right sites for your online advertising campaign, also find out what these sites offer beyond the banner. By extending your media buy, you could reap the benefit of package deals that include discounted prices or promotional add-ons, thus extending the overall effectiveness of your campaign.

Online Ad Placement Is Critically Important

We have been concentrating on the creative and direct response aspects of online advertising, but let us not forget that placing your ads appropriately is just as important to your lead- or order-generation success. Media research will uncover a multitude of potential sites for placement, and selecting both the right medium and the right placement schedule takes skill. This is where some of the advertising networks and media services, referenced earlier, can be very helpful.

Obviously, you will want to select sites that you believe appeal to, or target, your ideal types of prospects. As with traditional print media and direct mail or telemarketing lists, you should work your way down in priority from most- to least-targeted Web sites. An easy way to start if you have had success with traditional media is to map those media to what may be available on the Web. The growing popularity of the Internet has paid off in the fact that virtually every publication with any kind of sizable circulation either has a Web site or participates in one. Similarly, many direct mail lists on the market have Internet counterparts—chances are the list owner is on the Web or the mailing list is available with e-mail addresses. At the very least, the types of individuals found on that list would have an affinity to a Web site somewhere.

Use this marketing information to point yourself in the right direction. Again, start with the most targeted Web sites—those that seem to perfectly target your audience—and work your way down to Web sites that may only partly target your audience.

If you are targeting software developers, for example, you would first concentrate on Web sites that appeal directly to software developers—sites sponsored by developer associations or user groups, specialized publications, developer conferences, and so on. You could either stop there or extend your research to the next category—Web sites that appeal, in part, to software developers. These might be sites sponsored by more-generalized information technology publications and conferences, or some of the technology "supersites" referenced earlier.

You might then choose to go one step further, supplementing your media buys with specific pages on search engines that software developers are likely to use. In many cases, you can arrange for your banner ad to appear on a search engine only when certain keywords are searched on by the visitor.

Purchasing the media can get complicated, because not all sites sell online advertising in the same way. This is yet another area in which the Web is a unique medium: It cannot be sold on the basis of *when* an ad appears (the day or time) because time is irrelevant in cyberspace. It is also difficult to "guarantee a circulation" as in print advertising, or to determine a quantity as in direct mail, so most ads are sold on the basis of *number of impressions*—how many times your ad actually appears.

That does not mean the number of people who see it, just the number of times it shows up. That is an important distinction. To see why, try this experiment sometime: Visit a Web site with advertising and go to a single page on which an ad appears. Instead of navigating around the site, just keep reloading the page several times and keep your eye on the ad. Each time you reload, it is likely that the ad will change, because it is in rotation with other ads. After several times of reloading the page, you will probably see the first ad again. Each time you see that same ad counts as one impression.

Some online advertising media are sold using other criteria. In some cases, for example, you pay for click-throughs, not for impressions. Be sure to understand how the pricing works when you are planning your media strategy.

The whole area of media pricing is now undergoing change due to new ways in which online advertising is being analyzed. An online advertising report issued in May 2000 by AdKnowledge (*www.adknowledge.com*) is an example of this trend. The report analyzed over 150 million banner ad views from the results of numerous online ad campaigns. Interestingly, only 24 percent of the conversions to sales came from prospects who clicked on the banner ad. Thirty-two percent of the sales came from users who had *viewed* an ad, but *did not click*. The remainder of the sales came from repeat customers, whether or not they had initially clicked on the ad.

This fact brings up the need for a different perspective on tracking and analyzing banner ad effectiveness. The report suggests that *nonclick conversions to sales* are an important component of online advertising. And yet, most media, and most advertisers, analyze and depend on "cost-per-click" data.

Online advertising can be placed on traditional Web sites, but there are Internet service providers and networks that are so huge that they hold real promise for targeted online advertisers. Obvious examples include America Online, CompuServe, Prodigy, AT&T's WorldNet, and MSN. There are other services, which may be lesser known but could be useful as new advertising outlets. One example is Juno (*www.juno.com*). Juno began offering free e-mail service with no Internet access required in early 1996, and by 1999 had over 6½ million accounts on record. Every time users open their e-mail, they receive highly targeted e-mail advertising, including banners, pop-ups, and "product order micro-sites." Yet another "hidden" media source might be large companies' intranets that accept advertising.

Other Important Facts about Online Advertising

There are some additional facts that it is important to understand about advertising online:

- Online advertising can be purchased directly from the Web site owner or through Web advertising networks. There are also services that facilitate free online advertising through trade, exchange, and reciprocal link programs, such as LinkExchange, mentioned earlier.

- Banner ads in particular have a promotional life of about *15 days*. Prepare several banner ads in advance of a campaign and ask for your ads to be rotated periodically.

- Banner ads can be created and placed on very short time frames. That makes it easy to pull ads that are not working or add them to new sites very rapidly. More elaborate online ads may take longer to create.

- Online ads and direct mail can be tested similarly. Consider testing not only media placement, but also different offers and different creative approaches. Because of short time frames, you can change entire online ad programs quickly, so testing and program modifications can occur almost in real time.

- Try placing your online advertising on your *own* Web site. This is useful if you want to draw attention to a special promotion, offer, or contest by providing a prominent link to it. You could also benefit from placing a banner ad on your own site that integrates visually with an ad you are running. The on-site ad will reinforce your advertising and provide a convenient link to a Web response form from your home page for visitors who came to your home page as a result of the ad.

- Check with media sources for technical restrictions for online ads. You will generally need to keep graphics simple and file sizes small. You may also need to resize the ad for use on different sites.

- Make online ads more dynamic and eye-catching by incorporating motion and multiple frames.

- Incorporate new technology into online ads as appropriate, but do not assume that every prospect will have the software or hardware necessary to take advantage of it. Given the rise of rich media, consider testing rich media ads against traditional ads.

- Always test online ads and their links before going live. Look at ads through different browsers and on different computers. Be sure to check that your ads are appearing on the sites as contracted, and that the links you specified are working properly.

- Find out in advance what the site or advertising network offers you in terms of tracking capabilities so you can measure and analyze the effectiveness of your advertising.

- Use online advertising in association with other media. For example, coordinating the placement of online advertising with traditional media, such as print advertising or direct mail targeting the same audience, can lift awareness and response. After the campaign is running for a while, the online ads can be used to reinforce the advertising and provide a means for generating online inquiries.

- Analyze the results of online advertising campaigns as you would any other media. Don't just look at click-throughs; look at responses. Technology is available to track "view-throughs" as well. View-throughs represent individuals who view the ad but don't click on it. Various research studies done on view-through visitors suggest that they are, in fact, good prospects, because they remember a company's advertising and return to the site at a later time.

Newsletter Sponsorships: For IT Marketers, It Could Be the Better Way to Advertise

One of the fastest-growing areas of the Internet is e-mail newsletters, as mentioned in the previous chapter. An important aspect of these newsletters is that more and more of them accept advertising, commonly called "sponsorships." E-mail newsletters are often free to the subscriber, but they include a limited amount of advertising from sponsors to offset the distribution cost. Advertising is usually in the form of a small segregated area at the top or bottom of the newsletter, or sometimes embedded into the newsletter text. The ad typically is a text-only ad set off by itself. Some newsletters permit advertisers to sponsor an entire issue of a newsletter so no other ad is seen in that issue, only the sponsor's. If the e-newsletter publishes an HTML version, your sponsorship could be very much like an online ad.

As mentioned in the previous chapter, newsletter sponsorships generally seem to pull very well. In fact, they often tend to pull a higher click-through rate than banner ads. With a cost that is generally equivalent to banners, newsletter ads are an attractive media buy. You may have to pay more for special placement in the newsletter, but if it positions your ad higher in the newsletter, it could pay off in an increase in click-throughs. Writing these little ads is a challenge, though, since marketers typically are restricted to a small number of words.

There are some distinct advantages to this type of advertising:

- Advertising that appears in an e-mail newsletter, even though it is text only, is almost guaranteed to be read. This is because newsletter subscribers tend to read the newsletter carefully; otherwise, they would not subscribe to it. As they read the newsletter, they cannot help but come across the sponsor's ad.

- Most e-mail newsletters are free to subscribers, and their publishers ask for nothing more than an e-mail address; however, the newsletters cover certain very narrow topics. Because of this targeted content, readers self-qualify as a legitimate targeted audience. Newsletter publishers can certainly give you circulation figures, but they typically will not release specific data about any subscribers. In some cases, newsletter publishers will share subscriber data with you in aggregate form so you know more about the types of readers. Some newsletters might also rent their subscriber lists.

- A newsletter ad can become even more effective when it incorporates a link to a specific Web response form or other Web page that further promotes the advertiser's product or service. Many e-mail programs provide the ability to directly link to Web pages, but to accommodate those that do not, it is wise to include the complete link address (including *http://www* if it is a Web link). Industry reports suggest over and over again that such links from newsletter ads are very effective. I have seen a number of reports of banner ads testing against newsletter ads, with the newsletter significantly outpulling the banner in most cases.

- Some newsletters are a hybrid between e-mail and HTML, and with these, there are additional advertising possibilities that may prove effective. Here, you can place a text-only ad in the e-mail newsletter, but you can also place a more graphic ad in the newsletter's HTML version. You may also be able to sponsor an entire column or page in the HTML newsletter.

Advertising Tip: Don't Forget Those Search Engines and Directories

A potential online advertising opportunity that's easy to overlook is search engine advertising. IT marketers who use this strategy successfully place ads on search engine pages that relate directly to their products or services. For example, a maker of a database product might place an ad that appears when a visitor searches on database, relational database, RMDB, etc. The ads can be either banners or text ads; text ads reportedly outpull banners, but it's worth a test. Large search engines are expensive, so purchase space selectively.

Online buying guides and directories present additional opportunities for marketers.

Incentive Programs: Another Form of Online Advertising

A growing area of online advertising is incentive programs. These programs reward the prospect or customer for providing information, taking an action, or making a purchase. This phenomenon deserves its own section because it is proving for some marketers to be a way to increase advertising click-throughs, acquire prospects, and even increase customer loyalty.

Incentive programs come in a variety of flavors, with the most common incentives being sweepstakes and contests, volume deals, and price breaks, according to Forrester Research. Also becoming increasingly popular on the Internet are online coupons and other forms of "instant-payback" programs.

Contests and sweepstakes are growing at a rapid rate, being legitimized by big-name marketers. For example, in December 1999, Compaq

Computer Corp. (*www.compaq.com*) cut a deal with Promotions.com (formerly Webstakes) to create custom sweepstakes-style promotions to run on Compaq's Online Services site.

As for online coupons, Forrester Research reports that they can send banner ad click-through rates as high as 20 percent. In fact, a study by NPD Online Research released in November 1999 showed that almost a third of the Internet population used online coupons in October, up from 23 percent earlier that year. The top two sites where coupons were being obtained, according to the survey, were Coolsavings (*www.coolsavings.com*) and ValuePage (*www.valuepage.com*). There is even a place where you can search out a free offer in the category of your choice—it is called The Free Forum Network (*www.freeforum.com*).

There are a wide variety of incentive programs, some initiated by marketers themselves. As you might expect, there are also numerous organizations on the Internet that specialize in online incentive programs. Following are just a few of the leading ones.

ClickRewards (*www.clickrewards.com*)

ClickRewards, operated by Netcentives, Inc., appropriated the frequent-traveler miles concept and applied it to the Web. Hence, they offer "ClickMiles" for shopping at participating Web sites. These ClickMiles can be converted into frequent-traveler miles on a one-for-one basis in several leading airline and hotel programs, as well as for other types of rewards.

Flooz (*www.flooz.com*)

Flooz positions itself as "the online gift currency." In 2000, Flooz launched "Flooz for Business" to encourage companies to use their e-mailed gift certificates for employee and customer rewards. Flooz certificates can be used at over 70 online stores. One of the twists to Flooz is that the company offers its B-to-B customers personalized home pages. That way, companies can send Flooz over a site that is customized to their own needs.

MyPoints (*www.mypoints.com*)

With over 8 million members and over 200 advertisers and partners participating in MyPoints and MyPoints BonusMail (e-mail advertising), MyPoints offers "rewards points" for purchase. Points may be redeemed for a variety of products and services from some 50 rewards providers. MyPoints also offers completely customized Private Label loyalty rewards programs used by such companies as American Express, GTE, and ZDnet. In 2000, MyPoints announced that it would acquire another leading online incentive company, Cybergold, and in 2001, MyPoints itself was acquired by United Airlines. The airline planned to merge its mileage reward program with MyPoints.

Online Advertising Is Undergoing Continuous Innovation

The dynamic nature of the Internet means that online advertising will be ever-changing. New strategies, techniques, and tools will continue to be introduced in an effort to improve the effectiveness of online advertising.

Some would say that affiliate marketing itself, which we discuss in detail in Chapter 11, is really a form of online advertising. Affiliate marketing largely uses banner ads placed on affiliate Web sites to drive traffic to sponsoring Web sites. In this context, affiliate marketing can be seen as a major online advertising innovation.

There are other innovations coming. In a May 2000 survey of ad agencies, Arbitron Internet Information Services found that Webcast advertisements—ads that use the Internet to broadcast a multimedia message—will grow rapidly. The study indicated that one out of five agencies buying online advertising uses Webcast ads, and 81 percent of the respondents said their use of Webcast advertising would significantly increase in the coming years.

Will banner ads and other forms of online advertising be better in the future? New technologies and advertising approaches almost guarantee it. A few examples: StickyAds by Spidertop (*www.spidertop.com*) are banners that keep clickers on the Web site where the banner appears, instead of leaving to go elsewhere. Eyeblaster (*www.eyeblaster.com*) is an "out-of-banner" rich media platform that floats ads across a Web page. The Cybuy banner (*www.cybuy.com*) allows purchases directly from banners in only three clicks.

In a *New York Times* article on May 7, 2000, two other emerging innovations in online advertising are mentioned: "follow-me ads" and "piggyback ads."

With follow-me ads, an Internet user is identified as the customer of a particular company. The customer's activity on the Web can then be tracked, and appropriate advertising can be served up to the customer as he or she moves from site to site. In this way, a customer of a particular advertiser will actually see different advertising from others using the Web.

Free Internet access services and other sites that give something valuable away require that the user of the service accept advertising. As a result, piggyback ads might appear over any Web site visited by the user. This technique could be effective in providing a distinct competitive advantage to the advertiser. Now the advertiser could have a banner ad appear at the top of a competitor's Web site.

Online advertising will continue to evolve—and the IT marketer will undoubtedly benefit from these advancements.

Public Relations on the Internet

IT marketers who have been around for awhile may look back upon the non-Internet days of PR with chagrin. The primary PR activity of writing and placing press releases was (and for some still is) a laborious, time-consuming, and sometimes thankless chore. The process was often a shot in the dark, since the marketer never knew if, or when, a publication would pick up a story.

Although the need for personal contact and follow-up still exists today, the Internet has revolutionized public relations, as it has every other form of business. The good news is that much of the basic press release process can now be automated and targeted with the help of the Internet. In some cases, very valuable services are available to the IT marketer for free.

PR Web (*www.prweb.com*) is one such example. PR Web's founders began with a simple mission in 1997: They wanted to distribute a press release over the Internet and found that there was no free service available. They grabbed the opportunity and now help over 4,000 companies (even the Fortune 500) distribute some 150 releases a day. It is as easy as submitting a form to get your press release electronically distributed to the right target media audience, and it will not cost you anything. PR Web is now on its way to becoming a true public relations portal. Its home page is packed with valuable information and links about public relations and Web promotion—everything from associations and clipping services, to directories and software, to banner exchanges and PR forums.

A number of other paid services exist, and they are no less valuable to an IT company's PR efforts. PR Newswire (*www.prnewswire.com*) is one of the industry's elders, established in 1954, that has kept up with the Internet-driven times. In addition to electronic release distribution, PR Newswire offers such sophisticated Internet PR services as "Virtual IQ," an investor relations Web site that looks like your own site but is created and maintained by PR Newswire; and "Company News On-Call," a complete and up-to-the minute three-year, archived database of all stories appearing on PR Newswire from your company. MediaMap (*www.mediamap.com*) is strong on the IT media side. The company offers 20,000 media contacts in high tech, business and finance, healthcare, and the consumer press, including both print and Web publications. You will find a complete list of U.S. technology media on their Web site.

Do not forget the major media outlets when big news breaks. You can reach all of them online, too. In fact, some leading newspapers have done an excellent job of adapting their businesses to the Internet. Among the most notable leaders in this area are *The Boston Globe,* which has spearheaded a major regional site, *www.boston.com*, extending far beyond the newspaper itself; *The New York Times* (*www.nytimes.com*), which has used a free subscription model to build its own Internet-based subscriber list; and *The Wall Street Journal* (*www.wsj.com*), which became one of the early leaders in creating a successful paid interactive edition. As for periodicals, you can find over 150,000 of them at *www.publist.com*, the "Internet directory of publications."

You know how difficult it is to get your hands on the editorial calendars of publications serving your audiences, and yet these schedules are invaluable for targeting publicity. Try "EdCals" (*www.edcals.com*), the site that does the work for you. Sponsored by Bacon's and MediaMap, EdCals is a subscription site that provides access to editorial calendars for both print and Web media. The service claims to cover upcoming stories and special issues from nearly every leading U.S. magazine and newspaper, and they will keep you personally updated on a weekly basis.

Many IT marketers are heavily involved in trade shows and conferences. Here, too, the Internet provides valuable assistance in the form of such sites as TSNN.com (*www.tsnn.com*). This portal for trade shows offers information about trade shows, conferences, and seminars worldwide, easily searchable by events, suppliers, and venues.

PR Opportunities on IT Sites

Information technology has its own collection of sites that consolidate information, often from the various publications these sites represent, and make it available in a single location. These sites are all important publicity outlets for IT companies. All of these sites feature late-breaking news and information that relates specifically to the information technology industry. Most of them have other services of interest to the IT marketer, such as free e-mail newsletters. These sites, further described in Chapter 10, include:

CMPnet (*www.cmpnet.com*)
One of the largest IT sites, CMPnet consolidates information from some 35 different Web sites, including *Computer Reseller News, EE Times, InformationWeek, InternetWeek, ISPs.com, Network Computing,* and *Windows* magazine.

C|Net (*www.cnet.com*)
C|Net is a large network of many computer-oriented Web sites, including News.com (do not be fooled by the name, it is IT news), Download.com, Shareware.com, and Shopper.com. In 2001, C|Net acquired two major IT information sites, TechRepublic and ZDnet (see below).

Internet.com (*www.internet.com*)
Internet.com is a major information site that incorporates EarthWeb, the ClickZ Marketing Network, and numerous other "channels."

IDG.net (*www.idg.net*)
IDG is a well-known publisher of just about everything in the computer industry with "World" in its title, such as *Computerworld, InfoWorld, Network World,* and *PCWorld.* In addition, IDG publishes The Industry Standard and "Dummies" books, and operates IDC, an IT research firm.

ZDnet (*www.zdnet.com*)
ZDnet, a property of C|Net, offers "channels" such as Benchmarks, Careers, E-Business, and ZDU (ZD University, online classes). ZDnet also features such publications as *Inter@ctive Week, Macworld,* and *PC Week.*

Using the Internet for PR Campaigns

IT companies can leverage existing marketing and promotional materials into full-blown Internet-based PR campaigns. One great way to do this is to create customer success stories and then get them placed on Web sites that target key audiences.

Other lead-generating PR opportunities exist for IT marketers. If you produce white papers, Bitpipe (*www.bitpipe.com*) can post them for Web distribution. Bitpipe powers the white paper database of ITWorld (*www.itworld.com*).

You can also make sure sites that carry product reviews and listings are covering your products. Multicity (*www.multicity.com*) started out by launching its products for Webmasters using free site product reviews. According to the e-newsletter *B2B Marketing Biz* (*www.b2bmarketingbiz.com*), Multicity carefully created wording to be used in submissions, making sure they wrote concise, action-driven statements for each of their five products. The company did extensive research online to find every important site that carried reviews and listings of products for Webmasters. They built a hit list of some 40 sites and updated it daily.

Multicity's strategy was to keep in touch with these sites and to treat them as if they were paid advertising. Contact was frequent, and the wording was consistent across all placements. As a result of this grassroots campaign, Multicity attracted 100,000 Webmasters to its software products.

7

Internet Events and Meetings

Event marketing plays a significant role in marketing IT products and services. IT marketers have long attended trade shows and conferences in an effort to get in front of "live" prospects. Most IT companies also use their own marketing and sales seminars to attract prospects to hear about products and services or see product demonstrations.

The Internet presents a compelling opportunity for marketers to transform live events into "net events." This rapidly growing, specialized area of Internet technology is already revolutionizing the way events are executed. Meta Group (*www.metagroup.com*) says that as much as 90 percent of global 2000 companies will be using Web conferencing by 2003. The technology has other applications important to IT companies, such as online collaborative meetings and distance learning. This chapter explores this potential and details some of the ways that IT marketers are using Internet events and meetings as part of their marketing programs.

Are Live Events Good Marketing Investments?

In my earlier days as a marketing communications manager for an IT company, I remember doing the "conference circuit" and the "convention route." Attending these events as an onlooker was far better than those dreaded times when my boss was a conference speaker or my employer had a booth. It meant countless hours spent on pre-event logistics, materials preparation, and shipping. When that nightmare was over, another began with booth duty on the floor of some nameless convention in a city that would have been fun if I had had the time and energy to see any of it. If you have had this experience, you know how unglamorous and exhausting event marketing and the travel associated with it can be, despite rumors to the contrary.

Actually, there was something even worse than conventions: company-sponsored seminar programs. The headaches were simply multiplied across cities that spanned the country—and so much more could go wrong.

All of these national events were expensive. Seminars, especially, were a financial drain. Fees, travel, and accommodations for guest speakers, along with travel and accommodations for all company personnel involved in the seminars, mounted up quickly. Add to that the cost of slide shows, handouts, signs, meeting rooms, coffee, and snacks (not to mention the cost of promoting the event beforehand and following up with attendees afterward).

However, the reality is that experiences with live seminars vary widely from company to company. When a company is successful, it means that seminar rooms are filled with "butts in seats." More importantly, the attendees are the people the company wants—prospects whom the sales force considers to be quality leads. In this case, the company will keep investing in live seminars.

Yet seminar disasters are not uncommon, either. There could be any number of reasons for bombing out. Perhaps the audience is not well targeted to begin with or the seminar content (which is the offer) is weak. Maybe the weather in a particular location is lousy or traffic is bad on the day of the seminar. Maybe the seminar is in downtown Manhattan—where most seminars seem to do poorly—or it could be that the product being promoted is a dog, so even a great speaker or an action-packed agenda will not save the day.

In some cases, what IT companies learn about their event marketing can be nothing short of shocking. Here is one scenario that is based on a true story:

A software company has routinely attended several trade shows for years. Someone in marketing analyzes the results and discovers that the most expensive show is actually generating the lowest-quality leads. When the costs of supporting that particular show and fulfilling the leads are added up, it is clear that the company has an ROI disaster on its hands. The marketing manager talks to the sales manager about it. He just shakes his head, laughs, and says, "Oh yeah, the leads from that show are junk. My salespeople do not even pay any attention to them." Truly chilling—an IT direct marketer's worst nightmare.

I hope this does not sound familiar, but it should be food for thought. Conventions and trade shows in particular should be evaluated carefully. These events tend to be far less effective than seminars in generating *qualified* leads, because the venue is very different.

If you have attended such shows, you know the score. You can go from booth to booth and pick up a slew of very expensive literature and a variety of giveaways free and without obligation, and in most cases you can remain totally anonymous while you scoop these goodies into a gargantuan convention bag. You can even participate in various games and contests and actually win something valuable—although you do not have the slightest interest in the exhibitor's product or service. At the end of this major trade show, all the exhibitors truck home with hundreds, or maybe thousands, of "leads"—only to discover that most of them are about as qualified to purchase as the people manning the hot dog concession stand at the trade show.

Of course, not all trade shows leave a bitter taste in marketers' mouths. I can recall hearing stories of technology companies whose marketing and sales staff come back from shows flush with hundreds of thousands of dollars' worth of business booked in a few days. Just as important, some very significant products are launched at trade shows. With shows, as with marketing seminars, fabulous success stories abound—as do unmitigated disasters. The trick is to learn how to use event marketing in a targeted, results-oriented way so you can achieve the former, not the latter.

The Typical Seminar Series

More and more, IT companies are scrutinizing their participation in live seminars and marketing events. They need to justify that seminars are worth the investment because the expense associated with a seminar program can be significant. To put this into perspective, we can examine a breakdown of estimated costs and the anticipated results for a ten-city marketing seminar series. We will make the following assumptions:

- The seminar will be a live, half-day event with free admission, held in ten U.S. cities in hotel meeting rooms.

- The sponsoring company will have to prepare a presentation, hire one or more guest speakers, and send a marketing coordinator and one speaker from corporate headquarters to every seminar.

- Handouts will need to be produced for an anticipated audience of about 500 people.

- A direct mail invitation will be sent to 3,000 prospects within 50 miles of each seminar site (30,000 prospects).

- The invitation will achieve a 2 percent response.

- Fifty percent of the respondents will *not* attend the seminar, even though they signed up for it. (This is a fairly typical "no-show" rate—the percentage of individuals who say they are coming to a seminar but do not show up.)

The accompanying chart (Figure 7.1) shows the costs and results for this ten-city live seminar program. Depending on the costs and results of other qualified lead generation activities you might conduct, this may or may not seem to be a reasonable cost. To get a true reading of any event's marketing value, you should track not just number of people attending, but also:

- The number of event attendees who were converted to customers.

- The length of the sales cycle associated with event attendees versus other types of prospects.

- The average sale from event-attendee customers versus other types of customers.

- The lifetime value of the event-attendee customers versus other types of customers.

	Typical Costs/Results
Seminar promotion: high quality direct mail invitation to 30,000 prospects (3,000 each of 10 sites), not including follow-ups, confirmations, or fulfillment	$60,000–75,000
Seminar presentation: one original of a typical slide presentation plus 10 copies for laptop or slide projector use	3,000–5,000
Hotel meeting rooms, including AV support and breakfast	10,000–15,000
Presentation hand-outs and related promotional material	5,000–6,000
Guest speaker fees and travel	30,000–40,000
Travel and accommodations for 2 people: 1 marketing person to be present at all 10 sites for registration/coordination, and 1 speaker from company headquarters	20,000–30,000
Total costs	$128,000–171,000
Number of invitations mailed	30,000
Response rate from the direct mail invitation	2.0%
Number of individuals registering	600
Number of individuals attending (50% "no-show" rate)	300
Average number of attendees per seminar	30
Cost per attendee	$427–570

Figure 7.1. Live seminar costs and results.

The Net Event

Even if your company is achieving substantial success with traditional event marketing, you cannot help but be intrigued by the "net event." The concept of replacing or augmenting traditional live events with Web-based online or "virtual" events has caught on quickly with business-to-business marketers. In fact, virtual events are booming on the Internet. To explore why, we can use the traditional seminar program as a point of reference. Despite the substantial face-to-face benefits of a live seminar, such a program can be:

- *A logistical nightmare.* Speakers and hotels need to be scheduled and managed, materials have to be in the right place at the right time, and prospects need to be invited in advance and registered on-site. The seminar is also dependent on things you cannot control, such as local traffic and weather conditions.

- *A substantial investment.* Costs for speaker fees, hotel rooms and food, travel, presentation output and equipment, and seminar promotion add up quickly. The seminar may also need last-minute support via telemarketing or fax if registration numbers are low.

- *A quality control challenge.* Ensuring that presenters are well prepared and materials are well executed, especially when the seminar takes place at numerous national or worldwide locations, is a difficult task.

- *A risky venture.* Even if everything is handled properly, the typical no-show rate at a live seminar can be 50 to 60 percent. Free seminars have become somewhat of a "commodity item," because there are now so many of them offered. As companies downsize and managers become overburdened, attendance at offsite seminars becomes difficult to fit into the workday. In fact, senior business executives rarely attend these events due to the intense demands on their time and their heavy travel schedules.

Here is the difference between a live seminar and a virtual seminar. The virtual seminar can:

- *Virtually eliminate logistical hassles.* Prospects are invited to come to a special URL in cyberspace instead of a physical place. You do not need to arrange for hotels and you do not need to ship anything anywhere. In fact, you do not even have to show up anywhere other than on the Web. Web traffic may be heavy, but it is better than the roads—and the weather is irrelevant.

- *Provide you with foolproof quality control.* The online seminar is totally controlled by you. The format, content, and timing are uniform and singular, and therefore completely consistent. You only have to create it one time no matter how many times someone sees it. Even if you execute the online seminar as a live event, it can be archived and repeated.

- *Attract qualified prospects.* The online seminar is more convenient for prospects or customers; they do not need to leave the office to attend. As a result, the virtual seminar has the potential to attract not only larger audiences, but also a greater number of senior executives. The online seminar is also a more novel and intriguing approach than a live seminar. As such, prospects might find it more compelling to attend.

- *Cost substantially less than live seminars.* Online seminars compare favorably to live events.

Earlier, we looked at the costs and results for a ten-city live seminar program. Now we can compare the costs and results for an online seminar program, using the following assumptions:

- The seminar will be a one-hour session, conducted entirely over the Web. The sponsoring company uses an outside firm to create and host the seminar.

- The sponsoring company will hire one guest speaker, who will provide a presentation for use on the Web. The guest speaker will also be available for an interactive question-and-answer session, which will be held during a few preappointed times via teleconference. Seminar visitors will be able to call a toll-free number to listen to the presentation while Web content is "pushed" over the Web. They will also be able to ask questions and listen to answers via telephone.

- A direct mail invitation will be sent to 30,000 prospects. They will be selected based on geographic areas that mesh with the live seminar program. We assume the same cost to execute the direct mail as with the live seminar program.

- The call to action in the invitation will instruct recipients to respond by coming to a special URL to register for the virtual seminar. They will still need to attend the seminar itself, so we'll assume the same no-show rate as with the live seminar.

Figure 7.2 indicates the costs and results for the online seminar.

Analysis of Live Seminar Program versus Online Seminar Program
The cost for the direct mail promotion is the same for both seminar programs. Despite the same promotional cost, you'll see that the online seminar costs less than the live seminar when all costs are considered.

	Typical Costs/Results
Seminar promotion: high quality direct mail invitation to 30,000 prospects (3,000 each of 10 sites), not including follow-ups, confirmations, or fulfillment	$60,000–75,000
Seminar presentation: creation and presentation of the complete online seminar, including design, content, and interactive teleconference session	30,000–50,000
Seminar Web hosting for one month	2,000–5,000
Guest speaker fee for the online seminar	3,000–5,000
Total costs	$95,000–135,000
Number of invitations mailed	30,000
Response rate from the direct mail invitation	2.0%
Number of individuals registering	600
Number of individuals attending (50% "no-show" rate)	300
Average number of attendees per seminar	30
Cost per attendee	$316–450

Figure 7.2.   Online seminar costs and results.

A direct bottom line comparison shows that the online seminar generates a lower cost per attendee than the live seminar. There are additional benefits that have not been factored in, however.

One potential benefit of the online seminar is the fact that the no-show rate tends to be somewhat lower than with live seminars. Given location and weather conditions, online seminars are "more dependable" in terms of generating lower no-show rates in general.

Another factor is that once a live seminar is concluded, it must be run again, live. With an online seminar, the marketer can get additional usage out of it by archiving the event on the Web. It can then be used several more times at a low incremental cost as a marketing tool, unlike the live seminar program, whose costs continue to go up every time it is presented at a new physical location.

This analysis of live seminars versus online seminars makes a compelling case for the use of Internet events.

Replacement or Enhancement?

Do you need to eliminate all live seminars and conduct online seminars instead? Not necessarily. You may still wish to hold live seminars in a few key cities so that you can tell your story face-to-face and your salespeople can "press the flesh." However, you can *supplement* your live seminar schedule with an online seminar that you promote only in secondary cities—so you can "be there" even if your live seminar is not.

You also can use an online seminar as a follow-up to a live seminar, inviting individuals who could not attend the live seminar to share in the experience online. Also, you can suggest that attendees to your live seminars tell their colleagues that they can attend a virtual seminar version of the live seminar.

After you create an online seminar, you can easily create another version of it for partner or reseller use. By archiving the online seminar, you can extend its value and use it for subsequent promotional efforts. In fact, an archived seminar can be promoted as a separate event, driving more prospects to it beyond its initial use. This means your investment is not "dead," as it might be with a live event; it "lives on" as a renewable marketing resource.

An Online Seminar Success Story

My agency has numerous stories about IT companies that have run successful online seminars. Since most of our clients are sensitive about releasing specific results, I am using my own agency's experience to demonstrate the real results that can be achieved with online seminars. We have run our own online seminars for several years, and each time we achieve results similar to the program described below.

Promotion

We held a marketing-oriented online seminar on October 25, 2000, and repeated this same seminar on November 2. We did extensive testing of direct mail and e-mail promotion based on previous seminar programs. Eighteen thousand three hundred individuals were reached using the following media:

- *Direct mail:* Twenty-five hundred oversized "postcard" invitations were sent to our in-house prospect list, and 8,200 were sent to two outside mailing lists. The direct mail invitation was a two-color self-mailing card, 6 by 11 inches, that featured the online seminar "B-to-B Internet Marketing: 7 Strategies for Success." The invitation said the seminar was based on my book, *Business-to-Business Internet Marketing*, 2nd edition. To respond to the direct mail, the prospect had to visit a special URL and sign up in advance of the seminar. The individual was asked to enter a "priority code" for list-tracking purposes. The only response path was an online response form.

- *E-mail*: One thousand sixty e-mail invitations were sent to our in-house list of permission e-mail addresses, and 7,600 e-mails were sent to six guaranteed opt-in e-mail lists. The e-mail briefly described the seminar and invited the prospect to a special URL, which was unique to each e-mail list. Again, the prospect needed to sign up in advance using an online response form. All registrants received confirming e-mails, as well as e-mail reminders the day before the seminar.

Seminar

I conducted the seminar using Placeware, which also managed the registration process. The seminar was a one-hour free event, a 45-minute presentation followed by about 15 minutes of questions. I presented the seven strategies and showed direct mail and Internet marketing examples via static Web-pushed slides. Attendees listened to my audio presentation via telephone. During the seminar, I used instant polling, slide annotation, whiteboarding, and the live demo feature. Attendees were able to ask questions at any time during the seminar via the online chat feature, but these questions were hidden from view and held until the end of my presentation. At the close of the seminar, attendees were "sent" to a special Resource Area Web site, which included additional information about the seven strategies, along with links to Web sites and online seminars referenced during the presentation.

Results

The results of the seminar promotion were as follows:

- Direct mail for the house list pulled a 3.6 percent response, versus an 8.9 percent response for the e-mail house list.

- Direct mail to outside lists averaged 0.6 percent, versus 1.3 percent on average for the opt-in e-mail lists.

- The overall response rate for the seminar was 3.6 percent, with 660 individuals registering for the seminar. A total of 295 individuals attended, which translates into a no-show rate of 55 percent. The percentage response and no-show rate was almost exactly the same as for an online seminar run six months earlier.

- Attendance to the first seminar was 186, and to the second session was 109. We used an interesting technique, a "second-chance e-mail," to provide an additional lift to response. We sent individuals who registered but did not attend the first seminar an e-mail reminding them of the second seminar. This e-mail resulted in a 7.2 percent response, netting another nine attendees at the second seminar.

We use a Web registration form that asks numerous qualifying questions. We then ask additional questions at the seminar's resource area. We continue to find that this seminar generates a very high percentage of qualified leads. We have, in fact, acquired new clients as a direct result of individuals attending the seminar. Figure 7.3 shows the Web page describing the seminar; Figure 7.4 shows one of the slides from the seminar.

Who Is Using Online Seminars Effectively?

There is widespread use of online seminars for marketing purposes among IT companies. Virtually every major hardware, software, networking, and service company seems to be using online seminars or Webcasts of some kind. A growing number of IT companies launch entire seminar series that run on an ongoing basis. The following are just a few examples.

AXENT (*www.symantec.com*)
AXENT Technologies merged with Symantec in December 2000. Prior to the merger, AXENT tested substituting live Webcast seminars for its traveling road show. According to the e-newsletter *B2B Marketing Biz* (*www.b2bmarketingbiz.com*), AXENT created a series of educational Webcasts targeting technical managers and tested a variety of tactics to promote them, including broadcast e-mail to a house list, advertising on the company Web site, notices in the company e-newsletter, newsletter sponsorships, and direct mail. AXENT found that the Webcast semi-

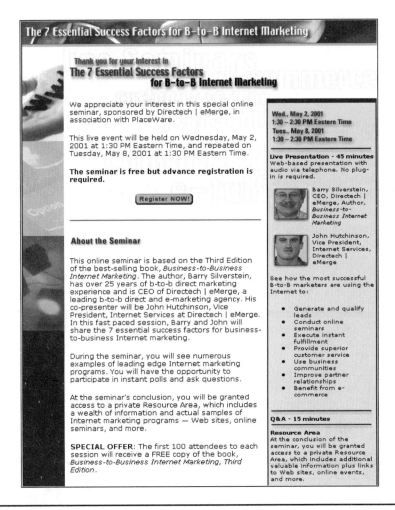

Figure 7.3. Recipients of direct mail and e-mail invitations are directed to this Web landing page to learn more about an Internet marketing seminar and to register online.

nars cost $21 per attendee versus about $175 per attendee for the live seminars. Lead quality improved as well: Online seminars produced about 30 percent hot and warm leads, whereas in-person events generated under 20 percent hot and warm leads. E-mail to the house list outperformed all other media used.

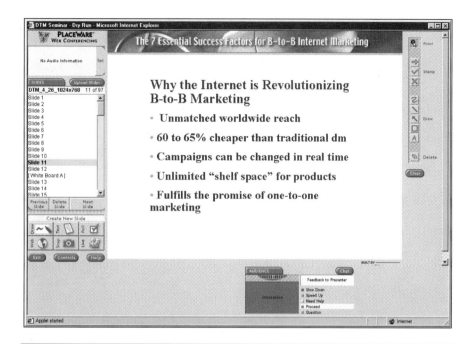

Figure 7.4. This is a slide from an Internet marketing online seminar, as it appears to a presenter using Placeware. Slides can easily be selected using the controls to the left. Annotation tools are to the right of the slide.

Centra BCN (Business Collaboration Network) (*www.centranow.com*)

Centra Software provides an online conferencing solution that incorporates the ability to do visual presentations with voiceover IP technology—you hear the sound through your computer, and if you have a headset, you can also interact by speaking through your computer. The software does not require a plug-in, but your computer must have a sound card and speakers, although a headset is recommended to use the full capabilities of the software. To showcase its technology, Centra features numerous online seminars through its "Business Collaboration Network."

Cisco Systems (*www.cisco.com*)

Cisco is a leader in online events, as they are in many other aspects of Internet usage. Cisco uses live broadcast seminars, simulated live broadcast seminars that are rebroadcast in different time zones, archived seminars for on-demand viewing, and chats as part of its online arsenal. Cisco attracted more than 30,000 viewers in their first year of operation, which began in January 1999. The company typically draws more than 1,000 simultaneous viewers from around the world to its live Webcasts, and an average of 2,500 viewers to on-demand events during the first 90 days of presentation. According to Cisco, the company can reach the same number of people at an in-person event with a Web event for about 10 percent of the cost of a seminar tour.

ITWorld (*www.itworld.com/webcasts*)

ITWorld, an IDG site, is a community for IT professionals. ITWorld offers its own online events, but also provides Webcasts sponsored by vendors. At ITWorld's Webcasts page, you'll find a variety of "short subjects," audiocasts, editorial Webcasts, vendor Webcasts, and presentations on IT careers and recruiting.

Oracle Internet Seminars (*www.oracle.com/iseminars/*) and Oracle eBusiness Network (*www.oracle.com/ebusinessnetwork*)

Oracle provides a very comprehensive "iSeminar" with both scheduled seminars and "on-demand seminars"—replays of previous events. The scheduled live seminars lead you through Oracle's "See, Try and Buy" process. In February 2000, Oracle raised the stakes in online seminars by introducing an "e-Business Network" which carries live "e-casts" of events and other streamed broadcasts on a regular basis. For example, its "View From a Suite" series features applications experts and other e-commerce leaders.

Placeware Seminars (*www.placeware.com/seminar*)

Placeware, an early leader in online conferencing, is particularly well suited to online seminars. This is because the Placeware "room" offers presenters the ability not only to show slides, but also to annotate those slides, create new slides on the fly, use a whiteboard, conduct instant polls, demonstrate anything on the presenter's desktop, and lead audience members through tours of Web sites. Placeware also lets audience members ask questions via conventional telephone or a chat function. Placeware is "firewall friendly" and does not require a plug-in. To promote its product capabilities, Placeware runs an extensive program of free online seminars, many of which cover general business, e-business, and marketing topics and feature well-known speakers.

Microsoft Multimedia Central (*www.microsoft.com/seminar*)

Microsoft's seminars for the most part are technical training, all easily accessible from one central page, now called "Multimedia Central." Multimedia Central connects you to every online seminar Microsoft runs. The company offers individual product-oriented seminars that you can instantly view on demand, as well as seminars within a series. Their "Complete Commerce" series, for example, is composed of four seminars, ranging from product overviews to detailed technical sessions.

The Net Event Is Not Without Technological Challenges

Early models for the Internet event were largely informational Web sites with a healthy dose of high-value "objective" informational content. Educational institutions, museums, scientific consortiums, and the like sponsored such sites. The Web is still populated with such informational sites, but commercialization has quickly taken over. Now companies with something to sell sponsor many informational sites. That is not necessarily a bad thing—you can still find some incredibly valuable, data-rich sites if you are willing to wade through an occasional sales pitch.

The marketing version of the Internet seminar or event combines the best of both the informational site concept with the concept of Internet-based education. Internet events can be anything from online trade shows and conferences, to Web-based seminars and symposiums, to Internet "talk shows" and presentations. Some of these are widely promoted and open to the general public, whereas others are invitation-only, private-access events. For the most part, these events are intended to promote something, so they are offered at no charge.

A major barrier for such events has been Internet technology itself. You cannot, of course, access Web sites without Web browser software. The two leading browsers are Netscape Navigator and Microsoft Internet Explorer. Current versions of these software products incorporate the Java programming language, which facilitates interactivity and multimedia. "Plug-ins," which enable sound and images to be sent across the Web, are also being built into current browsers so that they are already available without the need to download the plug-in. In some cases, limited sound and multimedia can be experienced on the Web *without* plug-ins using Java-based servers and other real-time technologies.

The most common implementation is "streaming," which replaces the need to download and launch a file to see or hear it. With streaming, after the applet is launched or the plug-in is installed, audio or full-motion video can be delivered in real time to the computer desktop.

The rapid adoption of streaming media promises to fuel the market for Internet collaboration, meetings, and events. The Internet Research Group says the market for streaming-media services will reach $2.5 billion by 2004, 20 times what it was in 2000. Vastly improved streaming technology, in combination with much faster Internet connections, will converge to turn Internet events and even e-learning into mainstream markets.

As just one example of the pervasive presence of e-learning, in June 2000 Barnes & Noble (*www.bn.com*) announced that it would develop its own "Barnes & Noble University" on the Web. This "free online education resource" offers e-learning taught by book authors. Obviously, it is also an opportunity for authors to sell more books. Behind the concept is a distance learning organization, notHarvard.com (*www.notharvard.com*), which creates "eduCommerce" Web sites.

The de facto standard for audio and video streaming is Real Networks' RealSystem software (*www.real.com*), although Microsoft's Media Player is gaining ground. RealSystem software is used to deliver content on more than 85 percent of all streaming media–enabled Web pages, according to the company. In June 2000, Real claimed that over 125 million unique RealPlayer users had been registered. The user base grows by over 200,000 users per day, an increase of more than 300 percent since the end of 1998. Users can download a free RealPlayer, through which RealAudio (sound) and RealVideo (full-motion video) can be received. RealPresenter permits PowerPoint slide shows to be enhanced with a synchronized audio track, and RealFlash enables animations that can be synchronized with RealAudio. Real products can stream both prerecorded and live presentations over the Web.

Real took another step toward dominating multimedia on the Internet with its purchase of Xing Technology in April 1999. Xing was the developer of MP3 software, used to stream music across the Web. At the same time, RealNetworks announced a partnership with IBM to create a universal standard for digital distribution of music.

Services such as Activate (*www.activate.com*), Yahoo! Fusion Marketing (*fusion.yahoo.com*), Education News and Entertainment Network's NetSeminar (*www.netseminar.com*), and Webcasts (*www.webcasts.com*) offer the ability to send "Webcasts" (live or prerecorded video presentations) in real time over the Internet, or take a telephone feed of audio, translate it, and broadcast it in real time over the Internet. Other companies are quickly entering this market. For example, Internet content delivery service Akamai Technologies (*www.akamai.com*) announced in June 2000 that it would offer online conference call services to telecommunications giants AT&T and WorldCom, among others. Earlier in 2000, Akamai acquired Internet-conferencing company Intervu, whose product NetPodium was popular for online conferences and seminars. This is useful for virtual seminars because it allows a speaker to use a telephone and his or her voice can be seamlessly transmitted to Web "listeners." The speaker can also be prerecorded, so the event can be staged "live" and it can be archived for ongoing use as well. Numerous technology conferences, trade shows, and symposiums have used live video streaming to put a unique twist on their offerings.

The most common form of Internet event presentation is currently the combination Web/teleconference event. Although a variety of technologies are used for implementation, the basic concept is the same: The attendee goes to a URL to see Web content but calls an 800 number to hear a synchronized presentation. Web content is "pushed" to the attendee's computer while the audio is sent via a telephone. The benefit is that no plug-in or sound card is required to participate, only a basic Web browser and a telephone, which is likely to be available to virtually any audience. Some technologies permit additional features, such as computer-based chat, instant polling, and live demonstrations.

Numerous providers of software and services have entered this market, and it is growing exponentially. For example, PlaceWare (*www.placeware.com*) provides live, interactive Web presentations for business use that can include hundreds and even thousands of attendees at a single event. PlaceWare is based on a "meeting room" concept that goes beyond passive Web-pushed content. It also allows participants to "talk" via online chat, while permitting the presenter to not only push Web pages, but also to conduct online demos and instant polls and to use an electronic whiteboard to enhance the online presentation.

Some solutions are provided over the Internet as a service, whereas others are software products. An essential difference is the combination of Web and teleconference, as described earlier, versus what is commonly known as "voiceover IP," which is voice delivered via the Internet. While voiceover IP quality has dramatically improved, it does require both a sound card and a computer headset if the participant wants to both hear and speak. Some solutions offer the option of both the teleconference and voiceover IP.

Astound (*www.astound.com*) and MShow (*www.mshow.com*) function as online event service bureaus, and companies such as Centra Software (*www.centra.com*) and Latitude Communications (*www.latitude.com*) offer Web-conferencing software products. Expect this area of Internet technology to expand dramatically in the next several years as service providers and software companies rush in to serve the market.

The marketing world has been waiting for a Web that can truly support full-blown multimedia, live audiovisual presentations, interactive live chat, and live videoconferencing. Streaming-media products take a giant step forward toward that ultimate goal. This technology is still partly dependent upon the vagaries of an Internet that is bloated with traffic, and the inadequacies of data transport pipes, delivery devices, Web servers, and receiving computers. But dramatic improvement is on the way. Broadband, which uses both cable and telephone lines, will increase the Internet's ability to handle the load, as will newer technologies such as DSL. Nevertheless, until these technologies are commonplace and available to the Internet majority, it may be risky to execute a virtual seminar that is completely live or wholly multimedia on the Web. The conservative strategy of using sound and motion selectively, supplemented with more-traditional communications such as a teleconferencing component, is likely to be a better bet until the technology advances even further.

Interacting live via a computer or by voice during the virtual event requires "chat," voice over the Internet, or online videoconferencing capabilities. Technologies that allow visitors to interact and ask questions live and online are being perfected. Interim solutions, such as the use of traditional telephone teleconferencing in combination with the virtual event or employing e-mail to respond to questions, are being used with considerable success to overcome early-adopter issues.

All of these advances are critically important to the proliferation of virtual events and virtual learning. Most marketers want to be in a position to replicate the content of a live seminar or leverage the investment they have already made in a CD-ROM, a slide show, or a videotaped marketing presentation for use on the Internet. Previously, the Internet was not the right venue for such heavy sound-and-motion content, but that is rapidly changing, and IT marketers will be the direct beneficiaries of advances in this area.

Types of Internet Events

It is possible to adapt practically every kind of live event into a virtual event that either *enhances* the live event or stands on its own. Following are some specific examples that are appearing in one form or another on the Web.

The Online Trade Show

These events seem to be most popular as enhancements to live shows, but they are even being used to replace live shows. One example of online trade show usage is that the show is already running as a live event and the show sponsor wants to extend its value to nonattendees. The sponsor creates a show-specific Web site and features some of the content from the live show. Aggressive sponsors offer special incentives to the exhibitors to advertise on the show site. An online trade show could be used as a "hook" for a live trade show, or it could completely replace a live trade show if desired.

The Online Seminar or Presentation

This is probably the most popular format, and the one with the most variations. These are the basic formats for the online seminar:

- *Scheduled live seminar.* The online seminar or presentation can be a "live" event held at an appointed time, during which a speaker is heard via a teleconference phone call or via audio streaming technology over the Web. The speaker can be heard *and* the presentation can be seen over the Web with audiovisual streaming. The speaker typically leads the visitor through a "slide" presentation of individual screens that are "pushed" over the Web. The speaker answers questions asked by participants via telephone, or takes questions via e-mail and answers them via e-mail, chat, or streamed audio over the Web. Audio portions can be recorded digitally for archiving purposes. This type of event can be enhanced with a mini-site or "resource area."

- *Scheduled prerecorded seminar.* The prerecorded format offers more flexibility in that it can be held at more times than the live session without the presence of the speaker. It is less flexible in that it does not allow for live interaction. Some presentations mix prerecorded sections with a live question-and-answer period to gain the benefits of both formats.

- *On-demand seminar.* This type of event has the most flexibility, in that it is available to the attendee at any time. Audiovisual content is typically available on-demand; for example, a video of a speaker can be played at any time. It can be appended to an existing Web site or be run as a special, invitation-only seminar or presentation. Typically, the on-demand seminar does not include a scheduled session or provide the ability to ask questions "live" online, except through e-mail. One option is to add a scheduled event, or to schedule a question-and-answer period at specific times, as an enhancement to this format. Another possibility is to accept questions online and answer them via return e-mail. Generally, the content of the on-demand seminar is organized into sections that can be easily navigated, so attendees can move through the seminar at their own pace.

The Online "Webcast"

This event is really a television or radio program broadcast over the Internet. It typically features a panel discussion or several speakers who offer short presentations, followed by a question-and-answer session, most often conducted via teleconference.

The Online Meeting

The online meeting can be anything: a sales meeting, user group conference, analyst meeting, press conference, and so on. A number of companies now routinely use the Internet for sales meetings and press conferences, and several companies have even experimented with online annual meetings.

The Online Chat

An online chat is a variation on the Web event which eliminates the slide show and allows an expert to informally converse with participants. This is conceptually the same as a teleconference, but it uses the Internet to facilitate the interaction instead of a telephone. Participants log into a chat room and ask questions of the expert. The expert answers the questions, and free-form commentary from all participants can occur as a result. Some participants prefer anonymity. Typically these sessions run anywhere from 30 to 60 minutes.

"Crossing Over" with Online Events

A developing trend is the increasing connection between offline and online events. Trade shows, for example, are moving toward not just promoting live events on the Internet, but sometimes running live Webcasts from the event, or posting videos of the event on the Web soon after its conclusion. Live seminar programs are also being captured on video and archived for Web use. For example, the Direct Marketing Association (*www.the-dma.org*) held two live seminars, one on e-commerce and one on e-mail marketing, in several cities during the spring of 2000. In late June, once these seminars were no longer offered live, the DMA sent an e-mail to members promoting the seminars again, this time as online seminars. The DMA had adapted the live seminars, added chat rooms so classmates could converse and bulletin boards to connect with the instructors, and offered them as on-demand Web events at a 20 percent discount for both.

Developing and Hosting the Internet Event

Before you rush off to cancel all of your live seminar programs, do yourself a favor: *Test* the online event on a limited basis with your target audiences. Admittedly, it is almost a "no-brainer" when it comes to comparing the costs/results from an online seminar to that of a live seminar program. A seminar held on the Web looks like the clear winner, but although the Internet event may seem to hold great promise, it is important to know if your audience will be accepting of this new marketing format.

Today, the Internet event seems to have its greatest appeal for audiences such as technical professionals—IT managers, networking managers, software developers, and the like. But as Internet usage increases, usage of Internet events will increase. As a result, such events could become attractive replacements for live events.

The Internet event should also be a particularly attractive venue for senior executives, who often do not have the time to attend an event in person. If you want to reach a high-level audience via the Internet, compare the pros and cons of a virtual event to these other "live" formats:

- *The teleconference, or teleforum.* This format is basically a seminar held via the telephone. It typically lasts about an hour, rather than the traditional half-day event, and is offered early in the morning so the executive can grab a cup of coffee and listen, perhaps with *The Wall Street Journal* at hand, before the responsibilities of the day distract him or her. With the right speakers and topic, the teleforum is a very powerful format—perhaps even more attractive than virtual events for high-level decision makers. If appropriate, teleforums can be enhanced by directing listeners to a URL to view Web-based content during the event.

- *The executive roundtable or briefing.* This variation of the seminar is a small live event with a restricted invitation list. It is usually open to senior executives by invitation only from the sponsoring company's CEO. The executive roundtable is positioned as an opportunity to participate in a discussion with peers. Sometimes the invitation to such an event is as exclusive as the event itself—it may be engraved, hand-addressed, or even include an executive gift.

- *The executive retreat.* The "retreat" is typically an executive symposium that includes one or more renowned speakers and is held in a world-class resort—with ample time for golf and other recreational opportunities. These formats, if well executed, can attract top executives who want to rub shoulders with "stars" like themselves. Of course, the expense associated with such events is significant.

If you are successfully holding teleforums, roundtables, or retreats for executives such as the ones described, do not scrap them all in favor of Internet events—test an online chat, online seminar, or other Web event first to see if it has the same appeal and staying power.

Guidelines for Developing and Hosting Your Own Internet Event

Following are some of the things you should think about when you are planning and executing your own Internet event.

Plan Your Event
What kind of event do you need? The Internet event is a customized Web application, and it will vary substantially based on the type of event you wish to execute, as well as the audience for the event. First,

map out your available options. Decide whether you will create the event entirely in-house or with the help of outside resources. Determine early whether you or another organization will do the Web hosting.

Develop the Event
Evaluate the needs of the target audience and develop an event well suited to that audience. Technology considerations are important, and they should be assessed during the development stage. Each of the following questions should be asked, because each requires a different kind of technological support:

- *Database integration.* Will you preassign individuals an access code and greet them at the "door"—or will you simply identify attendees when they arrive and sign in? Do you wish to prequalify attendees by asking them to register in advance, or is it acceptable to send them directly to the event?

- *Audiovisual requirements.* Do you intend to have one or more "live" speakers make a presentation or guide attendees through a section of the event? Will you use traditional telephone for the speaker(s), or will you do it all online using streaming audio? Do you wish to include sound and motion, and are you prepared to do so?

The "event concept" will ultimately guide the structure of the event, where the event is hosted, as well as the copy and creative execution.

In the case of a Web seminar, you may be adapting the content of a live seminar. Replicating the content is not as easy as it sounds: You will have to modify slides, scripts, and other materials so they are optimized for presentation on the Internet.

Critical Success Factors
In general, the same critical success factors that apply to live events apply to virtual events:

- *Guest speaker(s).* Guest speakers add credibility and prominence to a seminar. The guest speaker ideally should be a noted authority in the field, an analyst or consultant, or a journalist. The guest speaker can provide an aura of objectivity and impartiality to a seminar and helps draw a crowd. It is also appropriate for guest speakers to be from organizations that are partners or customers of the sponsoring company. There should be an opportunity for a question-and-answer session if possible.

- *Success stories.* Success stories, either told by customers or related by the company sponsoring the seminar, typically are well received at seminars. Seminar attendees like to hear about how problems were solved and challenges overcome.

- *"Exclusive" information.* Seminars that share some sort of exclusive information—such as the unveiling of survey results—have high-perceived value, especially if this information is conveyed by one of the guest speakers.

- *"Hot" topics.* Current in-vogue topics of interest to the target audience, combined with success stories or product demonstrations, can add to a seminar's success.

- *Interactivity.* For the virtual seminar, interactivity of some kind is essential. A demo that the prospect can control and a worksheet with a calculator are examples of interactive elements that work.

Establish a Structure for the Event

It is critical to construct an effective structure for your event with an intuitive navigational flow and organized content. The structure should be mapped out on a flow diagram that outlines the path that visitors will take from the time they enter the event. Factors to consider in creating a structure include the likelihood of repeat visits, the frequency of information "refreshment," and the segmentation of the site's content. Generally, each page of the event should be short and clean to minimize the need for excessive scrolling.

Depending on the event's complexity, it is generally a good idea to follow a modular layout. This allows the visitors to go to different areas based on their needs, interests, and time constraints. If the event is on-demand, attendees may want to check in at several times on several different days, in order to fit the event within their busy schedules. If you want the event to include any type of real-time presentation or a live "chat room" for online questions and answers, you will probably want to schedule these parts of the event at various specific dates and times, just as you would a live event.

Create the Content for the Event

All of the content for an Internet event should be "Web-ized." There is nothing worse than loading an event with copy and graphics that have not been modified for electronic consumption. Copy should be crisp and informative and be conveyed in readable, digestible chunks. The navigation template should be clean and attractive. Graphical elements should be designed to facilitate navigation.

If you are doing a Web seminar, using the content from a traditional seminar is probably a good place to start. Use the speaker's slides as a basis for the virtual seminar's graphics, and his or her notes as copy input. Do not try to use the materials as is—graphics typically will need to be rendered especially for the Web in an appropriate program, with the final graphic resolution at 72 dots per inch (dpi).

Simple animations, such as movement of type and graphics, should be used to enhance visitors' experiences. Most animations should be universally viewable without any special software. Graphic files should be kept small and manageable. Interactive forms should be designed for the lowest common denominator.

Research and Add Appropriate Technologies

Incorporate only those Internet technologies that will enhance your event, not detract from it or cause undue complications for event visitors. Options include database connectivity, dynamic HTML, use of cookies, push technology, Java applets, streaming audio and video, and electronic commerce.

When used appropriately, multimedia offers your visitors an enhanced experience, with the ability to click on images and interact with animated text and images. However, essential content should be available to the lowest common technological denominator. If you require plug-ins to hear sound or view motion, they should be optional, not required. Mirror any content so that participants will not miss anything if they do not use the plug-ins.

A word of caution, especially if you are targeting your event to individuals who work in larger corporations: Some corporate networks have firewall technology that might block certain plug-ins. Always suggest that the participant do a browser test prior to the event if plug-ins are used. It is important not to assume that everyone can see and hear your event as you intended it. Designing the event for maximum audience attendance is important.

Database integration adds an additional personalized dimension to Web events. Merging Web pages with online information provides data that can be used to dynamically generate Web pages on the fly, offering the option for heightened personalization and user feedback.

You have a wide range of databases from which to choose. Many of the larger, more-robust database products, such as Oracle and Sybase, can integrate with the Web, as can smaller programs such as Microsoft Access. Others, such as ColdFusion, are designed especially to act as a database interface to process database scripts and return the information within HTML.

Implementation options include password access, user profiles, and interactive online qualification forms for individual users. Such mechanisms allow for rapid and accurate tracking of attendance, as well as gathering information on attendees and their opinions. All of this information will be valuable in improving future virtual events.

Determine How the Event Will Be Hosted

The decision to host a virtual event hinges on several issues, including expected traffic, database requirements, multimedia technologies employed, and site security. If, for example, you are using streaming media, you will need a special Web server to accommodate the traffic, or a broadcasting service that can stream it for you. Examine and compare the options for internal versus external hosting.

When evaluating outside hosting services, look at the following criteria:

- Server hardware and software

- Redundancy and reliability of servers

- Connections and bandwidth available

- Space restrictions

- Data-transfer restrictions

- Availability of e-mail and autoresponders

- Availability of FTP

- Quality of access statistics

- Security

- CGI availability and support

- Java availability and support

- Database access

- Search capabilities

- Audio, video, and multimedia support as required

- Technical support

- Fee structure

Program and Test the Event

Before "going live," test all components of the virtual event thoroughly. Program and test all links, forms, and graphic files. Test all pages and any database integration from multiple Web browsers on different computer platforms. Test and evaluate all multimedia components to ensure that they are functional on the widest possible range of platforms. Evaluate the content for general clarity and readability. If possible, try out the event on staff, customers, or "friendly" prospects before making it widely available.

It also might be a good idea to post technical information at the event's URL to be certain that attendees can take full advantage of the event. I saw an excellent example of "covering all the bases" when I went to a company's event address to sign up. This company had included a page of instructions for "testing and optimizing" participation in the event, as well as a link to "test your browser." The company listed all the technical requirements for the event, along with a description of firewalls and how to work around them so the data portion of the online seminar would function properly.

Promote the Event

Promote the Internet event. (See the next section of this chapter for suggestions on event promotion.)

Evaluate the Results

Establish measurement criteria in advance so that you know how many individuals attended the event. Use qualification forms with offers within the event to identify and track quality leads. Compare the ROI of virtual event programs to the ROI you have achieved with traditional events. You may find that it varies based on the type of audience and the type of event. Use this analysis to plan and refine future Internet event programs.

Promoting Events Using the Internet

The Internet brings a whole new spin to promoting both traditional and Internet-based events. And as you might expect, services already exist to help event producers promote and host their events with little effort. If you hold a substantial number of events, you might want to look at these services: iNetEvents (*www.inetevents.com*), which provides a Web-enabled event management application that puts a "Web wrapper" around your event; b-there.com (*www.b-there.com*), an attendee relationship management engine; and iconvention.com (*www.iconvention.com*), providing associations with the means to extend physical shows into online vertical trading communities.

It is also a good idea to keep track of both live events and online events so you can be aware of trends. Here are some valuable resources:

- AllMeetings (*www.allmeetings.com*)—the best locations for meetings

- Go-events (*www.go-events.com*)—a comprehensive listing of business events

- EventWeb (*www.eventweb.com*)—an extremely useful event newsletter with a lot of Internet coverage

- MeetingEvents (*www.meetingevents.com*)—industry-related events

- SeminarFinder (*www.seminarfinder.com*), Seminar Information (*www.seminarinformation.com*), SeminarPlanet (*www.seminarplanet.com*), SeminarSource (*www.seminarsource.com*)—databases of seminar events

- TechCalendar (*www.techweb.com/calendar*)—technology-related events

- TSNN (*www.tsnn.com*)—a comprehensive listing of worldwide trade shows; this site merged with TSCentral.com in April 2001 to create the world's largest tradeshow portal.

Suppose you are promoting a traditional event, such as a free half-day seminar in ten cities. This might be what the promotional plan looks like:

1. Establish the dates and locations. Select list sources and target the appropriate audience within 50 miles of each city.

2. Create and mail an invitation. Include the traditional phone, mail-in, and fax-back response paths.

3. Follow up with fax and telephone confirmations to registrants.

4. Cross-promote the seminar with advertising and public relations activities.

Now see what happens when you enhance your promotion by using the Internet as a registration facilitator. You execute the same four steps, but you add a special seminar registration URL to the mail piece and promote it prominently. You urge prospects to visit the URL to receive further seminar details and to register online.

When the prospect arrives at the Web response area, you offer:

- A more-detailed agenda and description of the seminar, along with speaker photographs and biographies if appropriate.

- Directions, including printable maps, for each seminar location.

- Information about other events of potential interest to the prospect, including a list of Internet-based events for those prospects who are not in the ten-city area or cannot attend the live seminars but want more information about your company's product.

- An interactive registration form—perhaps with a special offer just for online registrants—so that prospects can register online and receive an instant acknowledgment. (Collect an e-mail address here and you can use it to remind the registrant of the seminar several times before the event. Use a Web-based database tool and you can capture the marketing information you obtain from the prospect "one time" instead of re-keying the information. Use it for future promotions and to track the prospect's activity.)

This relatively easy enhancement could have a significant impact on your seminar program—and your marketing ROI. Here are the six reasons why:

1. You may be able to reduce the cost of your direct mail seminar invitation by making it less elaborate and driving response to the Web—where they get full seminar details. Typical direct mail seminar invitations include a full agenda, speaker biographies, and location information. That takes considerable space to accomplish in a mailing piece. With the Web as your electronic information center, perhaps even an oversized postcard invitation would suffice.

2. Overall response to the promotion could increase because you have added a Web response path that some registrants may prefer to use. On the Web, they can get more information about the seminar without the need to speak to anyone, and they can easily register online.

3. Online registrants may be higher-quality prospects because they take the time to visit the URL, review detailed information, and complete the registration form.

4. Using a series of e-mail confirmations and reminders, which you send prior to the event, could reduce your "no-show" rate (which is typically 50 to 60 percent for live seminars).

5. Even if prospects visit the URL and do not come to the seminar, they have been made aware of your company, your seminar series, and other events you sponsor that may interest them.

6. Individuals who are outside the ten-city seminar area could visit the URL to learn more about your company and products and, as a result, become new prospects for you.

The incremental cost to your seminar promotion to achieve these potential benefits should be very low. If you have a Web site, the seminar URL could "hang off" of it. Creating the seminar response area is not a complicated task—it can be done by your in-house Web staff or be outsourced to an interactive resource. If you need comprehensive response management support, there are firms that handle online seminar registration and confirmation, along with maintaining your marketing database.

Use a similar strategy to promote other live events, such as your appearance at trade shows or conferences, sales meetings, press tours, and so on. Consider these additional promotional ideas:

- Place a Web banner ad on your own site to promote your appearance at a conference or trade show. Prominently feature your booth number and consider offering Web prospects something special if, when they visit your booth, they mention that they saw the promotion on your Web site.

- When you book any booth space or speaker from your company at a conference, be sure to see if the show's sponsor offers a Web site with links or special rates for exhibitors or speakers. Also see if you can offer "virtual" exhibit area admissions tickets to prospects, printable from your Web site.

- Collect e-mail addresses of trade show and seminar attendees and ask if you can communicate with them via e-mail. E-mail a questionnaire after the event to get their opinions and further qualify their interest.

- Collaborate with co-exhibitors at shows or co-sponsors of seminars to promote events via the Internet. Cross-promote each other's products via e-mail and your respective Web sites.

Promoting the Net Event

All of the techniques you would use to promote traditional events apply to promoting virtual events as well. You can invite people to a virtual event in the same way you invite them to a live event:

- Direct mail is generally the most effective medium for seminar invitations.

- Telemarketing can be effective when you are inviting a small number of people, or to follow up on direct mail.

- Print advertising can supplement direct mail for trade show and conference promotions.

- E-mail sent to prospects and Web banners placed on your own site, or on carefully selected sites, could be used to augment mail and telemarketing efforts.

- You could also use public relations to publicize your event, which might lead to mention in trade publications or even free links on appropriate Web sites.

With the likelihood that virtual events and seminars will become more common in the future, it might be interesting to test various methods of inviting prospects and customers to such events. For example, if you can obtain an opt-in e-mail list, you might want to test traditional direct mail against e-mail invitations to a virtual seminar to see which is more effective in generating attendance.

With a virtual event, you can eliminate the need for an "I will attend" mail, fax, or phone response. Instead, you can offer prospects the ability to register online when they arrive at the special URL of the event. If the event is exclusive, you can preselect a targeted list of people to invite, assign them individual access codes, and provide the codes on mailed or e-mailed invitations. Then, using a Web database program, you can actually "recognize" and greet them at "the door," when they come to the event. You can even encourage the prospect to share the access codes with colleagues, if you so choose, to extend the reach of the event.

Imagine receiving an elegant invitation to a virtual seminar with your own personal access code. Go to the seminar's special URL, enter your access code, and instantly, your name, title, company name, and address appear. You can verify it, or make changes as needed, online. The Web database records the changes and instantly updates the marketing database.

This technique is very appealing, because it suggests to the prospect that he or she is important to you, and that the event really is exclusive. In fact, it is the beginning of a marketing relationship that starts with the prospect's coming to the event and taking responsibility for updating his or her own database record.

Obviously, there is considerable value to you as the direct marketer, because you are getting the prospect not only to attend your virtual event but also to engage in a dialogue with you. If you include qualification questions for the prospect to answer, you will get to know even more about the individual. You will be able to use that data to help prioritize the prospect's interest, and you will continue to market to that prospect over time.

Unlike the traditional event, the virtual event is more "anonymous" and certainly not as personal. As a result, you do not have the same opportunity for your marketing and sales staff to meet the prospect face-to-face. That is why promoting the virtual event should extend beyond the initial contact. Once a prospect comes to your virtual event, you should immediately engage him or her, offering compelling reasons to "sign in" and stay awhile. You may not want to ask a lot of questions of the prospect at the beginning of the event because this may discourage continued interest. Instead, use a questionnaire during the event or at the end—and make a substantive offer for completing it.

Use the event as an opportunity to cross-promote other virtual and live events, and give the attendee the ability to return to the event by keeping it available on the Web for a period of time. After that, it is a good idea to archive your virtual event, perhaps on your Web site or at another special site, so that prospects can come back in the future. The virtual event also has the potential to continue a marketing relationship that can ultimately turn a prospect into a customer.

Holding Online Marketing Meetings

Could the Internet also change the nature of meetings, perhaps making face-to-face meetings, and the travel associated with them, a thing of the past? Services such as WebEx (*www.webex.com*) might lead you to believe that could happen. WebEx is one of the leading Application Service Providers in a growing number of companies entering the emerging Web-based collaboration services marketplace. WebEx provides its basic "Instant Meetings" service free for a small number of business users. Its paid "Premium Meeting" service adds participants and additional interactive features.

In November 1999, WebEx began partnering with MindSpring to offer "WebEx Office" to that ISP's small-business customers. It was part of a new portal, MindSpring Biz, now renamed Earthlink's business area (*www.earthlink.net/business*) after the acquisition of MindSpring by Earthlink. A small-business user can "open" a WebEx Office in moments and begin conducting meetings on the Web, collaborating and exchanging information in real time. WebEx Office features include linking to existing Web sites to serve as a private conference room, instant messaging, meeting scheduling, calendaring, and more.

Clearly, this is another opportunity for the IT marketer to leverage the Internet for both external and internal marketing-oriented meetings and events.

Using Distance Learning for Marketing

The natural evolution of online meetings and events is distance learning. Although distance learning and online training have been around for years, the explosion of the Internet has increased their penetration of the marketing world. They are now on the verge of mass adoption for general marketing use. According to IDC, Web-based training is expected to exceed $6 billion by 2002, growing at a compound annual growth rate of almost 95 percent. By that year, says IDC, technology-based training is likely to overtake instructor-led training. In a survey of corporate training managers, Corporate University Xchange (*www.corpu.com*) found that as much as 96 percent of corporate training will be conducted online by 2003.

In this area, it is the IT market driving early adoption because of the ever-increasing demand for technical training. Although educational programs may be beyond the scope of today's B-to-B Internet marketer, it is not difficult to imagine a future that involves extended customer service in the form of marketing-based online tutorials for prospects, modeled after earlier distance-learning efforts. Two of the reasons this will become more commonplace as a marketing technique are the widespread availability of multimedia tools, such as Flash and Shockwave, and the ever-increasing bandwidth to facilitate multimedia transmission.

Numerous companies have served the "e-learning" market for years, even before the Internet reached its current hot status. Typically, early leaders focused on IT technical training. One such company, CyberStateU (*www.cyberstateu.com*), today offers its "Synergy Learning System" to help reduce a student's total study time. The system combines multiple teaching mediums into a structured-learning environment, combining online lectures, reviews, assignments, and interaction with more-traditional books and video tapes. CyberStateU serves hundreds of leading companies, offering fully certified courses on behalf of Cisco, Microsoft, Novell, and others.

Now, e-learning is broadening its base and becoming a more accepted means of general business training. Newer organizations such as Digital Think (*www.digitalthink.com*) and SmartForce (*www.smartforce.com*) are typical of the "e-learning" trend. SmartForce runs Dell's online educational program, "EducateU." These and other services are expanding their offerings beyond IT learning as the education demands of general business continue to grow.

Another entry into this market, ZDUniversity, was originally an IT-oriented educational service, but it has evolved into the centerpiece of a new service launched by Ziff-Davis in October 1999 called SmartPlanet (*www.smartplanet.com*), now part of ZDnet. According to the company, SmartPlanet is a "personal online learning community—a uniquely rich and diverse Web destination for people seeking continuous personal and professional growth on virtually any topic or interest." The former ZDU will become part of SmartPlanet as the base for the "Computers & Internet Learning Zone." SmartPlanet has registered members, both free and paid, and will grow its user base via distribution and partner agreements. Time will tell whether such online learning communities will become models for the future of marketing-driven distance learning.

To apply distance learning as a marketing technique to reach larger organizations, the best solution might ultimately be establishing learning programs within each company. Here, such products as LearningSpace from Lotus (*www.lotus.com*) hold promise. LearningSpace Anytime 3.0, introduced in mid-1999, was the first Web-based product to give users the flexibility to learn either through self-paced materials, live interaction with others in a virtual classroom, or collaboration with others independent of time and place. This server software application can be accessed from either a Web browser or the Lotus Notes client. LearningSpace has been adopted by such organizations as Siemens Corporation, American Express, and online business education provider UNext.com.

8

Internet Fulfillment

The Internet is by design an exceptional fulfillment channel for IT companies. An IT company can easily fulfill and disseminate technical and marketing information via e-mail and the Web, replacing paper-based fulfillment almost entirely with e-fulfillment. This practice has already saved large IT companies millions of dollars, as they produce fewer data sheets and other forms of printed product literature in favor of posting HTML pages on their Web sites. The even greater advantage to Web-based fulfillment, however, is the ability to execute demos, trials, and actual delivery of software products online. By allowing customers to purchase products with a credit card and immediately unlock and download software, IT companies can literally change their traditional business model to an e-business model almost instantly.

This chapter discusses e-fulfillment and the dramatic impact it can have on the way IT companies market their products and services.

Traditional Fulfillment: An Aging Process

The inquiry fulfillment process has not really changed much from the early days of direct marketing. A prospect or customer receives a solicitation and responds in some way, and then the fun begins. The marketer responds to the inquiry via direct mail, sending data sheets, a catalog, or some other literature in a large envelope, sometimes with a personalized letter, often via first-class mail. Speed is of the essence, since inquiries are known to "cool off" in just a matter of days. Even though fulfilling requests for information is now database driven and somewhat automated, it still involves the labor-intensive and expensive practice of sending "literature packs" to hundreds or thousands of individuals.

The potential of the Internet in this area is almost too good to be true. It presents the IT marketer with the unique ability to electronically fulfill any number of inquiries online—no paper required!

Inquiries typically come from a variety of sources—advertising, direct mail, trade shows, public relations, and the like, but until you determine the quality of the inquiry, it should not be considered a "lead." Junk leads are not uncommon, and they can come in via any of the sources mentioned. But this is the point at which some IT marketers make either of two critical mistakes:

1. The marketer disregards the inquiry altogether, assuming it is "junk."

2. The marketer fulfills the inquiry through the standard fulfillment process, which generally means sending a costly full-color literature package, sometimes packaged in a presentation folder, via first-class mail.

Both of these responses are wrong. In the first case, discarding the inquiries means that the marketer is potentially losing some good leads—maybe even qualified prospects—which could be buried in a pile of generally unqualified inquiries. The problem is, the marketer will never know.

The alternative is not much better: By fulfilling the inquiry as if it were a qualified lead, the marketer wastes a lot of money. Some marketers even exacerbate the process by then sending these inquiries to their sales force. There is nothing worse for a salesperson than spending valuable time chasing an unqualified inquiry. If the salesperson continues to receive unqualified inquiries, he or she will lose all faith in the marketing organization.

That is why the most sensible way to handle inquiries at this stage is with a *two-step* process. It is okay to respond to unqualified inquiries. It makes more sense, however, to do it with a far less expensive mailing—perhaps a simple #10 envelope with a printed letter that acknowledges the inquirer's interest but asks several qualification questions on an accompanying reply card before additional information is sent. This simple strategy can save thousands of dollars.

Even so, numerous industry studies suggest that fulfillment is the Achilles' heel of a majority of IT direct marketers. Some companies do a shoddy job of it, hurting their corporate image in the process. Others may send the right materials; however, their turnaround time is anything but prompt.

Unfortunately, these examples are far from unusual. Industry studies support the fact that many companies are doing an inadequate job of qualifying and fulfilling inquiries. I have heard on more than one occasion that average time frames for fulfilling inquiries vary from two weeks to as long as three months. Some studies suggest that companies actually drop a significant number of inquiries from the fulfillment process altogether.

Although they may not openly admit it, the fulfillment process of many IT companies is in a shambles. Sometimes, it is because a company is overwhelmed with responses. Sometimes, the fulfillment process itself is flawed, or the system is inadequate, or the quality control is poor, or it is simply human error. Whatever the reason, the result is the same—an inquiry is mishandled, overfulfilled, or lost. That means a lead could be receiving inferior treatment and a potentially good prospect could be alienated.

The Transformation of Traditional Fulfillment

Fulfillment experts say that 48 hours should be the *maximum* amount of lag time between the time an inquiry is received and the time a contact is initiated by the company.

Interest in a product or service wanes from the moment a prospect or customer asks for more information until the moment the information is received. The competitive environment is such that, if that individual has a choice, he or she is just as likely to go to any company that provides the requested information first. Business is so time-driven today that the speed of information delivery is often as crucial as the information itself. Buying decisions are sometimes made on that basis. That is why experienced direct marketers know that they should never underestimate the positive and negative effects of fulfillment. This brings into question the whole process of traditional fulfillment itself. Here are the standard ways fulfillment is usually executed.

Direct Mail

Direct mail is still the primary means of inquiry fulfillment. Typically, an inquirer receives a basic fulfillment package—a letter, literature, and a reply card—by mail.

Traditional inquiry fulfillment seems to be a remarkably wasteful process. Examine your own fulfillment materials and those that you receive from other companies. You will notice that many direct marketers "overfulfill" by mailing out folders packed with expensive, glossy literature even to unqualified inquiries. Companies that should know better are sending bulging literature kits to reader-service inquiries, sometimes via first-class mail. This is a colossal waste of money and natural resources.

Traditional direct mail fulfillment has been improved with the use of electronically distributed fulfillment requests and inventory control procedures. Some marketers have set up automated 800 numbers connected to voice-response systems or autofax machines, which accept an inquiry and electronically transmit it to the fulfillment operation, which picks and sends the appropriate literature pack within days or sometimes hours. The direct mail fulfillment material itself may be pre-kitted, waiting for a laser-personalized letter and mailing label to be generated and affixed. In extraordinary cases, literature or other fulfillment materials may be sent via priority mail or overnight delivery services. Overnight delivery is less common in inquiry fulfillment, but it is becoming more common in order fulfillment. Larger mail-order companies contract with an overnight delivery service to reduce the shipping cost so that low-cost one- or two-day delivery can be offered to customers as a service enhancement.

Fax

Facsimile transmission is increasingly used to supplement or even replace direct mail fulfillment. Common among larger IT companies is fax-on-demand, or autofaxing. The inquirer calls a toll-free number and enters his or her fax number and a product code. The responding fax-on-demand system immediately generates a data sheet on the corresponding product and faxes it to the inquirer. This type of fulfillment is inappropriate if a color brochure or multipage booklet or manual must be sent, but it is acceptable for fast distribution of simple information. Its overwhelming benefit is the speed of response, which can offer a significant advantage in many cases. Sometimes, autofaxing is used to precede direct mail fulfillment.

Telephone

In the context of providing essential information immediately, the telephone can be a viable fulfillment medium. If an inquirer makes an inbound call to a toll-free number, the telemarketer can be trained to provide the caller with the necessary information by phone or offer to send additional information via fax or direct mail. Outbound telemarketing should only be used if the marketer believes the inquirer is a highly qualified prospect.

Behind each of these media is an inquiry-handling process of some kind. Some companies choose to handle inquiries themselves, whereas others hire fulfillment services to perform the task.

The Electronic Fulfillment Difference

Electronic fulfillment is fulfillment that is facilitated by the Internet. In its most basic form, electronic fulfillment is a simple e-mail response to an e-mail or any other kind of inquiry. Although e-mail is for all practical purposes still a text-only medium, it is useful in that you can send an immediate response directly to the inquirer's electronic mailbox. You can also embed Web links in your e-mail response so that the inquirer can visit a URL to receive additional information. Although not all e-mail programs support Web links, it is still good practice to mention URLs in e-mail.

Responding via e-mail can be effective and desirable, as long as the individual made the inquiry via e-mail or gave you permission to respond in that manner. (It is generally recommended that you ask the question, "May we communicate with you via e-mail?" on a reply card or during a telemarketing call.) Products are available to automate e-mail so that you can respond to multiple inquiries at once. With some e-mail communication products, you can "autorespond" to inquiries without human intervention.

Recent industry data suggests that current customers are more accepting of e-mail fulfillment than are prospects. However, an electronic inquirer would probably appreciate an e-mail response because it is immediate. Again, one of the biggest issues with fulfilling information requests is the time lapse between the act of inquiring and the receipt of information. E-mail is one way to close that gap and feed the need for instant gratification that is so prevalent today in marketing (and in life).

One application of e-mail fulfillment that seems to be accepted and appreciated is the e-mail newsletter, which has broad appeal to both customers and prospects. A prospect who is receptive to e-mail and is interested in a product or service is likely to subscribe to an e-mail newsletter that keeps him or her informed on a periodic basis about that product or service. This method of fulfillment is far less threatening than receiving a telemarketing call. The e-mail newsletter is likely to receive more attention and get read more often than traditional direct mail.

As discussed in Chapter 5, the e-mail newsletter is itself becoming a primary means of generating leads for business-to-business marketers. In the context of instant fulfillment, it is a remarkably efficient medium. Consider the fact that much of what you may now send in traditional printed form could be converted to e-mail newsletter format. It may not have the same appearance; today's e-mail is predominantly raw text with no bold, underlining, bullets, or graphic images. But that could be changing soon. E-mail programs are catching up, and it may not be long before they routinely incorporate HTML-like graphics.

Even with the basic e-mail newsletter, you have an opportunity to translate marketing material into a format that is widely accepted and read. As long as the e-mail newsletter has information of perceived value, and it is not merely a sales pitch, prospects and customers alike will read it. Just as important, you can rapidly build an e-mail list of subscribers who, at the very least, share the commonality of being interested in your e-mail newsletter topic. Sending your e-mail newsletter periodically not only gets your message to a target audience more than once, it also positions you as an expert. And e-mail newsletters are very inexpensive. Once you automate the e-mail process, the cost associated with e-mail distribution is almost insignificant. Compare that to traditional direct mail fulfillment.

The reader service number itself is undergoing change in the era of the Internet. Now several trade magazine publishers are providing Internet-based reader service numbers so that inquirers can respond online. Some of these services allow an advertiser to post electronic information at a special Web address, with a link to the advertiser's Web site. As a result, the inquiry can literally be fulfilled instantly instead of waiting days, weeks, or months, as might be the case with the traditional inquiry-handling process.

Dell Computer (*www.dell.com*) created an Internet version of the reader service number that it calls an "E-Value Code." Although Dell builds computer systems to individual specifications, they also know that certain preconfigured systems will be popular. Dell runs print ads promoting these systems and shows an E-Value Code with each of these systems. The interested prospect goes to the Dell Web site and enters the E-Value Code in the appropriate box on a Web page, and the site instantly returns information to the prospect about that particular system. That is e-fulfillment at its simplest and its best.

Other innovations promise to keep the Internet on the cutting edge of fulfillment. In May 2000, Digimarc (*www.digimarc.com*) announced a technology called MediaBridge which permits an invisible image to be embedded in a printed ad, brochure, or CD. Suppose the prospect is reading an ad with this invisible image. He or she can hold the ad up to a camera connected to the computer, and the invisible image will point the computer to the URL of a Web page. Print ads using this technology appeared for the first time in the July 2000 issue of *WIRED*. The magazine ran 30 of the ads and included an explanation with that issue. Digimarc ran a promotion giving away 25,000 "PC cameras." The technology has been licensed by several other publishers as well.

GoCode (*www.gocode.com*) uses barcode technology to achieve the same purpose. A barcode is placed in printed content, and then a barcode reader attached to the computer translates the barcode into the appropriate URL. FindtheDOT (*www.findthedot.com*) involves printing "Power Dots" in advertisements, in catalogs, and on business cards. Customers tap the Power Dot on ads of interest with a "Personal Information Assistant" (PIA), a little wireless hand-held device that is distributed free. The PIA wirelessly transfers the stored Power Dots to the user's PC and initiates a recognizable e-mail response from the specific advertisers of interest.

Creative use of imagery technology is also revolutionizing the visual quality of fulfillment. For example, MGI (*www.mgisoft.com*) offers the MGI ZOOM server, an imaging server that enables users to zoom in and examine items in very fine detail regardless of the bandwidth. The technology is being used by Internet retailers to give prospects and customers online close-ups of products.

The largest technology information providers have virtually made a business out of integrating their print publications, conferences and events, and the Internet—all in an effort to consolidate information and do a better job of serving prospects and customers.

IDG (*www.idg.net*) is a good example. IDG publishes *Computerworld, Network World, PCWorld*, and countless other magazines and books, including the successful . . . *for Dummies* series. IDG also sponsors numerous industry conferences and events, such as ICE, the Internet Commerce Expo.

One of IDG's big success stories on the Web is Network World Fusion (*www.nwfusion.com*). This sister Web site to the Network World publication requires separate registration. Web site visitors must complete an eight-page qualification form to gain access to the content, but the form is hardly a barrier: The Web site garnered 94,000 registered users in just its first 18 months. All of this Web activity caused IDG to develop its own search-and-access service, IDG.net, which now permits registered users to personally navigate over 140 Web sites.

IDG's integrated use of traditional publications, Web sites, conference events, e-mail newsletters, and online surveys is a model for the future of B-to-B Internet marketing. This whole concept of involving the online "reader" in a literal web of communications is a significant trend in the information-technology market that applies to all marketers. E-fulfillment is a logical alternative to direct mail and fax fulfillment for numerous reasons, not the least of which is the incredible cost-savings potential. Not only does e-fulfillment drastically reduce the cost of fulfillment, but it also removes the time-to-market factor.

E-fulfillment can quite literally happen instantly, at least on the Web. A prospect comes to a Web site, completes a Web response form, and clicks the Send button. With e-fulfillment, information can appear as an instant direct response to the request. There is no time lapse. Nothing has been available to the IT marketer that even comes close to such an idea. What is even more significant is the relative ease with which it can be implemented.

Means of Electronic Fulfillment

Electronic fulfillment can be implemented in two basic ways: "pull" and "push."

"Pulling" the Prospect to You

The Web Response Area

In Chapter 3, we discussed the effectiveness of Web response forms. A Web response area with a Web response form is the termination point for a campaign-specific URL. The inquirer visits the URL and finds information about the offer and the product or service being promoted, along with a Web response form.

The Web response form can really function as a gateway to a company's electronic fulfillment process. As an example, suppose a prospect receives a direct mailing from a company promoting a line of modems designed for small-business usage. The informational offer is a white paper, promotionally enhanced with the offer of a discount on the modems for an order placed within the next 30 days. The direct mail heavily promotes a special URL as the primary response path.

When the prospect visits the URL, there is a "welcome" page including links to pages with brief information about each of the available modems. Each page shows a picture of the product and highlights its specific benefits and features. At this URL, there is also a qualifying form that the visitor must fill out to get the white paper. The form has certain required fields. Once these fields are completed and the form is sent, the visitor can receive the white paper via ordinary mail. However, the visitor also has the option of receiving the fulfillment electronically because the completed form leads to a page that allows the visitor to unlock or download the white paper.

Now what about that discount offer? This can be fulfilled in a number of ways. After the visitor completes and sends the form, a discount coupon can be dynamically generated. By linking the visitor's ZIP code with a directory of resellers, the names and addresses of several dealers can be generated on the fly—so the visitor can actually be directed to the closest reseller.

With the addition of electronic commerce, the visitor could also use a credit card to purchase any of the modems online at the discounted prices—right from an order page. Alternatively, the visitor can be given an 800 number to ask questions, place an order, or inquire about where to purchase the products locally.

The near future promises an even more intriguing slant to this kind of electronic fulfillment. With Internet telephony on the horizon, this scenario can include an interactive online conversation with a live sales representative. If a visitor has questions while navigating the site, they can be answered on the spot, through the computer itself, or via a connection between the computer and the visitor's telephone.

The Web Site

Your corporate Web site can also be used to "pull" a prospect to your site with an electronic fulfillment center. In the preceding example, the incoming URL would terminate at a special "electronic door" into the electronic fulfillment center of your corporate Web site. The fulfillment center is a designated area of a corporate site, set up to collect leads and generate information in response to inquiries. In this area, the visitor would locate information about the modems and request the white paper or take advantage of the discount offer. Online ordering could also be offered in the fulfillment center. Services such as SubmitOrder (*www.submitorder.com*), a business unit of technology distributor Digital Storage, offer fully integrated "e-fulfillment" capabilities so companies can offload the e-commerce fulfillment headaches. Other services, such as eLeads from MarketSoft (*www.marketsoft.com*), provide Web-based lead management.

The response path to a more general electronic fulfillment center may not be as focused as a campaign-specific Web response form. However, it provides you with the ability to handle fulfillment in a centralized place, while exposing the visitor to a broader line of products.

E-mail

E-mail itself can act as a pull–push medium. After you begin to correspond with a prospect or customer via e-mail, you have established an ongoing dialogue. As part of that dialogue, you can encourage the individual in the context of e-mail to visit a Web site to get more information or to sign up for an e-mail newsletter. Advertisers that place their promotional messages in e-mail newsletters are for the most part advertising a Web site address. IT Internet marketers can make excellent use of e-mail in support of pull Web site areas by continuously reinforcing URLs in the body of e-mail messages.

One innovator in this area is MindArrow *(www.mindarrow.com)*, whose interactive "eBrochures" arrive via e-mail. The company's "Virtual Prospecting" system delivers a company brochure via e-mail and then analyzes which elements are most popular with viewers. The system has the ability to notify salespeople as to when prospects are reading the brochures and can track how long they looked at them and which products they found to be of interest.

"Pushing" Information to the Prospect

"Push" simply means taking information and sending it, or pushing it, to the prospect or customer. In that respect, e-mail is the simplest kind of push technology a marketer can use. Any promotional e-mail delivered to a prospect or customer is, in effect, pushed to the individual's mailbox. However, it is really the regular delivery of such e-mail, as with e-mail newsletters sent on a periodic basis, that turns e-mail into a push vehicle.

Push technology is most often defined as the process of pushing Web pages to someone's computer. The acknowledged pioneer of push is PointCast Inc., which was acquired in May 1999 by Launchpad Technologies, developer of the eWallet consumer shopping utility and an Idealab! Company. The acquisition led to the formation of a new company combining PointCast and eWallet called EntryPoint *(www.entrypoint.com)*. In the fall of 2000, Entrypoint merged with Internet Financial Network to become Infogate *(www.infogate.com)*.

Infogate is a free advertising-supported service that provides a personalized bar that sits on a user's desktop. Infogate offers instant access to news and information, e-commerce, resources, and search. A customized ticker delivers headline news and stock data to the desktop.

The push concept is not without its problems and controversies. In fact, by mid-1998, several push-technology vendors had gone out of business, and of the remaining companies, some had moved away from the push label. One of the reasons push may have run into trouble was that it ran into a technology wall. Early derivations of push were slow and intrusive. Because most targeted end users were in corporations or other organizations, information was sent across the Internet through a corporate network to the end user's desktop. The problem was that large files were being transferred, in some cases several times a day, to a corporate end user. If many corporate end users were using a push service, it was the corporate network that had to handle the load.

Despite these apparent shortcomings, push technology has been somewhat rejuvenated by new and improved products and services. In its new market-driven form, push technology could once again be an important way of reaching prospects, customers, and other constituents on an automatic, ongoing basis.

How would you apply push technology to your own electronic fulfillment? Instead of offering prospects or customers a few promotional pages to review when they visit your Web site or sending a periodic e-mail newsletter to their electronic mailboxes, you could deliver "personalized" Web pages with highly valued information to prospects and customers on a regular, complimentary basis. Prospects or customers would not have to go anywhere to gain access to the information they want—it would simply "appear" on their computer desktops.

This delivery method already is being used by major technology companies to automatically deliver software updates to customers. If push has a new life, it will probably be in the area of individualized corporate intranet and extranet use.

One vendor that has helped push move in this direction is Marimba *(www.marimba.com)*. Through its Castanet product suite, Marimba provides the ability to deliver what it calls "Internet Services Management" products for use across intranets and extranets. Specific customer examples include:

- Seagate Technology, which uses Castanet to deliver and update business applications such as sales forecasting and pricing information to its internal sales management, mobile sales force, and external OEM and distributor partners.

- Nortel Networks, which employs Castanet to provide uniform delivery and maintenance of its manufacturing test applications shared among internal employees and external contractors.

- Intuit, which embedded Castanet into its Quicken 99 personal finance software so millions of online users could receive software and information updates quickly and transparently.

In this context, push becomes an extension of a comprehensive Internet-based customer-service strategy. From a marketing perspective, what push really does is turn fulfillment into *cultivation*. Applied appropriately, push puts information into the hands of people who want it, regularly and automatically. They do not even have to ask for it more than once; it simply appears. With traditional media, a marketer would need to send a printed newsletter on a quarterly or bimonthly basis to accomplish this. The cost of database maintenance, print production, and mailing would be substantial. With the Internet, on the other hand, delivery is immediate and far more cost-effective.

This is no small issue for IT marketers who play in the business-to-business space. Products and services tend to be purchased by committees or groups in a business environment. The timing of purchases tends to correspond more to a company manager's available budget than to when that individual receives a promotional message. In the case of more-sophisticated, expensive products, there is often an evaluation-and-review process that could take considerable time before a purchase decision is made.

All of these factors contribute to the reality that, for many companies, the fulfillment of an inquiry is just the very first step in an ongoing mating dance between marketer and prospect. In some cases, a sales cycle can extend to 6, 9, 12, or 18 months or more. Periodic contact with the prospect during this extended period can be costly via traditional mail, and even more costly via telemarketing or sales calls, yet cultivating the prospect is imperative. Continuing to requalify the prospect's interest becomes just as important in an effort to get the cream to rise to the top.

With the inevitable dominance of the Internet as the core of business communication, it is likely that more and more business people will likely prefer to get their information electronically. IDC says that over 50 percent of online business people download information from the Internet several times a week.

Push technology offers a whole new form of fulfillment to marketers. Pushing information pages, special offers, and requalification forms to a targeted group of prospects could prove to be an expedient, low-cost method of direct marketing. It could extend the life of direct marketing campaigns and make them much more effective at an attractive incremental cost.

Push technology could offer a real service to prospects, fulfilling a need for automatically delivered information readily provided by marketers that "sponsor" its creation and delivery. If it is well executed, push technology could affordably and easily create a unique one-to-one relationship with prospects—a goal that many traditional high-end direct marketing programs strive for, but that is costly and logistically difficult to achieve.

Some Interesting Variations on Pushing Information

Some companies have made the most of the push concept and created what is, in effect, continuous Internet fulfillment. One interesting example is Individual.com *(www.individual.com)*, a unit of Office.com *(www.office.com)*. Individual.com (Figure 8.1) is the world's leading provider of free, individually customized news, information, and services to business people over the Internet. With over 1 million subscribers, Individual.com covers more than 1,000 topics, uses more than 40 news sources, and has information on more than 50,000 companies available. But the most interesting thing about Individual.com is the user's ability to create a completely customized news page and have it delivered daily to his or her desktop.

Basically, a user signs up for specific areas of interest through a simple registration process. The user's individual Web page contains his or her chosen topics, featured companies, personal stock quotes, and

Figure 8.1. With Individual.com, a user selects topic areas of interest and then receives relevant items on a personalized news page each day.

more. Each user receives a highly customized e-mail news briefing every business morning with headlines and summaries linked to stories on the individualized Web page. This is the ultimate in Internet fulfillment—free, valuable information, customized to your needs, available every day via e-mail or on the Web.

Another interesting example of Internet fulfillment of special relevance to IT marketers is a service from Hewlett-Packard called "Instant Delivery" (*www.instant-delivery.com*) (Figure 8.2). By installing free software that comes with an HP printer or is available via the Web, users get selected news and information delivered directly to their desktop printers. Instant Delivery records and remembers users' preferences. When information of interest in that category is available, the service delivers it over the Internet and prints it on the printer.

Of course, this is more than Internet fulfillment; it is an ingenious way for HP to keep in front of its customers and, incidentally, to make

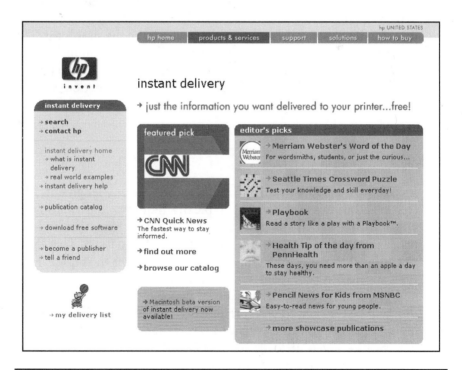

Figure 8.2. HP's "Instant Delivery" service automatically sends documents via the Web to a user's printer.

sure that those customers are consuming ink and paper which, hopefully, is ordered from HP!

The Unique Benefits of Fulfillment on the Internet

Regardless of the delivery method, electronic fulfillment can perform valuable functions that replace the need for paper-based fulfillment. These functions fall into several categories, listed here in order of "relationship intensity."

Acknowledgment

Just the act of immediately acknowledging an inquiry or order is a powerful communication technique. When a prospect or customer completes a Web response form and clicks the "Send" button, an acknowledgment page can instantaneously appear in response with the simple text, "Thank you. We have received your inquiry and will process it immediately." In a marketing world that has become depersonalized and automated, getting this type of acknowledgment in direct response to an action is reassuring. The impact of an Internet thank you cannot be minimized.

Confirmation

Electronic fulfillment can go beyond simple acknowledgment. The next step of a business relationship typically requires confirmation of specific information. When you call a toll-free phone number and place an order from a catalog, you interact with another person. This individual not only takes your order, but also confirms it over the phone. He or she typically will repeat your credit card number, verify your name and address, confirm the items you just ordered, and tell you the total amount that will be charged to your credit card. You will also know, before you hang up, when you can expect to receive the items you ordered. Often you will be given an order-confirmation number in case you have a problem with receiving the order.

If the same scenario just described takes place at a Web storefront today, the customer still has a need to know that the order has been confirmed. In fact, the need is greater, because there is no person-to-person voice contact—the order is being placed computer to computer.

Today's leading Internet-based order-generation companies recognize this. Most of them therefore build in a number of confirmation contacts that help to reassure the customer that the order has been properly filled. At the point of sale, for example, the customer is led through a question-and-answer process, entering necessary data along the way. At the end of this process, a built-in autoresponder feeds back all of the data at once, asking the customer to review it and make necessary changes before pushing the Send button one last time. This is an important step in the confirmation process, because the customer is taking responsibility for the accuracy of the transaction.

The next confirmation contact point is typically an e-mail to the customer restating the specifications of the order—now confirming that it was understood by the company and completing the confirmation loop by sending it directly to the user's mailbox. Confirmation at this stage is important for another reason—if the customer did not place the order, or the order is incorrect, the individual can take action at that point.

Finally, some Internet marketers take the confirmation process one step further, informing the customer that the order was shipped and when to expect its arrival. This step is obviously essential if there is a delay in the order, but it is just as useful and reassuring if the order is a normal shipment. Some marketers will include instructions for tracking the shipment at this stage, or even provide an online-tracking component to their Web site.

We have used an order-confirmation process as an example here, but confirmation just as easily applies to an inquiry from a prospect. It is particularly useful in confirming a prospect's attendance at a seminar, for example.

"Instant" Fulfillment

At its highest level of relationship intensity, electronic fulfillment functions as the channel for actual physical fulfillment. Again using traditional media as an example, fulfillment of an inquiry is most often handled through a paper-based transaction. In some cases, an inquiry may be fulfilled via fax, but most often the inquirer receives paper fulfillment, which may include a letter, data sheets, and brochures, perhaps packaged in a folder, all enclosed in a large envelope, and mailed or sometimes delivered via a package delivery service.

Even if the inquiry goes through a two-step fulfillment process, the individual receives, at the very least, a mailing with some additional information and a reply device designed to further qualify that person's interest. If the individual responds to this step, he or she will receive additional information from the marketer. Whatever the marketer sends, there will be a time lag unless the fulfillment is by fax only. That means a potentially hot prospect will continue to cool off as days or even weeks go by.

As previously discussed, traditional fulfillment is one of the weak links of the marketing process for many IT companies. Although it may be unrealistic to convert the entire paper fulfillment process to electronic fulfillment, moving toward fulfillment over the Internet has to be an attractive long-term alternative.

For one thing, electronic fulfillment is environmentally friendly. Traditional fulfillment is paper-based and labor-intensive. Electronic fulfillment, on the other hand, does not waste trees, ink, or time. It does not have to be produced in quantities of 1, 10, 50, or even 100,000. It does not have to be cut, folded, stapled, and inserted into folders and envelopes. It does not burden your staff (or postal service workers). In short, it saves natural resources, time, and money.

Now printed literature can have a longer shelf life, because time-sensitive information can just as easily be conveyed electronically, on the Web. Collateral materials can be mirrored electronically to leverage copy and artwork.

This extends far beyond the point of a casual convenience for prospects and customers. Electronic fulfillment is a desirable means of delivering information almost instantaneously—at a cost that is just too low to ignore. I have heard and read industry stories about large IT companies that are saving millions of dollars by replacing much of their printed fulfillment with electronic fulfillment. The need for printed literature still exists, but it can be substantially reduced with electronic fulfillment.

Electronic fulfillment provides customers and prospects with a new kind of "instant gratification." They can receive information instantly in an electronic form that can be viewed online or printed out and saved. They can just as easily unlock or download information of high-perceived value or software that they can demo, try, and buy, right from the computer desktop. Information can even be personalized to meet the individual's specific needs and be delivered free and on a regular basis to the individual's computer. Based on the individual's feedback, electronic fulfillment can be further tailored.

Electronic fulfillment thus becomes the beginning of a relationship. You can engage your prospect or customer in a dialogue, which allows you to continuously learn more about the individual's real needs. You can collect data from the prospect or customer by asking questions on electronic surveys and response forms and then turn the answers into *marketing intelligence*. You can then use this intelligence to build a highly effective communication program, tailored to individual needs. Database-driven electronic fulfillment ultimately meets the informational needs of many individuals, one person at a time.

Meanwhile, you drastically reduce the costs and lag time of traditional fulfillment. You develop an ongoing one-to-one relationship with the prospect or customer, learn more about that person's specific needs, and reap the financial and timesaving benefits of electronic fulfillment.

Instant Online Help

For IT companies, the help desk is a necessity, and now it can be fully Internet-enabled through the "intelligent" Web page, which knows what a visitor is doing, and can provide assistance on-demand. Intelligent software agents can respond to a visitor's question, for example, and even "learn" from the questions, offering more accurate answers as the process progresses. With the addition of such intelligent or active agents, marketers have the ability to feed individualized information to Web site visitors, based on the information visitors provide. For example, every time a prospect revisits a site, active-agent technology recognizes the visitor, calls up the visitor's profile, and guides the visitor to specific pages that would be of interest to him or her. Ultimately, targeted content can be delivered to each visitor to a site who is in the site's database.

Using push technology, the visitor does not even have to be online at the time. Active-agent technology also allows the marketer to communicate with that person proactively and automatically, transmitting relevant information to him or her as it becomes available.

Another form of instant online help is the comprehensive self-service system. Primarily for customer use, this system essentially allows a Web site visitor to resolve problems via a structured, intelligent online process. We discuss this in more detail in the next chapter.

One area of online help that is quite intriguing is "call-me" technology. Here is how it works: A visitor is navigating a Web site and comes across a product that seems interesting. The prospect has some questions that he or she wants to discuss with a salesperson immediately. The prospect clicks on a "Call Me" button found on the Web site. A dialog box pops up and requests the prospect's phone number. Meanwhile, the technology is alerting a salesperson and automatically calls the prospect.

When the salesperson engages the prospect on the phone, the technology can go a step further in the sales-assistance process. Now the salesperson can "take control" of the prospect's Web browser and actually walk him or her through product information, or redirect the prospect to other, more-appropriate Web pages. It is kind of like a virtual sales call. Obviously, the salesperson attempts to convert the prospect to a customer at the close of the session.

As these Internet telephony products and services become more available, usage will expand and extend into the area of online fulfillment. Imagine a marketing future in which both prospects and customers will largely be able to get all the assistance they require via the Internet, self-directed when necessary and enhanced by live sales support as needed.

Moving to Web-based Information Dissemination

Even if you acknowledge the need to move your paper fulfillment to the Web, how do you actually accomplish what could be a daunting, even overwhelming, task?

Start by doing a thorough inventory of all of your corporate literature and other collateral information. Determine which printed materials you currently use for fulfillment and how many different types of fulfillment packages you might have in existence.

Do a reality check: Are you sending too much literature to unqualified inquiries? Are you sending the right materials to qualified leads? Lay out all of the physical pieces you use for traditional fulfillment. Look them over and classify them as follows:

- General information about your company

- General information about product lines, services, or support

- Specific information about products or services, including data sheets, bulletins, and catalogs

Now reclassify these categories into "time-sensitive information" and "other." Put all the time-sensitive information in a priority pile. (Time-sensitive information is anything that will need to be updated periodically because of changes in specifications, deadlines, time limits, etc.)

After you have completed the classification process, you can begin to transition the printed literature to the Web. Convert the time-sensitive information first. It makes a lot of sense to look at electronic fulfillment as value-added fulfillment: Instead of arbitrarily loading all of your fulfillment literature onto the Web, focus on the information that is most time-sensitive and critical for the prospect to have immediately.

You have two basic options for electronic conversion of printed information: HTML pages and PDF files.

HTML Pages

To produce HTML pages, your printed literature will need to be converted to or written in HTML. Any graphics, illustrations, diagrams, charts, or photographs will have to be scanned or re-created. Depending on the way your information currently is stored, and the HTML tools you use to convert the documents, this could be a relatively easy task or a time-intensive, complex process.

Printed literature does not always transfer perfectly to the electronic medium. Dense blocks of text are difficult to read on a computer screen, some colors do not look the same, and photographs in particular can lose a lot of their definition on the Web because they must be converted to a lower resolution. You are wise to enlist the services of a creative resource skilled at electronic media.

HTML will probably continue to be the standard way of creating Web pages in the near term. Even with the proliferation of new technologies, HTML is prevalent across so much of the Web because it is universally viewable by any Web browser. As a result, if you are creating electronic fulfillment from scratch, you can probably use HTML as the safest "language" of choice. "Dynamic HTML" (DHTML) is also becoming more common. Basically, dynamic HTML adds more interaction and animation to HTML, breathing new life into it. One example of DHTML: When you go to a Web site and roll over a main link, you may see the contents for that link pop up on your screen. Then you can click on any of the sublinks. Although only the latest versions of Web browsers can view DHTML, its increasing usage probably means that HTML is likely to be with us for a while.

XML

The "competitor" to HTML is XML, the eXtensible Markup Language. XML usage is growing and it, too, could emerge as a standard way for exchanging data across the Internet. XML is an even more powerful language that incorporates document-management technology. According to industry reports in 2001, the XML standard will facilitate Web page development because it can be used to define what data page elements contain. Reportedly, Microsoft's ".Net" and Sun's "SunOne" will both employ XML.

PDFs

PDFs, or PDF files, are documents that are readable by the Adobe Acrobat Reader, which can be downloaded free at *www.adobe.com*. Adobe Acrobat has become the de facto standard tool for translating and posting printed literature to the Web. Once a piece of literature is in a PDF, it can be viewed in its "exact" format—with all typefaces, graphics, illustrations, and photographs in place—electronically.

To view the document, the visitor must have Adobe Acrobat Reader, but this program is free and can be downloaded from Adobe's Web site (through a link from your Web site, if you wish). Typically, the visitor downloads the PDF of interest and then opens it with Acrobat Reader on his or her desktop for viewing. The document can also be printed—but it cannot be modified in any way unless the visitor has the full version of Adobe Acrobat.

The PDF format avoids the time-consuming task of converting fulfillment literature into HTML, because converting printed documents to PDF is a fairly simple process of scanning and saving. You will notice that a majority of sites with heavy-duty information content that originated in printed format offer that content as PDFs.

After you have transitioned to electronic fulfillment, it is much easier to modify and disseminate content on the Web than via traditional methods. You can continue to convert printed literature into Web-based formats via HTML or as PDFs. Modifications can then be made in electronic format.

Electronic information dissemination has a number of benefits associated with it:

1. *Updating is easy and fast.* Unlike printed literature, you can update product information in real time and publish it to the Web on a moment's notice. This is a major benefit to companies that now depend on product data sheets and price lists. This type of information typically undergoes constant change. Printed formats take time to produce and the cost is high, especially for small print runs. Data sheets and price lists should be primary candidates for the transition to electronic information dissemination.

2. *Electronic product catalogs can be offered to prospects and customers.* As with a traditional catalog, the electronic catalog is a compendium of product information. Unlike a printed catalog, however, you can update the electronic catalog frequently and keep it current all the time. A properly designed electronic catalog can also be much easier to navigate and cross-reference than a printed catalog. Even if the catalog is for reference rather than for online purchase, it provides prospects and customers with an easy way to access information—and it provides you with a far less-expensive and more-timely marketing publication.

3. *Lead generation offer fulfillment is a natural for the Web.* You can encourage a prospect to respond via a campaign-specific URL and ask for a Web response form to be completed. When the form is sent, the prospect can instantly receive a copy of the offer (if it is information) or a demonstration or trial (if it is software). Electronic-offer fulfillment can eliminate the need for physical fulfillment or, at the very least, dramatically reduce the cost of traditional fulfillment as more prospects respond online. If you collect a prospect's e-mail address and ask permission to use it, you can then establish an e-mail communications program, again reducing the need for traditional mail contacts.

You could also use the Web to facilitate an online contest. A simple postcard mailing I received from one business-to-business marketer offered to enroll me in a monthly contest with cash prizes. The card carried a special number that when entered on the company's Web site (along with other information) would qualify me to win. This type of promotion is likely to generate a high number of "false positives"—individuals interested in winning, but not necessarily interested in the company's product—but it is an interesting concept that may have merit depending on the circumstances.

4. *The Web facilitates individualization of online fulfillment.* Here are a few examples:

   – Online fulfillment can be individualized by relating the response received to a question to the corresponding information. For example, when a prospect or customer responds to a certain question using multiple-choice answers, each of those answers could be linked to a particular Web page, or several answers could be combined to dynamically generate the specific information of interest to the inquiring individual.

   – Web sites with search tools allow visitors to find the specific information they are looking for, quickly and easily. The built-in search engine uses key words to search a database of Web pages and reports the result of the search to the visitor. Then the visitor can select the appropriate page from the list provided. Some sites license search technology from other vendors for use on their own sites. In fact, search engines are increasingly common on Web sites. As the amount and depth of content increases, search functionality will become a necessity for many sites.

   – "Solution databases" are increasing in popularity as marketers build areas into Web sites that help prospects and customers customize their search for solutions. In this online fulfillment application, a database of potential solutions is created and visitors are invited to define certain criteria to execute a search. The search then picks the most appropriate solution(s) and delivers the proper Web pages to the visitor. The visitor gets the impression that the solution has been customized to his or her needs when, in fact, it was simply assembled from information residing in a searchable database.

The CD/Web Connection

Now that virtually all PCs include high-speed CD drives, it is a rare software program that is delivered on diskettes. Most software, from operating systems to applications to games, is disseminated via CD or over the Internet. As a result, the CD is enjoying new popularity among business-to-consumer and business-to-business marketers alike.

Do you know anyone who *has not* received an America Online CD in the mail? AOL has grown its subscriber base to nearly 29 million, largely because of this direct marketing technique. I bought a music CD recently, only to find that America Online had worked a deal with the music company to put its software on it.

As a marketing medium, the CD has great value due to a number of significant benefits:

- CDs hold a huge amount of data, so a marketer is unlikely ever to run out of room, no matter how much information must be conveyed.

- Depending on the speed of the user's CD drive, a CD can contain remarkably sophisticated programs, incorporating everything from sound to motion to movies to fully integrated multimedia productions. With newer CD drives, speed will not be an issue; in fact, a CD-ROM that runs at "20X" is twice as fast as a T1 Internet connection, and now "50X" drives are becoming standard. The implications are that CDs can offer much faster delivery of graphics-rich, data-intensive content than can the Internet for most users.

- CDs take advantage of the "one-to-many" software manufacturing principle: The first one, or the master, is expensive to produce, but subsequent copies are cheap. That is one of the reasons America Online can distribute millions of CDs through the mail.

- CDs are durable, lightweight, stable, nonmagnetic, and nearly indestructible. This makes them ideal for mailing purposes. They can be silk-screen printed with colorful graphics and packaged in everything from CD cases to simple paper covers. Because they are "hard goods," they have a perceived value associated with tangible items.

- CDs can be built as "hybrids"—they can feature "collaboration" between the content on the CD and content on the Web.

- A CD can be programmed to provide seamless access to a Web site through the user's Web browser.

Some marketers have figured out a way to turn the CD/Web connection into a direct marketing concept. They utilize the CD as the core of a promotional mailing to select prospects, using Web-style content on the CD, and tell the recipients to go to a Web site or call an 800 number to unlock the CD content. Of course, the CD content better be worth it. This is no different from getting a "key" from a software vendor to unlock and use a program from a CD, but it is a novel way to leverage the CD/Web connection.

The Kiosk/Web Connection

Although kiosks are primarily used in a retail environment, their time may be coming as a viable IT marketing tool that puts even more prospects in touch—literally—with your products.

Interactive kiosks with touch screens are now in use as informational vehicles in malls, retail stores, and airports. A shopper with no computer skills can walk up to a mall kiosk and locate stores. In the retail store, the shopper can locate departments and read about the day's sale items.

Now there is a growing trend for kiosks to be Web-enabled. A kiosk can be designed to house local versions of Web sites and pages so that a connection to the Internet is unnecessary. Web-enabled kiosks suggest a host of future possibilities for business-to-business marketers. They may be particularly effective in reaching the growing SOHO (Small Office Home Office) shopper.

Suppose just such a shopper walks into an office superstore during a lunch hour. The shopper finds that there are not enough salespeople, so he or she walks over to the touch kiosk prominently displayed at the front of the store. With a few touches on the screen, the shopper can find and compare computers, or other products, and their prices. For example, let us say he or she is looking for a new computer printer. Your company, which manufactures the printer, happens to be running a special that month, and you have purchased advertising space on the chain's kiosks.

The shopper notices your kiosk banner ad and touches it. The banner ad links to local Web pages that you downloaded from your corporate Web site. Those pages were electronically transmitted earlier that month to the chain's advertising department, which distributed the pages to the store kiosks.

The shopper sees that you are offering a special in-store discount on a particular model. The shopper touches an area on the screen, and an in-store coupon instantly comes out of the kiosk's thermal printing unit. The shopper looks for and finds the printer, likes its features, and likes the discounted price even better. She decides to buy the printer and take advantage of the special price.

In fact, the Internet is now being used to enhance the traditional in-store retail experience. Kmart and Sears already offer access to online information to shoppers via in-store intranet kiosks.

Internet-enabled kiosks are making their move not only in stores, but in places where businesses can reach business people—like airports. Typically, these are kiosks that are really enhancements to phone service, offering business travelers the ability to send a fax or check e-mail, but it may not be long before they also allow travelers to request information online or even place orders for products online.

Telecommunications carriers are also using touch screens with telephones and mini-kiosks to enhance telephone service. These interactive devices may not be Internet-enabled today, but they could be in the future. The technology to turn kiosks into freestanding Web stations is already here—it is just a matter of implementing it. Airlines are already offering online kiosks for e-ticketing at airports, and e-mail access at airports is becoming more common.

And it will not end there. The Internet is making its appearance in the most interesting, and sometimes unusual, places. Some bank ATMs now offer Web browsing. And now Web pages are popping up in office building elevators and even restrooms.

Future Information Dissemination Channels

You are likely to see many variations on a theme when it comes to future information dissemination. Some emerging concepts promise to make future electronic fulfillment even more effective. One area of fast growth on the Web in the business-to-business space is the *Web community*—a kind of online mall, but with true community components, such as discussion forums, chats, newsletters, job banks, and more.

The Web community is a place where information—lots of it—is shared by companies with common interests or goals. The information providers pool their information to an information publisher, which sponsors a single "supersite" to disseminate the information.

Web communities function as large electronic directories or catalogs of information for a rich variety of sources, each of which is available on or accessible through a single site. Communities also offer information providers the ability to interact with their constituencies and effectively expose new audiences to the providers' messages. In most cases, communities are free to users, as long as the users register (and therefore provide contact information that can be used by both the community and the participating information providers).

In addition to communities whose primary goal is to disseminate information, there are now business-to-business communities whose primary goal is to sell products from a single location. These communities are especially interesting because they are redefining the rules of e-commerce. Typically, a consortium of companies agrees to place its products for sale on a single site, providing customers with a single point of contact, a single invoice, and centralized order processing. These companies extend their presence, their buying power, and their market by collaborating.

Communities have become such a significant trend, in fact, that an entire chapter (Chapter 10) has been devoted to the topic.

Creating Online Demos and Trials

Online fulfillment holds great promise in the context of printed information that is converted to the electronic medium, but there is an even more exciting aspect to electronic fulfillment—online demos and trials.

The Web has become a major marketing medium for IT marketers, primarily software companies, that now use it as a giant arena for delivering online product demonstrations and trials. An "online demo" of a software product can be executed in a few different ways. Probably the least desirable is an actual interactive demo that happens on the Web in real time. A "live" demo can be affected by too many factors beyond the marketer's control—the Internet connection or Web traffic, the nature of the user's transmission device, the target computer's capabilities, and so on. Nevertheless, some marketers execute fast-running live demos in real time right over the Web.

An alternative is the online demo that simulates the product's capabilities or includes a partially live demonstration. This type of demo is more of a guided tour or walk-through of the software—it allows some limited, preprogrammed interaction by the prospect in an effort to convey the basic product benefits and features. A product tour can also be executed in the context of an online seminar, in which a presenter walks through the demo as part of the agenda. A demo of this sort can be even more effective if it is tied together with an offer of a full CD demo—which the prospect can request in return for completing a Web response form.

The most common demo format is the download. And yes, there is an entire Web site devoted to software downloads at, where else, *www.download.cnet.com.* The download typically is a compressed file that the prospect copies, expands with common utility software, and then opens on the computer desktop in "offline" mode. The download has several advantages:

- The prospect does not have to be online to interact with the demo. The demo runs off of the prospect's computer, not off of the marketer's Web site.

- The demo can contain multimedia (sound and motion), as well as interactivity, which is unencumbered by technology issues surrounding electronic media transmission.

- The demo can be delivered online, instantly and free—the prospect does not have to wait for a disk or CD to arrive.

- The demo can also be set up as a *trial*—it can be the real software product that the prospect tries for a period of time and then purchases if desired. In such cases, the software is programmed to time out after 30 or 60 days.

Order E-Fulfillment and Distributing Live Products over the Internet

Order e-fulfillment is crucial to the success of any e-commerce operation. It appears, however, that for many companies, e-fulfilling orders is no easy task. In May 2000, Bain & Company in association with Mainspring issued a series of studies that suggested order e-fulfillment needed to be significantly improved. During Mother's Day 2000, the studies said, as many as 30 percent of all orders were unfulfilled.

The ultimate in instant gratification is when a customer can receive a live product online. Entire companies are being built around the concept of electronic product delivery—some at the outset, and some because they have no choice.

Consider the case of Egghead, a company that, at its high point, sold software in 250 retail stores. But then, on the verge of bankruptcy in January 1998, Egghead announced that it would close its remaining 80 stores, change its name to Egghead.com (*www.egghead.com*), and move its entire sales operation to the Web. The company literally reinvented itself as an online merchant and aggressively marketed its products through affiliate programs. Now Egghead.com offers a discount software superstore, a computer-products superstore, an online liquidation center, and online auctions at its heavily trafficked site. In July 1999, Egghead.com merged with Internet rival Onsale.com (*www.onsale.com*) in a deal valued at $400 million.

Although there are endless numbers of companies selling and delivering software via the Internet, more than a few are inventing entirely new ways to fulfill their customers. CyberMedia (*www.mcafee.com/cybermedia*) was so successful at it, they were purchased by the McAfee Software Division of Network Associates. CyberMedia saw the potential of e-fulfillment and created a novel product called Oil Change, which has become a software bestseller. You install Oil Change on your PC and it checks the software you have, goes on the Internet, and finds, downloads, and installs the appropriate updates, patches, and bug fixes for more than 6,500 software programs. Oil Change costs less than $50 and is continually updated via the Internet on a subscription basis for a few dollars a year. It could represent a new class of facilitating software that will make the Internet all the more useful for the business person and consumer alike.

Anything that can be committed to an electronic format can be distributed live over the Internet. Any product with information at its core can be delivered over the Web. Information products—research reports, survey results, white papers, subscription e-mail newsletters, and the like—are all being sold electronically.

It is not only IT companies that are succeeding at selling information electronically. One of the non-high tech B-to-B success stories on the Internet is *The Wall Street Journal Interactive Edition* (*www.wsj.com*). The venerable business daily has aggressively marketed its Internet version with a two-week free trial, offering print subscribers the special price of $29 annually, versus $59 for new, nonprint subscribers. Publisher Dow Jones wisely made sample content from the Interactive Edition available free on the Web site so nonsubscribers could see its value. The Interactive Edition already has a paid subscriber base of several hundred thousand. Media reports in May 2001 indicated that *The New York Times* would follow suit with paid services.

The line between electronic inquiry fulfillment and order fulfillment continues to blur. IT marketers are anxious to find new ways to qualify prospects, shorten the sales cycle, and, if possible, get prospects and customers to purchase over the Internet. Even if the product itself is not Web-deliverable, product update and service information can easily be delivered electronically via e-mail or over the Web.

Internet-enabled delivery of products obviously goes beyond the scope of electronic lead fulfillment. It is an area the IT marketer should carefully watch. As information and services become products, the Internet becomes a powerful delivery channel for them.

Ultimately, the potential for order e-fulfillment is virtually unlimited for IT marketers. The cost reduction associated with order e-fulfillment is tantalizing. According to the Organisation for Economic Co-operation and Development (*www.oecd.org*), it costs just 50 cents to distribute a software product electronically versus $15 traditionally. And it doesn't have to be just software.

Airlines and e-travel services are seeing enormous benefits from order e-fulfillment. Airlines encourage online customers, particularly business travelers who order last-minute tickets, to use electronic ticketing instead of paper tickets. E-tickets have substantially reduced the cost of doing business for airlines, and the growth of e-ticketing by airlines and travel services such as Biztravel (*www.biztravel.com*), Expedia (*www.expedia.com*), and Travelocity (*www.travelocity.com*) is expected to skyrocket. By eliminating the physical packaging and documentation for a software product, the entire cost structure of marketing and sales can shift dramatically. For IT marketers, e-fulfillment could be a dream fulfilled.

E-Fulfillment Resources and Services

Listed here are just some of the many services available to IT marketers which may help facilitate e-fulfillment. Numerous customer relationship management (CRM) products and services now include e-fulfillment components, so if you need a broader solution, you would be wise to expand your search to CRM tools. We discuss CRM in further detail in the next chapter.

DHL (*www.dhlmasterclass.com*)
DHL, an air express company that specializes in international package delivery, offers a site called DHL Masterclass to assist small and medium-sized companies transition from traditional to e-business. The site includes resources, information and tips on fulfillment, logistics, customer-relationship management, and supply chain management.

FedEx (*www.fedex.com*)
FedEx has taken a new turn in e-commerce and fulfillment by announcing a service to help small and mid-size companies build online stores. The FedEx service links the company's electronic delivery and tracking capabilities to each online store, which can be set up in a matter of minutes.

MarketFirst (*www.marketfirst.com*)
MarketFirst is a software company that provides a true end-to-end, comprehensive automated marketing platform. MarketFirst offers a marketing knowledge base, campaign design and execution technologies, workgroup collaboration, real-time media preference management, and reporting and measurement capabilities in an integrated, open-computing environment. Their "eMarketing Blueprint" applications are templates that get systems up and running quickly. MarketFirst also offers Web-hosting services to allow immediate implementation of automated marketing programs. IT users include Autodesk, Quantum, and SalesLogix.

MarketSoft (*www.marketsoft.com*)
MarketSoft has a solution that it says solves the lead-management problem. MarketSoft's eLeads is an Internet-based system that combines e-business with traditional selling models to ensure that the right

leads get to the right people at the right time, measuring results as part of a closed-loop process. MarketSoft's eOffers improves the timeliness and relevancy of offers and promotions delivered to customers. Both products combine to form The Marketing Network, which the company says can accelerate buying cycles and sustain the growth and retention of new customers. IT users include Compaq, Covad, Ingram Micro, and Microsoft.

NetQuartz (*www.netquartz.com*)

If you use trial downloads or CDs to sell software, NetQuartz offers an interesting product called LinkStudio that lets you track, control, and communicate with your prospects over the Internet while they are running your trial. When prospects actually run the trial, LinkStudio informs you, and a built-in e-mail service allows communication with each active user during the trial. LinkStudio also handles beta feedback, online software rental, license management, and secure rights management.

Netship (*www.netship.com*)

Netship allows small and medium-size businesses to set up their own nationwide distribution network. Netship has networked over 450 Netship centers across the United States through its Web site to provide local support, competitive rates, and service through major shipping carriers. Netship centers act as virtual warehouses, holding inventory and picking, packing, and shipping orders on demand. Using Netship.com, a company can get instant online quotes and up-to-the-minute shipment, warehousing, packaging, fulfillment, tracking, and inventory control. Netship is operated by Parcel Plus, Inc., a major package-delivery franchiser.

SubmitOrder (*www.submitorder.com*)

Claiming to have coined the term *e-fulfillment,* SubmitOrder.com is a pure play e-fulfillment service provider. The company provides e-fulfillment customers with everything from Web site development to inventory management, order fulfillment and processing, "pick, pack, and ship" services, and integrated call center services. E-fulfillment strategic planning and integration, e-tail distribution, customer response, and e-tail business support are also parts of the service. Users of SubmitOrder.com include ZanyBrainy.com, MuseumCompany.com, and indulge.com.

UPS (*www.ups.com*)

UPS, the world's largest express carrier and package-delivery company, has done nothing short of reinvent its traditional business to become an e-fulfillment and e-commerce leader. In April 2000, UPS received the prestigious MIT Sloan School of Management "Clicks & Mortar" Award for "the greatest advancement in integrating both physical and online business practices." UPS has developed the fastest and most advanced Internet-based package-tracking system, along with UPS Document Exchange (the digital Internet delivery service), eVentures (an e-business incubator for Internet start-ups), and UPS OnLine Tools (which enables businesses to integrate transportation information throughout their Web operations and other business processes). In April 2000, UPS Capital Corporation, the financial services arm of UPS, announced that it would offer B-to-B customers the first fully integrated means to link the delivery of goods with information and the accelerated delivery of funds via EBPP (electronic bill presentment and payment) solutions.

9

Internet Customer Service

Customer relationship management (CRM), second only to e-commerce, has become the fastest growing area of Internet marketing. AMR Research (*www.amrresearch.com*) estimates that the market for CRM will grow to $16.8 billion by the year 2003, from $3.7 billion in 1999.

In many ways, the Internet has become a symbol of the ultimate customer relationship for both business-to-consumer and B-to-B marketers. That, at least, seems to be the case among many of the top e-commerce players. Over 90 percent of these leaders are committed to customer loyalty programs, according to a 1999 research study by IDC. Close to three-quarters of the firms researched use personalization and mass customization to help increase customer retention, and almost half of them are modeling the Lifetime Values of their customers.

Numerous studies support the fact that building customer relationships is far and away the most important undertaking for the Internet marketer. April 2000 statistics from the Boston Consulting Group indicate that 28 percent of all online purchases are unsuccessful. Twenty-three percent of online shoppers who have unsuccessful experiences say they will not buy again from the site at which they encountered a problem. March 2000 studies jointly conducted by Bain & Company and Mainspring show that online retailers lose money on shoppers who visit only once, but that repeat purchasers spend more money over time. Customer loyalty went beyond dollars alone. The studies found that an online shopper who purchased apparel from a Web site referred three people to that site after his or her first purchase. A purchaser of consumer electronics, after ten purchases from a Web site, referred 13 people to that Web site. In short, happy online customers are a great source for word-of-mouth advertising.

eCRM, or electronically serving a single customer's needs in an individualized fashion, 24 hours a day, 7 days a week, anywhere in the world—even with a customer base of thousands or millions—is now a reality. Innovations such as customer self-service areas, Internet-based help desks, intelligent search engines, solution databases, and "call-me" buttons on Web sites are making this kind of customer service a new standard. The Internet presents a cost-effective and lasting way of building all-important relationships with customers. As a result, the Internet is fulfilling the promise of a true one-to-one marketing medium.

In this chapter, we look at what the Internet has to offer to IT marketers who want to build and enhance relationships with their customers.

Building Better Customer Relationships

The business reality of today and tomorrow is that customers have many choices—and they are exercising their options aggressively. As one piece of evidence of the dramatic shift in customer loyalty, you would be hard-pressed to find any IT manager at a sizable company in the world today who would brag about his or her fierce loyalty to a single computer manufacturer. There still may be "IBM shops" or "HP departments"—but commingled hardware is as common in most IT organizations as coffee and creamer are in the company cafeteria. That is why one of the fastest growing businesses in the IT industry is systems integration. If anything, hardware and software companies are developing products that work better together with their competitors' products than ever before. Now, a major computer company's service organization is often as skilled in servicing its competitors' products as it is in servicing its own gear.

This is just as true of any customer-driven business. Unfortunately, your customer is just as likely to be your competitor's customer. Buyers are not exhibiting the kind of loyalty that may have anchored their purchases in the past. Products have become commodities, and choices are many. Where loyalty does exist, it is frequently connected to the service and support provided by a company rather than to the product itself.

The issue of customer loyalty has pervaded business to such an extent that perhaps the number one business book topic in the past few years (other than the Internet) is customer service and customer loyalty. There are business conferences and seminars devoted to customer service, magazines that highlight it, and Web sites that discuss it, such as CRMCommunity (*www.crmcommunity.com*), CRMDaily *(www.crmdaily.com)*, and CRMGuru (*www.crmguru.com*).

Marketers now use numerous programmatic techniques to attack the issue of customer loyalty. Arguably the best-known customer loyalty program in existence is the frequent traveler program. Pioneered by major airlines, frequent traveler/frequent buyer programs now abound. Hotels and rental car companies have them. Restaurants participate in them. Some credit card companies turn them into "Membership Miles" (American Express) or other kinds of frequent-purchase rewards programs.

To what extent do the airlines' frequent traveler programs really create loyal customers? Opinion is mixed. Although frequent business travelers will often select an airline because they are building mileage credit, they will just as often join numerous airline frequent traveler programs so that they can switch airlines with little downside effect when the need arises. Industry data seems to suggest that the top priority of most frequent business travelers is flight schedule, not the mileage credit accumulated in an airline's frequent traveler program, which brings into question the effectiveness of such programs in truly cementing customer loyalty.

Brand preference in the airline industry may be a bad example. Domestic flights have so proliferated that one airline's schedule is sometimes indistinguishable from other airlines. Frequent travelers complain that the same is true of the service. The fact is that the traveler has so many choices that no airline is a clear-cut winner. That phenomenon is pervasive in other businesses as well. Look at the credit card, automobile, and gasoline industries.

Competition always seems to exist for IT marketers as well, whether it is direct or indirect. Even channel conflict can play a role in fostering unwanted competition.

The trick, then, is to create reasons, even opportunities, for your customers to gravitate toward you when the need arises. More to the point, your goal should be to *create loyal major customers*—buyers who continue to do business with you, preferably building a more important mutually beneficial relationship with your company over time.

Using the Internet to Learn What Customers Want

There are two basic strategies you will need to employ concurrently to build better customer relationships with the Internet: maintaining ongoing relationships with your most-valued customers, and moving other customers up "the marketing pyramid" so that they can reach most-valued-customer status.

Maintaining Ongoing Relationships with Your Most Valued Customers

What do *you* value most about a business relationship? Is it the fact that the other party knows you personally? Understands your needs? Keeps in touch? Makes you aware of valuable offers, new products, and other useful information? Provides you with superb service? Solves problems quickly and to your satisfaction? Remembers what you like? Makes it worth your while to continue the relationship? Shows appreciation for your business?

It is probably all of these things—some of which may be more important to you than others. It is that complex thing called the business relationship, and understanding all of the attributes of the business relationship, that is the beginning of successful customer relationships.

By combining database-marketing technology with the customer-enhancing power of the Internet, it is within your reach to develop a one-to-one relationship with your customer. In fact, it is the Internet that now offers marketers the missing piece of the customer relationship puzzle: real-time interactivity.

You can start at the most basic level of Internet customer marketing by implementing an *e-mail customer survey*. Collect customers' e-mail addresses, construct a simple survey that polls them about their needs, and send it out. Make it easy for customers to respond—tell them to simply put X marks next to multiple-choice answers. Provide a space for additional comments, but keep open-ended questions to a minimum. Then ask your customers to reply to the e-mail survey by a specified date.

Alternatively, invite customers via e-mail to participate in the survey by visiting a special URL. Set up a Web page of questions, similar to a Web response form. That way, you can employ a user-friendly format to take the answers to survey questions.

Your customers have a vested interest in providing you with feedback. Some companies spend thousands of dollars holding in-person focus group sessions with a small number of customers to learn about their needs. Others invest in telemarketing surveys that never get through to a majority of their customers. A customer e-mail survey offers you the opportunity to inexpensively break through to many customers at once and get useful data quickly. Traditional direct mail customer surveys are known to generate 15 percent, 20 percent, or even higher response rates. You should be able to achieve that kind of response with a customer e-mail survey.

If you are in a position to go beyond the e-mail survey, you should consider building some sort of customer relationship program via the Internet, if only with your most-valued customers. Your program could be as simple as a periodic e-mail newsletter delivered to a customer's e-mail box each month or as elaborate as a menu of customer-driven information choices, personalized to each individual's special requirements and needs, or it could become the Internet version of a *customer loyalty program.*

IT marketers are executing Internet-based customer programs that are models for success. For example, some years ago, IBM *(www.ibm.com)* created a customer contact program called *Focusing on You* that makes methodical use of a customer marketing database and uses the Internet as the information delivery vehicle. IBM diligently captures customer data and aggressively applies it in a "consensual database program" to understand and meet customer information needs on a completely individualized basis.

Focusing on You is not based on pie-in-the-sky technology—it relies primarily on e-mail and the simplest of Web site pages. The real key is the strategy behind *Focusing on You,* as Michelle Lanter Smith, direct marketing manager for IBM, explains:

> *It is very tempting as the marketer of a product or service to try to control the messages you want delivered to your customers. However, in today's reality of competition and easy access to numerous sources of information, it is not a strategy that will work very long or very well. Customers know that they have much more power than they had yesterday, so they expect to be able to control the information they receive, especially from a large vendor like IBM. With the* Focusing on You *program we give them that power. We ask them to tell us*

what they want to hear about (they select from topics listed on an interest profile) and then we store this information along with demographic data on a relational database.[1]

You can see from this program description that IBM's philosophy is to *empower* the customer in the relationship. The company lets customers make the decision as to what they want to receive in the way of information, and even how they wish to receive it.

The benefits of a program such as *Focusing on You* extend beyond the value inherent in building solid customer relationships:

- The data received directly from the customer is "much more valuable than purchased data," says Lanter Smith, because it is straight from the source. Because the data is not being filtered through another party or purchased from an outside source, IBM gets to hear what its customers want, first hand.

- Lanter Smith reports that the company has seen "significantly higher responses in many instances" when comparing e-mail campaign messages to direct mail results. Results are fast, too—one e-mail campaign generated one third of all responses in just 24 hours. Additionally, there is some evidence that pass-along of e-mail is beating direct mail pass-along by two to one.

- The program is extremely cost-effective because it relies heavily on e-mail marketing. Lanter Smith estimates that sending customers traditional printed materials, such as brochures and binders, as part of a one-to-one customer relationship program is "at least 10 times more expensive" than e-mail communications.

Moving Your Customers Up the "Marketing Pyramid"

The second basic strategy is to move other customers up the marketing pyramid—until they reach most-valued-customer status. The marketing pyramid is a visual way of depicting customer value. It helps you separate customers into groups, typically from the greatest number of customers at the bottom of the pyramid, to the smallest number of customers at the top.

Look at the marketing pyramid in Figure 9.1 and you will see that there are five segments, from A at the top to E at the bottom. As customers move from E up to A, they are building a relationship with your company. For example, perhaps the customers in segment E purchased a single product from you, but the customers in segment C purchased several products along with support services.

As customers move up the marketing pyramid, they increase in value to your company. In most IT companies, you will find that the number of customers in each successive segment is smaller. That's why the customers at the top are the most valuable, because they do the most business with your company. Some customers may never get there, but cultivating customer relationships will surely move others to that "Golden Triangle" at the top of the pyramid. The very special customers in the Triangle may make up only 20 percent of your customer base,

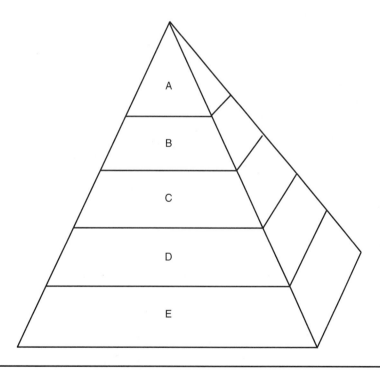

Figure 9.1. The "Marketing Pyramid" shows audience segments from largest and least important (E) to smallest and most important (A).

but they could be responsible for 80 percent of your revenue. (This, by the way, is the "80/20 Rule," a common marketing paradigm.)

One logical way to move customers along is "upselling." Upselling is a technique that marketers can use to encourage customers to purchase additional products or services.

IT marketers are experts at upselling. If someone purchases a computer system directly from a computer manufacturer, he or she will undoubtedly be a target for upselling. Not only will customers receive notification of the availability of other computer systems, perhaps at preferred customer pricing, they will also receive a host of promotions from other company divisions. They may, for example, receive a catalog of software marketed by the manufacturer that relates specifically to the system purchased. They may also be notified of supplies or accessories available directly from the manufacturer (sometimes called "aftermarket selling"). They will almost certainly be solicited by the company's service organization.

The customer upselling practice has been easy to implement through telemarketing, direct mail, and retail outlets, and it is now possible to implement it online with newer database-driven Web technologies. Marketers can use the information from their customer databases to dynamically generate Web pages that are individualized to a customer's needs. Pages can even be generated on the fly as a customer "walks through" a Web site.

The potential for upselling and cross-selling products to customers is sure to increase dramatically as the appropriate Internet tools increasingly become available. In fact, just the very concept of customized Web pages is likely to drive customers higher up the pyramid.

We can use IBM as an example in this section as well, because the company has recognized the value of its top customers via its "Gold Service" program. IBM created Gold Service to recognize special corporate customers more than five years ago and has expanded it to more than 300 corporate customers. Today, each Gold Service customer gets access to a special IBM Web site developed just for the organization's individual needs.

IBM encourages usage of the special site by direct mailing Welcome packages to every executive and IT staff member at the customer's location. The Welcome package includes a personal profile survey that helps IBM personalize all further communications. Virtually 100 percent of the respondents choose e-mail as their preferred method of correspondence.

According to e-newsletter *B2B Marketing Biz* (*www.b2bmarketingbiz .com*), IBM reports that average revenues for accounts enrolled in the Gold Service program increase by more than 30 percent per year. Response rates to e-mailed offers can reach as high as 16 percent, with up to 22 percent of responses coming from colleagues of users in the database who received pass-along e-mail offers.

Internet-Based Customer Service

Customer service is a primary area that can keep your customers satisfied and intensify their relationship with your company. Internet-based customer service can now incorporate customer call centers built on Internet telephony technology, interactive chat rooms, and 24-hour-a-day, 7-day-a-week customer service support areas with "smart" databases that help customers solve their own problems.

How important is customer service? A study released in November 1999 by Servicesoft (now part of Broadbase) indicated that 87 percent of online shoppers who spent $2,000 or more on the Web in the past six months will abandon a merchant's Web site and click to a competitor's if they experience bad customer service. Seventy-nine percent of these shoppers said they have increased their patronage and spending on a Web site when the customer service experienced is favorable. The study, conducted by Socratic Technologies, surveyed a total of 836 online customer service users during October 1999.

New customer service products abound—some of which are remarkable. Following is a sampling of just some of the innovative companies offering products and services in this burgeoning area.

Aspect *(www.aspect.com)*

Aspect's approach is to create a "Customer Relationship Portal," a package of software products that perform a range of Customer Relationship Management tasks. The company claims that its "multimedia" portal makes it possible to accept contacts from customers via fax, e-mail, the Web, and the telephone and route them to a single contact center, where agents can handle all media according to established criteria. Agents can then communicate with Web customers using text chat, IP telephony or whiteboarding, or answer e-mail with software that allows them to reply using prewritten responses.

ATG *(www.atg.com)*

ATG's "Dynamo Server" is a high-powered personalization engine that drives customized Web pages and enables scalable CRM and e-commerce solutions to be implemented. This is the technology behind the "My Sun" page (Figure 9.2) described in Chapter 3.

BEA *(www.beasys.com)*

The BEA E-Commerce Transaction Platform is used by such companies as Amazon.com, FedEx, Kaiser Permanente, DIRECTV, and United Airlines. Amazon.com uses it to help its customers shop for an increasing variety of products over the Web. FedEx uses it for its package-tracking

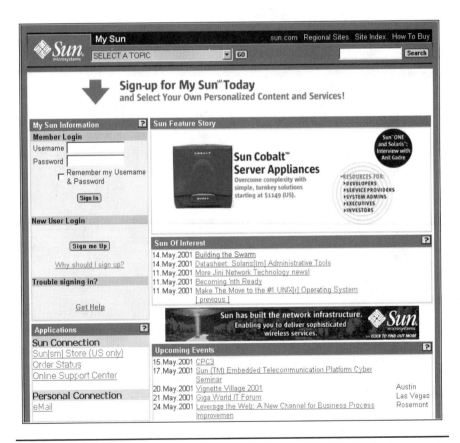

Figure 9.2. The "My Sun" page allows customers to change the look and feel of the page, set personal links, customize a stock portfolio, and more.

and logistics system, which handles an average of 36 million transactions daily to track 3 million packages delivered to 211 countries every weekday.

Bowstreet *(www.bowstreet.com)*

Bowstreet's "Business Web Factory" uses templates that contain data, behavioral information, procedures, and business policies so that programmers can quickly establish Web pages. With the templates in place, nontechnical managers can then create their own Web sites for a customer or groups of customers, simply by linking the templates that define customer relationships.

Brightware *(www.brightware.com)*

Intelligent agents are one of the keys to facilitating personalized customer service on the Internet. Brightware offers Answer Agent, which fields questions from customers and replies itself via e-mail. Answer Agent generates information for customers on the fly, based on the questions asked, right up to the point of ordering, if appropriate.

Broadvision *(www.broadvision.com)*

Numerous companies provide Internet-based personalized customer communications solutions, but it was Broadvision that first appropriated and trademarked the concept of one-to-one marketing on the Internet. Broadvision One-to-One is a software application system for large-scale personalized Internet, intranet, and extranet business applications. As one example of its success, Broadvision reports that it helped GE Supply achieve a 90 percent unassisted order rate, with a 42 percent increase in the size of online orders.

ePage *(www.epage.com)*

ePage is a solution developed by HomePage.com, a home page Application Service Provider. ePage allows users to easily create a personalized Web page for each customer where product information is stored and managed. Customized information, such as product warranties, owner manuals, purchase and customer service records, is maintained to create a one-to-one relationship.

E.piphany *(www.epiphany.com)*

A comprehensive solution of interest to IT marketers might be the E.piphany e.4 System from E.piphany. This Enterprise Relationship

Management suite of 16 Web-based, packaged solutions is designed to "mass customize 1-to-1 interactions," says the company. With such users as Charles Schwab, Hewlett-Packard, KPMG, and Wells Fargo, the company's technology is helping to drive the concept of one-to-one customer relationship-building.

eShare Technologies (*www.eshare.com*)

A total-solution provider of Customer Interaction Management (CIM) solutions, eShare Technologies has more than 2,200 customers in over 30 countries, including AOL, AT&T Worldnet, and Lycos. The company offers unified Web and telephony interactive customer contact management, including e-mail response, real-time customer interaction, chat and bulletin boards, instant messaging, and inbound/outbound and contact management.

Kana *(www.kana.com)*

There is now an entire breed of software serving what is known as the "Online Customer Management (OCM) market" which, by 2002, should reach close to $700 million, says Forrester Research. Kana is a leader in OCM (or eRM, Enterprise Relationship Management), and it has acquired a number of companies in pursuing an aggressive growth strategy. In December 1999, Kana acquired Business Evolution, Inc. (BEI), a supplier of Web-based customer assistance and support software, and NetDialog, a provider of self-service customer care solutions. In 2000, Kana merged with a leading provider of customer self-service, Silknet. One of the first vendors to successfully enter the customer support market, Silknet created eService customer interaction software, an enterprise-wide Web-based customer interaction application that extends beyond a company's call center out to the customer. It integrates multiple means of customer interaction, allowing the management of phone, e-mail, and Web communications, all in one application. In early 2001, Kana merged again with Broadbase, a CRM software vendor.

LivePerson *(www.liveperson.com)*

LivePerson's technology allows visitors to e-commerce sites to engage in real-time text conversations with customer service representatives. Customers can instantly chat online to ask questions, make inquiries, and receive assistance from "live people." LivePerson acts as a service bureau or network, so no hardware or software installation is required. Over 1,500 Web sites currently use LivePerson's solutions.

NativeMinds *(www.nativeminds.com)*

NativeMinds creates "vReps," or virtual representatives (Figure 9.3), automated customer service and support agents who answer customer questions via conversational dialog. NativeMinds says vReps can answer queries directly in real time, enable users to find information quickly and give feedback, encourage return visits and longer stays, lead users through the process of choosing and buying things, be aware of what users are looking for, provide information on customer habits, and escalate to a live representative or automated e-mail response when necessary.

Net Effect *(www.neteffect.com)*

Acquired in late 1999 by search engine AskJeeves, Net Effect provides a live help service, using a client's own customer care agents or those provided by Net Effect in partnership with major national call centers. Net Effect's service enables real-time, text-based conversations between e-businesses and their customers, and users include VerticalNet, The Right Start, and Southwestern Bell.

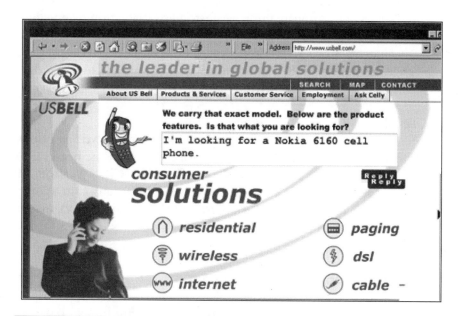

Figure 9.3. A NativeMind automated "vRep" answers questions and guides a customer in this demonstration of a typical session for a hypothetical telecommunications firm.

Net Perceptions *(www.netperceptions.com)*

In May 1999, Net Perceptions won the first-ever MIT Sloan E-Commerce Technology Innovator Award for "the technological innovation with the greatest potential to further revolutionize Web-based commerce." That technology is collaborative filtering: real-time recommendation technology that learns more about each customer's individual needs and preferences with every interaction and then makes increasingly personalized product and service recommendations.

PeopleSupport *(www.peoplesupport.com)*

PeopleSupport provides a suite of customized customer care services including live text chat, personalized e-mail reply, telephone services, and interactive self-help. The company offers complete outsourcing, software and infrastructure hosting, customer care consulting, and training. PeopleSupport's clients include Time-Warner, GE Card Services, Toyota, and CarParts.com.

Revenio *(www.revenio.com)*

Revenio's product, Revenio Dialog, is an e-marketing solution that helps marketers continuously improve customer satisfaction by engaging customers in ongoing, highly personalized "conversations" or dialogs across any channel. Revenio Dialog automates the process of responding with timely and compelling communications to move customers more effectively across the sales cycle.

Teradata CRM *(www.teradata.com)*

Teradata, a division of NCR, provides advanced analytic solutions such as enterprise data warehouses. In April 2000, NCR acquired Ceres Integrated Solutions and one year later, Teradata CRM Version 4.0 was introduced. The solution takes advantage of information in a company's data warehouse, presenting marketers with analysis, action, evaluation, and learning from within one tool.

Internet Telephony and Customer Service

Internet telephony is poised to take off as technological barriers continue to fall. Frost & Sullivan says the "VoIP" (Voice Over IP) market will grow to close to $2 billion through 2001. Already several vendors have staked a claim in this arena, both on the product and the service provider side. The area with the most activity in this space is "Call Me." Marketed by different companies under different names, the concept is basically the same: A visitor comes to your Web site. He or she is interested in learning more about a product or service—more than the Web page provides. The visitor sees a "call-me" button on the page, clicks on it, enters his or her phone number and a query, and receives a phone call from a live sales representative within moments. Even more interesting, the sales rep can then lead the inquirer through a directed Web session by "taking control" of the browser and pushing select Web pages to the inquirer at appropriate times. "Call me" is being offered by an increasing number of telemarketing service firms who resell the Web-based software as part of a total customer service package.

Advanced forms of the technology ultimately will permit instant communication via the Internet, versus over a telephone, as computers are increasingly VoIP-enabled. A unique twist on this technology is provided through "Push to Talk" from ITXC (*www.itxc.com*). The company can launch a phone call from within a banner ad or an e-mail so anyone who clicks will be connected with a salesperson or product specialist.

In an earlier chapter, it was mentioned that HP integrated call-me technology within its e-mail newsletters so customers could instantly get assistance, right at the moment they were reading about something of interest. IBM reportedly added call-me buttons to some 500 pages throughout their Web site. One of the most consumer-friendly examples of this technology comes from the apparel marketer Lands' End (*www.landsend.com*). Lands' End employs call-me technology combined with online chat to allow its customers to either request an immediate telephone call, chat with a Lands' End representative via computer, or "shop with a friend" online.

Next on the technology horizon? The fully integrated "Web Center." The Web Center vision is to have customer communications from any electronic point routed through a central facility. This could be managed in-house or outside. WorldCom (*www.worldcom.com*) appears to be an early leader in the outsourced Web Center, according to *InformationWeek*. WorldCom's Web Center Service, says the magazine, takes voice calls, e-mails, faxes, and chat requests and routes them through its data center. The subscribing company's call center operators can then handle them as necessary, while also being able to view call-center performance data.

Moving to the One-to-One Customer Relationship

The very idea of developing a "one-to-one" relationship with a customer was little more than a marketing fantasy before the advent of database marketing. With advances in computer technology, marketers now have access to even the most sophisticated marketing database products on their desktops. Nevertheless, the tools themselves are not enough: first, there must be a *commitment* to the concept of one-to-one relationship marketing, and then, there must be a *strategy* behind it.

Web site analysis firm NetGenesis (*www.netgen.com*) goes so far as to formalize a process for "understanding your online customer." In their Design for Analysis methodology, NetGenesis cites the need to identify goals, define metrics, assemble data, and build baseline business metrics. According to NetGenesis, the real path to understanding the customer is applying these metrics "to solving real-world business problems."

In a January 2000 research note on CRM, Gartner Inc. (*www.gartner.com*) suggests that the customer database is at the core of any customer relationship management program. Gartner cites several key reasons for the prime importance of the customer database, including the fact that the customer database offers a "unified customer view" and permits "multichannel marketing."

There is little doubt that organizations have generally recognized the value of the customer. Many IT marketers now realize that building a "customer-centric" company is vital to corporate health and profitability, but even the most superb customer-oriented companies may still be far removed from anything resembling one-to-one customer relationships. One simple reason is that it often means changing attitudes, then business practices, and sometimes even the corporate culture.

In the May 2000 issue of *1 to 1* magazine, Cisco is mentioned as a company that has "virtually" reinvented itself around customer needs. Already a pioneer in creating a customer-focused Web site, Cisco publishes a print and online magazine, along with dozens of e-mail newsletters that are industry- and job-specific. Cisco offers all of these publications free to customers, but they are only sent with a customer's permission. According to the company, Cisco is pursuing a "personalized, dynamic, customer-driven content model."

Now, IT marketers are realizing that it pays to get customers involved in solving their own problems. Customer "self-service" is a growing part of Internet-based marketing, and it is saving customers and companies time and money. The MathWorks (*www.mathworks.com*), the world's leading developer and supplier of technical computing software, is a good example. The MathWorks was one of the first 100 companies to create a Web site. Customers of The MathWorks include technology companies, government research labs, and more than 2,000 universities. The company's primary product is MATLAB, a fundamental tool for engineering and scientific work.

The MathWorks puts a major business emphasis on its service and support Web capabilities. Each month, the MathWorks Web site gets 220,000 visits from 120,000 users who can access 13,000 HTML pages of information. The number one destination of those users is the service and support area, which includes the ability to get technical support, check order status and license information, get quotes for products and services, edit contact information, obtain prerelease "sneak previews," get downloads of product patches and updates, and gain access to the Help Desk and mini-courses. The most popular part of the service and support area is the company's solution-search database of over 10,000 cases, where customers can solve their own problems based on the experiences of other customers.

The move to customer self-service has paid off handsomely for The MathWorks. Now 90 percent of the company's technical support happens over the Web. Users visit the site at least once every one to two months. "It is not just about sales and marketing," says Patrick Hanna, Web manager for The MathWorks. "Our Web site includes full service and support. Service is the secret. If you do a good job at it, loyalty and repeat business will increase."

One-to-one customer marketing doesn't have to be nearly that complex. A March 2000 issue of the Peppers and Rogers newsletter, *INSIDE 1to1*, reported on Hewlett-Packard's efforts to improve upon product registration rates. For manufacturers, getting a customer who just purchased something to fill in that registration card is a major challenge. Yet, if the customer does so, the company collects customer data that can be used for further promotions. Hewlett-Packard implemented an automatic registration link: Each time a customer installs HP software, a window pops up on the customer's computer screen suggesting electronic registration. Then, within a minute of registering, the customer receives a personalized e-mail with a link to a Web page offering a coupon for an additional related purchase. This process, says the report, moved HP's registration rate from 5 percent to as high as 20 percent, although registration costs fell almost 90 percent.

In your role as an IT marketer, you can demonstrate your commitment to the concept of addressing customer needs individually. You can do this by establishing a relationship program that truly enables your organization to get closer to your customers, and you can use the Internet as a powerful relationship-building tool in your move toward one-to-one customer marketing.

The Personalization Phenomenon

Underlying one-to-one marketing is the rapid move toward Internet personalization. Whereas the original definition of personalization in marketing meant using a person's name or other personally related information in a communication, today it has taken on a much broader meaning. Personalization, in fact, often crosses lines with customization, which represents the packaging of information in a customized way. For example, Dell Computer (*www.dell.com*) customizes Web pages to meet the specific needs of its major customers. By customizing these "Premier Pages" for each customer, Dell provides a very personalized experience. More importantly, this customization makes it easy for customers to always know the discounts and other terms and conditions of their relationship with Dell, thus making it easy to do business with the company.

Another very effective example in the context of customer service is the way Amazon.com (*www.amazon.com*) advises its customers on purchasing. Amazon makes "instant recommendations" and relates books to "purchase circles" (which show who's reading what by company and town). Amazon also provides "1-click ordering" which customizes the ordering process so returning customers don't have to reenter basic data already on file. Amazon's innovation in 2000 was "New for You," a personalized page of buying recommendations that it creates for customers, reminding them to reference it via e-mail.

As mounting evidence of widespread Web personalization, you will notice the presence of "my" pages at a growing number of sites, in particular at portals and search engines. "My" pages give users considerable individual power to customize home pages and other Web pages to meet their specific needs. These pages typically use personalization engines and tools that provide users with choices, usually in the form of check boxes, from which to select personalization criteria. By answering a few simple questions, the user is instructing the Web site to "learn" his or her preferences, so a personalized page appears the next time.

Personalization isn't only for Web sites. More and more, e-mail programs are incorporating sophisticated use of personalization, not just within the e-mail copy, but within the e-mail strategy. Programmatic e-mail is used so that an individual receives the right e-mail at the right time. Today it is possible to design e-mail programs to "follow" a prospect and cultivate his or her interest, or to prompt a customer to purchase again when appropriate.

For a continuing dialogue about Internet personalization, check out the Web site *www.personalization.com*. It will provide you with more than you will ever want to know about the subject.

Another valuable source of information covering personalization as it relates to marketing and customer service is the print publication *1to1*. Published by *DIRECT* magazine in association with Peppers and Rogers Group, the acknowledged one-to-one pioneers, the publication reports on one-to-one customer marketing innovations. Check out the Peppers and Rogers Group Web site as well (*www.1to1.com*), itself an excellent example of a personalized site.

Also worthy of review is a report titled "Best Web Support Sites" published by the Association of Support Professionals (*www.asponline.com*). The 1999 report was significant because it suggested the broad implementation of personalization across the ten winning sites: Iomega, Cisco, Sybase, Microsoft, Intuit, Intel, Symantec, CambridgeSoft, Dell, and Macromedia. According to report editor Jeffrey Tarter, "There's a clear trend toward personalization and audience segmentation, deeper use of clickstream data, better online forums, and greater intelligence in search tools and knowledgebase design."

In the context of building customer relationships, there does appear to be strong evidence that customizing and personalizing the Web experience leads to greater customer loyalty and higher customer retention rates. However, personalization, customization, and one-to-one marketing are not gimmicks to dazzle or Band-Aids to fix poor service; one-to-one marketing is a strategy to which an IT marketer must make a serious commitment.

Five Ideas for Building a One-to-One Customer Relationship Program

IT marketers spend a lot of time, money, and effort in the acquisition of new customers, yet too many times, these same marketers underinvest in customer retention. That is wrong—because building a long-lasting customer relationship starts *after* the sale.

Treat Customers Like Prospects

Numerous industry studies show that the cost associated with customer retention is far less than the cost of customer acquisition. Sometimes the cost of keeping a customer is as little as 20 to 25 percent of the cost associated with acquiring a new customer. This could mean that for every dollar you spend acquiring a new customer, it will cost you just 25 cents to retain that customer.

This law of customer acquisition and renewal or retention is well known to fundraisers, subscription publications, and mail-order companies. When they evaluate their marketing efforts, they often find that they actually acquire new donors, subscribers, or customers at a *loss* but renew them at a profit. It may therefore take more than one year to make money on a customer.

This is the principle behind LTV—*lifetime value of a customer.* A customer's LTV becomes an important measurement criterion when you evaluate customer acquisition and retention. Look at the average number of years you retain a customer. Then look at the average value of that customer over that period of time. You will get a good sense of what that customer is worth.

If possible, apply this analysis to each individual customer and use it to rank your customers; in effect, you need to build your own statistically accurate version of the customer marketing pyramid. Then you can compare this data with the amount of money you invest in customer acquisition and retention. If you find, as many IT companies do, that you are investing far less in customer retention than in customer acquisition, consider the ROI impact of even a modest shift in the ratio. By investing in customer marketing programs—and improving your use of the Internet as a customer marketing and communications tool—you could get a substantial payback.

Attitude is just as important as the money you invest. That is why you should *start treating customers like prospects.* When you treat customers like prospects, you never assume they are comfortably yours forever. This is a fact of business life for IT companies. There are few customers who do not use products and services from multiple IT vendors. You recognize that customers always can choose to go elsewhere and that you need to do everything you can to make sure they do not. In fact, in the IT world, it often pays to help your customers *integrate* disparate systems, even those from competitors, so your customers trust you as a problem solver. The key point here is: *You never take customers for granted.* Rather, you create opportunities to reward their loyalty, delight them with superior service, and ensure that their interactions with you are positive, satisfying, and rewarding.

With your customer as a prospect, you can think of new ways to keep the flame burning in that relationship. Direct marketing is an excellent way to cross-sell, upgrade, and extend a customer's business relationship with you—and to get that customer to refer other prospective customers to you as well. Use direct mail and telemarketing in combination with e-mail and a customer-only portion of your Web site to build an ongoing relationship with customers. These media should be used in combination to inform *customers first* about new products or services, make special offers, invite them to special events, and encourage their feedback.

The Internet can help you put a large emphasis on customer service and support and build real value into the customer relationship. Web-based customer service can be open for business 24 hours a day, 7 days a week, anywhere in the world. Just as important, by servicing existing customers over the Internet and making it known on your Web site, you demonstrate to prospective customers the value you place on customer support.

Ask Customers What They Want—and Give It to Them

IT companies that are responsive to their customers are companies that *listen* to their customers. These companies provide easy ways for customers to offer their feedback and opinions—via phone, fax, mail, and e-mail, and over the Web. They encourage their customers to interact, they take customers' recommendations seriously, and they act on them.

With one-to-one Web technologies available, those IT companies that not only listen to their customers, but learn from their input and needs, will be the leaders in the Information Age. These are the companies that will be able to respond quickly and give customers what they want in real time.

IBM's *Focusing on You* program, described earlier, was built on asking customers what they want—and *giving it to them*. One of the company's key findings was that customers wanted to "direct the dialogue based on their own needs." IBM took the responsibility to reduce the amount of information directed to the customer—giving him or her the choice of what to receive. That choice made it easier for IBM to provide the customer with the appropriate product information, based on specific needs.

Because customers directed the relationship and were involved in a meaningful dialogue, IBM benefited from an important side effect of the program: Customers also updated their own records. This aspect of a customer relationship effort is just as significant, because database maintenance plays a large role in its successful implementation. When a customer updates his or her own database record, the data is more likely to be accurate.

Explore New and Innovative Ways to Encourage and Reward Customers

You do not necessarily have to establish an elaborate frequent buyer program to encourage and reward customer loyalty. Sometimes, just making customers feel special can be enough.

One way to do that is to keep in touch with your customers via e-mail. Another way is to establish a customer service center on your Web site. A customer service center is a tangible way to reward customer loyalty, especially if you are providing added value to the customer relationship.

Web-based customer service centers obviously offer service and support to users of your products, but you can go beyond that in a number of ways. For example, you might post white papers, special reports, or benchmark studies only in the customer section of your Web site and provide links to useful Web sites just for customers. You may wish to build in a self-service area where customers can use solution databases to solve their own problems, or perhaps you want to consider using Internet telephony to enhance communications with customers.

You could offer customers the option of signing up for e-mail newsletters or the option of receiving Web pages from you, delivered to their computers on a regular basis. You could use your Web-based customer service center as a "reward center" by offering customers incentives for purchasing certain products or for doing business over the Web. You could build a business-to-business portal that serves your company's business area or industry, and then give customers "special privileges" in using it. Whether you take small or large steps with Internet customer marketing, you are proving that you value the relationship you have with your customers.

Recognize the Differences between Classes of Customers—and Treat Customer Classes Differently

If you utilize database marketing effectively, you can use the information you gather about your customers to segment them and rank them, and then build individualized programs based on classes of customers. Use that marketing pyramid we discussed earlier. For example, you may wish to treat customers at the top of the marketing pyramid very differently from other customers. You may want to develop a special relationship with these highly valued customers, communicating with them more frequently via e-mail, enrolling them in preferred-customer clubs, and making them special offers on a regular basis.

You may also wish to develop a special program for resellers or partners. Business partners are a customer audience in and of themselves, and they should be treated differently and communicated with separately.

Make One-to-One Fun

The idea of a one-to-one relationship is that you get to know each of your customers, their attributes, and their individual needs over time. The more you learn about your customer, the more you can use the Internet to target individualized communications to your customer.

Building that relationship is a serious marketing process, of course, but it should also be fun for the customer. Having fun—providing the customer with an opportunity to smile or even laugh—is a part of relationship building that can endear your company to the customer because you make him or her feel good. The Web can be a playful place. Some IT marketers make excellent use of this characteristic, offering customers games, contests, and "cafes" where customers can do the cyberspace equivalent of leaning back, putting their feet up, and just relaxing. You can use the informality and interactivity of the Web in a good-humored and informal way to make your customers feel that your company is friendly, down-to-earth, and easy to do business with.

We have discussed a number of ways to implement Internet-enhanced customer marketing, but the bottom line is *customer database integration*. You need to have access to customer data and use it in a proactive yet appropriate fashion to build a long-lasting customer relationship program via the Internet.

With Internet-enhanced customer marketing, you have the potential to keep your most valued customers buying more, the ability to push other customers up the marketing pyramid until they reach "golden" status, and the likelihood of improved productivity and profits that come from the cost-effective implementation of superior customer service.

Building Customer-Driven Extranets

The culmination of one-to-one marketing is the creation of a customer-driven extranet, a Web site established by a company to specifically offer private or preferred customer access to information and order entry. The extranet can be implemented as a restricted area on an existing corporate Web site, or it can be built as a separate site. Either way, it makes it clear that the company believes in the credo "the customer comes first."

As just one example, IBM reported at a recent Internet marketing conference that the company created extranets with some of its key customers to encourage them to do business with IBM online. The move contributed to moving IBM's e-commerce revenues from $35 million a month in early 1998 to over $1 billion a month by December of that year. As an aside, IBM saved some $300 million in call center costs in 1998 by handling more customer service inquiries online.

A restricted access customer service area of a corporate Web site is, in effect, a version of a customer-driven extranet. Many companies establish such areas for customers only, so that they can interact privately with the organization or gain access to information intended only for them. For the most part, access is permitted via a simple password, which the company assigns or the customer selects. Invitation-only Internet events, discussed in Chapter 7, are also a form of extranet, because they are often delivered via a special URL and require passwords to enter.

Private-access customer areas and virtual events running over the Web may be acceptable solutions for some IT companies, but conducting business on an ongoing basis with customers and partners over the Internet could stretch the boundaries of any public Web site. An extranet may make more sense, if only because the load of real-time customer service and transaction processing could eat a Web server alive.

The customer-driven extranet is, of course, a major technological undertaking. The impact on the organization should not be minimized, as business processes themselves may undergo dramatic change. If systems serving customers within your company are not centralized, the extranet will likely not succeed.

However, if you have your organizational act together and you have the technology to back it up (either with in-house resources or through outsourcing), then the business benefits of a customer extranet can be huge. In larger companies, for example, the costs associated with customer service and support can be dramatically reduced by shifting much of the repetitive person-to-person contact to Internet-based communications.

There are also out-of-the-box extranet solutions that smaller IT companies can take advantage of, such as Intranets.com (*www.intranets.com*). Intranets.com offers a set of free services that allow you to establish private spaces where you can collaborate and communicate with external audiences.

Even if you believe in the value of a customer-driven extranet, where do you begin? Maybe it is obvious—but it all starts with what your customers want and need. As mentioned earlier, asking your customers what they want—and giving it to them—should be the driving force behind an extranet. Using database technology, you can accumulate profile data about each customer's relationship with your company, track the customer's interactions with you, and use this data to individualize communications with the customer. In addition, you can learn what customers might want built into an extranet to best meet their needs.

Internet-based customer service requires consideration of new forms of data. For example, transaction data is different from online interaction data. A customer's transactions represent the inquiries or orders you receive. Analyzing this data will help you understand the customer's need for information or buying pattern. But interaction data can offer insight into online behavior. This is the data that tells you how often customers access your Web site, which pages they access most, how they navigate the site, and so on.

You can also bring together product data with solutions and applications information and what-if scenarios so that customers can interactively learn how products apply to their specific needs or how to solve problems with your products. The MathWorks *(www.mathworks.com)*, mentioned earlier, is a good example of this. The company built a database of over 10,000 cases so customers could solve their own problems online. This concept—using database-driven Web technology to deliver voluminous information of value that helps customers solve their own problems—is an increasingly common practice among IT companies. The added benefit is in the fact that time-intensive customer interactions can be dramatically reduced.

Solutions-oriented content as part of an extranet is at once the most challenging and most exciting opportunity for both company and customer. Imagine, for example, a customer solutions extranet for your organization. It could take the form of a searchable database that cross-references solutions with your products. Customers could enter their desired parameters and immediately be greeted with a list of solutions that fit their needs. Web pages would be dynamically generated on the fly, based on preferences that customers establish in their user profile. New product information could be selectively displayed.

This solutions center could also be used as a sales tool to allow your direct sales force or partners to better match solutions with products your customers should be purchasing. Electronic fulfillment can be added to the mix so that customers could unlock or download relevant information.

Extranets can also become the core of a highly successful e-commerce strategy. Dell Computer's "Premier Pages" referenced earlier are proof that customer extranets work. With more than 58,000 Premier Pages users, Dell expects to take the next logical step by facilitating the integration of these pages with its customers' own accounting systems.

Extranets with highly personalized information are already widespread. Ultimately, you will be able to cost-effectively offer an even higher level of personalization to customers as Internet database technology continues to advance and the Internet and the telephone continue to converge. Not only will you serve up highly personalized information over your extranet, you will also be able to "watch" your customers navigate the extranet and provide live assistance to them when required.

A Checklist for Developing Customer Extranets

From a marketing perspective, here are some of the things you will need to consider as you create a customer-driven extranet:

- Learn what to build in to your extranet from customers. Listen to their input and give them what they need.

- Provide a secure path to your extranet that goes beyond password protection alone, especially if you will be using your extranet to transmit sensitive customer data or to accept orders. Be sure that your IT organization or outside service provider addresses any security issues up front.

- Utilize customer promotions to increase customer involvement with the extranet. Consider offering gifts or incentives to customers who provide you with case histories or successful experiences with your product that you can then post on the extranet.

- Actively promote the benefits of the extranet to the customer base. Get customers excited about it and build a business case for its ongoing usage. It will repay you many times over in time and money saved.

- Incorporate online forms that allow customers to easily create user profiles, change their profiles, and request information. Use a Web database that enables you to update customer data online. The cost of this database will quickly be offset by the time saved in one-step data entry.

- Create an online solutions center to provide added value to customers. Integrate the legacy customer database with the extranet so that you can generate customized content that is individualized to each customer.

- Create online fulfillment in conjunction with the solutions center. Allow customers to request and receive product literature in the way they prefer—via e-mail, fax, or traditional mail. Encourage them to go to the Web to unlock or download information directly from the extranet.

- Consider using "push" technology to deliver product information directly to your customers' desktops by request, via periodic e-mail newsletters or Web pages.

- Explore emerging technologies that link the extranet with Internet-based telephony to provide customers with a new level of personalized customer support.

- Establish online measurement criteria and do periodic customer surveys to analyze customer usage of the extranet, understand which areas of the extranet are most and least popular, and continuously improve the extranet.

Note

1. Michelle Lanter Smith, "One to One: Put the Customer in the Information Driver Seat and Build Better Relationships," *DIRECT MARKETING* (Hoke Communications, Inc., January 1998).

10

Internet Communities and Exchanges

Unlike any medium before it, the Internet creates a sense of community. Early on, there were newsgroups, bulletin boards, and chat rooms. It was IT companies, of course, that led the charge with bulletin boards to meet the needs of technical audiences with a hunger for information and advice.

Now, there are full-fledged communities—areas on the Internet that bring together people with something fundamentally in common. Many of these communities are designed for consumers to chat, trade, and interact. But perhaps the fastest-growing area of community is business-to-business, and here there are an ever-increasing number of business-oriented communities that bring together sellers with information-seekers, prospects, and buyers. One of the more mature community areas, in fact, is IT. IT communities exist for executives, developers, marketers ... just about any audience with a common interest.

Even more significant than communities is the growth of exchanges, or marketplaces. These exchanges, both public and private, are where business is being conducted between companies with common interests. In some cases, exchanges are completely changing the business model; for example, large companies are establishing private exchanges so suppliers can compete to win business.

The forward-thinking IT company can capitalize on the concept of community not only by participating in communities and exchanges on the Internet, but by creating one as part of a consortium or even independently. This chapter explores the marketing potential of communities and exchanges and suggests how to make the best use of them.

What Is an Internet Community?

An excellent frame of reference for the IT marketer when it comes to community is the user group. Most every IT company of substantial size has a user group—an organization of individuals, sometimes operated independently, who use the company's products. The user group typically has its own governing body, its own annual meeting, and today, its own Web site. An IT company listens hard to its user group, because this is a community that could do much good—or much damage—to the company's reputation. A user group is very much a community of people with a common bond—the company whose products or services these people depend upon.

A community on the Internet is, likewise, a group of people with something in common, getting together or collaborating in a particular area of cyberspace. But community on the Internet extends far beyond this basic definition. An Internet community seems to take on a life of its own and to almost share the personalities of its members.

We could probably consider the first primitive Internet communities to be bulletin boards, newsgroups, and chat rooms. Each of these means of communication brought together people in a common bond. Bulletin boards were early facilitators of community input, and they still exist today. They allow posting of comments and questions for all to see, but they typically allow neither privacy nor one-to-one communication. Nonetheless, a bulletin board does encourage a sense of community, since it functions kind of like an electronic corkboard where people can share their thoughts.

Newsgroups took the Internet concept of community a step further. Through a newsgroup, individuals can communicate interactively via e-mail. Most newsgroups "thread" the discussions so members can not only answer each other, but also read each other's answers. Since newsgroups tend to be formed around specific topics or interest areas, they function as mini-communities in their own right.

Chat rooms may be more like cocktail parties than communities. In this environment, individuals can spend time chatting interactively (in real time) with others. Again, everyone "overhears" the conversation (by reading the comments that fly back and forth) and anyone can participate. Although chat rooms have achieved some well-deserved notoriety for their frankness and sometimes sexual innuendo, chat has "matured" somewhat. Today there are business-oriented chat rooms in which serious topics are considered and discussed.

Now we will bring our consideration of communities up to the present. Chat rooms were in part responsible for spawning full-fledged Internet communities—entire slices of the Internet that appeal to certain segments of society, or people interested in a particular subject. Today there are thousands of such communities, and some of them, as you'll see in this chapter, are relevant to IT marketers.

Types of Communities

Online Service Providers

The first Internet communities with any kind of mass "membership" were the early online service providers such as America Online and CompuServe. The most successful has certainly been America Online (*www.aol.com*). Early in 2000, America Online drove the consolidation of online service providers by acquiring CompuServe (*www.compuserve.com*) and scooping up one of the two giants in the browser war, Netscape (*www.netscape.com*). As mentioned at the beginning of this book, America Online pulled off the merger of the century, of course, when it acquired the much-larger Time Warner.

America Online and CompuServe are Internet communities in their own right, although CompuServe started as primarily a business-oriented service provider and still maintains that orientation. Both services have grown from basic fee-based online service providers to full-fledged communities that offer their own unique spin on the Internet. Some of the data points are impressive. By mid-2001, America Online had grown to over 30 million users worldwide, 26 million of them in the United States. CompuServe counted 2.8 million users in its own right. Each day, America Online transmits 150 million e-mails and 656 million instant messages, and serves up 7.3 billion Web pages. Among America Online's properties are Digital City, the leading local online network; ICQ, the leading communication community; MapQuest, the leading mapping and navigation service: and Netscape Netcenter, with 34 million registrants.

It appears that America Online will continue to operate CompuServe as a separate service, leveraging its business expertise as a separate brand. Under America Online's stewardship, CompuServe, stagnant at about 2 million members, may be poised for future growth.

But as communities, CompuServe and America Online are two Internet giants serving millions of people, many of whom seek out others like them or with interests similar to theirs. This is the essence of the Internet community that marketers must understand: The Internet uniquely encourages a very personal kind of community, even though individuals may only know each other's e-mail addresses and never meet face-to-face.

As an IT marketer, think about how you can take advantage of these special communities. As you might expect, both America Online and CompuServe accept online advertising and other forms of paid promotion.

In relation to promoting your product or service to people in business, where your greatest sales opportunity probably is, look at CompuServe and the business-oriented portions of America Online as real opportunities to reach "captive" audiences. These two services can deliver huge audiences to you—and their members are people who are already active Internet users. By understanding how to appeal to certain segments of these audiences, you could uncover new prospects and get more business for your company.

America Online and CompuServe certainly are not the only service providers with huge installed bases. Others with millions of subscribers include Microsoft's MSN (*www.msn.com*), AT&T WorldNet Service (*www.att.net*), EarthLink (*www.earthlink.net*), which in 2000 merged with MindSpring, and Prodigy (*www.prodigy.com*), which is aligned with telco SBC.

Portals and "Vortals"

One of the most significant Internet developments in 1999 was the rise of the "portal." The portal is a Web destination or gateway—a site that visitors start at and return to often. Even that definition is changing fairly rapidly. Although a portal is one working definition, a "hub" is another. The hub might be more of a place that simply links to other Web sites without the clear objective of becoming a user's home page. In this context, some would consider America Online, CompuServe, and other ISPs' home pages to be portals. Portals are part search engine, part community, and part something else. "Vortals" emerged in early 2000 as a term used to describe vertical portals. There was so much portal activity from late 1998 through 2001 that you needed a scorecard to keep track of it.

In Chapter 4, we discussed the search engines-cum-portals in detail, so we won't repeat that here. However, let's touch on the highlights of the "portals war," which has been an important development in the evolution of the Internet. Here are just a few examples of the changes and consolidation in this area:

- Infoseek launched the GO Network in January 1999 with a major advertising campaign designed to pump new life into the brand. With its search engine at the heart of GO, Infoseek sought to stake its claim in the portal wars by bringing together a number of high-profile sites, such as Disney.com, ESPN.com, and Family.com, onto one accessible supersite, *www.go.com.* Now GO is part of the Disney Internet Group.

- In early 1999, Excite was purchased by @Home, which provides high-speed Internet access delivered via cable TV wire. Excite is one of the Internet's leading search and directory companies whose technology is licensed to other sites. @Home is a leader in "broadband," which many experts feel will be the answer to the Internet's future.

- Not to be outdone, Yahoo! *(www.yahoo.com)* purchased GeoCities *(www.geocities.yahoo.com)*, the Internet's largest community of communities. Then Yahoo! made the $6 billion-plus purchase of Broadcast.com, one of the Internet's leading broadcast facilities.

- In early 1999, Lycos announced its intention to merge with USA Networks. The on-again, off-again merger was one of the business world's most-watched stories of 1999. It finally collapsed three months after the announcement and Lycos instead merged with Spanish Internet company Terra Networks in October 2000.

All in all, the portal activity noted above represents a true convergence of the Internet and the media/entertainment business. And that, too, only supports the fact that the Internet is now reaching enough individuals to translate into *very* big business.

Although searching for information is likely to be the main reason a visitor comes to a particular portal, there must be far more available than a search engine to entice the individual user to visit and *return*. Most if not all portals now offer free e-mail, free chat, personalized pages, and other attractive services that make their sites "sticky." (This is a phrase that Internet watchers have coined to refer to a site's ability to keep users at its site for more time, rather than coming for just a brief visit. Time spent on a site is believed to translate into dollars, because the "stuck" visitor is exposed to more of the site's advertising and uses more of the site's services. This also promotes return visits and loyalty to the site, which are important factors in generating additional revenue.)

Some Internet observers believe sticky sites will become the only way to differentiate among the millions of options available to visitors. Ultimately, to keep sites sticky, portals and other sites are expected to offer Web-enabled database, word-processing, or scheduling tools—eventually creating competition for the programs that run on the PC desktop. As broadband becomes the preferred method of Internet access, portals can really burn rubber, offering heavy-duty applications previously only available on computers.

Are portals truly communities? Yes and no. Some of them are more like information networks than communities. But others, like Yahoo!, are very community-oriented. Yahoo! users can create their own "My Yahoo!" pages to personalize their experiences, and younger users can go to a special community just for them called "Yahooligans."

Here again, as with America Online and CompuServe, there are many opportunities for IT Internet marketers to capitalize on each portal's popularity—including carefully targeted online advertising, page links, discussion groups, and the like. If nothing else, be sure your Web site is linked to the appropriate areas of each portal, and be certain to construct your Web pages so they can be easily recognized by search engines. (See Chapter 4.)

Why else should the IT marketer care about portals? In the Internet future, you could be part of one, or you could decide to eventually build one of your own—if not for the outside world, then for your employees. In a February 8, 1999, cover story, the publication *InformationWeek* suggested that "a growing number of businesses are adapting the portal's gateway-to-the-world model as an efficient way for their employees to access critical information online." The article went on to report that "enterprise portals" will make it possible not only for companies to share internal information, but for employees to use the portal as a "starting point . . . to access real-time and historical information . . . all from their browsers."

Forrester Research (*www.forrester.com*) confirms that business portals will be an Internet force in the coming years, suggesting that they will drive a Web business information market that will reach $11 billion worldwide by 2004.

Auctions

Auction sites can be considered Internet communities in the sense that they bring buyers and sellers together with the common goal of conducting commerce. For the IT marketer, auction sites may provide useful opportunities to more widely promote products and services beyond traditional audiences.

The business-oriented virtual mall offers merchants an opportunity to associate as part of a group of merchants who take advantage of the publicity and e-commerce engine of a larger site. And whereas virtual malls may lack daily excitement, auction sites have brought a fast and furious brand of electronically enabled old-time commerce to the Internet. As such, auction sites have become a hot commodity on the Internet, even in the business-to-business space. Following are some auction sites and providers that are relevant to IT marketers.

eBay (*www.ebay.com*)

eBay, founded in 1995, is the auction site that started it all. It considers itself very much a community. As of the first quarter of 2001, the eBay community served 18.9 million registered users representing over 150 different countries. eBay operates sites in the United States, Canada, the

United Kingdom, France, Germany, Japan, and Australia. In 2000, the eBay community transacted over $5 billion in annualized gross merchandise sales, according to the company.

eBay pioneered online auctions: Sellers offer items to buyers who bid online. The highest bidder wins the item. Bids are acknowledged by e-mail. eBay sends an e-mail each time the bidder is outbid to encourage continued activity. Seller and buyer registration is free. eBay creates a true sense of community with its users through such areas as the eBay Café, a bulletin board where members can ask questions and make comments, and a mechanism for users to create their own personal-interests page.

eBay has made significant moves into the B-to-B space, and some of its activities should be of interest to IT marketers. The Business Exchange on eBay, for example, services the small-business marketplace. It provides a destination on eBay for businesses to buy or sell new, used, and refurbished business merchandise, including computers and related items.

DoveBid (*www.dovebid.com*)
DoveBid offers a portfolio of "asset disposition solutions" that includes live Webcast auctions, around-the-clock online auctions, sealed-bid Internet sales, and private-treaty Internet sales. DoveBid has conducted industrial auctions for over 60 years and has aggressively moved into the Internet auction business.

Egghead (*www.egghead.com*)
Egghead, which merged with Onsale.com in 1999, features both a traditional online store and clearance center—where you can buy computer, electronics, and office-related items—and an auction area. Each day Egghead opens a new set of auctions and posts thousands of items, including computers, peripherals, consumer electronics and more. With over 3 million registered users, Egghead's auction site is a major Internet auction for both consumers and businesses.

FairMarket (*www.fairmarket.com*)
FairMarket is not an auction site, but rather a developer of e-business selling and marketing solutions and a leader in dynamic pricing technology. FairMarket sets up and manages auctions for its clients, and also provides e-mail customer service support 24 hours a day, seven

days a week so inquiries from buyers and sellers can be answered promptly. FairMarket helped Dell design its DellAuction.com site, launched in July 1999, and continues to host it and provide technology and design support.

FreeMarkets *(www.freemarkets.com)*

FreeMarket is a "market maker," bringing together direct-materials purchasers from large consumer, high-tech, utility, and industrial products companies with sellers who manufacture or supply custom components and materials to the buyer's specifications. In the first quarter of 2000, FreeMarkets acquired iMark.com, an auction site for surplus equipment and inventory.

Online Asset Exchange *(www.onlineassetexchange.com)*

The Online Asset Exchange is included in this section in order to compare it to such sites as DoveBid and TradeOut (see below), even though it classifies itself as an exchange and not an auction. Buyers search from listed equipment and can submit an offer or a request for information directly to the seller via e-mail. The Online Asset Exchange claims to be the world's largest marketplace for used industrial assets. In first-quarter 2001, the Exchange had over $12.5 billion in listed assets.

Priceline *(www.priceline.com)*

Priceline.com is less of an auction site/community and more of a comparison-shopping site. Here, users bid on select items to see if they can "win" the item at the price that they wish to pay. Priceline created this type of consumer-bidding site and achieved notoriety for consumer bidding on airfares. Now Priceline has established bidding programs for hotel rooms, rental cars, new cars, home financing, and long-distance telephone service.

TradeOut *(www.tradeout.com)*

TradeOut.com is a leading business-to-business exchange connecting buyers and sellers of business surplus. TradeOut provides an opportunity for sellers of excess inventory, overstocks, and other surplus goods to find buyers, who may be wholesalers, discounters, or just companies looking for a good deal. In the conventional business world, sellers would typically have to pay a broker to unload the surplus, and the average buyer would often be closed out of this market. Using a model not unlike eBay (which is one of its major investors), TradeOut facilitates bidding on everything from computers and peripherals to office furniture and industrial equipment, charging its sellers a percentage of the transaction but allowing buyers to participate free.

Information Technology Supersites

In some respects, the Information Technology "supersites" are models for the information portal/community. These specialized sites consolidate information, often from the various publications they represent, and make it available in a single location. Some may consider them portals, whereas others may classify them as hubs. But they are communities in the sense that a visitor to one of these supersites can typically obtain free e-mail accounts, receive free e-mail newsletter subscriptions, connect with others in special-interest groups, and take advantage of online events and targeted programs. All of these sites feature late-breaking news and information that relates specifically to the information technology industry, and each provides important opportunities for advertising and publicity. These IT supersites include:

CMPnet *(www.cmpnet.com)*
One of the largest IT-focused supersites, CMPnet consolidates information from more than 35 different Web sites, including *Computer Reseller News, EE Times, InformationWeek, InternetWeek, ISPs.com, Network Computing,* and *Windows* magazine. Start at the home page and you will find all of them, including CMP's three true communities, TechWeb, Ch@nnelWEB, and EDTN Network.

- TechWeb *(www.techweb.com)*
  "The IT Network," as CMP calls it, provides news, downloads, services, resources, and community discussions. Within TechWeb is "PlanetIT" *(www.planetit.com)*, a true community carved out of the larger network especially for IT professionals. PlanetIT is organized into "Technology Centers" focusing on such specific areas as data management, desktop computing, e-business, networking, Web design, and others. Planet IT offers specialized resources, newsletters, roundtables, discussions, and more.

- Ch@nnelWEB *(www.channelweb.com)*

This CMP community (Figure 10.1) is very useful for IT companies with channel partners. (Is there an IT company that *doesn't* have them?) Ch@nnelWEB focuses on the specific needs of distributors, resellers, and partners, offering deep content and extensive services for this audience and advertisers interested in reaching them. This community includes "Solution Centers" such as Developer, E-Business, and Intranet; weekly Web chats; a connection to the Computer Exchange, which deals in used computer products, "VARBusiness University"; and more.

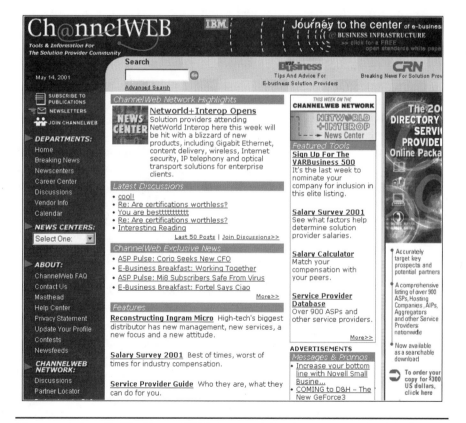

Figure 10.1. CMP's ChannelWEB is a specialized community for IT solution providers and VARs.

- EDTN Network *(www.edtn.com)*

    CMP's EDTN specializes in electronics design and is organized into such areas as News Center, Design Center, and Career Center. More of a network than an interactive community, EDTN is a hub-like site that points to partner sites such as Embedded.com, etown.com, and EE Product News.

ClNet *(www.cnet.com)*

ClNet is an extremely useful network for IT marketers. In itself, it is more of a portal than a community, connecting to other ClNet sites, including News.com (do not be fooled by the name, it is IT news), Builder.com, Download.com, Shareware.com, and Shopper.com. ClNet operates a technology auction area and offers over 25 "dispatches" (free e-mail newsletters) available in text or HTML. To keep abreast of everything on ClNet, sign up for the "CNET Digital Dispatch." ClNet also operates ZDnet, mentioned below. In April 2001, ClNet announced that it would acquire TechRepublic *(www.techrepublic.com)*, a leading IT community hub.

IDG.net *(www.idg.net)*

IDG.net is a gateway to the more than 250 publications and services Web sites of this corporate giant. IDG publishes *Computerworld, InfoWorld, Network World, PCWorld,* and *CIO,* along with the Internet-focused magazine *The Industry Standard.* IDG is also the creator of *"Dummies . . ."* books (the most successful book series ever) and operates IDC, an IT research firm. IDG also runs a major IT community called ITWorld *(www.itworld.com)*.

Internet.com *(www.internet.com)*

Internet.com is a major network that operates 170 Web sites, over 350 e-mail newsletters, over 400 online discussion forums, and more than 100 moderated e-mail discussion lists. It is organized into 16 "content channels," many of which are relevant to IT marketers. (Windows, Linux/Open Source, Web Developer, and ASP Resources are a few examples.) Internet.com now operates EarthWeb as one of its channels. EarthWeb was a large IT network in its own right. EarthWeb, Inc. sold its content business assets to Internet.com and announced in April 2001 that it would change its corporate name to Dice, reflecting its core business. Dice.com is the leading job site for IT professionals.

TechTarget (*www.techtarget.com*)

TechTarget is really a collection of search engines rather than a single site, and it claims to have monthly traffic of over 1.3 million IT visitors. TechTarget maintains a portfolio of Web sites in narrowly focused IT markets. Each business-to-business site features its own IT-specific search engine that provides rapid access to the most-relevant site-specific results. Each site also features an experienced editorial team that aggregates, organizes, and prioritizes all the relevant site-specific content on the Web and delivers it all in one place.

ZDnet (*www.zdnet.com*)

ZDnet is a subsidiary of C|Net, which acquired ZDnet from publisher Ziff-Davis. ZDnet's mission is to be "a premier 'full service' destination for people looking to buy, use, and learn more about technology." ZDnet combines content from such publications as *Inter@ctive Week,* *Macworld,* and *PC Week* with content from a host of online publications, and offers a significant online shopping area for prospective buyers of computers, electronics, and technology items.

Other Business Communities

There are many other business communities that could offer IT marketers the opportunity to reach new prospects and generate leads. Business communities are places where information—lots of it—is shared by companies with common interests or goals. The providers pool their information to a publisher or consolidator, who sponsors a single "supersite" to disseminate the information.

Business communities function as large electronic directories or catalogs of information for a rich variety of sources, each of which is available on or accessible through a single site. Communities also offer information providers the ability to interact with their constituency and effectively expose new audiences to the providers' messages. In most cases, communities are free to users, as long as the users register (and therefore provide contact information that can be used by both the community and the participating information providers).

Many of these communities are rapidly evolving into **marketplaces** or **exchanges,** where business is transacted between buyers and sellers. Both exchanges and private exchanges are growing rapidly. Forrester

Research (*www.forrester.com*) says these "eMarketplaces" will capture 53 percent of all online business trade by 2004. Gartner Inc. (*www.gartner.com*) reports that, as of January 2000, there were more than 300 such organizations. Gartner believes that they will account for almost $3 trillion in sales transactions by 2004. Boston Consulting Group (*www.bcg.com*) estimates that public exchanges could represent as much as $2.5 trillion in revenue by 2004.

Listed next are several business communities and exchanges that should be of interest to IT marketers.

Business Communities and Exchanges

BizProLink *(www.bizprolink.com)*
BizProLink is a network of 135 industry-specific business-to-business communities. A typical community includes industry news, resources, a business center, a discussion center, and an "eMarketplace" that contains business storefronts sponsored by advertisers, as well as an online auction. Several communities are IT-oriented, such as Networking B2B (*www.networking-b2b.com*) and Computer Software B2B (*www.computersoftwareb2b.com*).

CommunityB2B *(www.communityb2b.com)*
CommunityB2B is a source for comprehensive, targeted information on evaluating, purchasing, and implementing electronic B-to-B technology and solutions. The site provides interactive B-to-B peer exchange and networking and serves as a catalyst for exchanging B-to-B strategy and ideas. CommunityB2B is one of a family of technology communities run by DCI, a producer of technical conferences. Other sites include CRMCommunity.com, EACommunity.com, and DWCommunity.com.

ConcertGlobalMarket *(www.concertglobalmarket.net)*
ConcertGlobalMarket is part of the world's largest Internet-based B-to-B marketplace for indirect goods and services. It is a single point for information and services, providing buyers with access to supplier catalogs, and suppliers with a hosted application to manage inventory, orders, and catalog content. Concert is a joint venture of AT&T and BT.

Converge *(www.converge.com)*
Converge is an independent online marketplace where high-technology buyers and sellers connect, collaborate, and transact business. Converge

was formed by a collaboration of IT companies, including Compaq, Gateway, Hewlett-Packard, and NEC. In February 2001, Converge acquired NECX from VerticalNet. As a result, Converge can now serve over 20,000 trading partners globally, with access to more than 10 billion items valued at more than $30 billion.

Covisint *(www.covisint.com)*
Covisint is included as a leading example of a private exchange, although it is not directly related to IT. Founded by competitors GM, Ford, and DaimlerChrysler, the objective of the exchange is to greatly streamline the buying and selling process between auto makers and their suppliers. Covisint is creating a business community of buyers, sellers, designers, engineers, and third parties affiliated with the global automotive industry. Sellers of goods and services will be able to buy goods and services from their own suppliers. Covisint will also offer supply-chain services and auctions. Covisint says that by the end of 2000, the site had already transacted $350 million among its members. In May 2001, DaimlerChrysler conducted an international online auction on Covisint that involved five suppliers who exchanged some 1,200 parts at a value of over 3 billion Euros.

e2open.com *(www.e2open.com)*
e2open is a global marketplace where computer, consumer electronics, and telecommunications companies can plan, collaborate, manage, and execute supply-chain transactions over the Internet. Founders of e2open include Acer, IBM, Nortel, Panasonic, and Seagate. This private exchange offers design collaboration, supply-chain collaboration, and open-market capabilities to its members.

Exportall *(www.exportall.com)*
This informational site is included for IT marketers who are involved in exporting products. Exportall consists of two directories: a general one that visitors can access from the home page, and a country directory. Exportall also offers the latest international business headline news, online reports, and export tips. It includes information on every country in the world and resources for export and international business.

GE Industrial Systems EliteNet *(www.geindustrial.com)*
GE's EliteNet is a private exchange that connects GE Industrial Systems' Preferred Customers with critical information, resources, and management tools. EliteNet users have access to e-learning, e-business

updates, and detailed product specifications, along with on-line order management.

Manufacturing.net *(www.manufacturing.net)*

Manufacturing.net combines product and supplier databases with news, original editorial content, and powerful search-and-retrieval capabilities. It includes product information, economic statistics, and industry-specific news and research, focusing on design, automation and control, manufacturing processes, plant operations, and supply chain. The site draws from 23 magazines with a subscriber base of 2.35 million.

Office.com *(www.office.com)*

A venture of Winstar Communications, Office.com targets small and mid-sized businesses, offering them original content and selected third-party information for 150 industries, community areas, independent reviews, assessment tools, and one-click purchasing. In 2000, Office.com acquired Individual.com, a popular customized news service.

Oracle Exchange *(www.oracle.com)*

Oracle's aggressive move into e-everything is exemplified by Oracle Exchange, launched in mid-1999 as a hosted business-to-business trading network. Oracle first created "Auto-Xchange" for Ford, the world's first automotive online supply-chain network and the largest business-to-business electronic network, so the automotive giant could move its procurement operations to the Internet. Leveraging that experience, the database company then created Oracle Exchange, which offers "open e-business marketplaces that enable Internet supply chain networks to dramatically increase purchasing and operating efficiencies."

PeopleSoft Marketplace *(www.peoplesoftmarketplace.com)*

PeopleSoft got into the marketplace business in 2000 with this B-to-B trading exchange where customers, suppliers, and employees can collaborate and do business over the Internet. PeopleSoft Marketplace brings together select trading partners and suppliers and offers eProcurement to its users. The marketplace will continue to add such collaborative services as resource management, benefits, travel and expense, and recruiting.

VerticalNet *(www.verticalnet.com)*

VerticalNet is arguably the most successful operator of vertical trade communities on the Internet. VerticalNet offers nearly 60 vertical "communities" (Figure 10.2) in such specialized areas as communications, digital broadcasting, electronics, environmental, service, process, and science. Each of VerticalNet's communities is individually branded by industry and caters to individuals with similar professional interests. VerticalNet updates its editorial content daily on each site, encourages professionals to exchange ideas, provides a targeted area for buyers and sellers to do business with each other, and solicits advertisers for its "storefronts" on each vertical site. VerticalNet became one of the first such sites to launch its own online auction service in 1999. Despite its industry-leading success at public marketplaces, VerticalNet announced early in the second quarter of 2001 that it would refocus its business on creating software for companies to create their own private marketplaces.

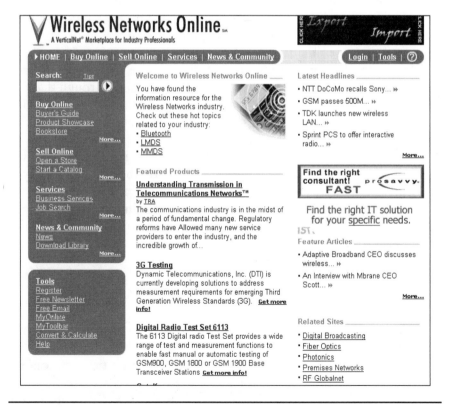

Figure 10.2. Wireless Networks Online is one of sixty specialized vertical communities offered by VerticalNet.

Yahoo! Industry Marketplaces (*industrymarketplaces.yahoo.com*)
In an effort to capitalize on the growth of B-to-B on the Internet, Yahoo! formed three distinct "Industry Marketplaces" in early 2001: Yahoo! IT Software Marketplace provides users with the ability to compare over 20,000 IT software packages, find information on tradeshows and seminars, and focus on the news from IT vendors and analysts. Yahoo! Electronics Marketplace and Yahoo! IT Hardware Marketplace are similar in nature.

Becoming Part of a Community

You can become part of most communities, as an individual or a representative of your business, by simply "joining." In some communities, joining is free. It takes nothing more than the process of completing and sending an online application and getting a user ID and password. Obviously, you could also become a paid advertiser.

In some communities, you may have to pay a membership or participation fee, or you may have to contribute part of the revenue you receive from the community if you sell something through that community. Some communities, such as virtual malls, may "rent" you virtual space on a contractual basis. Still others may ask you to "subscribe" for a certain period of time.

But this should not deter you from exploring the business viability of communities. Certainly, you can tell a lot about a community just by the companies it attracts. Typically, "name-brand" companies will not participate in a community that is not a legitimate operation.

Following is a suggested plan of action to help you evaluate communities for potential business participation.

Find the Right Communities

There are so many kinds of communities that you must first do a broad search to locate those communities that may have business or marketing value for you. You can start with the communities mentioned in this chapter, but there may be tens or even hundreds more that apply to your particular needs. Go to several of the portals mentioned earlier and use their search engines to help you locate appropriate communities. Remember that communities are not always identifiable as "communities"; they could be portals, hubs, virtual malls, auction sites, or any site where Internet users congregate regularly.

Narrow Your Options

Armed with this preliminary list of communities, begin to narrow your options by critically evaluating each site. First classify the potential communities into free versus paid sites. Then make sure you understand whom the community serves. You want to be certain that the target audience is appropriate for your product or service. Finally, determine from the information on the site which companies are involved in the community. You want to learn if your competitors participate. You also want to know whether or not the buyers and sellers are from companies that fit your company's own profile, and if they are the kinds of companies you want to do business with.

Then apply the following checklist to each community.

Which Free Services Are Offered?
Does the community offer free services you could take advantage of, such as e-mail, home pages, chat, discussion groups, etc.?

What Opportunities for Free Publicity Exist?
Does the community have areas in which your company, product, or service can obtain any of the following free:

- Listing in member or supplier directories

- Mention in discussion groups or chats

- Posting of press releases or product information

- Including a company profile

- Having speakers participate in online forums or seminars

- Posting of job openings

- Listing of your events in a community calendar

- Listing of your products or services in a buyers' guide

- Reciprocal linking to your site from the community and vice versa

What Opportunities for Paid Advertising and Promotion Are Available?

In evaluating paid opportunities, look at each possible activity from a media return on investment perspective. In other words, analyze the potential number of prospects you will reach and ask yourself if the dollars you are investing in the paid activity are reasonable on a cost-per-thousand basis. The smart way to go about it is to test a particular activity on a limited scale and see if the results warrant continued investment. The kinds of paid opportunities that may exist on community sites include

- Paid sponsorships of discussion groups or chats

- Paid sponsorships of site features, such as job banks and events

- Paid listings in directories and buyers' guides (Some communities provide different levels of participation so your products can be highlighted or you can be a featured supplier.)

- Fees/commissions for products sold

- Banner advertising on the home page or specific pages

- Paid sponsorship/advertising in a community e-mail newsletter

- Rental of e-mail subscriber lists

As with any business decision, weigh all the positives and negatives before you get involved in a community, even if participation is free. If your objective is to use the community for marketing purposes, you will have to invest time as well as money. It takes time to make use of a community's resources and build relationships with community members.

Often, the highest value you will get from a community is the *networking* value. View the community as a giant virtual meeting room.

The networking possibilities are limitless. If you look at the community as a place where unlimited networking potential can result in unlimited business opportunities, you will probably get more than you ever thought possible out of participating in one.

Should You Build a Sponsored Community?

A much larger decision than participating in an existing community is whether or not to build one of your own. As an IT marketer, why should you consider building a community in the first place? One reason is to establish a peremptory leadership position in a particular field.

Consider the case of Siebel Systems (*www.siebel.com*), a worldwide leader in sales-automation software. In February 1999, Siebel announced that it was launching a new business portal called Sales.com to serve the needs of sales professionals. Siebel partnered with Sun Microsystems, Dun & Bradstreet, and Miller Heiman to launch the site.

Sales.com provided, among other things:

- Sales tools to track and manage opportunities, accounts, contacts, calendars, and action items

- Up-to-the-minute information about public and private companies, customers, prospects, and competitors

- Personalized sales leads and fully integrated pipeline management, to build and manage sales opportunities

- Skills-enhancement services to help sales professionals continue to refine their sales skills by reading articles, receiving daily tips, and participating in a wide range of courses

- Networking services that allow sales professionals to build and leverage relationships through online communities and discussion forums

- A variety of online services including travel, a complete business center, and online shopping

This sponsored community was available first only to Siebel Systems customers, and then opened to all. In December 1999, Siebel announced that it was spinning off Sales.com as an independent, private company, having secured $27 million in private financing. This is a classic example of a visionary company's staking out new territory on the Internet and applying the concept of a business-to-business community to its own marketing and sales objectives.

Despite its early success as a free community site, Sales.com made a decision in 2000 to attempt to convert to a paid-subscriber site. It must not have been successful, because in the first quarter of 2001, Siebel announced it would shut down Sales.com.

Even though Sales.com succumbed to an economic downturn, the concept of a sponsored community lives on. In many respects, the emergence of private exchanges represents the evolution of the sponsored community.

The Use of Sponsored Communities by IT Companies Is Growing

IT companies serve identifiable audiences, such as developers and programmers, which often become strong affinity groups. A good example of this is the user group community, mentioned at the start of this chapter. Affinity groups naturally lend themselves to Web-based communities, and as a result, there continues to be rapid growth in these types of communities. Some communities are very clearly sponsored by a single company, with the goal of developing an affinity around that company's products or services, whereas others are communities that might be run by one or more sponsoring organizations to serve a market need.

A good example of a company-sponsored IT community is the Lotus Developer Network (*www.lotus.com/ldn*). This community, sponsored by IBM's Lotus subsidiary, appeals specifically to developers who work with Lotus products. The community includes information about training, events, and technical services. It also encourages developers to join in discussions. Developers can use the community free, or they can apply for a paid "Pro Membership" which adds a members-only Technical Forum and access to a special Knowledge Base.

Some IT communities develop an almost legendary and even fanatical following. Take Slashdot, for instance (*www.slashdot.com*), part of the Open Source Development Network (*www.osdn.com*), a division of VA Linux Systems. Slashdot, according to the *Washington Post*, is "the number one site for tech news and geek ranting."

Founded in 1997, Slashdot has acquired a reputation for being a freewheeling place that encourages unstructured, controversial sharing of opinions by Linux developers. As of May 2001, Slashdot was garnering more than 2 million unique visitors per month. That same month, Slashdot announced its availability on Palm-powered handheld devices.

Tools to Help You Build a Community or Exchange

Almost any IT company, no matter how small, can build at least a "destination site" on the Web. But it will probably take some specialized tools to build a true community or exchange. As with any Internet or software application, there are low-end (sometimes called "lite") and high-end versions. The tools mentioned next are a few examples of what is available to help you create a community or exchange, but they just scratch the surface.

Ariba *(www.ariba.com)*
Ariba is a major vendor in the B-to-B community and exchange space. Ariba claims to be "the largest worldwide business-to-business commerce network for operating resources on the Internet." Ariba.com creates a single network access point created for buyers and facilitates the transaction by acting as an intermediary. Such companies as Bristol-Myers Squibb, Cisco Systems, Federal Express, Hewlett-Packard, and Visa are client buyers. In the spring of 2001, Ariba announced a change of strategy, focusing its efforts on providing software to build and manage value chains for companies in certain vertical industries.

Comercis *(www.comercis.com)*
Comercis forms industry-specific communities that network professionals, vendors, distributors, manufacturers, and suppliers in a secure trade environment.

Commerce One *(www.commerceone.com)*
Commerce One offers a number of e-commerce community solutions, including MarketSite, a "trade zone" that competes with the previously mentioned Ariba. Commerce One created the Internet-purchasing system for General Motors.

Delphi *(www.delphi.com)*

Delphi has more than 750,000 registered members and 220,000 forums. Delphi forums allow members to create, control, and promote a virtual meeting place consisting of message boards, real-time chat, customized Web pages, integrated promotion, and electronic commerce. In mid-1999, Delphi introduced a unique twist to its forums called "Mention Marketing." This technology monitors Delphi's message boards for particular words that users might enter. These words would relate to a potential banner ad. So, for example, if a user types in the words "hard drive," Mention Marketing will detect it and trigger a banner ad from a computer vendor to appear at the bottom of the message board. This in itself is an interesting application of personalized advertising.

Excite *(www.excite.com)*

Excite, mentioned earlier in this chapter, is a portal that also provides the ability to start and join communities, as does the portal Yahoo! *(www.yahoo.com)*.

Involv *(www.involv.net)*

Most suitable for intranet usage, this free business-oriented service with home pages, polling and voting, a discussion board, task management, calendar, and shared links is positioned as "Web Teaming."

Participate.com *(www.participate.com)*

Participate.com offers larger companies outsourced online community-management services. Its clients include AT&T WorldNet, Quote.com, and The Street.

PurchasePro *(www.purchasepro.com)*

PurchasePro offers software to build online marketplaces that help businesses of all sizes buy, sell, and collaborate. PurchasePro also operates the Global Marketplace, interconnecting more than 140,000 businesses and powering hundreds of private and public marketplaces.

What to Build into Your Community

Suppose you have decided to consider building a community. How do you really go about it? Here is a basic plan.

Determine the Type of Community You Need

First decide if your community will target only employees (an intranet), customers or suppliers (an extranet), or a public community on the Web. Intranets and extranets will require special security measures to protect confidential information and limit access to authorized participants. You may wish to restrict access to a public community as well by establishing subscriber or membership rules. Your goal for a public community may be to gain widespread publicity, or you may wish to allow only qualified individuals to make use of the community's services.

Set Objectives for Your Community and Establish an Operating Budget

Set some realistic specific objectives for your community. With a customer community, for example, set a goal for how many customers you expect will participate. Project customer-service savings and revenue impact of the community. Also establish a community operating budget, both for start-up and ongoing development and maintenance costs. A community is more complicated to build than a basic Web site, and it potentially involves more back-end support because it is so interactive in nature. Be sure to anticipate the cost and manpower required to support the activity generated by a community.

Establish a Community Structure

Learn what a community is, how it operates, and what it includes by visiting other business communities and actively participating in them. Typically, you will want to consider including the following in your community.

Information Center
This is usually the heart of the community. Depending on the type of community you establish, this area would contain information about your industry, your company and other companies' products and services, white papers and special reports, directories (if appropriate), pertinent news, research links and tools, etc.

Community Services

As part of your community, you may want to provide value-added services to community members, such as a master calendar of events, selected links to other relevant Web pages, and an e-mail newsletter.

Interactive Areas

A key part of what makes a community a community is interactivity. The easiest way to offer interactivity is probably through the creation of a bulletin board. Beyond bulletin boards, interactivity can move from e-mail messaging to discussion forums to live chat rooms. It is recommended that you include at least one form of interactive technology, because this is a primary characteristic of a community. It is also a good idea to include an interactive feedback mechanism, even if it is a simple Web response form, to encourage community members to offer their comments and suggestions.

Conducting Business or Using e-Commerce

You will need to incorporate some combination of database and e-commerce technology into your community if you want to conduct business. E-commerce, of course, will be the heart of any marketplace or exchange you build. In this case, you should thoroughly review the chapters on Internet customer service (Chapter 9) and selling on the Internet (Chapter 12).

Involving Partners

Some partners may want to participate in co-founding your community, whereas others may want to be sponsors. Others may see the community as a way to increase their own exposure and sales opportunities. Partners that have a "brand name" can enhance the credibility of your community and make it all the more desirable to users. For more about partnering, see the next chapter.

Set Up the Back-End

As indicated above, a community is a more-complex and involved Web site. Do not underestimate the back end. Establish processes and procedures to service and respond to community members. Have a good, integrated Web database in operation. Ensure that all technologies you deploy in the community are pretested and are functioning properly.

Verify that your Web server or hosting service is adequate and that all activity can be monitored. Make sure everything is working—*before* you go live!

Launch and Publicize Your Community

Launching a Web community is a lot like launching a new product—and most IT marketers know what that involves. Use the same marketing tactics for launching the community as you would when launching a new product: Establish a publicity campaign, try to get press coverage, hold special events, and if appropriate, advertise.

Maintain and Grow Your Community

Once established, your community will require ongoing care and attention. A community is an active, vibrant place. Community members will expect content to be refreshed frequently, links to be working, discussion groups to be current, and interactive systems to be responsive. Maintaining the community is an essential part of its success. And it does not stop there—you should always be looking for ways to improve and grow the community.

11

Internet Partnering

In the information technology business, the 1990s saw the emergence of true "coopetition," as arch-rivals built pacts and formed alliances in hopes of collectively increasing revenues. IBM was at the center of two such deals in 1999, reaching agreements with Dell and EMC. Only a few years ago, these business alliances might have been unthinkable. Both Dell and EMC compete fiercely with IBM, the first going head-to-head in PC sales, and the second steadily increasing market share in computer storage systems, once an IBM stronghold. Yet IBM apparently saw value in cooperating with these competitors, finding a way to turn their opposition into a business opportunity.

In many respects, this is an indication of a business shift of remarkable proportions. And the Internet is, in part, responsible for this new business environment. With its natural alliance-building architecture, the Internet has broken down business barriers and caused partnering to flourish. The Internet has even spawned its own brand of partnering—affiliate marketing. The Internet is being used by many organizations to establish far-reaching alliances; in some cases, partners are even establishing entire information networks.

The significance of Internet partnering takes on special meaning for IT companies in dealing with the channel. Most IT companies could not drive the sales they need without channel partners, such as distributors and resellers. Here, the Internet shows great promise, since it facilitates cooperative Web marketing and lead distribution. But it can be a double-edged sword, because the IT company's Web presence could also create a direct conflict with its channel partners.

In this chapter, we discuss some of the positives and negatives of Internet partnering, and you will discover how IT companies can put it to best use.

Partnering—The Traditional Way

Partnering with other businesses certainly is not a new concept, even though partnering with competitors may be a new twist. For IT companies, "strategic alliances" are an increasingly common way of doing business. Companies with compatible products or services find that they can potentially reduce marketing and sales costs, provide a more comprehensive solution, and potentially increase revenues faster when they work together.

Partnering has brought great change to the information technology industry. Computer hardware and software companies often develop partnerships that are intended to present strong reasons to buy two or more products together rather than separately. These companies will sometimes involve a "channel partner," such as a VAR (Value-Added Reseller) or a distributor, which typically adds a service and support component to the package. In the best scenarios, the partners deliver a superior solution of high value. But if the partnerships go awry, the customer can be caught in the middle of a lot of finger pointing or, at the very least, a lack of coordination.

Nonetheless, partnering has its distinct advantages, and it has generally been successful as a way of doing business for IT companies. It seems logical, then, that the Internet would not only adopt the partnering model, but capitalize on it.

Before we explore Internet partnering, it is appropriate to first talk about some of the ways you can get the most out of traditional partner marketing relationships.

Cooperate But Do Not Capitulate

Cooperative marketing programs should be just that—cooperative. You and your partner should develop programs together, and you should agree on common objectives, offers, messaging, and logistics. But it is generally best for only one partner to take the lead—and usually it is the partner who is putting in the most money. If that is your company, you need to diplomatically take control of the program. Although you will work in a spirit of cooperation, you will also want to be sure that your company gets what it needs out of the relationship, that you can make the final decisions, and that you will get a reasonable return on your investment.

Accentuate Your Compatibility

Get to the root of what is fundamentally special about your partner relationship—and then highlight the benefits of it. You may want to develop special packages or offers that make it very attractive to purchase your products together with your partner's products. If the partner relationship involves service and support, this too could be a unique aspect of your sale. Whenever you sell jointly, convince the prospect that your partnership makes you stronger and differentiates you from the pack.

Centralize Lead Processing

If possible, centralize lead processing and fulfillment. If you are the lead partner, maintain management of the lead generation process. If leads go directly to partners, you immediately lose control over those leads—and your ability to track responses and analyze results is lost as well. If you must decentralize lead generation; at least establish and agree on methods to share, distribute, contact, and follow up on leads. This activity should be just as carefully managed and coordinated as joint sales calls.

Offer Resellers Turnkey Programs—and Make It Easy to Participate

Many IT marketers are involved in *channel marketing*—marketing products and services through VARs, retailers, distributors, representatives, agents, or other marketing partners that resell products. Computer hardware, software, and networking manufacturers have widely adopted this selling model to more effectively reach diverse markets, often on a worldwide basis. Insurance companies have long distributed their products and services through captive or independent agents.

Resellers are a special kind of partner. They especially like programs that support their business, but take very little effort on their part. If you want to support reseller partners, it pays to design direct marketing programs that are fast, low-cost, and easy to customize for resellers.

Consider doing "VAR versions" of your end-user promotions, and get larger VARs to sign on up front so you can simply tag them on to your existing program. It will be easier, faster, and cheaper for everyone.

Consider adding incentive programs for the sales teams of larger resellers—so they get excited about promoting your products over someone else's. Make sure the sales teams (yours as well as your partners') are informed of any direct marketing programs that you are executing on their behalf.

Support Partners with Traditional Direct Marketing

Supporting partners with traditional direct marketing is a common practice. Companies working as partners may co-brand advertising or direct mail promotions to take advantage of market conditions and benefit from joint marketing. Alternatively, the sponsoring company may execute a direct mail program and offer partners the opportunity of participating by printing versions of the piece with each partner's logo and call-to-action information.

Many information technology companies execute partner versioning as a routine part of a direct mail promotion. Several years ago, I was involved in a significant effort that brought together a major computer manufacturer with more than 50 software partners and resellers. The computer company was promoting a new hardware platform, and it was important to demonstrate that software vendors were building applications for and supporting the platform. The company aggressively solicited the participation of leading partners and offered to fund the majority of the promotional costs.

A core mailing package was developed. It included elements that could easily be versioned: an outside envelope with a glassine window that allowed a brochure to show through it, a laser-generated letter and reply form with the computer company's logo along with digitized logos of the partner companies, and a brochure that was designed as a template with common copy, except for a panel that could easily be versioned and was reserved for the partners.

A common informational offer was used for this program, but this offer was enhanced with a special purchase incentive unique to each partner. Partners were required to add training, additional licenses, or consulting as their "payment" for participating in the program. A few of the partners wanted their own unique versions of the program, which could be accommodated at an additional shared cost.

Many marketing lessons were learned from this campaign, among them:

1. The computer company could extend its reach well beyond its own customer and prospect base, reaching new audiences with an interest in specific software solutions. In fact, in many cases, it was the software that pulled the sale to the computer company.

2. The computer company could penetrate new vertical markets as a result of a software company's specialized product or industry strength. This opened new business opportunities that previously were not available.

Centralizing and consolidating the direct marketing campaign achieved a number of economies and efficiencies. Rental lists could be acquired at once, so duplicates could be eliminated across all mailings in advance. Materials could be printed at once for maximum efficiency. A single source managed the program, increasing program efficiency. All leads funneled through a single point of contact, increasing the efficiency of prospect contact and lead distribution and resulting in the ability to consolidate response management and results reporting. This made it much easier to evaluate the success of each individual mailing, as well as the overall campaign.

Partnered direct marketing programs need not be this elaborate to achieve results. I have seen partner versions of self-mailers and even postcards perform very effectively. As with any direct marketing program, the keys are good list selection, a strong offer, and creativity appropriate for your audience.

But today there is another weapon: the Internet. Now traditional direct marketing partner programs can be enhanced with the Internet in a variety of ways:

1. Using a partner-specific URL, you can direct leads to a special Web page that reinforces the benefits of the partnered program and captures responder information.

2. E-mail can be used to acknowledge information requests, confirm orders, and embed Web links to partners' Web sites.

3. You can keep partners informed of program activities via e-mail and can post direct mail samples for partners to review on the Web.

4. You can use a partner extranet to allow partners to view and order entire programs, distribute leads, track results, and monitor performance.

We discuss these ideas in more detail later in this chapter, but first, let us explore how partnering began on the Internet.

The Starting Point for Internet Partnering: Affiliate Marketing

It was Amazon.com (*www.amazon.com*) that created the first commercially successful affiliate marketing program, Amazon.com Associates. Amazon pioneered a method of partner or shared-revenue marketing that has become one of the fastest growing types of business on the Internet. Forrester Research (*www.forrester.com*) predicts that affiliate marketing will account for over 20 percent of online sales by 2003.

What exactly is affiliate marketing? Although the particulars change based on who is offering it and how it operates, the basic definition is the same: An affiliate marketing program is essentially a revenue-sharing program that uses the Internet to facilitate partnered selling.

Let's look at Amazon's affiliate model to explain the concept. It is a very simple yet ingenious idea. Anyone with a Web site (as long as it does not have questionable content) can become an Amazon Associate, free of charge. You simply sign up, agree to the company's terms, and link to Amazon.com's site through a variety of ways. For example, you can put a "button" on your home page, or use a search box link (which allows visitors to search Amazon for products from within your site), or link to individual products sold by Amazon. In all cases, links lead your Web site visitors directly to Amazon.com—through a unique URL that tracks activity back to you. This way, if a visitor purchases anything from Amazon through your site, you get paid a commission, based on the particular product purchased. You also get the benefit of an e-commerce "store" on your site, along with the legitimacy of the Amazon brand.

You become an "agent" or an Internet reseller for Amazon. You need not fill the order, collect money, or deal with customer service because Amazon handles all that. And since the company is so good at it, your Web site visitors have a positive buying experience through your site. It is an Internet variation of the old "drop-shipping" model used by mail-order companies. A mail-order company would offer a product it did not manufacture and make an arrangement with the manufacturer to ship the product, from its warehouse, directly to the customer. The mail-order company, as the middleman, would then bill the customer and pay the manufacturer.

Affiliate marketing is so uncomplicated and easy for both parties that it is possible for everybody to be a winner. There is little risk on the part of either the affiliate program sponsor or the affiliate. Setting up links is technically simple and inexpensive, and the very nature of the Web makes these links easily traceable. An affiliate can be as aggressive or passive as desired in promoting the sponsor's products. In some cases, the affiliate's primary objective may be to enhance a Web site's service component, so the added income from the program is just an added benefit. Other affiliates may be looking for a fast, easy way to get into e-commerce, or improve an established operation by adding an increased product line.

From the site visitor's perspective, an affiliate program is an added benefit. The visitor can now purchase products or services directly from your site. If those products and services are relevant to your site's topic area, then the visitor's experience is enhanced.

Making Affiliate Marketing Programs Meet Your Needs

Affiliate programs are both broad in reach and highly targetable. That means you can pretty much mold an affiliate program to your own needs.

For example, suppose you are a marketer of software targeted to businesses. If you were part of the Amazon Associates program, or another Internet bookseller's program, you could select appropriate books in the software category and sell them on your Web site. You are providing your site visitors with a service and gaining additional revenue at no cost. It really is that simple to make money with affiliate marketing.

The same principle applies to other affiliate marketing programs, from products to services to auctions. It is all in how you apply affiliate marketing to your own specialized IT marketing needs.

I have taken this approach with my own company. As an Amazon Associate, my company added a direct marketing bookstore to its Web site. It is completely flexible and uncomplicated. We choose marketing books (including my own) that are relevant to our site and write our own descriptions of the books. Each book has a special order number provided by Amazon, which links directly to the Amazon.com site, so visitors to our site can easily order these books. We also have a search box link, which makes it possible for visitors to buy anything Amazon.com sells.

For each item ordered through our site from Amazon, our company gets a small commission. We are providing a valuable service to our Web site visitors and enjoying the benefits of e-commerce—at no cost to the company. The income is modest, but the service we provide is invaluable. This is but one tiny example of how affiliate marketing can work for any company.

Does it work for IT companies? Consider the fact that Dell Computer (*www.dell.com*) announced its first-ever affiliate marketing program in March 1999. Launched with 50 charter members, the Dell program extended its products to more than 65,000 affiliate sites. By the end of 1999, Dell's program was expanded to the Asia Pacific region.

Despite the growth of affiliate marketing, there are some who believe the model is flawed. Critics say that affiliate marketing simply directs Web traffic to other sites, providing a quick exit door instead of keeping visitors captive. As a result, some companies, such as Iconomy (*www.iconomy.com*) and Escalate (*www.escalate.com*), offer to build "ready-made" Web stores that sit on a company's Web site, rather than send visitors to another site to make a purchase.

Tips on Becoming an Affiliate

In most cases, becoming an affiliate is as uncomplicated as signing up and linking to the affiliate sponsor's site. But there are a number of key considerations.

Choose Affiliate Programs Carefully
There are now thousands of affiliate programs available. Start by doing a survey of these programs to determine which fit with your site. Two of the best places to look are Associate-It (*www.associate-it.com*), which claims to be the "Web's biggest directory of Associate Programs," and Refer-It (*www.refer-it.com*), an Internet.com site. These two sites do an excellent job of providing general information about and providing search engines for affiliate programs. Between the two sites, you will find thousands of affiliate programs to review. Pick several that are rel-

evant to your business and then read the terms of every affiliate program very carefully. They are not all the same. Each may have its own unique twist. Be sure to understand the commitment required by the sponsor, and whether or not you will have to pay anything up front to participate.

Verify the Legitimacy of the Programs You are Considering

Do not assume that an affiliate marketing program or its sponsor is legitimate, just because you find it in a directory. If you are familiar with the name and the reputation of the company, there is probably little cause for concern. However, many affiliate program sponsors could be companies you never heard of before. This does not mean they are not legitimate, but do your homework. Make sure you are comfortable with the types of products the sponsoring company offers. Find out how long the sponsor's affiliate program has been in existence and how many affiliates are involved. Ask for references and check them out. Try to learn if there have been any complaints about the company by checking them out with local Better Business Bureaus or other such organizations operating on the Internet. It may even be worth it to go to a few of the sponsor's affiliate sites and order products through them to see how the sponsor handles your order. Determine if you can try the program for a limited period of time without obligation. This is a serious business decision. Make sure you are affiliating with a company that will not damage your own reputation.

Select Programs That Meet Your Web Site Visitors' Needs

Narrow down your selection to a few affiliate marketing programs that you feel best fit with your site. Typically, your affiliate program will be more successful if the sponsor's products or services are complementary to your own. As in the earlier example of selecting specific books from Amazon.com that might be of interest to a site visitor, you should think about working with merchants whose products relate to the products and services your company markets. Why do visitors come to your site, and what are they looking for? If the sponsor's affiliate program helps to answer these questions and supports the theme of your site or the business you are in, then it is probably a good fit.

Test One Program

You will probably be tempted to add several affiliate programs to your site. If you are new to affiliate marketing, however, you may want to approach it conservatively and test one program first. It is important to understand how affiliate marketing works and to see if your visitors will be receptive to it. You also need to make a commitment to the affiliate program, promoting it on your site and keeping the information relating to the program fresh.

Continuously Evaluate the Program and Add Other Programs Selectively

Keep a close eye on how well affiliate marketing works for you. Evaluate the sponsor's service and make sure your visitors are satisfied. Determine if you are getting what you anticipated out of the program. After you are comfortable with the concept of affiliate marketing, you could consider adding other programs to your site. But do so selectively. Typically, it is not productive to add multiple affiliate programs in the same category, for example. Make a commitment to one bookseller, or one computer products vendor. Otherwise, you may be offering your visitors too many choices and that could dilute overall ordering from your site. Affiliate programs should enhance your site, not take away from its effectiveness. If you fill your site with too many affiliate programs, your visitors may perceive that you are more interested in making money than servicing their needs.

Guidelines for Creating Your Own Affiliate Program

If you are interested in creating your own affiliate marketing program (i.e., a program in which you are the company doing the selling, rather than the affiliate), you will have a different perspective.

Establish an e-Commerce Operation First

Although some affiliate marketing programs share leads rather than revenue, the vast majority of affiliate programs are e-commerce programs. Do not even try to institute an affiliate program unless you already have a successful e-commerce operation or you are willing to make the investment in such an operation. If your objective is to fuel your e-commerce effort with affiliate marketing, you probably should consider a packaged solution or an affiliate marketing service provider. Following are some providers of affiliate marketing solutions:

BeFree (www.befree.com)
BeFree had over 2,800,000 affiliates signed up for some 200 merchants just one month after its November 1999 IPO was filed. BeFree mer-

chant clients establish "virtual storefronts" on affiliate sites, targeting specific merchandise to complement both the merchant and affiliate Web sites. BeFree's customers include America Online, Compaq, Gateway, Hewlett-Packard, and IBM.

ClickTrade (www.clicktrade.com)

ClickTrade targets small businesses and operates as part of Microsoft bCentral (*www.bcentral.com*). ClickTrade encourages small businesses to sign up as merchants in its "Revenue Avenue" area, a directory of over 7,000 affiliate programs that includes over 120,000 affiliates.

Commission Junction (www.cj.com)

Commission Junction is an affiliate marketing ASP that provides a turn-key solution for managing revenue-sharing relationships. CJ provides a network of more than 1,500 merchants and 350,000 content sites with affiliate marketing, management, recruiting, and administrative services on-demand. Participating merchants include eBay, Excite, HotJobs.com, Intranets.com, and Telocity.

LinkShare (www.linkshare.com)

LinkShare was one of the early providers of affiliate marketing programs. Launched in 1997, LinkShare was granted a U.S. patent in 1999 for the tracking technology behind its affiliate programs. In 2000, LinkShare launched a B-to-B network. LinkShare's 400 participating merchants include AT&T, BizTravel, Dell Computer, Delta Airlines, Handspring, McAfee.com, Priceline, and Verio.

Performics (www.performics.com)

Performics, formerly Dynamic Trade, positions itself as a full-service "pay-for-performance" vendor of online marketing tactics, including search engine optimization, partnering, and e-mail marketing channels. Clients of Performics include Bose, Discover, and Eddie Bauer.

Construct an Affiliate Program That Benefits Everyone

As the affiliate program sponsor, or merchant, your primary objectives are probably to extend your own company's awareness and reach, and increase your revenue. But you have a business obligation to construct a program that also benefits your primary customers (your affiliates) *and* your secondary customers (your affiliates' customers). Your affiliate program should be easy and uncomplicated for an affiliate to implement. Although you could charge an affiliate for participating in your program, most affiliate programs are free to the affiliate, so you may be less competitive if participation in your program costs money. Structure your compensation plan fairly so the affiliate benefits from your sales success. Typically, companies offer affiliates anywhere from 5 to 15 percent of the selling price of a product or service. Some programs may offer as high as 20 to 30 percent, but these higher amounts are usually doled out as special incentives or bonuses. Many affiliate programs are based on flat commissions, but there is some evidence that sliding-scale commissions are being adopted by merchants with products of varying value. A sliding scale may be appropriate if you want to reward affiliates for selling higher-priced products, and it could also differentiate your affiliate program from others. Remember, affiliates are really resellers that can contribute significant incremental sales at little cost to you, so make it worth their while to participate.

Work Out All the Details

There are numerous operational details you need to think about. For example, you could offer an affiliate program that has branding options. You may feel strongly about maintaining your identity on the affiliate program, or you may want to allow affiliates the flexibility to co-brand or "private label" your program. Under the private-label scenario, an affiliate could basically take your program and put its name on it. You could decide to implement a graduated revenue-sharing arrangement, whereby affiliates that sell more get a higher share of revenue. You need to determine what kinds of linking you will allow to your site, provide artwork and instructions, and set up a system that tracks affiliate activity. These are the kinds of details you will need to work out in advance, and each detail will have technical implications behind it.

Protect Yourself with a Legal Agreement

One of the advantages of affiliate programs is that you can grow a network of affiliates very rapidly via the Internet. If hundreds or thousands of Web site owners become your affiliates, it is unlikely that you will be able to screen each one and get to know them individually. They are not unlike VARs, albeit on a smaller scale when it comes to dollar volume. That is why a legal agreement is absolutely essential, just as it is for VARs. Before you sign on any affiliate, the affiliate should be required to accept the terms of your agreement. The agreement should include, among other things, a discussion of the business relationship you are establishing, your stand on ethics, terms of payment, and conditions of cancellation. You will probably want some language in the agreement that protects you and your site against fraud, unethical practices, and use of your program in association with any illegal or objectionable business activity.

Service Your Affiliates

Once your program is up and running, keep your affiliates informed via e-mail and by posting information on a special affiliates' page on your Web site. Report activity to affiliates on a regular basis and be sure to issue payments promptly. Ask your affiliates for feedback on how you can make your program better and what you can do to improve service. Affiliates not only are a valuable source of revenue, but they also can refer other affiliates to you and help you keep your finger on the pulse of Internet buyers.

Make a Long-term Commitment to Affiliate Marketing

After you are in the affiliate marketing business, look at it as a *business,* not just a marketing program. As a major distribution channel for your product or service, your affiliates are as important a channel as distributors, resellers, retailers, or a direct sales force. Do not underestimate the care and attention affiliates will require. You will need to consider an ongoing program of affiliate acquisition and retention, just as you would with prospects and customers. You will need to "police" your network as well as you can to make sure affiliates are legitimate and that they are playing by the rules. You will want to work out the details of building and maintaining relationships with your "affiliate community." Of course, you will also need to have a solid structure for standard affiliate reporting (both internal and reports to affiliates) and affiliate compensation.

Examples of IT-Related Affiliate Programs

Visit the two sites mentioned earlier, Associate-It and Refer-It, for the most updated listings of affiliate programs. Following are just a few examples of affiliate programs that are IT-related or of special interest to IT marketers.

Build My PC.com (*www.buildmypc.com*)

BuildMyPC is an Internet-based store that assembles computer systems to meet customer requirements. BuildMyPC offers a two-tier affiliate structure. For computer sales originating from an affiliate's site, the company pays a 1 percent commission. For sales originating from people referred to BuildMyPC's affiliate program by an affiliate, the company pays a one-half percent commission.

BuyTELCO (*www.buytelco.com*)

BuyTELCO is a clearinghouse for companies to purchase telephone services, selling everything from Internet access and frame-relay circuits to long distance and DSL. BuyTELCO has an affiliate program that lets affiliates decide what's best for their sites. They can link directly to the BuyTELCO home page, with access to the entire site, or only to those sections of the site that are of most interest to their customers. Affiliates create their own "BuyTELCO store" and earn commissions on the items they stock there. BuyTELCO also offers "PartnerPlace" (Figure 11.1), a program that allows system integrators and VARs to set up a telecom back office, or private extranet, that can be offered to customers.

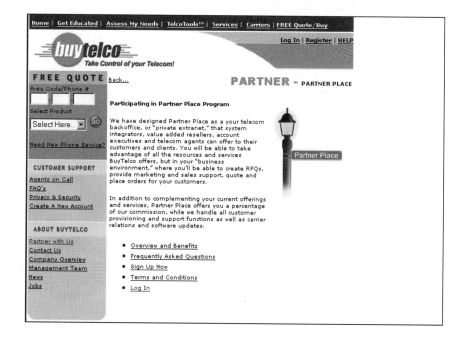

Figure 11.1. BuyTELCO offers an affiliate program as well as "Partner Place," which allows system integrators and VARs to set up a telecom back office, or private extranet, that can be offered to customers.

Dell (*www.dell.com; www.linkshare.com*)

Dell is generating $50 million a day in online revenue, and part of that comes from its "Dell Affiliates" program. Dell's program pays a 1 percent referral fee for qualifying sales. If you are interested in participating, you must sign up through LinkShare, which operates the Dell program.

GE Express (*www.geexpress.com*)

GE Express is a service that provides a single source for spare and replacement parts for major manufacturers' computers and related equipment. The company maintains a large inventory of quality parts and also provides a parts identification and hard-to-find sourcing service. Affiliates can earn a 3 percent commission on all orders placed from an affiliate site. GE Express pays commission as long as the purchase transaction is completed within 45 days of the referral.

HP Garage Affiliate Network (*www.hp.com/solutions1/garage/affiliates/index.html*)

This is not an affiliate marketing program in the true sense, but it is included because of its unique attributes. Basically, the HP Garage Affiliate Network puts small startups that use HP products in touch with companies that can offer them business services and expertise. Service categories include customer support, human resources, IT facility services, market research, mobile solutions, and public relations.

iGo (*www.igo.com*)

iGo is an online mobile-technology store that sells cellular phones, laptops, PDAs, digital cameras, voice recorders, and more. iGo's program offers affiliates a 7 percent commission on gross revenue for customers who purchase from iGo through an affiliate's site.

Outpost (*www.outpost.com*)

Outpost claims to be the world's largest online computer store, selling over 170,000 products. As with the Dell Affiliates program mentioned above, the Outpost program is managed by LinkShare, so affiliates must sign up via the LinkShare network.

Sundial.com (*www.sundial.com*)

Sundial.com retails wireless products and services online. Sundial.com partners with such well-known providers as AT&T, Omnipoint, Cellular One, US Cellular, AllTel, GTE, and SkyTel to offer wireless plans, phones, pagers, and even satellite TV systems. Affiliates earn 10 percent commission on all wireless products and services, and a $20 commission on each satellite TV system sold.

VeriSign (*www.verisign.com*) and Network Solutions (*www.networksolutions.com*)

VeriSign is a leader in security products used to authenticate sites to visitors. The VeriSign affiliate program is targeted to Internet Service Providers and Web hosting companies, allowing them to integrate digital certificates into their service offerings. VeriSign's subsidiary, Network Solutions, operates an affiliate program that has nearly 65,000 affiliates worldwide. Affiliates can earn 20 percent revenue share on Web address and bundled-services, 20 percent on Search/Submit, and flat fees on "ImageCafe" Web sites.

Using the Internet to Support Channel Partners

Whereas the affiliate program is the prevalent partner model on the Internet, the larger opportunity for IT marketers in terms of Internet partnering may well be in channel partnering.

IT companies that use retail, distributor, or reseller channels know that these forms of product distribution make it difficult to track sales and virtually impossible to capture the end-user customer. Customer end users are sometimes held at arm's length—unintentionally or purposely—by channel partners. Even worse, these customers become vulnerable to a company's competition because the reseller or retailer often does not have an exclusive relationship with the company and can therefore market competitive products to these customers.

As a result, the IT company misses the opportunity to communicate first-hand with a vast customer segment. These customers are no less important to the company, but they are "co-customers" of the channel partner. Marketing to this specialized customer base and building relationships with them becomes a complex and difficult challenge.

Just as important, the IT company needs to build an ongoing relationship with the partner organization itself. Large, global companies in particular could have a loose network of partners all over the world, some more loyal than others. How can a large company keep all of these various types of partners informed? And how can that company truly service their needs?

The Internet may help to solve this chronic business-to-business marketing problem. The Internet can help you know who your customers are when you rely on indirect sales channels. And the Internet makes it relatively easy for you to collaborate with resellers and other partners, sharing resources and cooperating on electronic marketing initiatives that could result in a substantial payback for a modest investment on the part of all partners. If you are the originating company, you can go a step further and enlist the assistance of partner organizations in reaching out to their extended customer family.

Reaching channel customers could be just the beginning of a deepening Internet relationship between companies and their partners. It therefore makes sense to fully explore the potential of sharing information on each other's Web sites, cross-linking, and extending electronic marketing activities.

As you might expect, there are already Internet-focused companies in existence that are capitalizing on the channel partner challenge. One of them, Asera (*www.asera.com*), offers an e-business solution it refers to as "demand chain management"—Web-based software that users configure to meet the needs of each channel. The solution addresses product lines, pricing, marketing, sales, and online order management, and is sold on a pay-for-use basis.

Building an Internet-based Channel Partner Program

The Internet can be as much an enemy as an ally in forging channel partnerships. That's because an IT company's Web presence can create the ultimate in channel conflict. An IT case in point came to light in "Avoiding Channel Conflict," a story that appeared in the March 2001 issue of *Line 56* magazine (*www.line56.com*). It was reported that Hewlett-Packard walks a fine line between selling directly and via its 40,000 North American resellers. HP tries to avoid undercutting its resellers in pricing. In addition, HP funnels leads via the Web directly to about 8,000 North American certified resellers. Resellers are required to report on the disposition of each lead.

There is little doubt that IT companies will increasingly rely on the Internet to help them maintain partner relationships and service channel partners. Of course, these business relationships are far more involved than the previously discussed affiliate programs. For the most part, the affiliate program concept relies on large numbers to succeed. The affiliate concept chains hundreds or thousands of other Web site owners together, working on the basis of exponentially increasing the sales of the originator. Although the originator "touches" the affiliates occasionally, the business relationship is more distant than with traditional partners. In most cases, the originator never meets or even speaks with the affiliate; the relationship is conducted via e-mail.

Here, on the other hand, it is likely that a business partner relationship has already been established, typically with a select group of companies. The partners are far more important in their relationships with the originating company. They were in place before the Internet was even considered as a marketing channel.

For Internet-based companies, the affiliate program may, in fact, represent the sole partner channel. But for traditional IT marketers rapidly transitioning to Internet marketing, the affiliate program is merely a nice bonus in terms of incremental revenue. For the traditional IT company, channel partners are more integral to the success of that company's entire selling model. In some cases, as with companies distributing products through distributors or master resellers, channel selling could be largely responsible for the company's profit or loss.

For these companies, then, the Internet is being used to facilitate communication and interaction between the company and the partner. In fact, this application of the Internet is probably even more significant than affiliate programs in the long run.

It is important to realize that the Internet itself will not compensate for a channel partner program that is unstable or poorly run in the first place. However, if your channel partner program is on solid ground to begin with, then using the Internet can have a major positive impact on channel partner programs.

There are several ways you can combine the traditional principles of partnering with the benefits of new media marketing.

"Web-ize" the Partner Relationship

Whether you are the company with partners, or the partner, you can quickly begin to make the Internet an integral part of your business relationship by collaborating on the Web. Encourage partners either to link to your site or to pick up and incorporate entire pages of information from your site into their sites. Provide partners with information from your Web site that you have repackaged for their use or offer to customize Web content for their sites. Give partners a graphic "button" or small banner that they can use on their sites to link to your site. If you are the originating company, offer partners a place on your site where they can post their information, perhaps in a "partner show-case" section of your Web site. Provide partners with their own unique order page to facilitate e-commerce.

Link Your Communications Electronically
Encourage e-mail communications between your organization's employ-ees and your partners' employees. With major business partners, you may want to agree on using portions of each other's networks selec-tively to facilitate communications.

Promote Your Partners in a Special Area of Your Web Site
IT marketers with significant partner relationships may want to pro-mote these relationships on their corporate Web sites. The most com-mon way to do this is by creating a special area on the Web site. This section typically describes the company's partner program (so the com-pany potentially can acquire new partners), highlights new partner participants, features news about partners, and provides links to part-ners' sites.

Establish a Partner Service Extranet
In Chapter 9, we discussed building a customer-driven extranet. You can do much the same thing with partners. There are two possibilities: You can create a private-access area of your company's Web site just for partners, or you can establish a private extranet that uses a separate URL to "hide it" from public view. In both cases, the primary objective is the same: to provide a site that services your partners. This site can be as simple or as sophisticated as you wish. You can start by using it as a central repository of all partner information—program details, agree-ments, promotions, and so on.

Ultimately, however, the greatest value of a partner extranet is *ser-vice*. You can use the partner extranet to offer a full range of promo-tional and marketing services to your partners. By establishing an order, delivery, and monitoring process up front, you will be able to offer part-ners a complete, one-stop resource for support.

You can also use the extranet to service the partner relationship by transferring paper-based systems to the Internet. For example, consider moving program and product ordering, lead distribution, results tracking, program monitoring, invoicing, receivables, and inventory tracking to the Internet over time. Create a self-service center where partners can resolve their own problems to cut down on telephone and face-to-face support. In other words, use the Internet to conduct business with your partners, not just as a marketing support medium.

Examples of IT Internet Partner Programs

Since information technology companies lead the market in using partners and the channel to distribute their products, they tend to have the most mature Web-based partner programs. Here are some examples.

Cisco (*www.cisco.com*)
Nearly 90 percent of Cisco's revenue goes through the channel, so you would expect Cisco to have a large, active partner and reseller program. Cisco introduced a new Channel Partner Program in mid-2001 that focuses, in part, on aggressively leveraging e-business. Cisco's established Internet presence will play a significant role in making the program a success.

IBM (*www.ibm.com/partnerworld*)
Take a good look at IBM's "PartnerWorld" and you'll get a real appreciation for just how comprehensive partner programs can be. PartnerWorld is a complete resource for IBM Business Partners, which includes marketing and sales, education and certification, technical support, financing, and more—all in one central location. The marketing and sales area is particularly impressive. It offers an entire co-marketing program of campaigns, events, and seminars; a marketing materials center with an "eLiterature Rack" and image library; and numerous sales tools, such as lead management and an "e-business value knowledgebase."

Intel (*channel.intel.com*)
The maker of the Pentium processor has an entire subsite off its corporate site just for the channel. Click on "Contents" and you'll see the depth of the site, from a new-visitor's center to general resources, including product and technical information, training, sales tools, global membership programs, and more. Intel's "e-Business Network" provides a centralized mechanism for serving partners with certification,

training, and business support. It includes a "Business Market Place," where channel partners can locate and link up with one another.

Microsoft (*www.microsoft.com/directaccess/partnering/microsoft/*)
"Microsoft for Partners" is itself a customer site that is accessible from the Microsoft.com home page. The Partners site links to four different areas: Microsoft Certified Partners, the Internet Services Network for ISPs and communications companies, "Microsoft Direct Access" for companies that sell technology and services, and the System Builder Program for OEMs.

Novell (*partnerweb.novell.com*)
Networking software company Novell's "PartnerWeb" (Figure 11.2) is interesting because it demonstrates how the Internet can be used to ad-

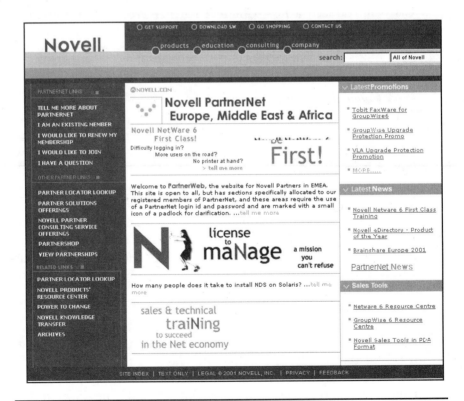

Figure 11.2. Novell's "PartnerWeb" addresses the needs of partners in a specific geographic region.

dress a specific geographic area's partner base. This comprehensive site services the company's partners in Europe, the Middle East, and Africa. In addition to standard links, the site allows partners to find information based on their functional areas: marketing, business manager, salesperson, and technical person.

Oracle (*www.oracle.com/partners/*)

Oracle has a large network of partners that includes hardware vendors, independent software vendors, and systems integrators that deliver applications and services based on Oracle's database. Oracle makes heavy usage of the Internet in servicing these partners. In addition, the company provides a solutions finder (*solutions.oracle.com*) that allows users to search on a combination of any word, company name, product name, industry, geography, business function, and operating system to locate the appropriate solution, and partner.

Partnering, Internet Style: What the Future Holds

In March 1999, Amazon.com and Dell "affiliated" in an unusual Internet business relationship that could be a forerunner of future Internet partnering. Each company agreed to link its site to the other's at the point-of-purchase pages. Dell customers have the option of purchasing a product from Amazon, and Amazon offers its customers Dell PCs on the way out of its electronic store.

The business reason for this partnership is simple—each company gains access to the other's customer base. In so doing, both companies share the potential to rapidly expand their businesses and attract new Internet buyers. The key word is "Internet" because the old direct marketing adage applies even to electronic audiences: Buyers tend to repeat their purchases *using the buying channel with which they are most comfortable.* Since Internet buying is a relatively new and growing phenomenon, reaching a large base of new potential *Internet buyers* at a reasonable cost, in association with another premier Internet brand, is like striking a vein of gold in cyberspace.

Dell was involved in another partnership formed in late 1999 with the goal of helping a chemical company move aggressively into e-business. Eastman Chemical began a partnership with Dell to offer its customers an opportunity to purchase discounted Dell computers. Eastman at the same time announced a partnership with UUNET (*www.uu.net*), the leading business Internet Service Provider, to allow Eastman customers the ability to sign up for UUNET's Internet service through Eastman and get a credit on their purchase.

You can expect to see many more of these partnerships, strategic alliances, and affiliations spring up on the Internet, even among competitors. It is too large a business opportunity to ignore.

"Collaborative selling" is another phenomenon that could shape the way businesses work together in the Internet-enabled future. iChannel from iMediation (*www.imediation.com*) is a software platform that helps companies support multiple sales models while accelerating the recruitment of business partners. This collaborative sales solution is in use by more than 70 companies, including the American Management Association, Hewlett-Packard, and Philips. WebCollage (*www.webcollage.com*) offers "interactive Web service syndication," which allows e-businesses to syndicate complete, interactive Web applications and share them directly through partner sites.

In the previous chapter, we referenced the rapid growth of communities and exchanges. Private exchanges, in particular, demonstrate the true principle of Internet partnering. Exchanges mentioned included Covisint, a collaboration of automotive manufacturers, and Converge and e2open, each founded by groups of competitive IT companies. Those entities could just as easily have been included in this chapter because they represent the remarkable rise of Internet partnerships.

The rapid growth of business-to-business communities and exchanges in particular suggests that Internet partnering will continue to be widespread. Many of these information economy business arrangements share a common goal: bringing together suppliers of products and services with qualified buyers who come to one place to shop. Several of these sites go beyond simply consolidating the information by also centralizing the purchasing process.

This phenomenon itself has far-reaching implications for IT companies that may be suppliers and buyers alike. Suppliers can participate in a consortium that spreads the Internet infrastructure costs across noncompeting "partners," achieves economies of scale by offering more and more products at little or no increase in promotional costs, and reaches a wider audience of prospective buyers than could be reached independently. Buyers gain the tremendous convenience of a single point of contact for locating and evaluating products, issuing purchase orders, procuring items, receiving invoices, making payments, and tracking orders. It is likely that with the proliferation of such consolidated buying sites, suppliers can ultimately reduce their costs and buyers can get better deals. In theory, at least, everyone wins.

As an IT marketer on the Internet, you have a whole new opportunity to extend the reach of your company through this type of Internet partnering. It might be as simple as linking your Web site to other partner sellers, or as serious as participating in a sellers' consortium. Whatever form of business venture you pursue, partnering could mean a new source of profits.

This is not the only form of partnering that will exist as the Internet economy matures. Chances are that if you are not already doing so, you will be partnering with your customers in a very real sense. As numerous books on the Internet's future point out, customers will drive companies to build entire marketing and business strategies around them. Models for the most successful companies doing business on the Internet are already built and, not surprisingly, they are all customer-driven. These new-age companies treat their customers as if they are strategic partners, encouraging them to play an integral part in molding the company's business.

Finally, as prospective business and consumer customers realize that they will have no choice but to navigate the waters of the Internet, they will turn to a new kind of partner—the "infomediary." As described by Hagel and Singer in their book, *Net Worth*, the infomediary, or information intermediary "will become the catalyst for people to begin demanding value in exchange for data about themselves. . . . By connecting information supply with information demand, and by helping both parties determine the value of that information, infomediaries will build a new kind of information supply chain."[1]

Hagel and Singer's infomediary of the Internet future could be the portal, community, or information network of today. Wherever the infomediary comes from, business-to-business Internet marketers will need to factor this new partner into the mix.

In some cases, the infomediary will become a true facilitator of buying decisions. Respond.com (*www.respond.com*) is an interesting example of the potential for matching buyers with sellers. Respond.com describes itself as a "request-driven lead generation solution provider" that matches up businesses with "purchase-ready" buyers. This Internet matching service, the first of its kind, puts prospective buyers in touch with sellers anonymously. The twist is that Respond.com lists product categories connected to forms that the prospect completes and sends. The prospect indicates interest in a particular product. Respond.com *removes the personal information about the prospect* from the form and forwards it to participating sellers via e-mail. The sellers then respond to the e-mail with information, which goes through Respond.com back to the prospect. In addition to its own branded matching service, Respond private-labels its "MatchSource" solution so that portals, search engines, directories, and other online communities can offer its business-matching service.

One way or the other, a significant success factor in IT Internet marketing is likely to be based on choosing the right partners. It is a strategy that should not be underestimated.

Note

1. John Hagel III and Marc Singer, *Net Worth* (Boston: McKinsey & Company, Inc., Harvard Business School Press, 1999).

12

Selling on the Internet

There is little question that the Internet has become a major sales channel for a wide range of businesses, including IT companies. In fact, many of them, including Cisco, Dell, Gateway, IBM, and Intel, have risen to the top as e-commerce leaders. But selling online has claimed casualties as well. The Internet landscape has recently been littered with unsuccessful Dot Coms whose online sales failed to meet their lofty expectations.

As a result, there is a new attitude toward selling on the Internet, not necessarily negative, but cautious and calculated. This is likely to be a good thing, because companies are more closely evaluating the risks as well as the rewards. Taking a lesson from the pure-play Dot Com failures, it is the "click and mortars" who are now finding that the best way to sell online is to integrate it with selling offline. E-commerce thus becomes one vitally important sales strategy, but not the only one.

This chapter examines what e-commerce leaders are doing to succeed, looks at some of the ways you can take advantage of e-commerce, and helps guide you toward avoiding the pitfalls and turning a profit online.

Putting the e-commerce Explosion into Perspective

Early interest in the Internet went beyond a better way to communicate or a more effective way to generate, qualify, and fulfill leads. The real power of the Internet, according to early adopter visionaries, was in its as-yet-untapped potential to be a major sales channel for marketers. E-commerce—generating revenue directly from electronic storefronts—was touted as the "killer application."

Initial optimistic expectations did not quite match reality. The year 1997 saw the growth of e-commerce, but it was slower than expected. This may best be explained by some of the early significant issues surrounding electronic commerce:

1. *Security and privacy.* Despite the attractiveness of online buying, considerable concern about the security of Internet-based transactions existed on the part of the prospective e-buyer. With the growing success of high-profile Internet merchants that use secure servers and the increasing number of security solutions now available, this issue began to diminish in importance. No less prominent, however, was the issue of privacy—not just privacy of credit card data, but the individual purchaser's privacy. It quickly became clear that organizations were capturing and accumulating personal data on prospective customers and buyers and that, in some cases, that data was being traded or sold. This issue continues to be one that could hamper e-commerce if it is not resolved.

2. *Infrastructure cost.* Internet marketers quickly realized that taking orders electronically required a whole different information infrastructure. Initially, e-commerce solutions were prohibitively expensive for all but the largest of companies. Many early e-commerce leaders designed their own systems from the ground up, but this was not a viable option for mass implementation. The market reacted as a number of vendors introduced lower-cost e-commerce solutions beginning in 1997. Now, many off-the-shelf solutions are available, even to small businesses. A whole new breed of solutions began popping up in late 1999: free e-commerce stores that basically use others' Web sites to sell-through products and services. E-commerce was further fueled by the widespread popular-

ity of auctions and, in the B-to-B space, business exchanges, discussed in Chapter 10.

3. *Regulatory environment.* Internet marketers were legitimately wary of regulatory controls that apply to commerce, such as the FTC's "30-day rule," and possible tax implications of doing business electronically. It was clear, however, that online sellers were able to achieve considerable e-commerce success despite these controls. By 1998, Internet commerce was fueled even further by a federal moratorium on sales taxes, although taxing online sales continues to be hotly debated by state and federal governments alike.

Actual business conducted online, as well as numerous predictions for future e-commerce sales, support the fact that the U.S. economy will increasingly depend upon the Internet as a leading commerce channel for goods and services. E-commerce has spread to worldwide markets as the Internet's penetration continued to grow exponentially. Here are just some of the validating statistics:

- A report released by Forrester Research (*www.forrester.com*) in March 2001 predicted that B-to-B e-commerce alone in North America would exceed $2.7 trillion by 2004. Gartner, Inc. (*www.gartner.com*) reported that B-to-B e-commerce reached over $430 billion by the end of 2000 and rose to almost $920 billion in 2001, a 112 percent increase. Gartner projects that B-to-B e-commerce will grow to over $8.5 trillion by 2005.

- Research firm IDC (*www.idc.com*) says that e-commerce will have a $5.3 trillion impact on the worldwide economy by 2005. IDC believes that 80 percent of business will be conducted online by 2003, and that $2 million per minute will change hands globally via the Internet by that same year. IDC's U.S. Small Business Survey, released in April 2000, predicted that over 70 percent of small businesses (those with fewer than 100 employees) would access the Internet by 2003, up from 52 percent in 1999. IDC says that 2.9 million small businesses, nearly half of them, will be selling online by 2003, a significant increase from 850,000 at the close of 1999.

- The lower cost structure of e-commerce is starting to pay off as well. IDC's U.S. eRetail Customer Acquisition Costs Forecast for 2000–2005 shows that the average online customer acquisition cost will level off to just under $120 in 2004 and 2005. (The customer acquisition cost, according to IDC, is the total sales and marketing expenses divided by new customer accounts.) For companies buying via the Internet, savings are just as significant. In a March 2001 study, Aberdeen Group (*www.aberdeen.com*) found that using the Internet to buy goods and services could save companies over 70 percent in purchasing time and costs. That translates into potentially $2 million dollars saved annually for an average mid-sized company.

Which companies are fueling the growth of e-commerce? It probably isn't surprising that the predominant players are IT companies. Researcher Jupiter Media Metrix (*www.jmm.com*) says that, by 2001, online sales of PC hardware grew to more than $5 billion from about $3 billion in 1999. Online sales of PC software grew to about $1.5 billion in 2001 from about $500 million in 1999.

Even more telling is *InteractiveWeek*'s "Interactive 500" list (*www.interactiveweek.com*), which ranks the "New Economy's" leading companies. In total, the Interactive 500 was responsible for over $183 billion in online sales during 2000, $100 billion more than in 1999. The December 2000 list, ranked on the basis of online revenue during 2000, gives eight of the top ten spots to IT companies. Leading the list is Intel, with almost $24 billion in online sales out of about $32 billion in total revenue. Rounding out the top five are IBM ($17 billion), Cisco Systems ($15 billion), Nortel Networks ($15 billion), and Dell Computer ($13.5 billion).

The Interactive 500 reveals something else about e-commerce. Although plenty of IT companies are peppered throughout the list, *InteractiveWeek* makes the point that fewer than 30 of the top 100 companies started out as Dot Coms. Just as significant, numerous brick-and-mortar companies made the 2000 list, proving that traditional companies are indeed claiming their place in cyberspace.

If one IT company has typified the movement to e-business, it is IBM. It has not only embraced the Internet, but has made it an integral part of its long-term business strategy. IBM was the subject of a December 1999 *BusinessWeek* cover story that reported that 25 percent of its revenue—about $20 billion—is "driven by e-business demand." The story indicated that ". . . about 75 percent of IBM's e-business revenue comes from sales of Net technology, software, and services . . . and not the old mainframe computers for which IBM is so well known."

The company adopted the term "e-business" and launched a massive advertising campaign in 1997. The campaign, which industry sources estimated to be in excess of $200 million, deluged virtually every media channel available (including television).

IBM was not just promoting e-business for others. The company aggressively began to practice what it preached. The company started the IBM Institute for Advanced Commerce, staffing it with over 50 scientists. In late 1999, IBM Global Services launched "e-business innovation centers" in four U.S. cities, with plans to open more in the United States and Europe. These physical locations give e-business customers access to IBM business strategists, marketing specialists, application developers, integration specialists, and interactive designers in one place.

In late 1999, IBM announced that it would launch a new enterprise information portal to allow its customers to easily access and search data across numerous sources. These are just a few examples of IBM's continuing foray into all things e-business.

Nevertheless, there is plenty of room for e-commerce opportunity, according to "The State of Online Retailing 4.0" released in May 2001, conducted by the Boston Consulting Group and released by Shop.org (*www.shop.org*). This fourth annual study of online retailing in North America projected 45 percent growth to $65 billion in 2001, with over $8 billion in computer hardware and software alone. As a percentage of total retail sales, online sales would represent about 2½ percent in 2001. Primary beneficiaries of online selling are the catalogers, according to the report. Companies that depend on catalogs found that about 40 percent of their online customers are new to the company, and 72 percent of online catalogers were profitable, versus 27 percent of Web-based retailers.

Dell: An IT Online Success Story

One of the stunning success stories in IT marketing is Dell Computer (*www.dell.com*), a company that, in April 2001, ranked first in global market share of computer systems. With annual revenues of $32 billion, the company ranks forty-eighth on the *Fortune 500* and number 10 on *Fortune*'s "most-admired" list of companies. Dell reports that more than 50 percent of its total revenue is Internet-enabled, which reached $50 million daily of online sales in 2000.

It's important to recognize that Dell was not a Dot Com, but rather a traditional direct marketer. In fact, it was Dell's "Direct" business model that allowed it to differentiate itself from competitors. The company's business strategy from the beginning was selling and servicing direct to the customer. There are no retailers or other resellers. As a result, everything Dell offers touches the customer without a middleman.

From Dell's perspective, this business model offers several unique advantages:

- *Price for performance.* By eliminating resellers, retailers, and other intermediaries, Dell believes it can offer more-powerful, more richly configured systems for the money than its competitors. Dell ensures this with an efficient procurement, manufacturing, and distribution process.

- *Customization.* Every Dell system is built to order. Customers get exactly, and only, what they want. Dell extended the build-to-order strategy to the Internet and pioneered online mass customization. Customized computer systems can be specified online and typically are delivered in 30 days or less.

- *Service and support.* Dell uses knowledge gained from direct contact before and after the sale to provide superior, tailored customer service.

- *Latest technology.* Dell's model means that the latest relevant technology can be introduced into its product lines much more quickly than through indirect distribution channels. Inventory is turned over every ten days or less, on average.

- *Superior shareholder value.* During its latest fiscal year, the value of Dell common stock more than doubled.

It was almost as if the Internet was invented for Dell to make its business model even better. Current Dell initiatives include moving even greater volumes of product, sales, service, and support to the Internet, and further expanding an already broad range of value-added services. The company says the Internet provides greater convenience and efficiency to customers and, in turn, to Dell. Today about 50 percent of its technical support activities and about 76 percent of Dell's order-status transactions occur online.

At the core of Dell's Internet business is, of course, its Web site, Dell.com. The site was launched in 1994 and added e-commerce capability in 1996. It is today one of the highest-volume Internet commerce sites in the world, receiving 40 million visits per quarter at 78 country-specific sites.

Dell's Web site has become a way to promote efficiencies throughout the company's business, including procurement, customer support, and relationship management. At Dell.com, customers may review, configure, and price systems within Dell's entire product line; order systems online; and track orders from manufacturing through shipping (Figure 12.1). At valuechain.dell.com, Dell shares information on a range of

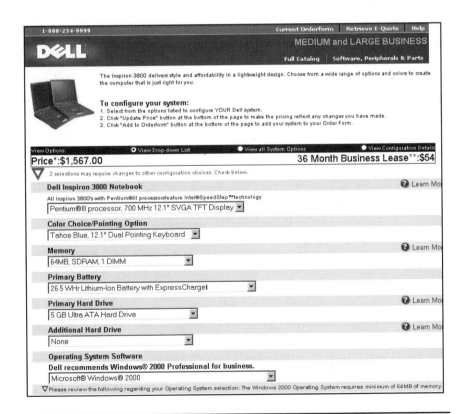

Figure 12.1. Customers can configure their own computers at Dell's Web site.

topics, including product quality and inventory, with its suppliers. Dell also uses the Internet to deliver industry-leading customer services such as "E-Support—Direct from Dell," which offers advanced online customer support; Dell Talk, an online discussion forum; and Ask Dudley, Dell's natural-language technical support tool.

Following are brief descriptions of some of Dell's major e-commerce initiatives.

Dell Premier Web Pages

More than 58,000 business and institutional customers worldwide use Dell's Premier Dell.com Web pages to do business with the company online. Premier Dell.com is a series of customized electronic store fronts/information portals for large customers. Premier Dell.com allows users to configure their systems in real time, with up-to-date pricing for each organization. Connecting this information resource to the customer's purchasing system is relatively straightforward if all the elements are in place.

The ultimate purpose of Premier Dell.com is electronic B-to-B integration. It starts with e-procurement, where the customer pulls information directly from the supplier's server into its purchasing system, creating an electronic requisition. After the requisition is approved, an electronic purchase order is created and sent via the Internet to the supplier. This hands-free process has the potential to dramatically reduce the cost of procurement, as well as reducing errors and cycle times in the purchasing process. Dell has implemented the solution in alliance with customers, choosing companies that are ready to invest the time and resources to strive to improve the way they do business.

One customer example of Premier Dell.com in the IT space is LSI Logic Corporation, a manufacturer of communications-chip solutions. According to Dell, LSI designated Dell as one of its standard suppliers for computer equipment. Employees began using Premier Dell.com to gather information, configure systems, and track orders. But when direct-ordering capability was added, efficiency really took off.

In June 2000, the company's procurement system was connected with their custom Premier Dell.com catalog. Now ordering direct from Dell with a paperless process is a way of life at LSI Logic's U.S. Operations. Employees no longer use time to research PC solutions for themselves. Instead, they are choosing to order directly from Dell. With standardized, preapproved options readily accessible on their custom Dell catalog at Premier Dell.com, they simply configure the system they need and initiate a purchase requisition. The electronic approval process allows them to track their requisition through the LSI Logic system. Once the order is electronically sent, they can monitor their purchase at Dell.com to find out when and how it will be shipped and when to expect delivery. The system can also be used to access technical data and track warranty status, parts orders, and service calls.

Another IT example is Exodus Communications, a provider of complex Web-hosting solutions. Exodus provides the network infrastructure for preconfigured systems in multiple Exodus Internet Data Centers worldwide. Using Dell's ".com configurator" and order-tracking software, Exodus can turn server orders in as few as five days. Working with Dell, Exodus created an integrated process that allows its systems engineers to create a .com configuration and then reference it for pricing, procurement, order tracking, support, and asset tracking.

The result from "e-orders" is flexibility, speed, efficiency, improved customer service, and asset management. Quoting and order processing are faster because a single configuration record can be carried from beginning to end without reentry. Electronic order entry reduces order processing time. The records in the order-management system have the Dell configuration files attached indicating support, limited warranty, and asset tracking.

DellHost

Leveraging its success in the server market, Dell turned to the Web site hosting business and introduced "DellHost" (*www.dellhost.com*) to help its customers get online. Through DellHost, Dell becomes a company's "Internet Presence Provider," offering space for Web pages and site support. DellHost is a comprehensive service that provides servers, setup, service, and support. As with Dell.com, Dellhost.com is a direct-to-customer site. DellHost even guarantees next-business-day setup on all dedicated hosting solutions.

In April 2001, DellHost received an award from *The Web Host Industry Review* for its e-commerce packages and was voted a Top Ten Host by *HostIndex*.

Dell Software and Accessories

Dell launched a separate site to sell software and accessories called Gigabuys in 1999, but in 2001 folded it back into Dell.com (*accessories.us.dell.com*). At the new Dell Software & Accessories site, customer can buy printers, scanners, software, accessories, multimedia, data storage, monitors, projectors, networking products, and even office products.

Dell Exchange

The Dell Exchange (*www.dellexchange.com*) is a three-part site: "TradeUps" allows customers to trade in an old system for a new Dell system; "Dell Auction" (*www.dellauction.com*) is a technology exchange that offers a way to buy and sell used and refurbished computers, peripherals, and accessories of any brand; and "Donation" leads visitors to the National Cristina Foundation (*www.cristina.org*), which helps disabled and economically disadvantaged children and adults obtain donated computers.

Dell Learning Center

The Dell Learning Center includes an online learning service called EducateU (*www.educateu.com*), offered in collaboration with SmartForce. EducateU is an online learning community that combines different learning elements with peer-to-peer and peer-to-mentor interaction to create an educational experience tailored to each individual student's needs. EducateU includes courses, a library of resources including articles and white papers, live and archived online seminars, chat rooms and threaded discussion groups, and 24-hour-a-day live help. A 1,200-course catalog covering topics ranging from home technology to IT certification is available online.

How e-commerce Works with Your Selling Model

Dell's selling model is 100 percent direct. But that isn't every company's selling model. Before you launch a serious e-commerce effort, consider how you sell now, and how the Internet works with your existing selling model. Next, we briefly examine the impact of electronic commerce on several common IT selling models.

The Retail or Mail-Order Model

Dell is, at its roots, a direct retailer. The retail model is basically one in which the customer makes a direct purchase from a location—a store. The store sells its goods to a customer, who must physically come in to make the purchase. If the store has the item in stock, the customer can purchase it immediately; otherwise, the item needs to be ordered and the customer needs to return to get it, or to have it delivered when available.

The mail-order model is a variation on the retail-store model. It simply uses a different distribution channel to complete the transaction. Here, the customer does not physically come to a place to purchase but rather orders an item via phone, mail, fax, e-mail, or the Web. Representative of mail order, probably more than anything else, is the catalog. It is no accident that many retailers have mail-order catalogs and many mail-order companies have opened retail stores. Why? Because the products are the same, only the distribution channel is different—so the basic underlying business process can be retained and applied to both selling models.

In many respects, Dell is both a store and a catalog. It is an electronic storefront with millions of items, which are classified and cross-referenced so that each product can be individually purchased by any number of criteria. Every product has its own description, its own order number, and its own price.

The Internet difference is that you can "visit" the catalog. You do not actually drive there, open physical doors, walk down the aisles, look at physical products, pay at the cash register, and leave with your purchase. You can say it differs from a traditional bricks-and-mortar store in that there is a loss of personal contact, the tactile browsing experience, and the immediacy of getting your merchandise on the spot, but consider the other benefits of the electronic store. You do not have to get in your car, drive there, and park. You can browse limitless "shelves" and visit whenever you want (even in your pajamas). You can find every product imaginable in stock, and never wait in line to make a purchase.

Other major IT retailers (those with stores and mail-order catalogs alike) have followed the lead of Dell and other successful online sellers by opening storefronts on the Web. If you sell your software, hardware, or networking products through stores or other direct-to-the-end-user locations, or through catalogs and mail order, you can quickly see how to apply this retail or mail-order model to your own brand of Internet-based order generation.

It is not surprising that on the business-to-business side, the first electronic merchants to succeed with Web stores were technology-based catalogers—sellers of multiple computer software, hardware, and networking products and services. Software merchants have even been able to fulfill the promise of instant product delivery by allowing customers to unlock and download live products upon purchase, but the marketplace has quickly extended far beyond that niche, and now virtually everything is, or will be, available for sale on the Internet.

A variant of the retail model on the Internet is the *virtual mall.* As with a traditional mall, a virtual mall is a collection of storefronts. Most malls are established primarily to sell to consumers, but an increasing number of malls feature business-oriented categories.

If you are considering participation in a virtual mall, be prepared to ask the mall manager a lot of detailed questions:

- How much *business* traffic does the mall generate?

- How many business-to-business advertisers are in the mall?

- Which categories are available, and do they appeal to business buyers?

- How is the mall promoted?

- How does the mall assist advertisers with Internet commerce in terms of technical support, activity tracking and reporting, and secure electronic commerce transactions?

- What costs are associated with being a mall participant?

Yet another Internet-based retail model is the *auction.* Auction sites are springing up on the Web to facilitate bidding on new and used products, services, and more. There are variations to auctions such as price-comparison sites and "name your lowest bid" sites. In fact, auctions and these related sites are one of the hottest growth areas on the Internet.

Although auctions are clearly designed to generate revenue for the sponsoring sites, there is a key characteristic they share that differentiates them from other e-commerce applications: Many auctions are also Internet-based *communities.* That is because the auction encourages ongoing interaction between buyer and seller, and often between seller and seller, via bulletin boards, newsletters, and community activities. Auctions, price-comparison sites, virtual malls, and other types of business-to-business communities were reviewed in detail in Chapter 10.

The Reseller Model

Many IT marketers rely heavily on distributors, resellers, or partners to generate revenue. This is very common in the high-technology sector, especially in a global economy where selling products might be more efficiently done through indirect channels.

Depending on the type of product or service you offer, the reseller channel may enhance or even dramatically change the item you sell. For example, a computer manufacturer's business systems are often bundled with a distributor's, reseller's, or partner's own products or services to create a total package or solution sale. The reseller "adds value" to the sale (hence the term "Value-Added Reseller," or VAR). The reseller channel may just as easily become an extension of the company's direct sales force (which, if it is not handled properly, can create channel conflict situations—harmful to prospects and customers alike).

Sony caused a furor in February 2000 when it launched SonyStyle.com (*www.sonystyle.com*) to sell consumer products online in Japan, effectively competing with its national dealer networks. Since Sony already owns 2,000 "Sony Shops" throughout Japan, the move could potentially cannibalize dealer sales.

How do you apply the reseller model to Internet-based order generation? Part of the answer depends on the type of relationship you have with your resellers and how they sell and deliver your products or services to the end user. Consider the concept of populating your resellers' Web sites with information you supply if resellers will allow it. Also consider the possibility of funding e-commerce initiatives with the goal of obtaining "site prominence" on resellers' sites for your products.

If appropriate, you could use the affiliate marketing model to offer resellers the ability to generate revenue by becoming an electronic conduit to your order-generation system. Amazon.com's Associates program passes through the orders from an associate's site via a link to the company's central order processing. The link identifies the associate with a code and the book ordered, connecting the two so that the associate can be credited for the sale.

You could provide each reseller "associate" with a unique order page on the Web, reflecting the special arrangement you have with that reseller. This can be done by setting up a basic Web page, modifying it for each reseller, and then linking the appropriate page through each reseller's site. Alternatively, you could authorize your resellers to use special pricing and part numbers on their sites so that the orders automatically pass through to your Web site and order fulfillment system.

Another possibility is to explore partnership opportunities that link your organization together with key resellers. Joint e-mail campaigns, combination banner ads, cooperative lead- and order-generation Web sites, and Web communities or "supersites" benefiting several noncompetitive organizations are just a few of the possibilities.

Review Chapter 11 on business-to-business partnering on the Internet for more about this selling model.

The Sales Force Model

If your company relies on your own telemarketers or a direct sales force to sell products, you are accustomed to the ongoing need to feed them qualified leads. In previous chapters, we discussed how the Internet can be used to generate and qualify leads, attract qualified prospects through Internet events, and instantly provide information to prospects and customers through electronic fulfillment.

Although the sales force model is likely to survive, it is undergoing dramatic change as IT businesses feel the pressure to cut selling expenses and improve sales efficiency. Sales force selling will always have its place in consultative and complex selling situations. It is difficult to replace a live sales call when it comes to selling highly technical or high-end products and services. Yet the Internet holds real promise as a tool for enhancing the sales process and for continuing the sales cycle in the absence of the salesperson.

Internet telephony offers one intriguing way to take advantage of sales force selling. Technologies that integrate telephony with the Web make it possible for telesales representatives to intercede during a prospect's Web session and assist the prospect by answering questions immediately. The technology is still in its early stage, but more and more sites are incorporating "call-me" buttons and other forms of Internet telephony. As a result, it may not be long before online ordering is enhanced with live voice support.

The Internet-enhanced sales force selling model can also facilitate the traditional sales call. A salesperson could walk into a prospect's office and make a sales presentation that was absolutely guaranteed to be consistently the same, anywhere in the world, regardless of that salesperson's personal knowledge base. That could happen by adapting a Web-based presentation, such as an online seminar, for the specific selling situation.

After an online seminar is created, it can be captured and modified for any salesperson to use. Loaded onto a notebook computer and called up locally through a Web browser, the seminar becomes an interactive sales presentation. The salesperson has instant access to it, without the need for an Internet connection. The salesperson can lead a prospect through a personalized one-to-one presentation, and the company has the assurance that the selling message is uniform and consistent. By connecting the notebook computer to a projection device, the salesperson can make the interactive presentation to many individuals at a single prospect or customer location.

Similarly, while in a prospect's office, the salesperson could access the company Web site or a private intranet or extranet to inform and educate the prospect and facilitate the sales process. If the prospect is ready to buy, contracts and product-ordering information could be available to the salesperson over the Web. The salesperson could even place an order and receive an instant electronic acknowledgment from the company—all while the salesperson is sitting right in the prospect's office.

Regardless of the selling model, Internet-enhanced order generation can have a dramatic beneficial impact on your sales process. You can either augment the way you sell products and services with the Internet or transition to the Internet and eventually replace your existing selling model with an Internet selling model.

The way you approach it is up to you, but whatever you decide, generating orders through the Internet is already offering significant business benefits and productivity gains to IT direct marketers. They are achieving increased reach into new markets, better support of customers, accelerated speed of order-taking and order fulfillment, and reduced selling costs.

A New Twist to e-commerce: The Shopping Bot

Enabled by powerful search-and-compare engines, the shopping "bot" brings a twist to e-commerce that has far-reaching implications for IT and other e-sellers. The shopping bot is an agent that basically searches the Web for products you want and then can not only bring back the results, but compare features and prices for you. As these bots continue to improve in quality and increase in popularity, they could ultimately change the very nature of e-commerce, putting the buyer in total control of the transaction.

Following are a few examples of bots.

www.mysimon.com

mySimon was selected by *Time Digital* as the best bot on the Web. By the end of 1999, mySimon could analyze specifications and prices of products from over 2,000 online merchants. You can compare prices by using model numbers or product names and, even better, you can get helpful "tutorials" on a product category, pick the features you want, and then compare available products and their prices, side-by-side. mySimon will even scour some online auctions as part of its service. In January 2000, ClNet acquired mySimon in a $700 million stock deal.

www.rusure.com

R U Sure is a "shopping agent" that actually resides on your Windows desktop. On the downside, you have to download it and you may consider it intrusive. On the upside, if you are a serious e-shopper, you might like having a permanently available comparison-shopping tool right there, all the time, which "turns on" when you visit a supported site.

www.dash.com

Dash is about cash. The approach of this shopping bot is to give you cash back, up to 25 percent, every time you shop online, along with special coupons and savings opportunities. Dash uses a "dashBar" that sits at the bottom of your Web browser and combines the typical comparison shopping with "coupon alerts," local weather and news, Web search, and other handy features.

www.respond.com

Respond.com (Figure 12.2) is not so much a shopping bot as a new breed of shopping service. By January 2000, Respond.com had 45,000 participating merchants, each of which pays varying fees for leads. The novel twist here is that a prospective buyer tells Respond.com what he or she is looking for and at what price. Respond.com acts as the middle-man, e-mailing the appropriate merchants with the request. The prospective buyer then receives offers from those merchants that want the business, kind of like a reverse auction.

How to Get an e-commerce Order Generation System Up and Running

The bottom line for IT marketers that want to sell over the Internet is that, one way or the other, they will need to have an e-commerce order generation system available to them. Although many IT companies may choose to outsource the entire system, or use someone else's system (such as a virtual mall or a service that creates an online store), others may

Figure 12.2.   Respond.com is a Web-based service that matches businesses with "purchase-ready buyers."

wish to make a long-term commitment to e-commerce by establishing their own system. To address this need, look at it from two different perspectives—modifying your existing order-generation system versus creating a new order generation system.

Transitioning from an Existing Order Generation System

Transitioning to the Internet from an existing order-generation system is no less challenging than building a system from scratch. You will need to conduct an audit of the existing system's order information and processing capabilities, as well as its technical infrastructure, to determine exactly what needs to be modified or added.

Of course, any order generation system, traditional or Internet-based, should be comprehensive from the start. You will need a closed-loop system that offers you the ability to

- Easily enter and maintain prospect and customer data

- Manage merchandise planning and product inventory

- Pick and process orders quickly and efficiently

- Provide responsive customer service

- Monitor order shipments

- Handle returns

- Invoice and reconcile payments and credits

It is important that the basic system be grounded in a solid database that retains both customer data and a history of customer transactions. You should be able to use this information to continuously update customer records and segment customers by key product and Recency-Frequency-Monetary (RFM) criteria: Which products are purchased when, how often, and for how much money.

The underlying technology is not insignificant. You need to evaluate existing databases and systems to be sure that they can be moved to the Internet. You may need to overlay new software tools onto parts of your system and replace other parts with new software. Equally important are the software and hardware servers and networking systems you will need to handle the anticipated e-commerce activity.

Although most direct marketers conceptually understand that generating orders through the Internet is essentially the same, there are aspects of e-commerce that are decidedly different. Making a commitment to e-commerce will require a marketer to focus on these major areas at a minimum:

1. *The "store" or electronic catalog.* The storefront or electronic catalog is the place you establish to let the visitor browse, learn

about products, and, potentially, purchase them. The most common customer-purchase model is a store with products that can be put into a "shopping cart." A visitor adds or deletes products to his or her shopping cart—typically an electronic inventory list of product names, numbers, and prices. When the visitor is finished shopping, he or she checks out—the point at which payment is authorized and the order is placed.

2. *The system behind the store.* Behind the store is the electronic infrastructure the marketer needs to have in place to run the store. This is the system that processes the order, verifies the credit card payment, picks the items for order fulfillment, triggers the shipping order, tracks the order, and updates the customer record. This system is also responsible for, or tied into, an inventory management system so that products can be replenished as necessary.

3. *The customer-service component integrated with the store.* A customer-service component that creates a sense of confidence and responsiveness is important to e-commerce success. There is a need for almost instantaneous response, because the Internet compresses everything into real time. Customers who order through the Internet will demand feedback at once. From their perspective, they are enabling the order process and facilitating product delivery by being on the Net in the first place.

More than anything else, successful e-commerce marketers convey the perception that they are truly on top of customer service. Organizations such as Federal Express (*www.fedex.com*) and UPS (*www.ups.com*) have gone beyond the boundaries of simple Internet order generation; they allow their customers to play a role in the order generation and fulfillment process. In fact, in many respects, it is the customers who actually drive the process. Try it for yourself: You can write your own shipping orders and track your own packages over the Internet.

Both FedEx and UPS are Internet innovators in their own right. FedEx pioneered online tracking and brought that capability to the Internet early on. Not to be outdone, UPS in April 1999 introduced UPS OnLine Tools, which e-commerce vendors can incorporate into Web sites so customers can calculate shipping costs, select and compare services, and track packages from order through delivery. UPS went a step further in

February 2000, forming an e-commerce subsidiary called eVentures that will perform back-end fulfillment functions for e-businesses.

The Internet shipping business was further enhanced with the introduction of iShip, a service that offers online buyers and sellers a one-stop package shipping and tracking solution. Online merchants can use iShip to ship packages cost-effectively and to manage shipments. Online buyers can choose carriers and can track deliveries through iShip. iShip is a service of Stamps.com (*www.stamps.com*), a provider of Internet-based postage and shipping services with over 300,000 customers. In April 2001, Stamps.com acquired competitor E-Stamp's patents and name.

What distinguishes outstanding Internet direct marketers is their ability to personalize the business transaction. Behind the friendly look and feel of such sites as Amazon and Dell is a marketing database strategy that clearly puts the customer first. Information must be available on a real-time basis so that pages can be personalized and updated on the fly. Amazon.com and other sites use something called "collaborative filtering" to accomplish this. And it appears that collaborative filtering is, in part, responsible for turning e-browsers into e-buyers. In October 1999, Nielsen's NetRatings released research that suggested that online merchants with personalized sites were converting browsers to buyers at a significantly higher rate, sometimes more than double those with nonpersonalized sites.

In fact, as database marketing becomes a driving force on the Internet, e-commerce is likely to become a whole new ball game:

> *Instituting database marketing on the Web will be like making the leap from playing checkers to playing multilevel niches. . . . The high level of segmentation granularity that can be achieved with interactive direct marketing is virtually unlimited. . . . Direct marketers can determine not only what products to display to a particular customer or customer segment, and what products to group together to improve cross-sell opportunities, but they can even determine finite levels such as which color product to feature based on customers purchase history.*[1]

Starting a New Order Generation System on the Internet

What if your IT company is brand new to order generation? Then the Internet is a good place to start—perhaps the only place you will really need. Most early Internet order generation systems were homegrown out of necessity, but now packaged systems are available that can get any IT marketer up and running quickly and cost-effectively.

E-commerce has now expanded so dramatically that there are a wide variety of packaged solutions offered by numerous vendors, priced from hundreds to hundreds of thousands of dollars. Some of these solutions are even being offered free, as long as the user agrees to utilize the seller's online e-commerce services.

One interesting example is Electrom.com (*www.electrom.com*), which claims to be the world's largest business-to-business e-commerce portal. Electrom.com, launched in November 1999, uses "SitePlugs" that work with Web design tools, such as Microsoft FrontPage 2000, to enable merchants to "plug in" e-commerce into their Web sites. Then the merchants can publish their site and Electrom will manage it from start to finish for up to 250 products, free of charge.

Even with the availability of off-the-shelf products and all-in-one resources, however, the implications of e-commerce on an organization's existing systems should not be minimized. Legacy systems, such as financial and accounting, and possibly the entire order processing and fulfillment system, will need to be tied together with Internet-based operations. Ultimately, any e-commerce initiative will need to be integrated into a company's operations to gain maximum efficiencies. This fact has never been more obvious than in the experience of traditional retailers transitioning to the Internet. For example, although 1999 was very much an e-Christmas, horror stories about retailers whose e-commerce systems crashed were not uncommon. Now, these same retailers have regrouped and are starting to outpace the Dot Coms in terms of well-executed e-commerce strategies.

The cost of a fully enabled e-commerce system should not be underestimated. Even in 1999, Gartner, Inc. (*www.gartner.com*) found that building an e-commerce Web site from scratch cost an average of $1 million, with 79 percent of the cost being labor-related.

Another major issue that should be addressed early on is whether or not you want to commit internal staff and resources to a major e-commerce effort. Maintaining an electronic store or catalog is no small feat. Products need to be photographed, scanned, and uploaded. Copy needs to be written and published. Order numbers and prices continuously need to be reviewed and updated.

That is just the creative side. An e-commerce operation requires serious site management on an ongoing basis. Maintaining pages and links and ensuring that all processes are in proper working order can be a laborious responsibility. At the very least, running an effective e-commerce operation will require a Web server that has the capabilities to facilitate online ordering and transaction processing.

Consider the following in evaluating Web servers:

- Languages and development tools

- HTML editors, search indexes, virtual servers, and other administration tools

- Security capabilities: protocols, authentication, and access control

- E-commerce features such as credit card processing

Should You Use a Web Hosting Service for e-Commerce?

Web hosting by an outside resource is an option that may make sense for many companies. If you choose to have your e-commerce site hosted by an outside service, you will want to review the ISP's full capabilities. Do not assume that every ISP can provide e-commerce hosting. ISPs typically offer the hardware, software, communications access, and service to host Web sites, but not all ISPs have experience with e-commerce business-to-business applications.

Here are some of the key questions you should ask of potential Web hosting services:

- How many customers do you have? How many of them are doing e-commerce?

- What do you provide in the way of security (firewalls, encryption, authentication, etc.)?

- How do you handle secure transactions (SSL, CyberCash, etc.)?

- What other e-commerce services can you provide (packaged solutions, back-end connections, analysis of site traffic, etc.)?

- What support do you provide in the following areas?

- – Online store software and services

- – Database connectivity

- – Server disk space

- – CGI scripting

- – Java and JavaScript

- – Authoring tools, such as FrontPage

- – Support for multiple languages

- – E-mail standards

- – E-mail virus scanning

- What are your technical and service capabilities?

  - – Guaranteed uptime

  - – Technical support availability (days and hours)

  - – Number of Web servers and number of sites per server

  - – Access capabilities (dial-up, 56K, 128K, T-1, T-3, ISDN, DSL)

  - – Data backup

  - – Site management

- What are your fees?

  - – Setup

  - – Monthly: based on which usage criteria?

  - – Other fees

Taking Orders Electronically

You do not necessarily have to transform your entire operation into an Internet-based business to take orders electronically. Today, scores of IT marketers straddle traditional and Internet order generation by supplementing their printed catalogs and mail-order marketing materials with the Internet.

The easiest way to start is to add the Internet as a response path to traditional order generation campaigns. If you generate orders via direct marketing, then you already have an established process to handle mail, phone, and fax orders. You could add an e-mail address, but that does not really facilitate the ordering process. Instead, consider adding a Web address that leads to a Web order form. Tell customers to refer to their printed catalog for complete product information while ordering on the Web. Set up a simple open-ended order form that mirrors one of your catalog order forms.

Even with this first small step toward full-fledged Internet order generation, you will have to establish security procedures so that the privacy of your customers' ordering and credit card information is protected.

Secure transactions are essential across the Internet, and this aspect of e-commerce cannot be a weak link. There were initial concerns about secure online ordering, but they are quickly vanishing with technological advances from companies such as CyberCash (*www.cybercash.com*). CyberCash pioneered major electronic commerce payment advances on the Internet. CyberCash enables merchants worldwide to accept multiple forms of payment including Secure Payment/SET, CyberCoin, and PayNow electronic check. In early 1999, CyberCash unveiled "InstaBuy.com" (*www.instabuy.com*), a one-click shopping service Web site, allowing consumers to sign up and make purchases from more than 85 online merchants. The consumer establishes an "InstaBuy wallet" which can be used to consolidate purchase information so it does not need to be reentered each time the consumer buys from a participating merchant.

Numerous other electronic-wallet services were introduced in late 1999 with the hope of increasing consumer and merchant interest in this nascent technology. Microsoft introduced "Passport" (*www.passport.com*), an e-wallet that allows e-buyers to input, edit, and send such purchase information as credit card numbers and shipping addresses to multiple merchants from a single place. Others, including American Express (*www.americanexpress.com*), Gator (*www.gator.com*), InfoGate (*www.infogate.com*), and NextCard (*www.nextcard.com*), are vying for top spots in this arena.

Anxious to purchase online from physical locations other than your computer? You can do it on ATMs with eStation (*www.estation.com*). eStation's technology turns ATMs into "virtual commerce" terminals. This new technology is now in use in Canada by food retailer Sobey's and by Canada Post.

"mCommerce," or mobile commerce, is also just around the corner. According to Cap Gemini Ernst & Young (*www.cgey.com*), mobile data application users will increase an average of 200 percent per year through 2005. More handheld devices than PCs will access the Internet within three years, according to analysts' predictions. This provides an even greater future opportunity for IT companies to capitalize on electronic commerce.

Innovative technologies and new avenues will continue to fuel the explosive growth of e-commerce. There is even a growing movement toward a standardized method of online payment using a new technology called ECML, Electronic Commerce Modeling Language. As of mid-1999, several leading companies, including America Online, IBM, Microsoft, MasterCard, and Visa, were working together in an effort to standardize and simplify the online purchasing process.

Several forms of security promise to make online ordering safer than ever. An especially hot technology area is the *digital certificate*. A digital certificate is a way of identifying the sender of a message or transaction, protecting that message, and then verifying that the original sender sent the message.

Here is how it works: You want to send a secure message. An intermediary via traditional mail, telephone, or in person verifies your identity. You then receive a digital certificate with a private key and a public key that will be used by the party who is receiving your message. You encrypt the data to be sent. The party receiving the data decrypts it with a private key and your public key. As a result, the receiving party knows it is really you who sent the message.

It may sound complicated, but standards already exist that are supported by both Netscape Communicator and Microsoft Internet Explorer (versions 4.0 and higher for each). The use of digital certificates is already growing rapidly among financial institutions.

Want to avoid taxes on those Internet orders? It is a complicated issue, but to date, the federal government continues to support a moratorium when it comes to taxing goods sold over the Internet. States are rushing to include the Internet in mail order tax legislation, but it is unlikely to slow down the growth of e-commerce.

Driving Traffic from the Internet to a Traditional Order Generation Channel

Another way to implement e-commerce is to use the Internet to provide incentives to prospective customers to go to a *traditional* retail location or reseller to purchase your product. You can accomplish this with Internet couponing.

Internet couponing promises to be a future growth area. According to research conducted by NPD Group (*www.npd.com*), 87 percent of online coupon users say they plan to use them again in the future, yet only half of Internet users know about online coupons. Surprisingly, over half of the online coupon users in the study were considered upscale, with household incomes above $45,000. One-third had incomes above $75,000.

Internet couponing is already available in the consumer market. "ValuPage" (*www.valupage.com*) offers supermarket coupons to consumers who come to the site and enter their ZIP code. Then, if there is a supermarket chain nearby, the consumer can print out a special ValuPage of items for which there are special discounts and take it to the store. At check-out, the ValuPage is presented to the cashier, who scans it and in return gives the consumer "WebBucks," which offer the consumer money off on any items purchased during the consumer's next shopping trip. There are more than a million ValuPage subscribers signed up.

With minor adaptation, IT marketers could apply this model to their own selling situations. For example, you could offer a prospective customer an Internet coupon that is redeemable through any of your traditional order-generation channels (e.g., a printed mail-order catalog, a reseller, or a retail store). The coupon could be generated on the fly, based on answers to qualification questions. It could be accompanied by specific redemption instructions that include the catalog's toll-free phone number, a reseller's local phone number, or the local address of a retail store.

The Business of Order Fulfillment

As part of even the most basic e-commerce operation, you will need a way to implement online order entry and fulfillment. Ideally, it will be an automated process so that the orders received over the Internet can be seamlessly handled through your existing order-entry system.

It may actually make more sense for you to outsource the entire order-generation process to an Internet order fulfillment firm. Outsourcing allows you to test the viability of e-commerce without committing internal resources to the operation, but it is generally a short-term strategy for any business that is serious about generating orders through the Internet.

This strategy is supported by a report released in February 2001 by Jupiter Media Metrix (*www.jmm.com*). The research firm found that 33 percent of online retailers would outsource their online shipping to outside firms in the next year to end the headaches of online order fulfillment. The report found that 44 percent of online retailers lose money on shipping and handling. Jupiter analysts believe these companies can save up to 25 percent in labor costs by "fulfillment nets," a type of private trading network, to automate drop-shipping processes.

It is likely that you will want to provide customers with everything in one place on the Web—product descriptions, special promotions, pricing information, online ordering, perhaps even interactive customer service. Ultimately, that requires an investment that goes beyond a one-time trial or a simple Web order form.

The extent to which you provide online ordering is really up to you. The variations are as unlimited as the potential. Insight Direct (*www.insight.com*), a business-to-business IT marketer of over 130,000 computer-related brand-name products, is a case in point. With a customer base primarily in the United States, Canada, the United Kingdom, and Germany, the company has been doing business on the Web since 1995, which has helped fuel its growth. Insight had 2000 sales exceeding $2 billion with annual sales growth of 34 percent. As early as 1997, Insight transitioned to a true one-to-one marketing approach, offering customized pages to key customers:

> . . . *despite the amount of purchasing data the company has on its customer base, Insight is only giving custom Web pages*

to those customers who are recommended by one of its 60 account managers.

Insight.com offers product listings, descriptions, specifications, and real-time pricing, including volume discounts for eligible customers. It also features "landing pads" from corporate intranets that allow multiple users to order from the site, special equipment configuration forms and Internet auction pages with bargain-priced items.[2]

In 1999, Insight innovated again by moving from customized landing pages for customers to fully customer-customized "eCatalogs."

Given the almost continuous flow of innovations in Internet technology, you can expect that generating orders through the Internet will change shape before your eyes. In early 1998, for example, a new kind of Web banner ad was introduced to the market that essentially enables banner-generated e-commerce:

Typically, online merchants place banner ads on other heavily trafficked sites like search engines in the hope that users will click on them and visit their sites. . . . banner ads with Enliven technology allow people to click on them and make a secure purchase without leaving the site they're currently visiting.[3]

Now ordering products from within banners and within e-mails is increasingly common. This intriguing development means that online advertising and e-mail can lead directly to secure online order forms, thus eliminating a lengthy sales process. Although such a concept would be most appropriate for impulse purchases or items that require minimal description, e-commerce banners and e-mail promise to shorten the sales cycle and turn clicks into cash.

Where to See IT e-commerce in Action

Many of the leading IT e-commerce sites have been referenced previously in this book. In Chapter 3, the "Baker's Dozen of IT Web Sites" includes Apple, Beyond, Cisco, HP, and McAfee, all of which are fine examples of e-commerce. Dell, covered in detail in this chapter, is also worth studying.

Several of the sites mentioned in Chapter 10 represent leading edge IT e-commerce, among them Egghead, BizProLink, Converge, and Verticalnet.

To locate additional IT e-commerce sites, the following resources are recommended:

- The Interactive 500 list at *www.interactiveweek.com*

- The NetMarketing 200 list at *www.btobonline.com*

- The Fortune e50 list at *www.fortune.com*

- The Red Herring 100 at *www.redherring.com*

Notes

1. Michael Rowsom, "Bridging the Gap from Traditional Marketing to Electronic Commerce," *DIRECT MARKETING* (Hoke Communications, Inc., January 1998).

2. Larry Riggs, "Made to Order: Insight Offers Business Clients Customized E-Catalog Pages," *DIRECT* (Cowles Media, January 1998).

3. Ken Magill, "Banners Say 'Buy' in E-Shift as Bauer Loads New Tech," *DM NEWS* (Mill Hollow Corporation, February 9, 1998).

13

Integrating Online and Offline Marketing

No IT marketer, even having read this book, should get the impression that it is time to abandon traditional marketing in favor of Internet marketing. Despite the growth and inevitable dominance of Internet marketing, other marketing channels such as advertising, public relations, and direct mail/telemarketing will likely continue to be essential components of the marketing mix. What will change, however, is the mix itself. It is not difficult to imagine, for example, that the time will soon come when all other marketing media support the Internet, rather than the other way around. The wise IT marketer will start preparing for this now.

As important today is the economic argument for Internet marketing. There is much evidence cited in this book that makes a case for marketing electronically, purely from a cost–benefit perspective. Although e-marketing is not a panacea, it presents compelling financial reasons for, at the very least, integrating e-mail, e-fulfillment, Web-based customer service, and other Internet-based promotions into existing marketing programs.

That is why this last chapter starts with the premise that "online" and "offline" marketing must be intelligently integrated—and that the best principles of traditional marketing must be applied to Internet marketing in preparation for migration to the Internet. We also consider how Internet marketing will fundamentally change the way IT companies market their products and services and what you will need to do to take advantage of the online and offline marketing in combination.

Online and Offline: The Reality of a Changing Marketing World

A little more than five years after the first commercial Web browser hit the market, the Internet became ubiquitous in business worldwide. It has been so widely adopted and is so pervasive that the press routinely refers to "the Internet economy." Nowhere has the impact of the Internet been more apparent than on the nation's stock markets, as Internet IPOs almost single-handedly fueled the Dow's record-breaking rise in 1999. The Internet has been the software industry's second coming, as its rise has already spawned a slew of under-40 billionaires (that is *b*, not *m*). A whole new breed of Internet-only companies have become a breeding ground for countless innovations.

Just as quickly, however, did business conditions turn around in late 2000 and early 2001. There was trouble in paradise; Dot Coms started bleeding red ink. Some went bust. Venture capitalists and the market looked for profits instead of promises.

It is reassuring to know that direct marketing itself continues to outpace overall sales growth in the United States by 54 percent, according to the Direct Marketing Association's May 2001 report, *2000 Economic Impact: U.S. Direct & Interactive Marketing Today*. The DMA says that direct marketing revenue reached $1.73 trillion in 2000, with direct marketing sales growth expected to be about 9.6 percent annually through 2005. B-to-B direct marketing sales in 2000 grew to almost $793 billion, more than a 12 percent increase from 1999.

The DMA report also indicated that U.S. consumers and businesses spent $24.2 billion on goods and services as a result of direct marketers' online media expenditures in 2000, representing a 75 percent increase over 1999. Direct marketing companies spent $2.8 billion on interactive media marketing in 2000, an increase of about 70 percent over 1999.

The DMA's fourth annual *State of the Interactive/E-Commerce Marketing Industry* for 2000 indicates that almost seven out of ten companies say that interactive media is meeting or exceeding their expectations. The percentage of profitability achieved by companies that conduct Web transactions online rose to 69 percent in 2000 from 49 percent the year before. Nevertheless, only 57 percent of consumer companies and 35 percent of B-to-B companies utilize their Web sites for online transactions.

When you open up the electronic black box and look inside, Internet marketing is, basically, *electronic direct marketing*. It is not all that different from what direct marketers have been working toward all along, even though it has uniquely different qualities and requirements. The migration to Internet marketing implies many things for all of us in marketing, not the least of which is a fairly dramatic shift in the way marketing dollars will be allocated in the future. Internet marketing could turn marketing budgets upside down and even lead you to rethink how a marketing organization should be staffed. These are not insignificant issues for IT marketers.

The experience of the successfully launched Dot Coms proves that offline was as important as online marketing. Those that survived did so in part because they used offline marketing to build awareness for their brands. Without offline marketing, how many of these brands would have been noticed by the clicking public?

Heed this as an important lesson. The Internet is a grand and powerful marketplace, a medium that now reaches over 130 million people in the United States alone. But it is also an emerging marketplace, a very fragmented medium with millions of places people can go. Standing alone, it is not yet as effective as it can be in combination with other media.

Most IT marketers would not use a single marketing medium to launch a new product. They know that trade magazines, for example, will accomplish one kind of objective, and direct mail and telemarketing will accomplish another. The most successful marketing programs still *combine and integrate* media to increase efficiency and maximize results. That's why, despite the turmoil caused by changing fortunes and a weakening economy, IT marketers have not run away from the Internet; rather, they have run toward online and offline integration.

No lesser a world-class IT marketer than IBM is proving the point. IBM combined TV, print advertising, direct mail, and online media to support its Global Business Intelligence Solutions Group in a major worldwide integrated campaign with a $30 million budget, *Advertising Age* reported in September 1999. Advertising in business magazines and newspapers was carefully woven together with direct response television, radio, and banner ads on select Web sites, supported by a 250,000-piece mail drop. During 2001, according to *The Wall Street Journal*, IBM increased its ad budget by 17 percent to support its software products. A new IBM campaign launched in March 2001 invested 15 percent or more in online advertising—double the norm, says *The Journal*.

If you consider the Internet to be *one* of your arsenal of marketing weapons, rather than the *sole* weapon, your chances of success will be that much greater. It is likely that, someday, the Internet will become the most powerful weapon available to you. But not many IT marketers would be ready to risk abandoning every other form of marketing just yet.

How, then, can you most effectively integrate "online" and "offline" marketing today?

Your Market and Your Audiences Will Determine How You Integrate Online and Offline Marketing

As this book points out, Internet marketing is emerging as an inevitable way of doing business for IT marketers. Yet, if you have ever done targeted marketing, you know that *audiences* drive the effectiveness of direct marketing activities. That is why it is essential to understand where your market is today, and how accepting your audiences are of Internet marketing.

First consider the market you are in. How actively do your competitors utilize Internet marketing? (You will find out a lot about that just by visiting their Web sites.) How do they speak to their audiences?

Would you classify *your target audience* as early adopters of Internet technology, or laggards? How your various target audiences and constituencies respond to Internet marketing is a key consideration. You are undoubtedly familiar with the technology adoption curve, popularized by Geoffrey Moore (*www.chasmgroup.com*) in his landmark technology marketing books, *Crossing the Chasm* and *Inside the Tornado*. The curve basically defines the stages of acceptance of a technology product. Every product has a group of people who are its "early adopters"—individuals who will try the product before anyone else and, potentially, lead the market in the product's initial usage and ultimate acceptance. There is also a segment of the product's potential audience that will be far more conservative in adoption, lagging behind and, in some cases, never using it.

Although the Internet itself is now in a stage of mass adoption, you need to apply the technology adoption curve to your target audiences. Which are the audiences who will be very accepting of Internet marketing—the early adopters? Which audiences will be less receptive or even resistant to Internet marketing?

IT professionals—CIOs, software developers, and programmers, for example—will obviously be early adopters, but what about other business audiences? Where do sales and marketing people fit into your target industries? Financial managers and purchasing agents? Human resources managers? CEOs? *Which industries* are more likely to accept Internet marketing? *Which size* companies? The fact is, no one can be absolutely certain, because Internet marketing is still relatively new.

That means you may need to do some solid research to determine how *your* audiences will react to Internet marketing. Closely follow the practices of your competitors and your industry. Watch where they are focusing their efforts. Also, keep a close eye on the traditional media that target your prospect and customer audiences. Are they reporting about the Internet and the Web more frequently? Do they have companion Web sites that serve your audiences? Are there other Web-based information providers beyond your competitors who target your audiences? Are Internet marketing conferences springing up in your target industries? These are all strong signals that Internet marketing is, if not already accepted by your target audiences, rapidly gaining acceptance.

It will just be a matter of time before Internet marketing is commonplace, but you may have an opportunity right now to decide whether you will lead or follow with Internet marketing in your specialized area. Which will it be?

How to Integrate Online and Offline Media in the Internet Marketing Era

A second key factor to consider is how you will integrate the Internet with other media. Your media strategy—the way you use media and the mix of media you use—may change radically in the future. Begin the transition to Internet marketing *now*—by making the Internet a more prominent and integral part of your media mix.

Next we examine how media integration will shift from the use of traditional media to the increasing use of electronic media. Figure 13.1 is a classic example of media integration dominated by "offline" media. Note the following:

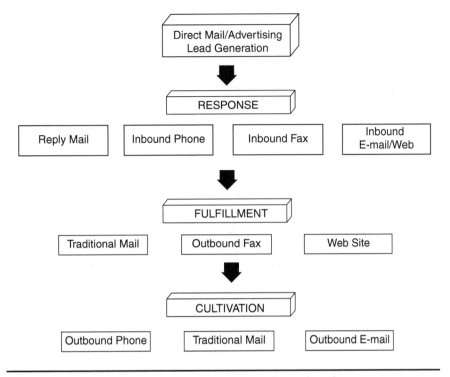

Figure 13.1. Media integration chart with traditional media.

1. *Lead generation.* Direct mail and print advertising are the primary media utilized to generate leads.

2. *Response.* Responses come in via reply mail, inbound phone calls to a toll-free number, faxes of the reply device, inbound e-mail inquiries, or inbound Web via a Web response form.

3. *Fulfillment.* Fulfillment takes place using traditional direct mail or outbound fax. In some cases, the respondent can be fulfilled instantly by receiving information or an offer at the Web site.

4. *Cultivation.* The respondent's name, address, phone number, e-mail address, and answers to qualifying questions are collected at the response stage and used to initiate a cultivation process. This process uses outbound telemarketing, traditional mail, and outbound e-mail to periodically contact and requalify the prospect.

Next you can see media integration in the era of the Internet. Figure 13.2 is an updated version of the media integration chart with an emphasis on e-marketing. Note the following:

1. *Lead generation.* Leads are generated from any source. In the future, e-mail and the Web may very well outpull other media as the primary lead source, so electronic lead generation will become more essential as time goes on.

2. *Response.* Responses come in via reply mail, inbound phone calls to a toll-free number, faxes of the reply device, inbound e-mail inquiries, or inbound Web, as before. It is likely, however, that the Web will become the primary response path in the future because it will be so much easier for the respondent. Web responses arrive via a designated, campaign-specific URL that leads to a Web response area with a Web response form that collects not

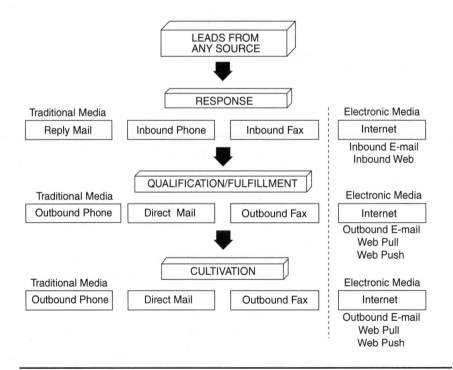

Figure 13.2. Media integration chart emphasizing electronic media.

only basic contact information, but answers to qualification questions. Prepare for Web responses to be the predominant form of inquiry and, eventually, order.

3. *Qualification and fulfillment.* Notice that the e-marketing future calls for a single-step qualification and fulfillment process. Today, traditional media are still being used to qualify and fulfill leads in a two-step process, but soon the process will be more heavily weighted to the Internet, which will combine qualification and fulfillment. This transition is already taking place.

    With the online lead qualification process happening in real time, marketers will be able to instantly deliver individualized fulfillment content to all types of prospects based on their interest and qualification level. This content could be delivered via outbound e-mail or, more likely, through individualized Web pages targeted to the prospect's specific interests and needs. Standard text-only e-mail will suffice for fast acknowledgments and "instant response," but eventually, e-mail will routinely include graphics and embedded Web site links, enhancing the e-mail fulfillment process. Fulfillment on the Web will occur via a routine Web response area process, as well as at Web sites. Fulfillment will also be "pushed" via the Web to a prospect's desktop if appropriate.

    The cost-savings implications of electronic fulfillment to marketers, and the ease of use to respondents, are so extraordinary that you should anticipate this type of fulfillment becoming the norm rather than the exception.

4. *Cultivation.* The cultivation process will be easier and more automatic with electronic media. Marketers will routinely use outbound e-mail for promotional purposes to communicate periodically, relying on e-mail newsletters, which will be sent to qualified prospects and customers who have consented to e-mail use. E-mail will routinely embed Web page links, which go to surveys, forms, and specialized Web pages. Prospects and customers will be pulled to Web sites and extranets via ongoing informational programs, which may include special promotions and content. Web content will also be pushed to the desktops of interested prospects and customers on a regular basis. As part of the cultivation process, Internet-based customer service will rule the relationship.

An Example of How to Execute Online-Offline Marketing

You can apply the principles of online-offline marketing today to reduce the overall cost and increase the overall efficiency of your marketing efforts even if you are still at the beginning of the Internet marketing curve. Following is an example.

Suppose you are organizing a traditional in-person marketing seminar targeted to a particular audience. It is a free half-day event to be held in five key cities. You need to make sure the seminar is well attended by the right prospects. What is the best way to promote it? If you used offline marketing alone, as you've probably done in the past, here is what you would do:

1. Establish the dates and locations, select list sources (including any in-house lists), and target the appropriate audience within 50 miles of each city.

2. Create and mail a direct mail invitation including a full agenda, dates and locations, and all other pertinent details. Include the traditional phone, mail-in, and fax-back response paths.

3. Follow up to non-registrants with a direct mail postcard to encourage them to reconsider. Follow up with fax and telephone confirmations to individuals who registered and said they would attend.

4. Cross-promote the seminar with traditional advertising and public relations activities.

Now what if you add the Internet *as an integral part* of the promotional plan? Here is how your original plan would be modified:

1. Establish the dates and locations, select list sources (including any in-house lists), and target the appropriate audience within 50 miles of each city. During the audience selection process, research additional opt-in e-mail lists that may be available. Also compile an in-house list of e-mail addresses for use in the promotion.

2. Create and mail an oversized postcard, considerably less expensive than the direct mail invitation referenced above, that pro-

motes the seminar. Instead of including all the details, provide a toll-free phone number for more information, but strongly encourage the prospect to visit a special Web page that fully describes the seminar. Let the Web page act as an electronic invitation that provides:

- A more detailed agenda and description of the seminar, along with speaker photographs and biographies if appropriate.

- Directions, including printable maps, for each seminar location.

- Information about other events of potential interest to the prospect, including a list of Internet-based events for those prospects who are not in the five-city area or cannot attend the live seminars but want more information about your company's product.

- An interactive registration form—perhaps with a special offer to encourage registering—so that prospects can register online and receive an instant acknowledgment. Collect an e-mail address here and you can use it to remind the registrant of the seminar several times before the event. Use a Web-based database tool and you can capture the marketing information you obtain from the prospect "one time" instead of rekeying the information. Use it for future promotions and to track the prospect's activity.

3. Follow up to nonregistrants with an e-mail if you have their e-mail addresses, or if necessary with a direct mail postcard to encourage them to reconsider. Follow up with e-mail at least twice to individuals who registered, said they would attend, and provided their e-mail addresses. Use fax and telephone confirmations only when e-mail addresses are not available.

4. Cross-promote the seminar using online advertising and public relations targeted to your audience rather than traditional advertising. Appropriate media might include mentions and sponsorships in e-mail newsletters, promotions on pertinent community sites, and banners/interstitials placed on targeted Web sites.

Notice in this example that there was a true interrelationship of online and offline marketing. You did not completely eliminate offline marketing; instead you used it to push prospects to the Internet. By using online and offline marketing in this way, you are likely to have a significant impact on your marketing ROI as you take advantage of the growing dependence on, and preference for, the Internet. The bottom line is this:

1. *You reduce the cost of your direct mail seminar invitation* by making it less elaborate and by driving responses to the Web—where they get full seminar details. You provide additional helpful service to prospects by acknowledging their registrations instantly online and by offering exact seminar locations with maps.

2. *Overall response to the promotion could increase* because you have facilitated response by adding a Web response path. This will probably become the preferred method of response in the future for most B-to-B audiences. On the Web, respondents can get more information about the seminar without the need to speak to anyone, and they can easily register online.

3. *Online registrants will likely be higher-quality prospects* because they take the time to visit the URL, review detailed information, and complete the registration form.

4. Using a series of e-mail confirmations and reminders, which you send prior to the event, *could significantly reduce your "no-show" rate* (which is typically 50–60 percent for live seminars). E-mail is much less expensive than telephone calls and even faxes. It goes directly to the recipient and is likely to be read.

5. Even if prospects visit the seminar Web page and do not come to the seminar, *they have been made aware* of your company, your seminar series, and other events you sponsor that may interest them.

6. Individuals who are outside seminar cities could visit the seminar Web pages to learn more about your company and products and, as a result, *become new prospects for you, even if they cannot attend the live event.*

The incremental cost to your seminar promotion to achieve these potential benefits should be very low. In fact, you are replacing the cost of a direct mail invitation and potentially direct mail and telephone follow-ups with the much less expensive use of a modest direct mail piece, Web pages, and e-mail. If you have a Web site, the seminar Web page could "hang off" of it. Creating the seminar response area is not a complicated task—it can be done by your in-house Web staff or outsourced to an interactive resource. If you need comprehensive response management support, there are firms that handle online seminar registration and confirmation, along with maintaining your marketing database.

The Impact of Internet Marketing on the Marketing Organizations of IT Companies

Most IT marketers are familiar with their role as a change agent in their companies. In recent years, database and direct marketing have catapulted the marketing organization to prominence, as an increasing emphasis on measurable results has struck a responsive chord with senior management.

IT marketing managers are now as likely to be held accountable for generating and qualifying leads as sales managers are for closing them. Senior marketing strategists are no less important to a company's inner management circle than are operating officers. The title "chief marketing officer" is emerging among larger and even some smaller companies as marketing gains prominence.

The rise of the Internet can enhance the position of marketing executives, managers, and the entire marketing organization within your company. Most senior business executives already acknowledge that the Internet will fundamentally change the way their company does business. They are also likely to acknowledge that it is the marketing organization in the company that is on the leading edge of that change. In a Direct Marketing Association interactive survey, 47 percent of the respondents said the electronic media function in their company reports to the marketing area.

The vast majority of Web sites are, first and foremost, marketing and sales sites. That reality has already resulted in many B-to-B companies gaining a leadership position in Internet lead generation and electronic commerce. In fact, more companies today are moving rapidly toward becoming "e-businesses." It is therefore unlikely that you will meet with much resistance from a company's senior management *outside* the marketing organization when publicizing the notion that Internet marketing is necessary and desirable. After all, these same senior managers are in the midst of developing strategic business plans that will leverage the Internet as a means of business process improvement.

IT executives are aggressively lobbying their companies for Internet-related dollars on a regular basis so that they can implement intranets and extranets. Corporate Web sites are reaching a level of importance well beyond the marketing area, especially for public companies. The Web site is becoming an "enterprise information portal": the repository for all corporate information and the conduit to get that information out to every one of the company's audiences—not just prospects and customers, but investors, analysts, the press, business partners, suppliers, employees, and prospective employees. Even more so, the rush to e-commerce will put the Internet front and center as the primary sales channel for an increasing number of companies.

Ironically, the most skepticism or resistance to Internet marketing may actually come from *within* the marketing and sales organizations. Why? Because of the FUD factor: fear, uncertainty, and doubt. These are likely to accompany any fundamental change to business as usual—and the change will be dramatic and all-encompassing with Internet marketing.

The Impact on Marketing

Even in an IT company, the marketing organization will likely face the challenge of reexamining marketing objectives, priorities, strategies, and tactics. Marketing managers may need to recast their programs, reshuffle their media mix, reorient their staffs—and perhaps even replace some staff with interactive media specialists.

The entire marketing organization will need to learn, and to teach the company, new ways of information delivery and response management. Marketing databases and database marketing programs will revolve around the Internet. Fulfillment priorities will change as instant response and electronic fulfillment become the norm. E-mail is becoming an accepted form of external marketing communication. The U.S. Postal Service and others will get into the fray as they provide certification of e-mail delivery.

Advertising, direct mail, and telemarketing usage could shift dramatically as these media begin to play a more subordinate role to the Internet and the Web. Chances are that traditional media will not disappear, but they will follow behind the Internet, relinquishing their former leadership position. Media convergence already exists. Web site addresses are everywhere, and the Web is fast becoming a primary response path for IT marketers. Direct mail and direct response advertising are even now being aggressively used to lead a prospect to a Web response form, an Internet event, or a corporate Web site. "Integration" will take on a whole new meaning as the Internet emerges as the core of a company's marketing programs, with all other media revolving around it and playing a supporting role.

With it all, some difficult budgeting and staffing decisions will need to be made. Internet marketing will require the marketing manager to accommodate entirely new budget line items (e.g., e-mail delivery, development of virtual events, online advertising campaigns, participation in communities, management of affiliate programs, creation of Web pages, maintenance of Web sites, electronic fulfillment and response management, Web server expenses, etc.). Decisions will not always be clear-cut as marketing melds with information technology and budgets become the shared responsibility of more than one department.

On the staffing and resources side, Internet marketing could cause a massive shift in hiring or training the types of individuals who work in a marketing organization and the kinds of outside services that need to be procured.

Internal resources may very well be skewed toward the Internet. Instead of the typical advertising and media personnel, marketing communications project supervisors, marketing service managers, or even direct marketing specialists, a marketing organization may need a cadre of Internet marketing experts. This could be a team of Internet marketing strategists, interactive producers, new media specialists, Web writers, and interactive designers—but it also may need to include a new addition to marketing: a "marketologist." The marketologist will be part marketer, part Webmaster—someone who understands the unique combination of marketing and technology that Internet marketing demands.

The Impact on the Marketing/IT Departments

The Internet has spawned some unholy alliances, not the least of which is between IT and marketing departments. In larger companies, these two contrasting functional organizations already find that they must work hand-in-hand to deliver Web content over the Internet, and the need will soon go beyond Web sites alone.

The IT department could be a potential internal barrier to an Internet marketing initiative—not because IT managers want to derail marketing, but rather because they legitimately need to control network traffic and user needs. That is a major part of their responsibility. As marketing "messes around" with e-mail and the Web, some IT managers may get more than nervous. IT's support of corporate intranets is a given—but Web sites, virtual events, or extranets that utilize heavy-duty marketing database engines, include online transaction processing, incorporate voiceover IP, and require the implementation of electronic commerce are something else again. This is the kind of stuff that could choke band-width, melt servers, and bring a corporate network to its knees.

That is why the "marketologist" could be a key person in the marketing organization. It is the marketologist who will need to speak IT's language, work the relationship, and make sure that the needs of Internet marketing can be accommodated by the corporate IT group. It is the marketologist who will need to understand what the internal IT organization can and cannot provide, and help make the decision, if necessary, to outsource Internet marketing to the appropriate Internet service providers.

The Impact on Sales

For the sales organization in an IT company, the transition to Internet marketing will be no less dramatic and, potentially, more traumatic. The lead generation and qualification process may not fundamentally change, even though the requirements for information input and dissemination may be drastically different. However, Internet-enabled partnering and electronic commerce initiatives could turn a company's entire sales process upside down.

As electronic commerce becomes easier and more cost-effective to implement, IT companies are now shifting some if not all of the traditional telephone or face-to-face selling to Internet-based selling. "Call-me" buttons and live-text chat on Web sites will become the norm. Telesales may very well become Internet-based as telephony and the Internet converge. Sending voice over IP (Internet Protocol) is already technically feasible. As demand for these applications grows, prospects or customers will go to the Web instead of the telephone to ask for information, solve their own problems, and, when necessary, engage in a sales or service dialogue on demand. In short, customers will drive the interaction process.

Banks of telemarketers may actually find their work shifting from inbound telephone calls to inbound e-mail and Web inquiries. Telesales specialists will be retrained to "watch" a visitor navigate a Web site, be available when the visitor clicks a call-me button, and intercede when that visitor needs more information—pushing Web pages to the visitor if necessary. Outbound telemarketers will just as likely be communicating via the Internet as over a telephone.

The direct sales force in an IT company is likely to change in complexion as well. In-person sales calls may still occur, but they will increasingly be enhanced or sometimes replaced by Internet conferencing. It may begin with just a telephone call that is enhanced with Web support. The salesperson will conduct a phone conversation but will suggest to the prospect that he or she go to the Web to view some information.

The IT salesperson of the future might arrange a virtual meeting over the Web with a prospect, perhaps including live videoconferencing. The prospect, of course, could be anywhere in the world. At this virtual meeting, the salesperson will make eye contact and walk the prospect through a visual presentation on the Web, leading him or her along with live voice. The salesperson will be able to stop at any point and take questions. The salesperson could show the prospect video clips of customer testimonials and success stories, or maybe the salesperson will invite the prospect to view and interact with a real-time product demonstration, right then and there.

If a face-to-face meeting is warranted, the salesperson will undoubtedly bring along a notebook computer that has presentations and demonstrations preloaded. He or she might connect to the Internet while in the prospect's office and guide the prospect through an online presentation, seminar, or demonstration on the Web. This might be an opportunity to have the prospect access an online calculator or analyzer to see the ROI benefits of the company's proposed solution.

Presenting the Case for Internet Marketing

In your role as a marketer, you will now become responsible for obtaining full management support and educating the entire organization about the inevitability of Internet marketing. You know the politics of your company—who the movers and shakers are, where the influence is, who calls the shots. You will have to use this intelligence wisely to elicit broad-based support for dramatic change.

You will, in effect, need to establish your own internal public relations program for Internet marketing. Plan it carefully and execute it wisely, for it will help shape the future of your marketing organization and your job. And who is your ally in all of this? The Internet itself. As you have seen in this book, the Internet is a business phenomenon of unprecedented proportion. IT marketing success stories are being written daily, and all of them can be found on the Internet.

In presenting the case for Internet marketing to your organization's management, use the Internet and its vast resources for credibility and validation. Rely on the major search engines and other information search sources, along with industry-specific sites, to get the ammunition you need. Use industry data and reports from the traditional press to enhance credibility.

Start with some of the gateway sites, which provide countless links to the relevant sites you will need to find. One such gateway is the outstanding site, *www.ceoexpress.com.* This "launching pad" for managers opens a wide door to all kinds of information and research about business in general. It is well organized, it is easy to use, and it offers plenty of links to sources that will be useful to you. Other valuable resources are listed in Appendix A of this book and linked on the book's companion Web site.

Focus on the Quantifiable Business Benefits of Internet Marketing

Selling the concept of Internet marketing to senior management and to the various groups, departments, or divisions within your company should be supported with facts. There is plenty of evidence, much of it presented in this book, to support the accelerated movement toward Internet marketing.

To make your argument all the more effective, focus on the *quantifiable business benefits* of Internet direct marketing:[1]

1. The most successful Web marketers are integrating the Web with other media.

2. Internet direct marketing is 60–65 percent cheaper than traditional direct mail marketing.

3. Internet direct marketing campaigns can be changed in real time.

4. The Internet provides "unlimited shelf space" for products.

5. The Internet provides worldwide reach for your company.

6. The Internet makes one-to-one marketing a reality, if it is executed properly.

Next we consider each of these benefits individually.

1. The most successful Web marketers are integrating the Web with other media.

   Internet and Web marketing should not occur in a vacuum. Market forces suggest that Internet marketing will eventually be the predominant form of marketing, but it will not replace the effectiveness of *combining and integrating* electronic and traditional media.

   Use the right combination of media to most effectively reach your target audience. Print advertising may continue to generate awareness for your company, your products, and your services, and direct mail may continue to generate and qualify leads. Do not abandon these media prematurely, but in every case, *integrate* the Internet into your media plans and *escalate* your use of Internet marketing.

   Whenever possible, establish a campaign-specific URL that leads to a Web response area designed to capture and qualify a lead. Ask prospects and customers to provide e-mail addresses, and request permission to communicate with them via e-mail. Use direct mail and advertising to drive people to Web response forms and your Web site. Support your Web activities by leveraging the messaging and offers from other media and making everything work together.

2. Internet direct marketing is 60–65 percent cheaper than traditional direct mail marketing.

Research by The Yankee Group (*www.yankeegroup.com*) indicates that Internet direct marketing represents a *threefold cost savings* for direct marketing. Moreover, The Yankee Group says that Internet direct marketing can bring *up to ten times the return* of a traditional direct marketing campaign, when considering original and follow-up campaigns applied to the same product. The areas in which you will achieve the largest savings are likely to be fulfillment, delivery, medium used, and analysis. The economics of Internet marketing make a compelling case for gradually moving promotional dollars from other media to Internet forms of promotion. Cost alone should not drive marketing decisions, but cost-effectiveness and media efficiency are powerful motivators for choosing one medium over another.

Electronic media turn traditional media cost structures upside down. With Internet marketing, there is nothing to print and mail; there are no advertising materials to reproduce and no telemarketing calls to handle. Web sites can reach one, a hundred, a thousand, or a million prospects or customers for about the same cost. With the proper in-house tools, e-mail can be widely distributed without unit-cost implications, as with direct mail, and, at least so far, the Internet is a tax-free commerce zone.

The Internet is just as significant a cost-savings medium in product distribution. According to the Organisation for Economic Cooperation and Development (*www.oecd.org*), it costs $1 to distribute an airline ticket electronically versus $8 traditionally. It costs just 50 cents to distribute a software product electronically versus $15 traditionally.

Use the growth of Internet marketing as a springboard for evaluating your media investments and product marketing and distribution costs on a dollar-for-dollar basis. Compare and contrast the total marketing costs for a direct response advertising, direct mail, or telemarketing campaign versus an Internet-based campaign. If it is feasible, establish head-to-head tests of one medium against the other. Keep audience criteria, the offer, and the basic creative approach the same. Evaluate which medium produces the

- Highest response rates

- Highest-quality leads

- Best conversion of responses to leads

- Best conversion of leads to sales

- Shortest response-to-lead-to-sale time frame

3. Internet direct marketing campaigns can be changed in real time.

One of the Internet's major strategic advantages as a marketing medium is the campaign time to market. Advertising campaigns depend on publication close dates; monthly publications generally require materials 30–45 days prior to an issue date. Typical direct mail campaigns take from 6 to 10 weeks to execute. Even telemarketing campaigns may take several weeks to organize and execute.

Time frames associated with Internet marketing are considerably shorter than traditional media time frames. For e-mail, copy can be written and then distributed almost instantly once e-mail addresses are obtained. The majority of responses to e-mail campaigns typically is received within 48 hours. Web pages can quickly be written, designed, and published to the Web using commonly available tools on almost any computer. Web pages and Web banner ads can literally be changed overnight if need be. Entirely new banner ad campaigns can be created and uploaded within days, making it possible to shift marketing gears quickly based on audience reaction and response.

Electronic media today have no time constraints associated with their availability. Information can be available instantly on the Web or distributed instantly via e-mail, regardless of the audience size. Electronic fulfillment is available for instant unlock or immediate download. "Real-time marketing" becomes a reality under this scenario. Although it can be both a blessing and a curse, it can lead to new opportunities for instant evaluation and on-the-spot campaign reengineering.

4. The Internet provides "unlimited shelf space" for products.

Amazon.com migrated from millions of books to tens of millions of books, videos, CDs, electronics, household items, and countless other products more rapidly than any "bricks-and-mortar" operation could ever conceive of doing. Companies that sell on the Internet can challenge convention by making limitless numbers of products available in an electronic store because, if the product is appropriately described and marketed, the buyer does not need to see and touch it.

The vastness of cyberspace is a marketing benefit like no other. Only the Internet can act as a virtual warehouse, extending your inventory and presenting any number of products at any time to customers and prospects anywhere.

5. The Internet provides worldwide reach for your company.

A company of virtually any size can reach out to the world with its message, products, and services. There are countless stories of tiny organizations, even one-person operations, marketing and selling products and services over the Internet. No other medium provides the low-cost coverage of the Internet, no other form of communication the worldwide penetration of the Web. Small organizations can appear to be large and, more important, they can gain the same marketing advantage on the Internet as do corporate giants.

With no time zones and no meeting protocol, electronic business can be conducted 24 hours a day, seven days a week, in every corner of the world—and the Internet marketer need never leave his or her office. This factor alone fuels the growth of the Internet as a medium of unlimited potential on a worldwide scale.

6. The Internet makes one-to-one marketing a reality, if it is executed properly.

One-to-one marketing is, at its heart, the simple notion of building a relationship that extends from one party to another. If the individualization of the Internet is maximized, one-to-one marketing can be a powerful and lasting way of doing business.

More than that, Internet marketing could create a one-to-one standard for doing business worldwide, and with that will come the availability of mass-market tools that will ensure its continued existence.

As with most information technologies, early products are introduced to the marketplace at premium prices. After competitors enter the market and the product category becomes both accepted and desirable, prices begin to moderate. Often, "light" versions of products enter the market to serve the low end.

Already, we have seen the migration toward lower-cost e-mail and Web tools. In many cases, e-mail software and Web browsers are now bundled in free with ISP Internet access services. The same is becoming true of Internet database marketing tools and e-commerce applications. High-end comprehensive solutions will always be available at premium prices, but lower-cost products with limited functionality will suffice for a large part of the market. That means that one-to-one marketing, e-commerce, real-time collaboration, and other Internet advances could reach well beyond a small percentage of Internet marketers. In fact, Internet marketers can purchase e-commerce services on a subscription or service bureau basis, avoiding the internal cost of establishing such an operation.

In the final analysis, you will not only need to convey the specific benefits of Internet marketing—you will also need to spread the word throughout your company that it will be *a profitable venture*. There are certainly up-front and continuing costs related to Internet marketing, but a thorough analysis should show that Internet marketing compares very favorably to the use of traditional media and marketing methods.

The Internet Marketing Audit

An audit is a first step in analyzing your existing use of Internet marketing and moving forward with wide-scale implementation. Use the audit checklist shown in Figure 13.3 to help assess your "Internet marketing readiness"—to define and answer questions and determine needs. This will help you as you begin to formulate a comprehensive action plan.

The Internet Marketing Action Plan

By completing the Internet Marketing Audit Checklist, you have taken a first important step in assessing your overall readiness for the transition to Internet marketing. Soon, you will see how to use the checklist to help develop a specific action plan for implementing Internet marketing, but first, we need to address several important factors that will have an impact on your plan.

Does your organization currently have, or do you plan to add within 12 months:	YES	NO
A corporate network (LAN and/or WAN)	❏	❏
Communication via e-mail *outside* your organization	❏	❏
A corporate Web site	❏	❏
In-house	❏	❏
Outsourced	❏	❏
An intranet	❏	❏
In-house	❏	❏
Outsourced	❏	❏
An extranet	❏	❏
In-house	❏	❏
Outsourced	❏	❏
A Webmaster, or someone primarily responsible for corporate Internet usage	❏	❏

Do you currently use, or do you plan to use within 12 months:		
Direct mail and other traditional media to drive traffic to your Web site	❏	❏
The Web as a response path in direct marketing campaigns	❏	❏
Campaign-specific URLs to track response by campaign	❏	❏
Web response forms to capture leads	❏	❏
Outbound e-mail as a promotional response, fulfillment, follow-up or continuity medium	❏	❏
Links to other Web sites	❏	❏
Online advertising such as banner ads, interstitials, or e-mail newsletter sponsorships as appropriate	❏	❏
Online events or seminars	❏	❏
Online informational fulfillment	❏	❏
Online demos and trials, if appropriate	❏	❏
Distribution of live products over the Internet, if appropriate	❏	❏

Figure 13.3. Internet marketing audit checklist. (*continued on next page*)

Do you currently use, or do you plan to use within 12 months:

Participation in Web communities	❏	❏
A Web community of your own	❏	❏
Participation in affiliate programs	❏	❏
An affilitate program of your own	❏	❏

Does your Web site or extranet currently have, or do you plan to add within 12 months:

Web response pages or response forms	❏	❏
An Internet-integrated database component for capturing/tracking visitor data	❏	❏
Web database capability to dynamically generate personalized pages on-the-fly	❏	❏
Automated e-mail response capability	❏	❏
Cookie technology for visitor tracking	❏	❏
Electronic (online) fulfillment	❏	❏
Electronic solutions center: matching products/services to customer or prospect needs	❏	❏
Internet-enhanced customer marketing: private access customer areas or extranets	❏	❏
Electronic commerce: order entry, processing, tracking	❏	❏
Support of partners via the Internet, if appropriate	❏	❏

Figure 13.3.   Internet marketing audit checklist. *(continued from previous page)*

Developing the Action Plan

Although each Internet Marketing Action Plan will be unique to a marketing organization's specific needs, these are the basic steps to follow in developing your own action plan:

1. *Assess your Internet marketing readiness.* Now is the time to evaluate your organization's Internet marketing capabilities. You need to be ready to transition to Internet-based marketing now. Use the Internet Marketing Audit Checklist to assess your readiness.

   Do not let the assessment process deter you. The fact is that most of the business-to-business marketing world is just beginning to apply Internet marketing in a disciplined, integrated way. The important thing is to understand your current state of readiness and recognize where you are today—and where you will need to be.

2. *Prepare your management for the Internet-dominated future.* The Internet has already captured top-of-mind awareness among senior management at many companies. You should have little resistance to the adoption of Internet marketing, but you will need to be an advocate. Make sure your management understands the value of Internet marketing and recognizes its inevitability. Share Internet marketing information from authoritative sources with your management. Make sure they know what their competitors are doing. Use the resources in Appendix A for your research.

   If you are in a position to do so, serve on or chair a committee in your organization that is charged with developing a strategic plan for using the Internet as a business, not just a marketing tool. Chances are, management is already on a course to use the Internet strategically as part of the company's overall business plan—so you can take advantage of that business condition to benefit your own marketing program.

   With senior management already aware of and planning for the ascension of the Internet, you have a rare opportunity to position Internet marketing and electronic commerce as a logical subset of your organization's entire Internet business plan. By riding the plan's coattails, you can push Internet marketing a lot further, a lot faster. Organizational acceptance and support of Internet marketing will be your ultimate reward.

3. *Develop the action plan.* Some organizations are more technologically ready than others are, and some marketers may be further ahead than you are. Although IT marketers are leading the charge, different companies are in different stages of readiness or implementation. After all, Internet marketing that is measurable is, for many, a new concept.

   As with any good marketing plan, your Internet marketing action plan should include:

   – Objectives: general and specific

   – Products and services to be promoted

   – Competitive environment

   – Market opportunities

- Marketing program strategy

- Audience characteristics and selection criteria

- Media usage and integration

- Offer development

- Creative execution

- Lead qualification, lead fulfillment, and response management

- Lead and sales tracking

- Response and results analysis

- Measurement criteria

- Technical requirements for implementation

- Staffing and organizational needs

- Program budgets and schedules

Implementing the Action Plan

The action plan should allow for a transitional stage, a period of time during which you consciously move your marketing programs more and more toward Internet marketing. Recognize that your plan should be flexible and may need to undergo continuous refinement and modification as conditions in your market change.

Refer to the Internet Marketing Audit Checklist and work toward turning the "no" answers into "yes" answers over time. Be sure your company is in a position to support current and future Internet marketing initiatives. If possible, help your company develop criteria for the acquisition of technology that will be required to implement Internet marketing on a broad scale. Lobby for assistance from outside resources and outsourcing of Internet services if needed to support Internet marketing initiatives.

Use the media integration plan outlined earlier to capitalize on the Internet trajectory. Start to integrate the Internet with your use of traditional media if you have not already done so. Test the effectiveness of the Internet as a lead generation and qualification medium. Compare Internet marketing campaigns with traditional media campaigns. Closely monitor Internet usage and evaluate results.

Increase your reliance on the Internet as time progresses, especially if prospects and customers seem receptive to Internet marketing. Let your audiences drive your use of the Internet—*ask them* how they wish to receive information and if the Internet is the medium they most prefer. Ask them for permission to use e-mail to communicate with them, and determine if they have an interest in having Web pages delivered directly to their desktops. Survey your customers regularly on their acceptance of Internet marketing.

Establish promotional guidelines that require consideration of the Internet in every marketing program. Do not execute any marketing program that does not have an Internet marketing component, and always take the time to spread the news internally (and externally if appropriate) of your Internet marketing successes.

In-House or Outside?

As part of your Internet marketing action plan, you will want to decide whether or not you will be in a position to implement programs in-house or with the assistance of outside resources. To help you make that decision, it is probably a good idea to identify the deliverables and analyze each in relation to your in-house capabilities. Figure 13.4 is just one example of such an analysis. You will note that some deliverables are handled with a combination of in-house and outside resources. It is likely that your situation will change and that at times you may have to outsource only part of the responsibility for some Internet marketing deliverables.

Suppose you decide to run a virtual seminar, for example. If that event includes streaming sound or video, you may want to use an outside resource—a Web-hosting service that has the server capacity and capability of handling streaming media. This may be a more desirable solution than burdening your in-house Web server. Also keep in mind that it may take more than one outside resource to meet your needs at any given time. A Web-hosting service would be a good resource for the technical implementation of a virtual seminar, but you may also need an outside interactive agency to create and execute the virtual seminar itself.

Staff Requirements for Internet Marketing

Earlier we mentioned the fact that you might have to retrain existing staff or even replace them with interactive marketing specialists. As Internet marketing continues to grow in importance for your organization, it would be prudent to analyze marketing staff requirements and make adjustments in the future.

Plan Deliverable	In-house	Handling: Outside
Technology		
Internet access		X
E-mail capabilities		
Marketing e-mail address for inquiries	X	
Broadcast capabilities for		
e-mail promotions and e-mail newsletters		X
Web capabilities		
Corporate Web site hosting	X	
Web response areas and forms	X	
Marketing database integration	X	X
E-commerce applications		X
Maintenance and Back-office		
Web site on-going maintenance		X
Electronic response and lead management		X
Marketing database management	X	X
Managing Web site links	X	
Managing e-mail newsletter programs	X	
Managing customer extranet	X	
Managing partner extranet	X	
Creation and Execution		
E-mail	X	
Updating Web site pages	X	X
Web response areas and forms	X	
Banner ad campaigns		X
Virtual events		X
Order generation		X
Electronic fulfillment materials	X	
Web community activity	X	X
Participation in others' affiliate programs	X	
Management of own affiliate program		X

Figure 13.4. Analysis of Internet marketing action plan deliverables.

In some cases, you may be better off contracting outside freelance resources or working with interactive agencies on a project or program basis. Very often, outside resources have a level of expertise and a team of skilled professionals already working in a cohesive group. You might not be able to match this expertise with existing in-house staff, and personnel situations or budgets may prevent you from recruiting the necessary personnel.

Whether you are evaluating outside resources or planning to add in-house staff, the following job descriptions might be helpful to you. These are generally the types of positions that should be considered in staffing an Internet marketing function. All of these individuals should have a demonstrated comfort level with Internet technology, and all should at least be familiar with basic e-mail and Web tools.

Internet Marketing Manager

- Manages programs, personnel, and budgets

- Motivates, leads, and supports the Internet marketing group

- Is responsible for training of group personnel

- Ensures that policies and procedures are followed

- Assigns responsibilities, tasks, and schedules

- Makes hiring, promotion, and compensation recommendations

- Tailors job descriptions to personal goals of personnel

- Maintains marketing partner relationships

- Interfaces with senior management regarding Internet marketing strategies

Marketologist

- Participates in developing a strategic Internet marketing program

- Maintains high level of knowledge of Internet and Web technologies

- Recommends new technologies in collaboration with IT department

- Acts as marketing liaison with internal IT resources and outside resources

- Manages Internet marketing media plan

- Measures and analyzes Internet marketing program results

- Acts as marketing strategist for creative execution

Internet Marketing Producer

- Facilitates the execution of Internet marketing strategies

- Works in close collaboration with marketologist, media, and creative personnel to build interactive programs

- Develops, applies, and integrates Internet technologies and implements programs

- Publishes and maintains Web pages

Internet Marketing Media Specialist

- Researches Internet media and develops Internet media plans

- Places Internet media

- Evaluates and analyzes results of Internet marketing programs

Internet Marketing Creative Specialist: Copy

- Helps develop Internet marketing creative strategies

- Works in close collaboration with Internet marketing team

- Researches competition

- Writes copy for e-mail, online advertising, and Web forms and pages

Internet Marketing Creative Specialist: Art

- Helps develop Internet marketing creative strategies

- Works in close collaboration with Internet marketing team

- Creates graphics and graphic design for Web pages, response forms, and online advertising

The Internet Is Part of a Changing Marketing World

In the era of Internet direct marketing, leads may come into your marketing pipeline from any source, qualified or unqualified. However, the e-mail and Web response paths may turn out to be the channel through which you acquire your *highest-quality leads*. Eventually, it may be the channel of preference for many prospects and customers.

If this is the trend in Internet-based lead generation, it bears careful watching in your company. It implies that it will be more important than ever to utilize the Internet to generate and qualify leads in the first place, *because chances are they will be better quality leads*. Of course, it will be imperative to include a Web response path in your direct marketing promotions as the Web becomes the preferred method for response.

It will increasingly be common for IT marketers to accept lead generation program responses via campaign-specific URLs leading to Web response forms and pages, or by establishing full-fledged response centers on their Web sites. Prospects will get what they need through electronic fulfillment on Web sites, with the availability of information unlocks or downloads providing marketers with a distinct advantage over competitors. In many cases, customers already purchase products or services online, unlock purchased software or information instantly, or subscribe to services that offer to review, cull, and deliver Internet-based information to them.

One of the strengths of Internet marketing will be its ability to facilitate prospect and customer cultivation. As e-mail becomes an accepted means of marketing communication to reach qualified prospects and customers, you will be able to use it as a promotional vehicle to update key constituents on a periodic basis. The e-mail newsletter is gaining wide acceptance as a format, as both customers and qualified prospects elect to subscribe to such publications.

Areas of Web sites increasingly are dedicated to customers, and extranets have evolved into customer and key prospect information and service centers. Web-based communications, in the form of Web sites that customers and prospects visit or Web pages that are pushed to customer and prospect desktops, are commonplace.

You can see the implications of Internet marketing just by noting how it pervades every step of the lead generation and qualification process. At this point, the Internet components do not replace other media—all media work together in a closely coordinated effort, supporting one another. Prospects need to be able to choose the way they wish to respond and receive information. This is a key concept, because it is will define the future of marketing communications: Prospects and customers will define the way you, the marketer, communicate with them. They will drive the communication process instead of the marketer.

This fundamentally changes the marketer/prospect relationship forever. With the empowerment of the prospect, and the rise of true permission marketing, the marketer's role will be to deliver what the prospect asks for, when the prospect asks for it, using the delivery channel of the prospect's choice. With the emergence of one-to-one customer relationships, the IT marketer will need to learn from the customer's interactions with the marketer and use that data to continuously refine the customer-marketing program.

This is only the beginning. At its current rate of adoption, Internet marketing is no longer an option but a necessity. With its true cost-saving and timesaving benefits, as well as the growing demand by prospects and customers, the Internet will become the core medium in the entire marketing process.

In many respects, Internet marketing has now come full circle. IT marketers who are moving aggressively toward it recognize that it does not work in a vacuum; that to be most effective, marketing programs need to integrate Internet advertising with traditional forms of advertising, and that traditional forms of fulfillment and customer service need to meld with e-business practices.

Forrester Research, in a 1999 report on "Driving Site Traffic," coined a phrase that could define this emerging intermingling of media: *synchronized advertising*. Forrester says the concept is to link "traditional advertising's branding strength with the Web's power to tailor messages based on a consumer's media consumption and purchase behavior."

Beyond that, says Forrester in a 2000 report, is the next marketing frontier, "presence awareness." Forrester defines presence awareness as "the ability to know a person's availability and status across all communication channels." Forrester sees presence awareness as a kind of "electronic peripheral vision" that Internet-based applications will someday incorporate. This means marketers will have a more in-depth understanding of what customers and prospects want, and when they want it, regardless of how they interact with the company. With the advent of wireless communications, this concept could extend even beyond today's physical boundaries.

These possibilities make the future all the more exciting for IT marketers. The real way to succeed with Internet marketing may well be to view it as the logical extension of the marketing process, integrated seamlessly with traditional marketing in a way that almost disregards the differences and capitalizes on the combined strength of both.

A Final Word

Technological change is driving our world, and the Internet is at the center of it. The Internet's inevitability, its wide adoption as an interactive communications tool, and its emergence as a system of commerce have converged on direct marketing and the marketing world in general, and the change is rapid and dramatic.

What is becoming clear, however, is that the free ride is over. Now the Internet is really getting down to business. The weaker Dot Coms are being weeded out by economic realities. Companies with an inadequate e-commerce infrastructure or poor Internet customer service are failing.

Web-based publishers of free information are reevaluating their business strategies, looking at the interactive edition of *The Wall Street Journal* as an example. WSJ.com is the Web's largest paid-circulation site, with 574,000 online subscribers. The *Journal* has succeeded where many others have failed, not only maintaining both print and online versions of the publication, but building a sizeable online base of paid subscribers.

The rules of Internet marketing are continuously being rewritten, which is why this book's Web site is an important source of updated information.

Internet marketing is now in a phase of maturity well beyond its early experimental stage. E-commerce is in its third generation. A June 2000 E-tail Economic Study conducted by McKinsey/Salomon Smith Barney suggests that it is those e-tailers that cross the lines between stores, catalogs, and e-commerce that will survive. "Pure plays," or

Internet-only retailers, lose money every time they sell anything, according to the study.

Database-driven Internet personalization is now standard practice. One-to-one relationship marketing is fast becoming a necessity in e-business. eCRM (Customer Relationship Management) is one of the hottest business sectors. Already, IT marketers large and small are using Internet marketing today to generate and qualify leads, hold successful Internet events, execute instant fulfillment, enhance customer relationships, and generate orders. They are joining Web communities and, in some cases, starting their own portal-like communities. They are building affiliate marketing programs, engaging in collaborative selling, and forming new kinds of Internet-based partnerships.

All kinds of advances are driving the Internet, and Internet marketing, to new heights, some of which today might still seem fantastic. Convergence of the Internet and telecommunications, the connections between the Internet and cable television, the onward march of broadband, voice-based Internet access, and the emergence of a truly wireless Internet will do much to drive widespread adoption. Other trends, such as the growth of ASPs (Application Service Providers), will bring sophisticated e-commerce and e-business applications to even the smallest of companies. Backwards integration of the Internet into bricks-and-mortar companies, which are using the Internet to run their traditional businesses, will have a far-reaching effect. The June 2000 approval of a federal e-signatures bill will make digital signatures as legal as those executed on paper. Broadening demographic usage of the Internet, from teens to seniors and men to women, will continue to spread its popularity. The reliance on e-mail by every consumer and business person will likely cause it to dominate every other form of communication, even the telephone. And we haven't even begun to explore the potential of a wireless Internet.

These are vast, fundamental changes. Despite the Dot Com setbacks of early 2001, the Internet economy is well entrenched, and we are only at the beginning of the Information Age.

And what of IT marketing? I have worked with IT companies for over two decades. I learned about the awesome power of direct marketing and witnessed firsthand what it could achieve. As a direct marketer who cut his teeth on direct mail, at first I found the swift move to Internet marketing unnerving. I am a complete convert now.

The adoption of the Internet reminds me of the desktop-publishing revolution. I remember when typesetters and paste-up artists were swept away by the flood of computer technology, some doubting it would take hold. Now everything in every design department at every ad agency and publication is done on computer disk. The productivity and quality improvements have been monumental. No one looks back upon the "good old days" of typesetting and manual paste-up with fondness anymore.

Fortunately, it is *marketing* that early on drove the growth of the Internet, and it is marketing that will now be one of its primary beneficiaries. Internet marketing is becoming the new direct marketing because of its inherent direct marketing power. After all, isn't Internet marketing in reality interactive, personalized, one-to-one direct marketing? Even more than that, the Internet is the marketing medium that can *truly complete the selling cycle* by letting prospects not only learn about a product online, but inquire about it and, when they are ready, actually buy it online. If Internet marketing is applied intelligently, it can fulfill the promise of direct marketing in the "Age of the e": totally measurable, results-oriented, repeatable, and highly efficient.

To survive and thrive, you, as an IT marketer, must fully embrace Internet marketing You must integrate it into your overall marketing strategy, capitalizing on the combined strength of online and offline media. And if you're to succeed, you will understand that the Internet is destined to become the central core of your marketing strategy.

The demarcation between traditional marketing and Internet marketing is blurring rapidly, and it is not merely in marketing. In fact, the entire business world is adopting the Internet as a business platform. The Disneys of the world are buying into it, and the Procter & Gambles of the world are advertising on it. It is the Ciscos, Dells, and IBMs of the world that are leading the revolution. And it is the Amazons, eBays, and America Onlines that are reshaping business as we know it.

Internet marketing is the new marketing, based on timeless marketing principles, that will drive IT marketing now and in the future. I have personally witnessed this transformation in my own direct marketing business. Our clients now use traditional media to drive prospects and customers to Internet events and Web sites. E-mail, newsletter ads, online advertising, and Web sites are becoming the primary marketing media of choice, working in conjunction with traditional direct mail and advertising to *improve the marketing ROI.*

I know for certain that the fundamental principles of direct marketing will not only survive—they will flourish as the basic tenets of Internet marketing. I am enthusiastic and positive about the emergence of Internet marketing and its still-promising future. It has so much to offer to so many—with such extraordinarily compelling and proven benefits. In the end, it is all about building better, more productive relationships with prospects and customers ... the simplest of notions, but all the more challenging to achieve as marketing becomes more sophisticated and complex. For IT companies, Internet marketing will ensure fulfilling and rewarding marketing relationships ... and ultimately, measurable marketing that leads to real profits.

Note

1. Melissa Bane (director of Internet market strategies, The Yankee Group), "Is Successful Web Marketing a Myth?" Sales and Marketing Series: *Web Marketing—Myth and Reality* (presentation given by Massachusetts Software Council, February 6, 1998).

Appendix A: Other Resources

Web Sites Mentioned in This Book
(in order of appearance; first reference only)

Chapter 1: How IT Marketers Can Put the Internet to Work

www.internetwk.com	*InternetWeek* magazine
www.datamation.com	*DATAMATION*
www.emarketer.com	eMarketer
www.cyberatlas.internet.com	CyberAtlas
www.statmarket.com	Internet statistics, updated daily
www.idc.com	International Data Corporation
www.gartner.com	Gartner, Inc.
www.bcg.com	Boston Consulting Group
www.internetindicators.com	Univ. of Texas's Center for Research in Electronic Commerce
www.the-dma.org	Direct Marketing Association
www.forrester.com	Forrester Research
www.neci.nec.com	NEC Research Institute
www.cmpnet.com	CMPnet
www.cnet.com	C|Net
www.idg.net	IDG.net
www.internet.com	Internet.com
www.zdnet.com	ZDnet
www.ftc.gov	Federal Trade Commission
www.interactiveweek.com	*Inter@ctive Week* magazine
www.webos.com	WebOS
www.aol.com	America Online
www.prodigy.com	Prodigy
www.netzero.com	NetZero
www.altavista.com	Alta Vista
www.yankeegroup.com	The Yankee Group
www.amazon.com	Amazon.com
www.webtv.com	WebTV

www.microsoft.com	Microsoft
www.wgate.com	WorldGate Communications
www.directechemerge.com	Directech	eMerge
www.dell.com	Dell Computer
www.cisco.com	Cisco Systems
www.intel.com	Intel Corporation

Chapter 2: How IT Marketers Can Benefit from the New Direct Marketing

www.speechworks.com	SpeechWorks
www.digiscents.com	DigiScents

Chapter 3: Making the Most of Your Web Site

www.hot100.com	Hot 100
www.netscape.com	Netscape
www.greenfieldonline.com	Greenfield Online
www.netratings.com	Nielsen/NetRatings
www.apple.com	Apple Computer
www.beyond.com	Beyond.com
www.hp.com	Hewlett-Packard
www.ibm.com	IBM
www.macromedia.com	Macromedia
www.mcafee.com	McAfee Associates
www.msn.com	Microsoft Network
www.oracle.com	Oracle Corporation
www.siebel.com	Siebel Systems
www.sun.com	Sun Microsystems
www.worldcom.com	WorldCom
www.netgen.com	NetGenesis
www.webtrends.com	WebTrends
www.netiq.com	NetIQ
www.o-pinion.com	OpinionLab
www.hitbox.com	HitBox
www.sales.com	Sales.com
www.bmcsoftware.com	BMC Software
www.b2bmarketingbiz.com	B2B Marketing Biz
www.agilebrain.com	AgileBrain
www.dbazine.com	DBAzine
www.nextslm.org	NextSLM

www.qualityofexperience.org	QualityofExperience
www.addme.com	AddMe

Chapter 4: Using Search Engines and Newsgroups

www.metrics.com	Software Metrics
www.searchenginewatch.com	Search Engine Watch
www.about.com	About.com
www.ask.com	Ask Jeeves
www.directhit.com	Direct Hit
www.excite.com	Excite
www.webcrawler.com	WebCrawler
www.google.com	Google
www.hotbot.com	Hot Bot
www.lycos.com	Lycos
www.northernlight.com	Northern Light
www.yahoo.com	Yahoo!
www.compuserve.com	CompuServe
www.liszt.com	Liszt
www.ibiblio.org/usenet-i/home.html	Usenet Info Center Launch Pad
news.announce.newsgroups	Newsgroups
news.announce.newusers	Newsgroups
news.answers	Newsgroups

Chapter 5: The Ins and Outs of E-mail

www.messagingonline.com	Messaging Online
www.optinnews.com	Opt-in News
www.jmm.com	Jupiter Media Metrix
www.imtstrategies.com	IMT Strategies
www.spamlaws.com	Laws about unsolicited e-mail
21stcm.com	21st Century Marketing
www.directmedia.com	Direct Media
www.amlist.com	ALC
www.idglist.com	IDG List Services
rentals.postmasterdirect.com	NetCreations' Postmaster Direct
www.webconnect.com	Worldata's WebConnect
www.yesmail.com	YesMail Network
www.mcsetraining.com	Landing page for Sento Corporation

www.imakenews.com	I Make News e-newsletter publishing
www.topica.com	Topica
www.clickz.com	ClickZ Network
www.zoomerang.com	Zoomerang.com
www.keyva.com	Keyva Technologies
www.messagemedia.com	MessageMedia
www.digitalimpact.com	Digital Impact
www.responsys.com	Responsys
www.exactis.com	Exactis.com
www.m1to1.com	Peppers & Rogers Group
www.egghead.com	Egghead
www.indimi.com	Indimi
www.mediasynergy.com	Media Synergy's Flo Network
www.bluestreak.com	Bluestreak
www.britemoon.com	Britemoon
www.mindarrow.com	MindArrow
www.zaplet.com	Zaplet
www.lifefx.com	LifeFX

Chapter 6: Internet Advertising and Public Relations

www.iab.net	Interactive Advertising Bureau
www.adrelevance.com	AdRelevance
www.unicast.com	Unicast
www.engage.com	Engage
www.doubleclick.net	DoubleClick
www.ad-venture.com	adVENTURE Internet Marketing Network
www.b2bworks.net	B2BWorks
www.247media.com	24/7 Media
www.b2bfreenet.com	B2BfreeNet
www.adnetwork.linkexchange.com	Microsoft's LinkExchange
www.alexa.com	Alexa
www.enliven.com	Enliven
www.iq.com	IQ Commerce
www.ilor.com	iLOR
www.wired.com	Wired Digital
www.adknowledge.com	AdKnowledge

www.juno.com	Juno
www.compaq.com	Compaq Computer Corp.
www.coolsavings.com	Coolsavings
www.valuepage.com	ValuePage
www.freeforum.com	Free Forum Network
www.clickrewards.com	ClickRewards (Netcentives, Inc.)
www.flooz.com	Flooz
www.mypoints.com	MyPoints
www.spidertop.com	Spidertop
www.eyeblaster.com	Eyeblaster
www.cybuy.com	Cybuy
www.prweb.com	PR Web
www.prnewswire.com	PR Newswire
www.mediamap.com	MediaMap
www.boston.com	*The Boston Globe*
www.nytimes.com	*The New York Times*
www.wsj.com	*The Wall Street Journal*
www.publist.com	PubList
www.edcals.com	EdCals
www.tsnn.com	TSNN
www.bitpipe.com	Bitpipe
www.multicity.com	Multicity

Chapter 7: Internet Events and Meetings

www.metagroup.com	Meta Group
www.symantec.com	Symantec
www.centranow.com	Centra Software
www.itworld.com/webcasts	ITWorld Webcasts
www.oracle.com/iseminars/	Oracle Internet Seminars
www.oracle.com/ebusinessnetwork	Oracle eBusiness Network
www.placeware.com/seminar	Placeware Seminars
www.microsoft.com/seminar	Microsoft Multimedia Central
www.bn.com	Barnes & Noble
www.notharvard.com	notHarvard.com
www.real.com	Real Networks
www.activate.com	Activate
fusion.yahoo.com	Yahoo! Fusion Marketing
www.netseminar.com	Education News and Entertainment Network's NetSeminar

www.webcasts.com	Webcasts
www.akamai.com	Akamai Technologies
www.placeware.com	PlaceWare
www.astound.com	Astound
www.mshow.com	Mshow
www.centra.com	Centra Software
www.latitude.com	Latitude Communications
www.inetevents.com	iNetEvents
www.b-there.com	b-there.com
www.iconvention.com	iconvention.com
www.allmeetings.com	AllMeetings
www.go-events.com	Go-events
www.eventweb.com	EventWeb
www.meetingevents.com	MeetingEvents
www.seminarfinder.com	SeminarFinder
www.seminarinformation.com	Seminar Information
www.seminarplanet.com	SeminarPlanet
www.seminarsource.com	SeminarSource
www.techweb.com/calendar	TechCalendar
www.webex.com	WebEx
www.earthlink.net/business	Earthlink Business
www.corpu.com	Corporate University Xchange
www.cyberstateu.com	CyberStateU
www.digitalthink.com	Digital Think
www.smartforce.com	SmartForce
www.smartplanet.com	SmartPlanet
www.lotus.com	Lotus

Chapter 8: Internet Fulfillment

www.digimarc.com	Digimarc
www.gocode.com	GoCode
www.findthedot.com	FindtheDOT
www.mgisoft.com	MGI
www.nwfusion.com	Network World Fusion
www.submitorder.com	SubmitOrder
www.marketsoft.com	MarketSoft
www.entrypoint.com	EntryPoint
www.infogate.com	Infogate
www.marimba.com	Marimba

www.individual.com	Individual.com
www.office.com	Office.com
www.instant-delivery.com	HP's "Instant Delivery"
www.adobe.com	Adobe
www.download.cnet.com	Download.com
www.onsale.com	Onsale.com
www.mcafee.com/cybermedia	CyberMedia
www.oecd.org	Organisation for Economic Cooperation and Development
www.biztravel.com	Biztravel
www.expedia.com	Expedia
www.travelocity.com	Travelocity
www.dhlmasterclass.com	DHL
www.fedex.com	FedEx
www.marketfirst.com	MarketFirst
www.netquartz.com	NetQuartz
www.netship.com	Netship
www.ups.com	UPS

Chapter 9: Internet Customer Service

www.amrresearch.com	AMR Research
www.crmcommunity.com	CRMCommunity
www.crmdaily.com	CRMDaily
www.crmguru.com	CRMGuru
www.aspect.com	Aspect
www.atg.com	ATG
www.beasys.com	BEA
www.bowstreet.com	Bowstreet
www.brightware.com	Brightware
www.broadvision.com	Broadvision
www.epage.com	ePage
www.epiphany.com	E.piphany
www.eshare.com	eShare Technologies
www.kana.com	Kana
www.liveperson.com	LivePerson
www.nativeminds.com	NativeMinds
www.neteffect.com	Net Effect
www.netperceptions.com	Net Perceptions
www.peoplesupport.com	PeopleSupport

www.revenio.com	Revenio
www.teradata.com	Teradata CRM
www.itxc.com	ITXC
www.landsend.com	Lands' End
www.mathworks.com	The MathWorks
www.personalization.com	Personalization.com
www.1to1.com	Peppers and Rogers Group
www.asponline.com	Association of Support Professionals
www.intranets.com	Intranets.com

Chapter 10: Internet Communities and Exchanges

www.att.net	AT&T WorldNet Service
www.earthlink.net	EarthLink
www.go.com	GO Network
www.geocities.yahoo.com	GeoCities
www.ebay.com	eBay
www.dovebid.com	DoveBid
www.fairmarket.com	FairMarket
www.freemarkets.com	FreeMarkets
www.onlineassetexchange.com	Online Asset Exchange
www.priceline.com	Priceline
www.tradeout.com	TradeOut
www.techweb.com	TechWeb
www.planetit.com	TechWeb's "PlanetIT"
www.channelweb.com	Ch@nnelWEB
www.edtn.com	EDTN Network
www.cnet.com	C|Net
www.techrepublic.com	TechRepublic
www.techtarget.com	TechTarget
www.bizprolink.com	BizProLink
www.networking-b2b.com	Networking B2B
www.computersoftwareb2b.com	Computer Software B2B
www.communityb2b.com	CommunityB2B
www.concertglobalmarket.net	ConcertGlobalMarket
www.converge.com	Converge
www.covisint.com	Covisint
www.e2open.com	e2open.com
www.exportall.com	Exportall

www.geindustrial.com	GE Industrial Systems EliteNet
www.manufacturing.net	Manufacturing.net
www.peoplesoftmarketplace.com	PeopleSoft Marketplace
www.verticalnet.com	VerticalNet
industrymarketplaces.yahoo.com	Yahoo! Industry Marketplaces
www.lotus.com/ldn	Lotus Developer Network
www.slashdot.com	Slashdot
www.osdn.com	Open Source Development Network
www.ariba.com	Ariba
www.comercis.com	Comercis
www.commerceone.com	Commerce One
www.delphi.com	Delphi Forums
www.involv.net	Involv
www.participate.com	Participate.com
www.purchasepro.com	PurchasePro

Chapter 11: Internet Partnering

www.iconomy.com	Iconomy
www.escalate.com	Escalate
www.associate-it.com	Associate-It
www.refer-it.com	Refer-It
www.befree.com	BeFree
www.clicktrade.com	ClickTrade
www.bcentral.com	Microsoft bCentral
www.cj.com	Commission Junction
www.linkshare.com	LinkShare
www.performics.com	Performics
www.buildmypc.com	Build My PC.com
www.buytelco.com	BuyTELCO.com
www.geexpress.com	GE Express
www.hp.com/solutions1/garage/affiliates/index.html	HP Garage Affiliate Network
www.igo.com	iGo
www.outpost.com	Outpost
www.sundial.com	Sundial
www.verisign.com	VeriSign
www.networksolutions.com	Network Solutions
www.asera.com	Asera

www.line56.com	*Line 56* magazine
www.ibm.com/partnerworld	IBM's "PartnerWorld"
channel.intel.com	Intel Channel Partners
www.microsoft.com/directaccess/ partnering/microsoft	"Microsoft for Partners"
partnerweb.novell.com	Novell's "PartnerWeb"
www.oracle.com/partners	Oracle Partners
solutions.oracle.com	Oracle Solutions Finder
www.uu.net	UUNET
www.imediation.com	iMediation
www.webcollage.com	WebCollage
www.respond.com	Respond.com

Chapter 12: Selling on the Internet

www.aberdeen.com	Aberdeen Group
www.jmm.com	Jupiter Media Metrix
www.shop.org	Shop.org
www.dellhost.com	DellHost
accessories.us.dell.com	Dell Accessories
www.dellexchange.com	Dell Exchange
www.dellauction.com	Dell Auction
www.cristina.org	National Cristina Foundation
www.educateu.com	EducateU
www.sonystyle.com	SonyStyle.com
www.mysimon.com	mySimon
www.rusure.com	R U Sure
www.dash.com	Dash
www.stamps.com	Stamps.com
www.electrom.com	Electrom.com
www.cybercash.com	CyberCash
www.instabuy.com	InstaBuy
www.passport.com	Microsoft's Passport
www.americanexpress.com	American Express
www.gator.com	Gator
www.nextcard.com	NextCard
www.estation.com	eStation
www.cgey.com	Cap Gemini Ernst & Young
www.npd.com	NPD Group
www.valupage.com	ValuPage

www.insight.com	Insight Direct
www.btobonline.com	BtoBOnline
www.fortune.com	Fortune
www.redherring.com	Red Herring

Chapter 13: Integrating Online and Offline Marketing

www.chasmgroup.com	Chasm Group
www.ceoexpress.com	CEO Express

Web Sites of Interest to the IT Marketer

There are potentially hundreds of Web sites that might be of interest to an Internet marketer. The best way to find them is to use the major Web search engines, entering combinations of appropriate keywords. After you find a site of value to you, be sure to add it to your browser as a "bookmark."

In an effort to reduce your search time, I have compiled and categorized a list of sites, along with a brief description of each, that I think you might find especially useful. All of these sites are linked on the book's companion Web site.

All of these URLs starts with *http://* which most browsers recognize, so I have not listed it. URLs typically are not case-sensitive, but it is best to enter addresses in all lowercase.

Barry's Favorite E-mail Newsletters about Marketing

(Subscribe free at the sites listed below)

www.1to1.com	Peppers and Rogers—Marketing 1to1
www.b2bmarketingbiz.com	B2B Marketing Biz
www.btobonline.com	B2B Alert
www.channelseven.com	Channel Seven
www.clickz.com	ClickZ Today
cyberatlas.internet.com	CyberAtlas
www.digitrends.net	Digitrends and eBiz Daily
www.ecommercetimes.com	E-Commerce Times
www.emarketer.com	eMarketer

www.wdfm.com	Larry Chase's Web Digest for Marketers
www.webpromote.com	Web Promote Weekly
www.wilsonweb.com	Web Marketing Today

Advertising, Direct Marketing, Marketing, and Sales

www.1to1.com	Peppers and Rogers Group
www.adage.com/interactive	Advertising Age Interactive Daily
www.admedia.org	The "Internet Advertising Resource Guide"
www.adresource.internet.com	Ad Resource from Internet.com
www.ana.net	Association of National Advertisers
www.brandchannel.com	All about brands
www.btobonline.com	BtoB magazine
www.builder.cnet.com	How to build better Web sites
www.clickz.com	Internet.com's ClickZ Internet Marketing Network
www.digitrends.net	Digitrends
www.directechemerge.com	Information for business-to-business and IT direct marketers
www.dmnews.com	DM News
www.dmplaza.com	Direct marketing resource site
www.ecommercetimes.com	e-Commerce Times
www.emarketer.com	eMarketer news and statistics
www.emarketingmag.com	eMarketing magazine
www.freepromote.com	Free Web site promotion
www.imarketingnews.com	iMarketing News
www.industryclick.com	*DIRECT* magazine
www.justsell.com	Sales portal
www.linkpopularity.com	Web page rankings
www.marketing.org	Business Marketing Association
www.marketingcentral.com	MarketingCentral portal
www.marketingclick.com	MarketingClick community
www.mediadirector.com	High-tech media
www.mediafinder.com	Media information
www.myprospects.com	My Prospects (create lists)
www.optinnews.com	Opt-in News
www.professionalcity.com	Resource center with a Marketing subsite

www.promotingyoursite.com	Profit Zone
www.publist.com	PubList, Internet directory of publications
www.shop.org	An association of Internet retailers
www.smei.org	Sales and Marketing Executives International
www.srds.com	SRDS—list information online
www.targetonline.com	*Target Marketing* magazine
www.technologymarketing.com	*Technology Marketing* magazine
www.the-dma.org	Direct Marketing Association
www.usps.gov	U.S. Postal Service, "Internet Branch"
www.wdfm.com	Web Digest for Marketers
www.webpromote.com	WebPromote e-mail marketing information
www.wilsonweb.com	Wilsonweb's Web marketing information

Internet Advertising Networks and Placement

www.247media.com	24/7 Media
www.ad-venture.com	ad-VENTURE Internet Marketing Network
www.b2bworks.net	B2BWorks Network
www.doubleclick.net	DoubleClick
www.webconnect.com	Worldata's WebConnect

Affiliate Marketing Directories

www.associate-it.com	Associate-It
www.cashpile.com	Cash Pile
www.refer-it.com	Refer-It

Business Information

www.all-biz.com	The "all business network"
www.bannerstake.com	Keyword competitive research
www.business2.com	*Business 2.0* magazine
www.ceoexchange.com	Online topics and discussion for CEOs

www.companysleuth.com	Competitive intelligence
www.countrywatch.com	Country-by-country news
www.emarketer.com	eMarketer news and statistics
www.fastcompany.com	*FAST COMPANY* magazine
www.firstgov.gov	U.S. federal government search site
www.forbes.com	*Forbes* magazine
www.fortune.com	*Fortune* magazine
www.gomez.com	Gomez Web site ratings
www.hoovers.com	Company information
www.ideacafe.com	A nifty site for small businesses
www.inc.com	Small/medium-sized business Web site
www.infousa.com	Information for small business
www.localbusiness.com	Local business news Web site
www.netlibrary.com	Net Library
www.nyt.com	*The New York Times*
www.thomasregister.com	*Thomas Register of American Maufacturers*
www.uspto.gov	U.S. Patent and Trademark Office
www.wsj.com	*The Wall Street Journal*
www.your-nation.com	Compare country-to-country demographic data

E-mail/E-Marketing List Vendors, Services, and Technologies

www.21staz.com	21st Century Communications
www.amlist.com	American List
www.cmgdirect.com	CMG Direct
www.digitalimpact.com	Digital Impact
www.e-dialog.com	e-Dialog
www.exactis.com	Exactis
www.imakenews.com	iMakeNews
www.indimi.com	Indimi
www.marketfirst.com	Market First
www.marketsoft.com	MarketSoft
www.mediasynergy.com	Media Synergy
www.messagemedia.com	Message Media
www.netcreations.com	Net Creations
www.radicalmail.com	Radical Communications
www.responsys.com	Responsys

www.topica.com	Topica
www.worldata.com	Worldata
www.yesmail.com	Yes Mail

Internet and Internet News

www.businesstech.com	Internet technology for business
ebiz.businessweek.com	*Business Week*'s "e.biz"
www.cio.com	*CIO* magazine
www.commerce.net	Industry consortium for Internet commerce
www.darwinmag.com	*Darwin* magazine
www.hot100.com	The hottest Internet sites, and more
www.internet.com	All things Internet
www.internetworld.com	Internet World
www.news.com	C|Net's news site
www.onmagazine.com	Time's *On* magazine
www.thestandard.com	*The Industry Standard* magazine
www.wired.com	Wired News

Internet Research

www.aberdeen.com	Aberdeen Group
www.activmedia.com	ActivMedia
www.computereconomics.com	Computer Economics
www.commerce.net/research	Commerce.net and Nielsen Media Research
cyberatlas.internet.com	CyberAtlas
www.cyberdialogue.com	Online research
www.ecommerce.gov	U.S. Department of Commerce e-commerce site
e-commerce.research.ml.com	Merrill Lynch E-Commerce Reports
www.emarketer.com	Comprehensive statistics
www.forrester.com	Forrester Research
www.gartner.com	Gartner, Inc.
www.greenfieldonline.com	Greenfield Online
www.iab.net	Internet Advertising Bureau
www.idc.com	IDC
www.jmm.com	Jupiter Media Metrix

www.npd.com	NPD Group
www.netratings.com	Nielsen/Net Ratings
www.statmarket.com	Daily Internet statistics
www.webcriteria.com	Web Criteria
www.webreference.com	Web Reference site for Webmasters
www.webtrends.com	Web Trends
www.yankeegroup.com	Yankee Group

Launching Pads, Time Savers, and Cool Things

www.555-1212.com	Telephone lookup
www.biztravel.com	Business travel
www.ceoexpress.com	Information starting point
www.corporateinformation.com	Corporate information
www.dictionary.com	Word definitions
www.download.com	Software downloads
www.hightechgateway.com	Launching pad for high tech
www.jumbo.com	Free and shared software downloads
www.learn2.com	Learn about anything
www.mapquest.com	The Internet's premier mapping service
www.productnews.com	Thousands of products in one place
www.smartship.com	Consolidated shipping information
www.spyonit.com	Spy On It Web search service
www.stpt.com	My Starting Point
www.technewsworld.com	Real-time tech news
www.techsavvy.com	Tech Savvy
www.weather.com	Check the weather anywhere
whatis.techtarget.com	Plain-English definitions for tech

Leading Information Technology Supersites

www.cmpnet.com	CMPNet
www.cnet.com	C|Net
www.idg.net	IDG Net
www.internet.com	Internet.com
www.techrepublic.com	Tech Republic
www.techtarget.com	TechTarget
www.zdnet.com	ZDnet

Web Portals and Search Engines

www.about.com	About
www.allonesearch.com	All One Search
www.altavista.com	Alta Vista
www.ask.com	Ask Jeeves
www.go.com	Go
www.google.com	Google
www.excite.com	Excite
www.hotbot.com	HotBot
www.lycos.com	Lycos
www.msn.com	MSN
www.netscape.com	Netscape
www.northernlight.com	Northern Light
www.webcrawler.com	WebCrawler
www.yahoo.com	Yahoo!

Direct Marketing and Internet Marketing Books Selected for the IT Marketer

These books can be purchased through this book's companion Web site (an Amazon.com affiliate) or through any online or retail bookseller.

Cliff Allen, Deborah Kania, and Beth Yaeckel, *One-to-One Web Marketing*, 2nd edition.
　A comprehensive guide to one-to-one marketing on the Web with lots of examples, tips, and techniques.

Rick Bruner, Leland Harden, and Bob Heyman, *Net Results.2: Best Practices for Web Marketing*.
　Textbook-style but with useful advice on brand building, direct marketing, and more.

David D'Alessandro, *Brand Warfare:10 Rules for Building a Killer Brand*.
　Brand-building from the CEO of John Hancock.

George Duncan, *Streetwise Direct Marketing*.
　A DM pro covers the gamut of direct marketing.

Lois Geller, *Response! The Complete Guide to Profitable Direct Marketing*.
> A DM guru shares tips.

Seth Godin, *Permission Marketing*.
> An e-marketing classic by an Internet visionary that gets to the heart of a key Internet marketing issue: Prospects will ultimately call the shots by giving marketers permission to send them marketing messages.

Bernie Goldberg, *How to Measure Lead Generation Programs* and *The Lead Generation Enigma: Why Salespeople Don't Like Leads and What to Do about It*.
> Small books with a big message.

Denny Hatch and Donald R. Jackson, *2,239 Tested Secrets for Direct Marketing Success*.
> A compendium of advice from DM pros. Encyclopedia of what to do (and what not to do), with pearls of wisdom from all corners of the direct marketing world.

Shel Holtz, *Public Relations on the Net*.
> How to use the Internet for PR.

Susan Jones, *Creative Strategy in Direct Marketing*.
> How the creative side of DM works.

Shannon Kinnard, *Marketing with E-mail*, 3rd edition.
> A comprehensive resource for e-mail marketers.

Michael McGrath, *Product Stratetgy for High Technology Companies: Accelerating Your Business to Web Speed*.
> More than 250 examples from high tech companies.

Kim MacPherson, *Permission-based E-mail Marketing That Works!*
> E-mail tips and techniques.

Geoffrey A. Moore, *Inside the Tornado* and *Crossing the Chasm*.
> Moore studied Silicon Valley companies and wrote *Crossing the Chasm*, which became a marketing classic. In this book, he explores the

technology product life cycle and shows what companies go through to achieve marketing success. This and the previous volume are must-reads for IT marketers.

Edward L. Nash, *Direct Marketing: Strategy, Planning, Execution*, 4th edition.
One of the most comprehensive overviews of direct marketing. Includes details of database marketing, infomercials, and interactive marketing. Also information on planning, mailing lists, print media, and more.

Don Peppers and Martha Rogers, *One to One B2B; Enterprise One to One: Competing in the Interactive Age;* and *The One to One Fieldbook.*
Any book by the acknowledged one-to-one experts will be worth the read.

Mary Lou Roberts and Paul Berger, *Direct Marketing Management.*
How to manage direct marketing programs.

Stevan Roberts, *Internet Direct Mail: The Complete Guide to Successful E-mail Marketing Campaigns.*
A comprehensive primer on e-mail marketing.

Ernan Roman and Anne Knudsen, *Integrated Direct Marketing.*
Roman was writing about integration long before it reached its current "hot-topic" status.

Don Schultz and Philip Kitchen, *Communicating Globally: An Integrated Marketing Approach.*
Strategies for worldwide integrated marketing.

Arthur Sculley and William Woods, *B2B Exchanges: The Killer Application in the Business-to-Business Internet Revolution.*
An essential guide to exchanges.

Patricia B. Seybold, *Customers.com* and *The Customer Revolution.*
This best-seller and its follow-up book share strategies for orienting your company to customers, including in-depth examples of companies that use the Internet to do it right.

David Shepard, *the New Direct Marketing: How to Implement a Profit-Driven Database Marketing Strategy* .
The emphasis is on data.

Thomas M. Siebel, *Cyber Rules*.
Strategies for excelling at e-business by the founder of Siebel Systems.

Joseph Sugarman, *Marketing Secrets of a Mail Order Maverick*.
One of the true direct marketing visionaries, Joe Sugarman has done it all and is more than willing to share his war stories and strategies for success with readers.

Donna Baier Stein and Floyd Kemske, *Write on Target: The Direct Marketer's Copywriting Handbook*.
Good advice for writing direct response copy.

Bob Stone, *Successful Direct Marketing Methods,* 7th edition.
Probably the most-authoritative text on direct marketing, covering every aspect in plenty of detail.

Susan Sweeney, *101 Ways to Promote Your Web Site*.
Details numerous ways to advertising, promote, and generate public relations for any organization's Web site.

Joan Throckmorton and Thomas Collins, *Winning Direct Response Advertising: From Print through Interactive Media*, 2nd edition.
Another living legend in the direct marketing business, Joan Throckmorton takes you through the whole gamut of direct marketing—advertising, mail, and interactive.

Lester Wunderman, *Being Direct: Making Advertising Pay*.
This book was authored by one of the greats of the direct marketing business. Combines autobiography with advice and wisdom—and shares Wunderman's vision of where direct marketing is headed. Entertaining and insightful.

Robbin Lee Zeff and Brad Aronson, *Advertising on the Internet,* 2nd edition.
Covers Internet advertising in depth.

Jan Zimmerman, *Marketing on the Internet,* 5th edition.
Updated fifth edition is a comprehensive guide to marketing on the Internet. Includes the ABC's of Internet marketing, how to create and distribute info-tools, how to create a Web site, multimedia, e-commerce basics, and more.

Appendix B: Glossary of Direct and Internet Marketing Terms

80/20 Rule. Also known as "Pareto's Principle." States a comparison of relative weight in marketing terms, such as "20 percent of the customer base generates 80 percent of the company's sales."

Affiliate, Associate. Affiliate marketing is a form of partnering that has been popularized on the Internet. Basically, a Web marketer offers affiliates the opportunity to share in revenue by getting referral fees or sales commissions on goods and services sold via the affiliate's Web site. The affiliate (associate) is an organization or firm that participates in an affiliate marketing program.

AIDA. A direct marketing concept that represents the way a respondent is engaged: Awareness, Interest, Desire, Action.

Audience. Typically, the individuals you are trying to reach with a direct marketing campaign. In business-to-business marketing, a commonly held theory is that there is no single large audience, but rather audience segments. (See also *Segmentation.*)

B2B; B2C. "B2B" or B-to-B refers to business-to-business, which means businesses that market directly to other businesses; "B2C" is business-to-consumer, or businesses that market directly to consumers.

Bandwidth. The amount of data that can be transmitted in a fixed amount of time. For digital devices, the bandwidth is usually expressed in bits per second (bps) or bytes per second. For analog devices, the bandwidth is expressed in cycles per second, or Hertz (Hz).

Banner, banner ad. A small advertising area on a Web site.

Benefit. What an individual derives from a product or service; what a product or service really does for the prospect or customer.

Bingo cards, bingo leads. Cards or leads that are returned with little or no information to enable the marketer to qualify the leads; "raw" responses.

Bookmark. A Web site or page saved via the Web browser for future reference.

BRC. Business Reply Card.

Broadband. A very high speed means of transmitting data now being used by cable and telephone companies to provide Internet access.

Browser.   The software that allows viewing of HTML documents or Web pages. The two leading browsers are Netscape (Navigator or Communicator) and Microsoft Internet Explorer.

Business reply.   Mail that carries a business-reply permit so that it can be returned at the marketer's cost.

Cable modem.   A modem that facilitates Internet access via television cable (See *Broadband*).

CGI.   Common Gateway Interface. Programming used most often to enable interactive forms and counters.

Channel marketing.   Marketing done to or through other channels, such as retailers, distributors, and resellers.

Chat.   Generally refers to online dialogue, typically conducted via e-mail.

Click, click-through.   The advertising version of a "hit"—when the viewer of a banner ad clicks on it; or clicking on an area of a Web page to open a link.

Closed-loop system.   Generally refers to a lead generation and fulfillment process in which the lead goes from an inbound response through qualification, fulfillment, follow-up, and conversion to sale, with tracking and feedback mechanisms established along the way.

Community.   A Web site, newsgroup, or discussion group that shares common characteristics. Web-based communities share information and provide services to community members.

Compiled list.   A list that is composed of names and addresses, telephone numbers, and/or e-mail addresses from nonresponse sources, such as directories or phone books.

Cookie.   A piece of data sent by a Web server to the visitor's computer to identify that visitor's computer when it connects again with the Web page.

CPM.   Cost per thousand. Applies to purchasing media, usually print advertising, mailing lists, and broadcast; also for banner ads.

Cross-functional direct marketing.   Marketing to multiple individuals or decision makers in different functional areas within a company.

Customer.   An individual who does business with a company; typical classifications are former, dormant, active, or current. Customers can also be ranked based on purchase criteria. (See also *RFM*.)

Cyberspace.   The imaginary location of the Internet.

Database, database marketing.   A computerized file of information about individuals, which includes basic contact information, response and/or purchase history, and other historic, transactional sales and marketing data. Database marketing is the practice of using databases to improve the marketing process.

DHTML. Dynamic HTML. Provides additional interactive capabilities beyond HTML. (See also *HTML*.)

Dimensional. Any mailing that is odd-sized or three-dimensional in nature, such as a tube or box.

Direct marketing, direct response. The discipline of results-driven, response-oriented marketing. Direct marketing includes any medium used responsively, including direct response advertising, direct mail, telemarketing, direct response television, direct response radio, and interactive media.

DNS. Domain Name System (or Service). An Internet service that translates domain names into IP addresses. Because domain names are alphabetic, they're easier to remember. The Internet, however, is really based on IP addresses. Every time you use a domain name, a DNS service must translate the name into the corresponding IP address. For example, the domain name www.example.com might translate to 198.105.232.4. The DNS system is, in fact, its own network. If one DNS server doesn't know how to translate a particular domain name, it asks another one, and so on, until the correct IP address is returned.

Download. The process of copying a file from one place to another, usually from a Web server to a computer.

DSL. Digital Subscriber Line. A technology that uses basic telephone lines to provide Internet access at very high speed.

E-business. The general term, popularized by IBM, for conducting business electronically.

ECML. Electronic Commerce Modeling Language. An emerging standard for universal acceptance of online payments.

E-commerce. The general term for selling online.

E-mail. Any electronic message sent over a network.

E-mail newsletter. A periodic news publication, sent in the form of an e-mail.

Exposures. See *Impressions*.

eXtensible Markup Language (XML). An emerging standard for Web page creation that may someday replace HTML.

Extranet. An Internet-enabled network designed primarily for a company's internal use, but also allows access to select outsiders, such as customers, partners, and suppliers in.

FAQs. Frequently Asked Questions.

Feature. What a product does; a product attribute or quality, unrelated to how it benefits an individual.

Flame. A negative response to unsolicited e-mail.

Flash. A bandwidth-friendly and browser-independent vector-graphic animation technology. As long as different browsers are equipped with the necessary plug-ins, Flash animations will look the same. With Flash, users can draw their own animations or import other vector-based images. Flash animation can only be created using the Flash animation application from Macromedia Inc. Flash was known as FutureSplash until 1997, when Macromedia Inc. bought the company that developed it.

FSIs. Free-Standing Inserts. Advertising inserted into or with publications.

FTP. File Transfer Protocol. The protocol used on the Internet for sending files.

Fulfillment. Generally refers to materials sent in response to an inquiry, or to the process of sending those materials.

GIF. Graphical Interchange Format. An electronic-image file format. Often used to refer to any graphic image on a Web page, other than a photograph.

Guestbook. Typically, a registration area on a Web site.

Hit. An interaction or request made to a Web server. A page can be "hit" numerous times by one visitor, and therefore hits are not a measure of the number of visitors.

Hits. The number of clicks to a Web page.

Home page. The primary page of a Web site.

Hosting. Typically provided by an Internet service provider, the process of setting up a Web server and administering a Web site.

House list, house file. A mailing list or database of prospects or customers that belongs to a company; could be maintained in-house or by an outside firm.

HTML. The HyperText Markup Language used so that browsers can view words on Web pages. Most text on Web pages is created in HTML.

HTTP. HyperText Transfer Protocol.

Hybrid list. Typically a compiled list that has been enhanced with response data or additional marketing information.

Hyperlink. A link to a Web page.

Icon. A graphic, picture, or small graphic element.

Impressions. The number of times a banner ad appears in an established period of time, typically a month.

Interactive media. Usually refers to the Internet, World Wide Web, and CD-ROMs; also means any medium that encourages interaction.

Internet. A computer network of networks; the world's largest network allows computers to connect with one another.

Internet address. Any location on the Internet. A "URL" (Uniform Resource Locator) is one form of address that points Web browsers to a particular Web page.

Internet Explorer. Microsoft's Web browser.

Interstitial. Web advertising that appears or "pops up" between Web pages.

Intranet. An Internet-enabled network used internally by a company or organization.

IP. Internet Protocol. (See *TCP/IP*.)

ISP. Internet Service Provider.

Java; Java applets. A language developed by Sun that has become the basis for many Internet applications; scripting or applications driven by Java.

JavaScript. A scripting language developed by Netscape to enable Web authors to design interactive sites. Although it shares many of the features and structures of the full Java language, it was developed independently. JavaScript can interact with HTML source code, enabling Web authors to spice up their sites with dynamic content. JavaScript is endorsed by a number of software companies and is an open language that anyone can use without purchasing a license. It is supported by recent browsers from Netscape and Microsoft, though Internet Explorer supports only a subset, which Microsoft calls Jscript.

JPEG. Joint Photographic Experts Group. Refers to a compressed graphic image format.

Keycode. A code assigned to a list to identify it as part of a mailing. The code could also represent other criteria, such as geography, company size, industry type, job title, etc.

Lead. Generally, a prospect that has not yet been qualified.

Lead processing. The process of qualifying, fulfilling, distributing, and tracking leads.

Listserv. An automatic mailing list server developed by Eric Thomas for BITNET in 1986. When e-mail is addressed to a LISTSERV mailing list, it is automatically broadcast to everyone on the list. The result is similar to a newsgroup or forum, except that the messages are transmitted as e-mail and are therefore available only to individuals on the list. LISTSERV is currently a commercial product marketed by L-Soft International. Although LISTSERV refers to a specific mailing list server, the term is sometimes used incorrectly to refer to any mailing list server. Another popular mailing list server is Majordomo, which is freeware.

Login. To make a computer system or network recognize you so that you can begin a computer session. Most personal computers have no login procedure; you just turn the machine on and begin working. For larger systems and networks, however, you usually need to enter a username and password before the computer system will allow you to execute programs. Alternative spellings for login are log in, logon, and log on.

Mailbot. An automatic e-mail responder or response program.

Marketing database. (See *Database*.)

Marketing Pyramid. A tool that can be used to break audiences into identifiable segments.

Match code. A code used to identify a specific name and address record. Usually the match code is made up of some combination of pieces of data from the name and address and other identifiable data.

Megabyte. (a) When used to describe data storage, 1,048,576 (2 to the 20th power) bytes. Megabyte is frequently abbreviated as M or MB. (b) When used to describe data transfer rates, as in MBps, it refers to 1 million bytes.

Micro-segmentation. The process of dividing an audience into very small, identifiable segments based on defined criteria or combinations or criteria.

Modem. Acronym for modulator-demodulator. A modem is a device or program that enables a computer to transmit data over telephone lines. Computer information is stored digitally, whereas information transmitted over telephone lines is transmitted in the form of analog waves. A modem converts between these two forms.

MSA. Metropolitan Statistical Area. A geographical area encompassing a city.

Netiquette. Good manners on the Internet; i.e., not sending spam, respecting others' privacy, etc.

Netscape. The company that pioneered the Web browser, first with Netscape Navigator.

NCOA. National Change of Address processing or program.

Nixie. Mail returned with a bad address.

OEM. Original Equipment Manufacturer.

Offer. The "underlying" offer is the company, its products and services, and the perception of those things by a particular audience. The "direct marketing" or "promotional" offer is the incentive offered by the advertiser/marketer to elicit a response.

Online. Usually refers to being on the Internet or on the Web; connected to a network.

OS. Operating System. The most important program that runs on a computer. Every general-purpose computer must have an OS to run other programs. Operating systems perform basic tasks, such as recognizing input from the keyboard, sending output to the display screen, keeping track of files and directories on the disk, and controlling peripheral devices such as disk drives and printers.

Package. Generally refers to a direct mail package, which typically includes an outer envelope, letter, brochure or other inserts, and a reply device.

Page. (See *Web page.*)

PDF. Portable Document Format. A form of publishing that retains the original document's characteristics; created by Adobe.

Perl. Short for Practical Extraction and Report Language. A programming language developed by Larry Wall, especially designed for processing text. Because of its strong text-processing abilities, Perl has become one of the most-popular languages for writing CGI scripts. Perl is an interpretive language, which makes it easy to build and test simple programs.

Permission e-mail, permission marketing. The concept of sending e-mail or marketing only to individuals who give their permission to receive the marketing messages.

Personalize. Direct mail that utilizes the individual's name or other unique data that is referenced in the copy.

Plug-in. Software that "plugs in" to a Web browser to enable added functionality, such as the receipt of sound or multimedia. See also *Flash; Shockwave.*

POP. Point of Presence. The physical place of connection from a computer to the Internet.

Portal. A destination site on the Web; can be an outgrowth of a search engine, or a specialized destination such as a business-to-business portal.

Premium. An offer or incentive for responding.

Prospect. An individual with the potential to purchase a product or service.

Pull. Generally, interactive media that draws ("pulls") the user to it, such as a Web site.

Push. Generally, interactive media sent ("pushed") to the user, such as outbound e-mail or Web pages delivered to a user's computer.

Qualification process. The process of qualifying a prospect to determine likelihood of purchase.

Qualification questions. A set of questions designed to qualify and prioritize prospects prior to advertising.

Reader service number. Numbers assigned by publications to handle inquiries to print advertising.

RealAudio. The de facto standard for streaming audio data over the World Wide Web. RealAudio was developed by RealNetworks and supports FM-stereo-quality sound. To hear a Web page that includes a RealAudio sound file, you need a RealAudio player or plug-in, a program that is freely available from a number of places. It's included in current versions of both Netscape Navigator and Microsoft Internet Explorer.

RealVideo. A streaming technology developed by RealNetworks for transmitting live video over the Internet. RealVideo uses a variety of data-compression techniques and works with both normal IP connections and IP Multicast connections.

Relationship direct marketing. Direct marketing that is intended to build an ongoing relationship through periodic contact over time.

Reply device. A reply card, reply form, or any other response piece that the respondent returns to the marketer.

Response list. A list made up of individuals with a propensity to respond, based on the fact that they responded to something already; typically, a list of subscribers, members, buyers, donors, etc.

Response management. The process of managing responses or leads from the time they are received through conversion to sale.

Response path. Any method established to facilitate a response, such as a business reply card, inbound fax, inbound telephone, e-mail, or a Web URL.

RFM. Recency/Frequency/Monetary data, which helps determine the value of a customer. Recency refers to when the customer last purchased, frequency to how often, and monetary to how much money was spent.

Rich media. The term generally applies to online advertising that incorporates multimedia, sound, motion, interactivity, or e-commerce.

Rollover. Moving the cursor over a specific area of a Web page.

Screen. Typically refers to the administrative, mailroom, or receptionist screening process of mail or phone calls in a larger company.

Search engine. A program that accesses information via a process of matching keywords; there are numerous search engines on the Web.

Segmentation. The process of dividing an audience into identifiable segments based on defined criteria or combinations of criteria.

Selection criteria. Refers to the available data used to select segments of mailing lists, such as geography, size of company, industry, job function, job title, etc. Selection criteria typically add to the CPM of a rental list.

Self-mailer. A mailing piece that is self-contained.

SET. Secure Electronic Transaction protocol for e-commerce payment transactions.

Shockwave. A technology developed by Macromedia, Inc. that enables Web pages to include multimedia objects. To create a shockwave object, you use Macromedia's multimedia authoring tool called Director, and then compress the object with a program called Afterburner. You then insert a reference to the "shocked" file in your Web page. To see a Shockwave object, you need the Shockwave plug-in, a program that integrates seamlessly with your Web browser. The plug-in is freely available from Macromedia's Web site as either a Netscape Navigator plug-in or an ActiveX control. Shockwave supports audio, animation, and video and even processes user actions such as mouse clicks. It runs on all Windows platforms as well as the Macintosh.

SIC. Standard Industrial Classification code. A common list selection criterion. An SIC is used to represent a specific industry or an industry segment, such as "Computers" or "Hospitals."

SOHO. Small Office Home Office. A rapidly growing business segment.

Source Code. Program instructions in their original form. The word *source* differentiates code from various other forms that it can have (for example, object code and executable code).

Spam. Unsolicited or unwanted e-mail.

SQL. Structured Query Language (pronounced either "see-kwell" or as separate letters). SQL is a standardized query language for requesting information from a database. The original version, called SE-QUEL (Structured English Query Language), was designed by an IBM research center in 1974–1975. SQL was first introduced as a commercial database system in 1979 by Oracle Corporation.

SSL. Secure Sockets Layer. A protocol developed by Netscape for transmitting private documents via the Internet. SSL works by using a private key to encrypt data that's transferred over the SSL connection. Both Netscape Navigator and Internet Explorer support SSL, and many Web sites use the protocol to obtain confidential user information, such as credit card numbers. By convention, Web pages that require an SSL connection start with *https:* instead of *http:*.

Sticky sites. Web sites that use techniques to get visitors to "stick," or stay on the site and return to the site; these techniques may include free e-mail and incentive offers.

Streaming. Generally refers to sending audio or video across the Internet. (See also *RealAudio, RealVideo.*)

Surfing. Reviewing Web sites or moving through Web pages.

Suspect. A potential prospect.

Targeting. The most common direct marketing practice; the practice of identifying an audience or audience segment, developing an offer for that audience, and promoting it through creativity that is appropriate for that audience.

TCP/IP. Transmission Control Protocol/Internet Protocol. The suite of communications protocols used to connect hosts on the Internet. TCP/IP uses several protocols, the two main ones being TCP and IP. TCP/IP is built into the UNIX operating system and is used by the Internet, making it the de facto standard for transmitting data over networks. Even network operating systems that have their own protocols, such as Netware, also support TCP/IP.

Telemarketing, telesales. Telemarketing refers to inbound or outbound prospect or customer contact via telephone with the objective of promotion or qualification. Telesales is the same process but with the objective of selling a product or service.

Universe. The total number of individuals who conceivably could be reached with a specific direct marketing campaign.

UNIX (Pronounced "yoo-niks"). A popular multi-user, multitasking operating system developed at Bell Labs in the early 1970s. Created by just a handful of programmers, UNIX was designed to be a small, flexible system used exclusively by programmers. Although it has matured considerably over the years, UNIX still betrays its origins by its cryptic command names and its general lack of user-friendliness. This is changing, however, with graphical user interfaces such as MOTIF.

Upload. The process of sending a file from a computer to a server or another computer. (See also *FTP.*)

URL. Uniform Resource Locator. An Internet location, most often a Web address.

Usenet. An Internet-related network that includes e-mail and newsgroups.

VAR. Value-Added Reseller.

Variable. Usually refers to a field on a database in which information changes based on the individual record. The variable can then be used in direct mail copy or a telemarketing script to build a relationship with the individual. An example might be the amount of money a customer spends with a company in a year, which would vary from customer to customer.

Versioning. Using variables to create versions of direct mail copy to personalize and appeal to specific characteristics. In business-to-business direct mail, versioning by industry or job function has generally been shown to increase response rates.

Viral marketing. Marketing that spreads rapidly via e-mail or other Internet communications. Viral marketing refers to e-marketing that encourages customers, prospects, or site visitors to recruit others, who recruit others, and so on.

Virtual event, online event, Web event. An event that occurs online, via the Web.

Visit. One user accessing one Web site at any given time.

Webmaster. Typically, an individual in an organization responsible for the organization's Web site and, sometimes, for Internet usage.

Web page. An individual document on a Web site or on the Web. A Web page can be heavily graphical and can include sound, photography, multimedia, and interactivity, based on the technologies used to create it.

Web response form. A form designed to capture visitor contact and often qualification information.

Web site. A collection of pages on the World Wide Web.

WWW, World Wide Web. The area of the Internet that contains HTML.

XML. See *eXtensible Markup Language*.

Index

\<TITLE\> tags, 85–86, 87
@Home, 130, 251
1to1 magazine, 234, 237
21st az Marketing, 108
24/7 Media, 129
80/20 Rule, 226
101 Ways to Promote Your Web Site
    (Sweeney), 78
2000 Economic Impact: U.S. Direct
    & Interactive Marketing
    Today (DMA), 4

A
Aberdeen Group, 302
About.com, 89–90, 91
acceptance
    of e-mail, 102
    of Internet, 8–9, 16
accessibility of Internet, 5, 6–7, 31–33
accessories, selling, 307–308
Acer, 261
acknowledgement benefit of fulfill-
    ment, 200
action plan development for direct
    marketing, 29
ad-blocking software, 130
addresses (e-mail), changing, 122
AdKnowledge, 138
Adobe Acrobat Reader, 206
AdRelevance, 124
ADSL (Asymmetric Digital Subscriber
    Line), 7
adVENTURE Internet Marketing
    Network, 129
Advertising Age, 330
advertising online, 124–145. *See also*
    affiliate (associate) programs;

banner advertising; events
    online, promoting; public
    relations online
advertorials, 125
animated GIF ads vs. rich media,
    135
awareness generated from, 128
best practices in, 131–136
buttons, 125–126
call to action in, 133
click-throughs, 138, 140
communities for, 266
contests for, 142–143
coupons, 127, 143, 324
directories for, 82, 84, 142
effectiveness measurement of, 140
event promotion, 136
exchange, 139
extramercials, 126
eye-catching, 139
"feeder" medium, 131–132
follow-me ads, 144–145
free, 139
games, 127
growth of, 124
impressions for purchasing, 77, 138
incentive programs, 127, 142–144
innovations in, 144–145
interstitials (pop-ups), 126
life of, 139
Messaging Plus ads, 126
newsgroups for, 96, 97, 116
newsletters (e-mail) for, 113–115,
    135, 140–142
"on-site" banner ads, 51, 139
out-of-banner rich media, 144
piggyback ads, 145

placement importance, 120,
136–138
precampaign teasers, 135–136
purchasing, 137–138, 139
reciprocal links, 76, 139
responses from, 128, 133–134, 140
return on investment (ROI), 124
rich media for, 135, 140
search engines for, 137, 142
skyscrapers and boxes, 126
sponsorships (newsletters), 114,
135, 140–142
StickyAds, 144
Superstials, 126
sweepstakes for, 142–143
testing, 135, 139, 140
trade, 139
traditional media and, 140
traffic generation for Web sites,
131–132, 134
updating ease of, 139
view-throughs, 140
Webcast ads, 144, 164, 168
Webmercials, 126
Web sites for, 51, 138
within-the-ad responses, 133–134,
326
advertorials, 125
affiliate (associate) programs, 279–289.
See also affiliate (associate)
programs, creating; partnering
Amazon Associate program,
279–280
BuildMyPC, 286–287
BuyTELCO, 287
choosing programs carefully,
281–282
Dell, 288
"drop-shipping" model, 280
effectiveness measurement of, 283
flexibility of, 280–281
GE Express, 288
growth of, 279
HP Garage Affiliate Network, 288
iGo, 288
legitimacy of programs, verifying,
282
needs, meeting with, 280–281, 282
Network Solutions, 289
Outpost, 288
"ready-made" Web stores vs. links,
281
Sundial.com, 288–289
testing, 282–283
VeriSign, 289
affiliate (associate) programs, creating, 283–286. *See also*
affiliate (associate) programs
BeFree, 283–284
branding opportunities, 285
ClickTrade, 284
Commission Junction, 284
commitment to, 286
compensation plan, 285
details, working out, 285
e-commerce establishing for,
283–284
e-mail for, 286
legal agreement, 285–286
LinkShare, 284
link strategy, 285
Performics, 284
private-labels, 285
reporting system, 285, 286
servicing affiliates, 286
storefronts (virtual) for, 283–284
aftermarket selling technique, 226
AgileBrain, 67, 68
AIDA (Awareness, Interest, Desire,
Action) formula, 40
Akamai Technologies, 165
ALC, 109
"alert services" for traffic generation,
61

alerts using e-mail, 111
Alexa, 130
AllMeetings, 176
alt (alternative topics), 94
AltaVista, 13, 79, 85–86, 87, 88,
    90–91
Amazon.com
    Associate program, 279–280, 295
    customer relationship management
        (CRM) of, 236
    Internet impact on marketing, 14,
        20–21
    traffic generation by, 63
American Express, 323
America Online (AOL). *See* AOL
America Online/Roper Starch
    Cyberstudy, 8–9
AMR Research, 219
animated GIF ads vs. rich media, 135
animations for events, 173
announcements using e-mail, 111
AOL (America Online)
    advertising, 128, 138
    community, 249–250
    Internet impact on marketing, xxvi,
        10, 12
    newsgroups, 94
Apple, 56
Application Service Providers (ASPs),
    35–36
Arbitron Internet Information Services,
    144
archiving advantage of events, 156,
    157
Ariba, 269
Arthur Andersen, 9
article summarization in newsletters
    (e-mail), 113
Asera, 290
Ask Jeeves, 91–92
ASP (Association of Support Profes-
    sionals), 58, 237

Aspect, 227
ASPs (Application Service Providers),
    35–36
Associate-It, 281
associate programs. *See* affiliate
    programs
Association of Support Professionals
    (ASP), 58, 237
Astound, 166
Asymmetric Digital Subscriber Line
    (ADSL), 7
ATG, 228
ATMs, 323
AT&T, 6, 138, 165, 250, 261
attachments, e-mail, 118
auctions, 253–256, 310
AudienceNet, 126
audiences' role in integrating online
    and offline marketing,
    331–332, 354
audio file in e-mail, 119, 120
audiovisual requirements for events,
    171
autofaxing for fulfillment, 188–189
automating mailings, 122
autoresponders
    e-mail, 121
    fulfillment using, 190
    traffic generation from, 61
"Avoiding Channel Conflict," 290
Awareness, Interest, Desire, Action
    (AIDA) formula, 40
awareness generation
    advertising for, 128
    banner ads for, 128
    integrating online and offline
        marketing for, 338
    "presence awareness" frontier,
        359–360
    promoting events online for,
        179
AXENT, 159–160

B

B2BfreeNet, 129

B2B Marketing Biz
    on customer relationship manage-
        ment (CRM), 227
    on e-mail, 105, 109, 116
    on public relations, 148
    on seminars (online), 159
    on Web site effectiveness measure-
        ment, 67

B2BWorks, 129

back end
    of communities, 272–273
    of e-mail, 122

Bacon's, 146

Bain & Company, 214, 219

bandwidth concern, 6–7

Bane, Melissa, 345

banner advertising, 127–131. *See also*
        advertising online; affiliate
        (associate) programs
    ad-blocking software, 130
    attention, competing for, 132–133
    awareness generation from, 128
    best practices in, 131–136
    buying services for, 129–130
    call to action in, 133
    competitor's site, placing banners
        on, 130
    conversion rate for, 128, 138
    creation of, 128–129
    decline of, 124, 125, 128
    e-mail vs., 101
    exchanging, 130
    Graphic Interface Format (GIF), 127
    life of, 139
    media buy, extending, 136
    offer in, 133
    placement services for, 129
    precampaign teasers, 135–136
    promoting events online with, 179
    responses from, 128, 133–134

rich media and, 130–131, 132,
        133, 135, 144
    search engines, banner ads on, 137
    smart links, 130
    testing, 135
    updating ease of, 139
    Web Response Forms (WRFs) and,
        71–72, 127, 134
    Web sites for, 51
    within-the-ad responses, 133–134,
        326

"Banners Say 'Buy' in E-shift as Bauer
        Loads New Tech" (Magill),
        326

barcode technology, 191

Barnes & Noble, 131, 164

BEA, 228–229

"before, during, and after" approach,
        111

BeFree, 283–284

best practices in advertising, 131–136

"Best Web Support Sites," 237

Beyond.com, 57

Bezos, Jeff, 14

Bitpipe, 148

biz (business topics), 94

BizProLink, 260

Biztravel, 215

blast (mass mailing), 109

blocking Web site access, 64

Bluestreak, 119, 131

BMC Software, 67, 68

Booz-Allen & Hamilton, 56

Boston Consulting Group, 3, 15, 219,
        260, 303

Boston Globe, The, 33, 146

bots (intelligent agents), 79, 80

boundlessness of Internet, 14–15

Bowstreet, 229

branding opportunities, 285

brick-and-mortar companies and
        selling, 299, 302

"Bridging the Gap from Traditional Marketing to Electronic Commerce" (Rowsom), 318
Brightware, 229
Britemoon, 119
broadband, 7, 166
Broadcast.com, 251
broadcasting (mass mailing), 109
Broadvision, 229
brochureware as Web sites, 48
browser software for events, 163
Bruner, Rick, 101
b-there.com, 176
B-to-B (business-to-business), 17
budget for community building, 271
BuildMyPC, 286–287
bulletin boards, 248
business communities and exchanges, 259–264
business influenced by Internet, 2–4, 9, 17–19, 33
business-to-business (B-to-B), 17
Business-to-Business Internet Marketing (Silverstein), xxv, xxvii, 158
BusinessWeek, 302
buttons
    for advertising, 125–126
    on Web sites, 53–54
buying services for banner ads, 129–130
BuyTELCO, 287
BYOBroadcast, 119

C
call-me (telephony) technology, 204, 220, 232–233, 312
call to action
    advertising, 133
    intersponding, 39
    Web Response Forms (WRFs), 70
CambridgeSoft, 237

Canadian market, 33–34
Cap Gemini Ernst & Young, 323
caps, avoiding, 123
Castanet, 196
catalogs online, 207, 309, 316–317
CD/Web connection, 209–210
Centra BCN (Business Collaboration Network), 161
Centra Software, 166
ceoexpress.com, 344
Ch@nnelWEB, 256–257
channel marketing, 275, 276–277
channel partners, 289–295. *See also* affiliate (associate) programs
    Cisco, 293
    demand chain management, 290
    e-mail for, 292
    extranets for, 292–293
    IBM, 293
    importance of, 289–291
    Intel, 293–294
    link strategies, 291, 292
    Microsoft, 294
    Novell, 294–295
    Oracle, 295
    promoting partners on Web sites, 292
    servicing partners, 292–293
    Web sites for, 291–292
"chat" capabilities, 166, 168, 249
Cisco Systems
    blocking Web site access, 64
    customer relationship management (CRM), 234, 237
    Internet impact on marketing, 3, 7, 9, 21
    lead generation and qualification, 57
    partnering, 293
    selling online, 302
    seminars (online), 161–162
classes of customers, treating differently, 241

ClickRewards, 143
click-throughs, 138, 140
ClickTrade, 284
ClickZ, 113, 114, 127
CMPnet, 5, 112, 126, 147, 256–258
C|Net, 5, 112, 126, 147, 258, 314
ColdFusion, 174
"collaborative filtering," 318
"collaborative selling," 296–297
Comercis, 269
comments tag, 85
Commerce One, 269
Commission Junction, 284
commitment to affiliate programs,
        286
communications intimacy from
        Internet, 19–20
Communications Week, 2
communities and exchanges online,
        247–273. *See also* communi-
        ties and exchanges online,
        building
    advertising opportunities of, 266
    auctions, 253–256, 310
    BizProLink, 260
    bulletin boards, 248
    business communities and ex-
        changes, 259–264
    chat rooms, 249
    CMPnet, 256–258
    C|Net, 258
    CommunityB2B, 260
    ConcertGlobalMarket, 260
    Converge, 260–261, 296
    Covisint, 261, 296
    DoveBid, 254
    e2open.com, 261
    eBay, 253–254
    Egghead, 254
    exchanges (marketplaces), 247–248,
        259–260
    Exportall, 261

    FairMarket, 254–255
    finding, 264–267
    FreeMarkets, 255
    free services of, 265–266
    fulfillment, 212
    GE Industrial Systems EliteNet,
        261–262
    growth of, 247
    IDG.net, 258
    Information Technology supersites,
        256–259
    Internet.com, 258
    Manufacturing.net, 262
    networking value of, 266–267
    newsgroups, 249
    Office.com, 262
    Online Asset Exchange, 255
    Oracle Exchange, 262
    PeopleSoft Marketplace, 262
    portals, 251–253
    Priceline, 255
    private exchanges, 296
    publicity opportunities of, 265–266
    service providers, 249–250
    services of, 265–266
    TechTarget, 259
    TradeOut, 255–256
    user groups as, 248–249
    VerticalNet, 262–263
    vortals (vertical portals), 251
    Yahoo! Industry Marketplace, 264
    ZDnet, 259
communities and exchanges online,
        building, 267–273. *See also*
        communities and exchanges
        online
    Ariba, 269
    back-end of, 272–273
    budget for, 271
    Comercis, 269
    Commerce One, 269
    community services of, 272

database technology for, 272
Delphi, 270
e-commerce technology for, 272
Excite, 270
growing communities, 273
information center of, 271
interactive areas of, 272
Involv, 270
launching, 273
leadership position from, 267–269
maintaining communities, 273
needs determination for, 271
objectives for, 271
Participate.com, 270
partners for, 272
publicity for, 273
PurchasePro, 270
sponsored communities, 267–269
structure for, 271–272
testing, 273
tools for, 269–270
CommunityB2B, 260
Compaq, xxvi, 13, 142–143, 261
compatibility, accentuating for
    partnering, 276
comp (computer-related topics)
    newsgroups, 95
compensation plan for affiliate
    programs, 285
competition
    integrating online and offline
        marketing and, 332
    Internet as research tool, 18
    keywords, researching, 86–87
    names in keywords, 84
    search engines for researching,
        86–87
    Web site, placing banners on, 130
CompuServe, 94, 138, 249–250
Computer Associates, 11
Computer Industry Almanac, 14
Computer Software B2B, 260

ConcertGlobalMarket, 260
conferencing, 19
confirmation benefit of fulfillment,
    200–201
content tips, 54, 173
contests, 142–143
continuous fulfillment, 198–199
contributions to newsgroups, making,
    97
Converge, 260–261, 296
conversion rate for banner ads, 128,
    138
cookies for traffic generation, 61–62
Coolsavings, 143
cooperation vs. capitulation for
    partnering, 275–276
copy for Web Response Forms
    (WRFs), 73
copywriting tips, 50, 123, 173
Corporate University Xchange, 182
cost-effectiveness
    of e-mail, 100–101
    of events online, 155, 156
    of integrating online and offline
        marketing, 338, 339
    of Internet, 20, 31–32, 346–347
    of newsletters (e-mail), 113
    of promoting events online, 178,
        179
cost per action (CPA), 108
cost per thousand (CPM), 108
costs of order generation systems, 319
cost to end user, e-mail, 104
couponing, 127, 143, 324
coverage by search engines, 5, 79
Covisint, 261, 296
CPA (cost per action), 108
CPM (cost per thousand), 108
crawlers, 79, 85–86
CRMCommunity, 221
CRM (customer relationship manage-
    ment) online, 219–246

80/20 Rule, 226
aftermarket selling technique, 226
Aspect, 227
ATG, 228
BEA, 228–229
Bowstreet, 229
Brightware, 229
Broadvision, 229
call-me (telephony) technology,
    204, 220, 232–233, 312
classes of customers, treating
    differently, 241
customers, treating like prospects,
    238–239
database technology for, 222, 223,
    234, 242, 244
e-mail for, 110, 240
ePage, 229
e.piphany, 229–230
eShare Technologies, 230
extranets for, 242–246
Focusing on You (IBM), 223–224,
    240
frequent-purchase rewards pro-
    grams, 221
fun for, 241–242
global marketing and, 37
"Golden Triangle" of marketing
    pyramid, 225–226, 242
growth of, 219
importance of, 219–220, 227
Kana, 230
lifetime value of a customer, 238
listening to customers, 239–240
LivePerson, 230
loyalty, 220–221
marketing pyramid, moving
    customers up, 222, 224–227,
    242
"My" pages for, 51, 62–63,
    236–237
NativeMinds, 231

Net Effect, 231
Net Perceptions, 232
"New for You" pages for, 63, 236
newsgroups for, 94
newsletters (e-mail) for, 223,
    240–241
one-to-one relationship, moving to,
    234–237
order generation systems, 317–318
PeopleSupport, 232
personalization phenomenon,
    236–237, 244
products and services, 227–232
"Push to Talk" technology, 233
Revenio, 232
rewarding customers, 240–241
"self-service," 234–235
"solution databases" for, 244
surveys (e-mail), 115–116, 222–224
telephony technology, 204, 220,
    232–233, 312
Teradata CRM, 232
upselling technique, 226–227
valued customer relationships,
    maintaining, 222–224
Voice Over IP (VoIP), 232–233
Web Center, 233
Web sites for, 240
word-of-mouth advertising, 220
CRMDaily, 221
CRMGuru, 221
Crossing the Chasm (Moore), 331
cross-promotion, 179, 181
cultivation
    from integrating online and offline
        marketing, 333, 334, 335
    from "push" technology, 196–197
cultural differences and global mar-
    keting, 37–39
currency differences and global
    marketing, 38
customer bases, sharing, 295

customer relationship management. *See* CRM
customer success stories for public relations, 148
customer transition with "mini-sites," 67
customization of selling, 304, 325–326
CyberAtlas, 2–3, 14
CyberCash, 322
CyberCoin, 322
CyberMedia, 214
CyberStateU, 183
Cybuy, 144

D
DaimlerChrysler, 261
Dash.com, 314
database marketing
    direct marketing and, 24
    intersponding and, 42
database technology
    for communities, 272
    for customer relationship management (CRM), 222, 223, 234, 242, 244
    for e-mail, 107
    for events, 171, 174
    for fulfillment, 208
    for newsletters (e-mail), 113
    for order generation systems, 316, 318
    for promoting events online, 180–181
    for traffic generation, 51, 62–63
    for Web Sites, 51, 62–63
DATAMATION, 2
DBAzine, 67, 68
decline of banner ads, 124, 125, 128
Del, 295
deliverables, Internet Marketing Action Plan, 354, 355

Dell Computer
    customer relationship management (CRM), 236, 237, 244
    Dell Exchange, 308
    DellHost, 307
    Dell Learning Center, 308
    Dell Premier Web pages, 306–307
    Dell Software and Accessories, 307–308
    fulfillment, 191
    Internet impact on marketing, 11, 21
    lead generation and qualification, 57–58
    partnering, 274, 281, 288
    selling online, 302, 303–308
Delphi, 270
demand chain management, 290
demos online, 212–213
descriptions and search engines, 87, 88
DHL, 216
DHTML (Dynamic HTML), 53, 205–206
Digimarc, 191
DigiScents, 33
Digital, xxvi
digital certificates, 16, 323
Digital City, 250
Digital Impact, 117
Digital Millennium Copyright Act, 16
Digital Storage, 194
Digital Subscriber Line (DSL), 7, 32
Digital Think, 183
DIRECT, 237
Directech | eMerge, 18–19, 118
Direct Hit, 92
"Direct Insight Online," 118
direct mail
    e-mail vs., 100–101
    events using, 157–158
    fulfillment using, 188

promoting events online with, 180
direct marketing, 23–45. *See also*
    global marketing; Internet
    marketing; intersponding
    model
action plan development for, 29
database marketing and, 24
future vision of, 30–31, 211–212,
    295–298, 360–363
growth in, 329
importance of, xxvii–xxviii, 4
integrating Internet with traditional
    media, 29
Internet marketing readiness
    assessment, 28–29
mail-order marketers, 25, 309
management preparation for, 29,
    344–349, 352
partnering and, 277–279
response paths (multiple), 25
return on investment (ROI) and,
    23, 346
toll-free 800/888/877 telephone
    numbers, 24–25
traditional media, subordinate to
    Internet, 26–28
transformation of, 24–31
transitional marketing strategy,
    28–29, 328–363
Uniform Resource Locators
    (URLs), 26, 34–35
Direct Marketing Association. *See*
    DMA
Direct Media, 109
directories, 82, 84, 142
discussion groups, e-mail, 116. *See
    also* newsgroups
Disney.com, 251
distance learning, 164, 182–184
DMA (Direct Marketing Association)
    on direct marketing, 26
    on e-mail, 100, 106, 115

on events online, 169
on Internet impact on marketing, 4,
    5, 329–330
on privacy, 55
DMA Insider, The, 115
DMOZ Open Directory Project, 82
DNS (Domain Name System), 16
"Do It Again" category of visitors, 56
domain name suffixes, 49
Domain Name System (DNS), 16
Dot Coms' impact on Internet market-
    ing, xxv, 4, 13–14
DoubleClick, 129
double opt-in, 100
DoveBid, 254
download.cnet.com, 213
downloading
    fulfillment from, 213
    instructions in Web Response
        Forms (WRFs), 73
    times of Web sites, 54, 55
drop-down menus of Web sites, 53
"drop-shipping" model, 280
DSL (Digital Subscriber Line), 7, 32
Dun & Bradstreet, 267
Dynamic HTML (DHTML), 53,
    205–206

E
e2open.com, 261
eAdvertising Report, 125
"early adopters," 331, 332
EarthLink, 12, 182, 250
Eastman Chemical, 295
E*Banners, 131
eBay, 253–254
ECML (Electronic Commerce Model-
    ing Language), 323
e-commerce. *See also* Internet market-
    ing; selling online
    affiliate programs and, 283–284
    revenue statistics, 3, 14, 21

technology for communities, 272
EdCals, 146
editorial calendars, 146
EDTN Network, 257–258
EducateU, 308
Education News and Entertainment, 164
effectiveness measurement. *See also* cost-effectiveness; Web sites effectiveness measurement
  of advertising, 140
  of affiliate programs, 283
  of events, 176
  of keywords, 85
  of Web Sites, 48, 52–55
efficiency improvement from Internet, 18–19
e-fulfillment. *See* fulfillment
Egghead, 117, 214, 254
eLeads, 194
e-learning, 164, 182–184
Electrom.com, 319
Electronic Commerce Modeling Language (ECML), 323
electronic direct marketing. *See* Internet marketing
electronic malls, 35
electronic-wallet services, 322–323
e-mail, 99–123. *See also* newsgroups; newsletters (e-mail)
  acceptance of, 102
  addresses, changing, 122
  advantages of, 100–102
  affiliate programs using, 286
  alerts using, 111
  announcements using, 111
  attachments, 118
  audio file in, 119, 120
  automating mailings, 122
  autoresponders, 121
  back end preparation, 122
  banner advertising vs., 101

"before, during, and after" approach, 111
building your own list, 107, 112, 123
caps, avoiding, 123
channel partners using, 292
copywriting, 123
cost-effectiveness of, 100–101
cost per action (CPA), 108
cost per thousand (CPM), 108
cost to end user, 104
customer relationship management (CRM) using, 110, 240
database technology for, 107
direct mail vs., 100–101
discussion groups, 116
double opt-in, 100
embedded ordering capability in, 326
event-driven e-mail, 111
events using, 158
facial images in, 118
follow-ups using, 110–111
"forward to a colleague" theme, 121
fulfillment using, 189–190, 194–195
HTML e-mail, 118
inbound e-mail, 102–103
innovation, 118–120
lead generation and qualification using, 102
length of, 123
lists, 106, 107–109, 123, 179
management, 117, 119–120
mass mailing (blast, broadcasting), 109
merge purge, 108
negative responses to, 122
opt-in lists, 99–100, 107–109, 112, 123
opt-out (unsubscribing), 106

outbound e-mail, 103–106,
109–116
outsourcing, 117
partnering using, 278
permission (opt-in) marketing, 99,
102, 105–106, 107
personalization of, 117, 122
privacy, 104–105, 106, 123
production time savings using, 101
promoting events online using, 180
response path using, 102–103
responses, 101, 109, 122
return on investment (ROI), 101
rich media features, 119
risk, limiting, 105–106
spam (unsolicited e-mail), 99, 102,
104–105
subject line, 122
surveys using, 115–116, 222–224
"tell a friend" theme, 121
text, 123
traffic generation for Web sites,
123
unsolicited (spamming), 99, 102,
104–105
usage statistics, 100
user's mailbox and, 104
viral marketing, 120–121
Zaplets, 119
eMarketer, 2, 9, 100, 125
EMC, 274
Emerging Interest, 119
Engage, 126, 129
engineering- vs. marketing-driven,
xxvi–xxvii, 1
Enliven, 130–131
Enterprise Relationship Management
(eRM), 230. *See also* CRM
(customer relationship
management)
EntryPoint, 195
ePage, 229

e.piphany, 229–230
eRetail Customer Acquisition Costs
Forecast, 302
eRM (Enterprise Relationship Management), 230. *See also* CRM
(customer relationship
management)
errors in Web sites, checking for, 53
Escalate, 281
eShare Technologies, 230
ESPN.com, 251
eStation, 323
European market, 34, 37–38
European Union Data Protection
Directive, 105
event-driven e-mail, 111
events online, 149–184. *See also*
events online, developing;
events online, promoting
archiving advantage of, 156, 157
AXENT, 159–160
broadband for, 7, 166
browser software for, 163
Centra BCN (Business Collaboration Network), 161
"chat" capabilities, 166, 168
Cisco Systems, 161–162
cost-effectiveness of, 155, 156
direct mail for, 157–158
distance learning, 164, 182–184
e-learning, 164, 182–184
e-mail for, 158
growth of, 149
ITWorld, 162
live seminars, 151–154, 157, 166
logistical problems eliminated with,
154
meetings online, 168, 181–182
Microsoft Multimedia Central, 163
no-show rate reduction from, 156
offline and, 169
on-demand seminars, 168

Oracle eBusiness Network, 162
Oracle Internet Seminars, 162
Placeware Seminars, 158, 162
plug-ins for, 163
prerecorded seminars, 166–168
presentations (online), 167–168
qualified prospects from, 154–155
quality control of, 154
response rates, 158–159
seminars (online), 167–168
services for, 164–166, 181–182
software for, 165–166
streaming media, 163–164, 166
success story, 157–159, 160, 161
supplementing live seminars with,
    157
technological challenges of, 163–166
teleconferencing, 165, 169–170
trade shows (online), 146, 167
trade shows (traditional), 149–151
virtual vs. live seminars, 154–156
Voice Over IP (VoIP), 165
Webcasts, 144, 164, 168
events online, developing, 169–176.
    See also events online; events
    online, promoting
animations, 173
audiovisual requirements for, 171
content for, 173
copywriting, 173
database integration for, 171, 174
effectiveness measurement of, 176
exclusive information in, 172
executive events, 170
firewalls and plug-ins caution, 173
graphic files, 173
guest speakers, 171–172
hosting, 174–175
hot topics for, 172
interactivity for, 172
multimedia, 173
planning, 170–171

retreats, 170
return on investment (ROI), 176
roundtables or briefings, 170
structure for, 172
success factors, 171–172
success stories for, 172
technologies to enhance, 173–174
teleconferencing, 165, 169–170
testing, 169, 173, 175
events online, promoting, 176–181.
    See also events online
awareness increase from, 179
banner advertising for, 179
cost-effectiveness of, 178, 179
cross-promotion, 179, 181
database technology for, 180–181
direct mail for, 180
e-mail addresses from, 179
e-mail for, 180
invitations, 180–181
no-show rate reduction from, 178
print advertising for, 180
prospects increase from, 179
public relations for, 180
qualified prospects from, 178,
    180–181
registration facilitator from,
    177–179
response increase from, 178
services for, 176
telemarketing for, 180
traditional promotions, 177
trend tracking, 176–177
Web sites for, 179
EventWeb, 176
eWallet, 195
eWEEK (PCWEEK), 2
Exactis.com, 117
exchange, advertising, 139
exchange service for selling, 308
exchanges (marketplaces), 247–248,
    259–260

exchanging banner ads, 130
Excite, 85–86, 87, 88, 92, 251, 270
exclusive information in events, 172
executive events, 170
Exodus Communications, 307
expanding markets and territories, 36–37
Expedia, 215
Exportall, 261
eXtensible Markup Language (XML), 206
extramercials, 126
extranets
    channel partners, 292–293
    customer relationship management (CRM), 242–246
    Internet marketing and, 7–8, 33
    partnering, 279
Eyeblaster, 144
"eye candy," 47
eye-catching advertisements, 139

F
facial images in e-mail, 118
FairMarket, 254–255
Family.com, 251
FAQs (Frequently Asked Questions) of newsgroups, 95
fax for fulfillment, 188–189
fear, uncertainty, doubt (FUD) factor, 340
Federal Trade Commission (FTC), 5–6
FedEx, 9, 216, 317
"feeder" medium, 131–132
FindtheDOT, 191
firewalls and plug-ins caution, 173
flames, 80
Flash technology, 131
flexibility of affiliate programs, 280–281
Flooz, 143
Focusing on You (IBM), 223–224, 240

follow-me ads, 144–145
follow-ups using e-mail, 110–111
Ford, 261
form response analysis for Web sites, 65
forms on Web sites, 42–43, 47, 49, 50, 69–71
Forrester Research
    on advertising, 124, 142, 143
    on affiliate (associate) programs, 279
    on communities, 253, 259
    on e-mail, 100, 101
    on Internet impact on marketing, 4, 359–360
    on selling online, 301
Fortune, 303
Fortune 350, 327
"forward to a colleague" theme, 121
free
    access providers, 13, 32
    advertising, 139
    links, 75–76
    services of communities, 265–266
Free Forum Network, The, 143
FreeMarkets, 255
Frequently Asked Questions (FAQs) of newsgroups, 95
frequent-purchase rewards programs, 221
Frost & Sullivan, 232
FTC (Federal Trade Commission), 5–6
FUD (fear, uncertainty, doubt) factor, 340
fulfillment, online, 185–218. *See also* fulfillment, traditional
    acknowledgement benefit of, 200
    advantages of, 200–204
    automatic, 199–200
    autoresponders for, 190
    barcode technology, 191

call-me (telephony) technology,
204, 220, 232–233, 312
catalogs, 207
CD/Web connection, 209–210
communities, 212
confirmation benefit of, 200–201
continuous fulfillment, 198–199
cultivation from "push" technology, 196–197
database technology for, 208
demos online, 212–213
DHL, 216
downloads for, 213
Dynamic HTML (DHTML),
205–206
e-mail for, 189–190, 194–195
eXtensible Markup Language
(XML), 206
FedEx, 216
future of, 211–212
help (instant) from, 203–204
HTML pages, 205–206
images technology for, 191–192
individualization of, 208
inquiry-handling, 197, 215
"instant" fulfillment, 201–203, 214
integration trend, 192, 333, 334,
335
intersponding, 43–45
Kiosk/Web connection, 210–211
lead generation and qualification,
197, 207
link strategy for, 189
MarketFirst, 216
marketing intelligence from, 203
MarketSoft, 194, 216–217
moving to, 204–211
NetQuartz, 217
Netship, 217
newsletters (e-mail) for, 190–191
"one-to-many" principle, 209
order fulfillment, 214–215, 325–326

PDF files, 206–207
printed information conversion,
205–207
product distribution, 214–215
"pull" technology, 193–195
"push" technology, 195–200
qualified prospects, 197
reader service numbers for, 191
services for, 216–218
"solution databases" for, 208
speed of, 190
SubmitOrder, 194, 217
telephony technology, 204, 220,
232–233, 312
trials online, 212–213
updating ease and speed, 207
UPS, 218
Web Response Forms (WRFs) for,
72, 73, 193
Web sites for, 194
fulfillment, traditional, 185–189
autofaxing for, 188–189
direct mail, 188
fax for, 188–189
inquiry-handling, 186–187, 188
lead qualification, 186–187
"overfulfill," 188
qualified prospects, 186–187
speed of, 186, 187–188
telephone for, 189
fun for customer relationship management (CRM), 241–242
future of Internet marketing, 30–31,
211–212, 295–298, 360–363

G
games caution for Web sites, 55
games for advertising, 127
Gartner, Inc.
on communities, 260
on customer relationship management (CRM), 234

on Internet impact on marketing, 3,
14
on selling online, 301, 319
Gateway, 13, 261
gateway pages, 76
Gator, 323
GE Express, 288
GE Industrial Systems EliteNet,
261–262
GeoCities, 251
Georgia Tech, 79
GIF (Graphic Interface Format), 127
Giles, Lee, 79
global marketing, 31–39. *See also*
direct marketing; Internet;
Internet marketing
accessibility of Internet for, 5, 6–7,
31–33
Application Service Providers
(ASPs), 35–36
business influenced by, 2–4, 9,
17–19, 33
Canadian market, 33–34
cautions, 37–39
communications technology
improvements and, 32
cost-effectiveness of Internet for,
20, 31–32
cultural differences, 37–39
currency differences, 38
customer service, 37
electronic malls, 35
European market, 34, 37–38
expanding markets and territories,
36–37
free access providers, 13, 32
growth of, 34
humor differences, 38
Internet and, 15–16, 348
language differences, 38
Latin American market, 34
mirror sites, 35

opportunities of, 36
order processing, 35
Pacific Rim market, 34
partnerships, 37
privacy issue, 38
shipping, 38
tax differences, 38
technology improvements and, 33
translation tools, 35
Uniform Resource Locators
(URLs), 26, 34–35
United Kingdom market, 34
World Wide Web for, 34–35
GM, 261
GoCode, 191
Go-events, 176
"Golden Triangle" of marketing
pyramid, 225–226, 242
GO Network, 251
Google, 85–86, 87, 88, 92
graphic files for events, 173
Graphic Interface Format (GIF), 127
gratuitous responses caution, 97
Greenfield Online, 55
growth
of advertising, 124
of affiliate (associate) programs,
279
of communities and exchanges,
247
of customer relationship management (CRM), 219
of direct marketing, 329
of events online, 149
of global marketing, 34
of Internet, 4–5, 9, 14
of partnering online, 274–275
of selling online, 301–302, 303
guest speakers for events, 171–172

H
Hagel, John III, 297

Hanna, Patrick, 235
hardware impact from Internet, 9–11
headlines in Web Response Forms
    (WRFs), 72
help (instant) from fulfillment,
    203–204
Hewlett-Packard
    channel partners, 290
    communities, 261
    customer relationship management
        (CRM), 233, 235–236
    e-mail, 115
    fulfillment, 199–200
    lead generation and qualification,
        58
HitBox, 65
hits, 64–65
home pages
    intersponding and, 40
    keywords for, 86
    Web site design, 49, 52
HostIndex, 307
hosting
    business, 307
    events online, 174–175
hot100.com, 47
HotBot, 79, 85–86, 87, 92
Hotmail, 121
HotMedia, 131
hot topics for events, 172
HP Garage Affiliate Network, 288
HTML
    e-mail, 118
    newsletters, 113, 141, 142
    pages for fulfillment, 205–206
humor differences and global market-
    ing, 38
hyperlinks for search engines, 80

I
IAB (Interactive Advertising Bureau),
    124

IBM
    advertising, 131
    communities, 261
    customer relationship management
        (CRM), 223, 226–227, 233,
        240, 242
    Internet impact on marketing, 9,
        10, 330–331
    lead generation and qualification,
        58
    partnering, 274, 293
    selling online, 302–303
iChannel, 296
Iconomy, 281
iconvention.com, 176
IDC, 34, 182, 197, 219, 301, 302
IDG, 112, 192
IDG List Services, 109
IDG.net, 5, 147, 258
iGo, 288
iLOR, 131
image maps caution for search
        engines, 80
images technology for fulfillment,
        191–192
IMakeNews, 113
iMediation, 296
implementation of Internet Marketing
        Action Plan, 353–354
impressions, 77, 138
IMT Strategies, 101, 102
inbound e-mail, 102–103
incentive programs, 127, 142–144
Indimi, 118
Individual.com, 198
individualization
    fulfillment, 208
    intersponding, 40–42
industry practices and integrating
        online and offline marketing,
        332
iNetEvents, 176

InfoGate, 195, 323
"infomediary," 297
information access services, 5
informational Web sites for free links,
    76
information center of communities, 271
Information Technology. *See* IT
InformationWeek, 53, 233, 253
Infoseek, 79, 85–86, 87, 88, 251
infrastructure cost of selling online,
    300–301
in-house vs. outside resources, 354
Initial Public Offerings (IPOs), 4
Inktomi, 79, 88
inquiry-handling, 186–187, 188, 197,
    215
INSIDE 1to1, 117, 235
Inside the Tornado (Moore), 331
Insight Direct, 325–326
InstaBuy.com, 322
Instant Delivery, 199–200
"instant" fulfillment, 201–203, 214
Integrated Services Digital Network
    (ISDN), 7
integrating online and offline market-
    ing, 329–339
    audiences' role in, 331–332, 354
    awareness increase from, 338
    competition and, 332
    cost-effectiveness of, 338, 339
    cultivation, 333, 334, 335
    "early adopters," 331, 332
    example of, 336–339
    fulfillment trend, 192, 333, 334, 335
    industry practices and, 332
    lead generation and qualification,
        333, 334, 338
    media integration, 332–335
    no-show rate reduction from, 338
    offline marketing importance,
        330–331
    prospects from, 338

response increase from, 338
responses, 333, 334–335
success from, 345–346
"synchronized advertising," 359
traditional media and, 29
Intel, 9, 131, 132, 237, 293–294
intelligent agents (bots), 79, 80
Interact, 117
interactions of Web site visitors,
    tracking, 65
"Interactive 500," 302, 327
Interactive Advertising Bureau (IAB),
    124
interactive areas of communities, 272
InteractiveWeek, 9, 302
interactivity
    for events, 172
    for traffic generation, 63–64
International Communications
    Research, 18
International Data Corporation, 3, 14
Internet Advertising Bureau, 126
Internet.com, 5, 147, 258
Internet Explorer (Microsoft), 86–87,
    95, 163, 323
Internet Financial Network, 195
Internet marketing, 1–22. *See also*
    advertising online; communi-
    ties and exchanges online;
    CRM (customer relationship
    management) online; direct
    marketing; e-mail; events
    online; fulfillment; integrating
    online and offline marketing;
    Internet Marketing Action
    Plan; IT (Information Tech-
    nology) Internet marketing;
    newsgroups; partnering;
    public relations online; search
    engines; selling online; Web
    sites
    acceptance of, 8–9, 16

accessibility of, 5, 6–7, 31–33
Asymmetric Digital Subscriber Line
   (ADSL), 7
bandwidth concern, 6–7
benefits from, 344–349
boundlessness of, 14–15
broadband, 7, 166
business influenced by, 2–4, 9,
   17–19, 33
business-to-business (B-to-B), 17
communications intimacy from,
   19–20
competitive research tool, 18
conferencing, 19
cost-effectiveness of, 20, 31–32,
   346–347
digital certificates, 16, 323
Digital Subscriber Line (DSL), 7, 32
Dot Coms' impact on, xxv, 4, 13–14
e-commerce revenue statistics, 3,
   14, 21
efficiency improved from, 18–19
extranets, 7–8, 33
free access providers, 13, 32
future of, 30–31, 211–212,
   295–298, 360–363
global marketing, 15–16, 348
growth of, 4–5, 9, 14
hardware impact, 9–11
information access services, 5
Initial Public Offerings (IPOs), 4
Integrated Services Digital Network
   (ISDN), 7
Internet Service Providers (ISPs),
   12–13, 31–32
intranets, 7–8, 33
leveling effect of, 17
management preparation for, 29,
   344–349, 352
marketing medium, 4, 358–360
"massification" of, 6
networking impact, 11–12

one-to-one marketing with, 51,
   62–63, 348–349
penetration of business community,
   17–19
"presence awareness" frontier,
   359–360
privacy issue, 5–6
productivity reduction from, 18
quantifiable business benefits from,
   344–349
research tool, 18
sales channel from, 20–21
search engines' coverage of, 5, 79
service companies impact, 12–13
shelf space (unlimited), 348
software impact, 11
spamming, 5
"synchronized advertising," 359
television converging with, 15
traffic on, 5
updating ease of, 347–348
users reached by Internet, 16–17
wireless Internet, 7
Internet Marketing Action Plan,
   349–358. *See also* Internet
   marketing
contents of, 352–353
deliverables, 354, 355
implementation, 353–354
in-house vs. outside resources, 354
Internet Marketing Audit Checklist
   for, 349–351
Internet Marketing Creative
   Specialists positions, 357–358
Internet Marketing Manager
   position, 356
Internet Marketing Media Specialist position, 357
Internet Marketing Producer
   position, 357
management preparation, 29,
   344–349, 352

Marketologist position, 341, 342, 356–357
  outside vs. in-house resources for, 354
  readiness assessment, 28–29, 349–351
  staff requirements, 355–358
Internet Marketing Audit Checklist, 349–351
Internet Marketing Creative Specialists positions, 357–358
Internet Marketing Manager position, 356
Internet Marketing Media Specialist position, 357
Internet Marketing Producer position, 357
Internet marketing readiness assessment, 28–29, 349–351
Internet Research Group, 164
Internet Service Providers (ISPs), 12–13, 31–32
Internet Tax Freedom Act, 16
Internet to traditional order generation, 324
intersponding model, 39–45. *See also* direct marketing
  Awareness, Interest, Desire, Action (AIDA) formula, 40
  call to action, 39
  database marketing and, 42
  forms (interactive) on Web sites, 42–43, 47, 49, 50, 69–71
  fulfillment, 43–45
  home pages, 40
  individualized information, 40–42
  interactive part of, 41–42
  navigation of Web sites, 41–42, 49, 53–54, 86
  nonlinear vs. linear information, 39–41
  one-to-one communications intimacy, 41–42
  relationship changes from, 44–45
  responding part of, 42–43
  Web Response Forms (WRFs) and, 42–43
  Web sites and, 39–43
interstitials (pop-ups) ads, 126
intranets, 7–8, 33
Intranets.com, 243
Intuit, 196, 237
invitations to events, 180–181
Involv, 270
Iomega, 237
IPOs (Initial Public Offerings), 4
IpsosASI, 128
IQ Commerce, 131
ISDN (Integrated Services Digital Network), 7
iShip, 318
ISPs (Internet Service Providers), 12–13, 31–32
"Is Successful Web Marketing A Myth?" (Bane), 345
IT (Information Technology) Internet marketing, xxv–xxx, 339–343. *See also* Internet marketing
  direct marketing importance, xxvii–xxviii, 4
  Dot Com's impact on, xxv, 4, 13–14
  engineering- vs. marketing-driven, xxvi–xxvii, 1
  fear, uncertainty, doubt (FUD) factor, 340
  future of, 30–31, 211–212, 295–298, 360–363
  marketing organization impact from, 339–343
  resistance to, 340
  sales organization impact from, 342–343
  senior management and, 339–340

supersites, 256–259
"synchronized advertising," 359
Web site for, xxx
ITWorld, 148, 162
ITXC, 233

J
Java & JavaScript, 63–64
Juno, 138
Jupiter Communications, 130
Jupiter Media Metrix, 100–101, 125,
    302, 325
Jurvetson, Steve, 120–121

K
Kana, 230
Keyva Technologies, 116
keywords, 82–85. *See also* search
    engines
    <TITLE> tags, 85–86, 87
    comments tag, 85
    competition research for, 86–87
    competitors' names in, 84
    effectiveness measurement of, 85
    home pages and, 86
    meta-tags, 76, 84, 86–87, 88
    places for, 84–85
    plurals for, 83
    prioritizing, 83–84
    rankings of search engines and, 82,
        85, 86, 87, 88
    repeating caution, 81, 85, 88
    spamming with, 83
    title changes and, 81, 84
Kiosk/Web connection, 210–211
Knowledge Systems and Research, 9

L
Lands' End, 233
language differences and global
    marketing, 38

Latin American market, 34
Latitude Communications, 166
launching
    communities, 273
    products with "mini-sites," 66
Launchpad Technologies, 195
Lawrence, Steve, 79
leadership position from communities,
    267–269
lead generation and qualification
    e-mail for, 102
    events online for, 154–155
    fulfillment for, 186–187, 197, 207
    integrating online and offline
        marketing for, 333, 334, 335,
        338
    partnering for, 276
    promoting events online, 178,
        180–181
    Web Response Forms (WRFs) for,
        71–72, 74
    Web sites for, 47–56
"leaking leads," 71
learning service, 308
LearningSpace, 183–184
legacy systems and order generation
    systems, 319
legal agreement for affiliate programs,
    285–286
legitimacy of affiliate programs,
    verifying, 282
length of e-mail, 123
leveling effect of Internet, 17
LifeFX, 119
life of advertising online, 139
lifetime value of a customer, 238
Line 56 magazine, 290
LinkExchange, 130, 139
LinkShare, 284
link strategies, 75–77. *See also* search
    engines; Web sites
    affiliate programs, 285

channel partners, 291, 292
free links, 75–76
fulfillment, 189
gateway pages, 76
impressions and paid links, 77, 138
informational Web sites for free
    links, 76
meta-tags, 76, 84, 86–87, 88
newsletters for links, 77
paid links, 77
reciprocal links caution, 76, 139
reverse-search of competition, 87
search engines and, 87
smart links in banner advertising,
    130
Web links for fulfillment, 189
Web Response Forms (WRFs) and,
    73–74
listening to customers, 239–240
lists (e-mail), 107–109, 123
Listz, 95
LivePerson, 230
live seminars, 151–154, 157, 166
logistical problems eliminated with
    events online, 154
"Loitering" category of visitors, 56
LookSmart, 82
Lotus, 11
Lotus Developer Network, 268
loyalty of customers, 220–221
LSI Logic Corporation, 306–307
lurking, 95
Lycos, 79, 86, 88, 92–93, 252

M
Macromedia, 58–59, 131, 237
"Made to Order: Insight Offers
    Business Clients Customized
    E-Catalog Pages" (Riggs),
    325–326
Magill, Ken, 326
mail-order model of selling, 25, 309

Mainspring, 219
malls (virtual), 310
management
    of e-mail lists, 117, 119–120
    of order generation systems,
        319–320
management preparation for Internet
    marketing, 29, 344–349, 352
Manufacturing.net, 262
MapQuest, 250
Marimba, 196
MarketFirst, 216
marketing intelligence from fulfillment,
    203
marketing medium, Internet as, 4,
    358–360
marketing organization impact from
    Internet marketing, 339–343
marketing pyramid, moving customers
    up, 222, 224–227, 242
Marketologist position, 341, 342,
    356–357
marketplaces, 247–248, 259–260. *See
    also* communities and ex-
    changes online
MarketSoft, 194, 216–217
MarketTools, 116
"Massachusetts Miracle," xxvi
"massification" of Internet, 6
mass mailing (blast, broadcasting),
    109
matching services, partnering,
    297–298
MathWorks, 235, 244
MATLAB, 235
Maximum Press Web site, xxx
McAfee Associates, 59
McKinsey/Salomon Smith Barney, 360
mCommerce (mobile commerce), 323
measurement capabilities of Web sites,
    47
MediaBridge, 191

media buy, extending with banner
  ads, 136
media integration, 332–335. *See also*
  integrating online and offline
  marketing
MediaMap, 146
media outlets, 146
Media Player, 164
MediaPost Communications, 119
Media Synergy, 119
MeetingEvents, 176
meetings online, 168, 181–182
"Members-Only" Web site, xxx
merge purge, 108
MessageMates, 118
MessageMedia, 117
message posting, 96–97
Messaging Online, 100
Messaging Plus ads, 126
Meta Group, 149
meta refresh tags caution for search
  engines, 81
meta-tags, 76, 84, 86–87, 88
MGI, 192
Microsoft
  Access, 174
  communities, 250
  customer relationship management
    (CRM), 237
  events online, 164
  fulfillment, 206
  Internet Explorer, 86–87, 95, 163,
    323
  Internet impact on marketing, 2,
    11, 15
  Microsoft Network (MSN), 59
  Multimedia Central, 163
  partnering, 294
  selling online, 322
Miller Heiman, 267
MindArrow, 119, 195
MindSpring, 12, 182, 250

"mini-sites," 65–67
mirror sites, 35
misc (miscellaneous topics) newsgroups,
  95
MIT Sloan E-Commerce Technology
  Innovator Award, 232
mobile commerce (mCommerce), 323
Moore, Geoffrey, 331
MShow, 166
MSN, 138, 250
Multicity, 148
multimedia, 63–64, 173
"My" pages, 51, 62–63, 236–237
MyPoints, 143–144
mySimon, 313–314

N
Narrative Communications, 130
National Cristina Foundation, 308
NativeMinds, 231
navigation of Web sites, 41–42, 49,
  53–54, 86
Navigator (Netscape), 95, 163
NEC Research Institute, 4–5, 79, 261
NECX, 261
negative responses to e-mail, 122
NetCreations, 119
Net Effect, 231
net events. *See* events online
NetGenesis, 65, 234
NetIQ, 65
NetMarketing 200, 327
Net Perceptions, 232
NetPodium, 165
NetQuartz, 217
Netscape
  Communicator, 323
  lead generation and qualification,
    50–51
  Navigator, 95, 163
  Netcenter, 250
  search engines, 87

traffic generation, 63–64
NetSeminar, 164
Netship, 217
Networking B2B, 260
networking impact of Internet, 11–12
networking value of communities,
    266–267
Network Solutions, 289
Network World Fusion, 192
Net Worth (Hagel and Singer), 297
NetZero, 13
"New for You" pages, 63, 236
news.announce.newsgroups, 97
news.announce.newusers, 97
news.answers, 97
News.com, 126
newsgroups, 93–98
    advertising on, 96, 97, 116
    alt (alternative topics), 94
    audiences of, 94
    biz (business topics), 94
    categories of, 94–95
    community of, 249
    comp (computer-related topics), 95
    contribution, making, 97
    customer communication with, 94
    finding, 95
    Frequently Asked Questions
        (FAQs) of, 95
    gratuitous responses caution, 97
    lurking, 95
    message posting, 96–97
    misc (miscellaneous topics), 95
    news (Usenet news and administra-
        tion), 95
    online services and, 94
    posting messages, 96–97
    product/service fit with, 95
    proposals for starting, 97–98
    prospects from, 94
    qualifying, 95
    rec (recreation topics), 95

    reputation building with, 94
    request for discussion for starting,
        97
    research using, 94
    sci (science) newsgroups, 95
    search engines for finding, 95
    signature files for, 97
    soc (social issues), 95
    starting your own, 97–98
    talk (conversation), 95
    thread, staying on, 96
    topic, keeping on, 96
    traffic generation for Web sites, 94
    Usenet, 93
    Usenet Volunteer Vote Takers
        (UVT), 98
newsletters (e-mail), 111–115. *See
    also* e-mail
    advertising in, 113–115, 135,
        140–142
    article summarization in, 113
    cost-effectiveness of, 113
    customer relationship management
        (CRM) using, 223, 240–241
    database technology for, 113
    fulfillment from, 190–191
    HTML newsletters, 113, 141, 142
    links in, 77
    opt-in list building from, 112
    popularity of, 112
    promotion using, 112
    public relations using, 146
    relationship building with, 115
    revenue from, 113–114
    services for, 113
    sponsorships, 114, 135, 140–142
    subscription on Web sites, 51
    text newsletters, 113
    traffic generation from, 61, 113,
        114
news (Usenet news and administra-
    tion) newsgroups, 95

New York Times, The, 144, 146, 215
NextCard, 323
NextSLM, 67
Nielsen/NetRatings, 56, 125
nonlinear vs. linear information, 39–41
Nortel, 196, 261, 302
NorthernLight, 85–86, 87, 88, 93
no-show rate reduction
    from events online, 156
    from integrating online and offline marketing, 338
    from promoting events online, 178
notHarvard.com, 164
Novell, 131, 294–295
NPD Group, 143, 324

O
objectives for community building, 271
OCM (Online Customer Management), 230. *See also* CRM (customer relationship management)
offers
    banner ads, 133
    "mini-sites" for promoting, 66
    Web Response Forms (WRFs), 70, 73
    Web sites, 47, 49, 50–51, 55
Office.com, 198, 262
offline and online events, 169
offline marketing importance, 330–331. *See also* integrating online and offline marketing
Oil Change, 214
on-demand seminars, 168
"one-to-many" principle, 209
one-to-one
    communications intimacy, 41–42
    marketing with Internet, 51, 62–63, 348–349

relationship, moving to, 234–237
"One to One: Put the Customer in the Information Driver Seat and Build Better Relationships" (Smith), 223–224
Online Asset Exchange, 255
Online Customer Management (OCM), 230. *See also* CRM (customer relationship management)
online services and newsgroups, 94
Onsale, 117, 214
"on-site" banner ads, 51, 139
Open Source Development Network, 268
OpinionLab, 65
opt-in lists, 99–100, 107–109, 112, 123
Opt-in News, 100
opt-in (permission) marketing, 99, 102, 105–106, 107
opt-out (unsubscribing), 106
Oracle Corporation
    eBusiness Network, 162
    events online, 174
    Exchange, 262
    Internet impact on marketing, 11
    Internet Seminars, 162
    lead generation and qualification, 59
    partnering, 295
order fulfillment, 214–215, 325–326
order generation system, 314–324. *See also* selling online
    ATMs, 323
    banner advertising with embedded ordering capability, 326
    capabilities of, 316
    catalogs, 316–317
    "collaborative filtering," 318
    costs of, 319
    couponing, 127, 143, 324

creative part of, 319
customer-service component,
    317–318
customization for customers, 304,
    325–326
database technology for, 316, 318
digital certificates, 16, 323
Electronic Commerce Modeling
    Language (ECML), 323
electronic-wallet services, 322–323
existing system transition, 315–318
global marketing, 35
infrastructure behind store, 317
Internet to traditional order
    generation, 324
legacy systems and, 319
management of, 319–320
mobile commerce (mCommerce),
    323
order taking, 322–324
privacy issue, 322
Recency-Frequency-Monetary
    (RFM) criteria, 316
resources commitment to, 319
response path, adding to traditional
    order generation, 322
security, 322, 323
selling online and, 306–307
servers for, 320
shipping, 38, 318, 325
shopping cart capability, 317
starting new system, 318–320
storefronts, 306–307, 309, 316–317
taxes, 323–324
Web hosting services for, 320–321
within-the-ad responses, 133–134,
    326
Organisation for Economic Coopera-
    tion and Development, 46,
    215, 346
outbound e-mail, 103–106, 109–116
out-of-banner rich media, 144

Outpost, 288
outside vs. in-house resources, 354
outsourcing e-mail management, 117
"overfulfill," 188

P
Pacific Rim market, 34
paid links, 77
Panasonic, 261
ParaSoft, 53
Participate.com, 270
partnering, 274–298. *See also* affiliate
    (associate) programs; channel
    partners; CRM (customer
    relationship management)
    online
  channel marketing, 275, 276–277
  "collaborative selling," 296–297
  communities, 272
  compatibility, accentuating, 276
  cooperation vs. capitulation,
      275–276
  customer bases, sharing, 295
  direct marketing support for,
      277–279
  e-mail for, 278
  extranets for, 279
  future of, 295–298
  global marketing, 37
  growth of Internet, 274–275
  "infomediary," 297
  lead processing centralization, 276
  matching services, 297–298
  private exchanges, 296
  resellers, 275, 276–277, 310–312
  "strategic alliances," 275
  traditional, 275–279
  turnkey programs for, 276–277
  Uniform Resource Locators (URLs)
      for, 278
  Value-Added Resellers (VARs),
      275, 277, 311

Web sites for, 278
Passport.com, 322
PayNow, 322
PDF files, 206–207
penetration of business community,
    17–19
PeopleSoft Marketplace, 262
PeopleSupport, 232
Peppers & Rogers Group, 117, 235,
    237
Performics, 284
periodicals for public relations, 146
Permison, Jack, 116
permission (opt-in) marketing, 99,
    102, 105–106, 107
personalization.com, 237
personalization phenomenon
    customer relationship management
        (CRM), 236–237, 244
    e-mail, 117, 122
    traffic generation, 51, 62–63
piggyback ads, 145
Pitney Bowes, 100
placement of advertising, 129, 136–138
places for keywords, 84–85
PlaceWare, 158, 162, 165
PlanetIT, 256
planning events online, 170–171
plug-ins for events, 163
plurals for keywords, 83
PointCast Inc., 195
pop-ups (interstitials) ads, 126
portals, 89, 251–253
posting messages, 96–97
Postmaster Direct, 109
precampaign teasers, 135–136
prerecorded seminars, 166–168
"presence awareness" frontier,
    359–360
presentations (online), 167–168
price for performance, 304
Priceline, 255

print advertising for promoting events
    online, 180
printed information conversion,
    205–207
prioritizing keywords, 83–84
privacy issues
    e-mail, 104–105, 106, 123
    global marketing, 38
    Internet, 5–6
    order generation systems, 322
    selling online, 300
    Web site policy on, 55
private access from Web Response
    Forms (WRFs), 73
private exchanges, partnering, 296
private-labels, 285
PR Newswire, 146
Procter and Gamble, 21
Prodigy, 13, 138, 250
Prodigy Biz, 18
product distribution for fulfillment,
    214–215
product information in Web Response
    Forms (WRFs), 73
production time savings using e-mail,
    101
productivity reduction from Internet,
    18
product reviews and listings for public
    relations, 148
promotion. *See also* advertising online;
    events online, promoting
    newsletters (e-mail) for, 112
    partners on Web sites, 292
    Web sites area for, 47, 49, 50–51
Promotions.com, 143
proposals for starting newsgroups,
    97–98
prospects. *See also* lead generation
    and qualification
    from integrating online and offline
        marketing, 338

from newsgroups, 94
from promoting events online, 179
PR Web, 145
public relations online, 145–148. *See also* advertising online
CMPnet, 5, 112, 126, 147
CｌNet, 112, 126, 147
communities and, 265–266, 273
customer success stories for, 148
editorial calendars, 146
IDG.net, 5, 147
Internet.com, 5, 147
media outlets, 146
newspapers for, 146
periodicals for, 146
product reviews and listings for, 148
promoting events online, 180
services for, 145–146
trade shows for, 146
white papers for, 148
ZDnet, 5, 112, 126, 147
"pull" technology, 193–195
PurchasePro, 270
purchasing advertising, 137–138, 139
"push" technology, 195–200
"Push to Talk" technology, 233

Q

qualification. *See* lead generation and qualification
qualifying newsgroups, 95
quality control of events online, 154
QualityofExperience, 67–68, 69
quantifiable business benefits from Internet, 344–349

R

rankings of search engines, 82, 85, 86, 87, 88
reader service numbers, 191
readiness assessment, 28–29, 349–351

"ready-made" Web stores vs. links, 281
RealNetworks, 164
RealPlayer, 164
RealSystem, 164
Recency-Frequency-Monetary (RFM) criteria, 316
reciprocal links, 76, 139
rec (recreation topics) newsgroups, 95
Red Herring, 120, 327
Refer-It, 281
registration, search engines, 79–80, 85–86
registration facilitator from promoting events online, 177–179
regulatory environment of selling online, 301
relationship building with newsletters (e-mail), 115
relationship changes from intersponding, 44–45
relationships. *See* CRM (customer relationship management)
"remembering" visitors for traffic generation, 51, 62–63
repeating keywords caution, 81, 85, 88
repeat traffic. *See* traffic generation
reporting system of affiliate programs, 285, 286
reputation building with newsgroups, 94
request for discussion for starting newsgroups, 97
research tool, Internet as, 18
research using newsgroups, 94
reseller model, 275, 276–277, 310–312
resistance to Internet marketing, 340
resources commitment to order generation systems, 319
Respond.com, 297–298, 314, 315

response areas on Web sites, 47, 49, 50
response paths
    e-mail for, 102–103
    multiple for direct marketing, 25
    traditional order generation,
        adding to, 322
    Web sites, 54–55
response rates
    from advertising, 128, 133–134,
        140
    from banner ads, 128, 133–134
    from e-mail, 101, 109, 122
    from events online, 158–159
    from integrating online and offline
        marketing, 333, 334–335,
        338
    from promoting events online, 178
response times of Web sites, 54
Responsys, 117
resubmitting to search engines, 81
retail model, 308–310
retreats, 170
return on investment. *See* ROI
Reuters, 21
Revenio, 232
revenue from newsletters (e-mail),
        113–114
reverse-search of competition for
        links, 87
revisiting schedule of search engines,
        81, 84
rewarding customers, 240–241
RFM (Recency-Frequency-Monetary)
        criteria, 316
rich media
    in advertising, 135, 140
    in banner ads, 130–131, 132, 133,
        135, 144
    in e-mail, 119
Riggs, Larry, 325–326
ROI (return on investment)
    advertising online, 124

direct marketing, 23, 346
    e-mail, 101
    events online, 176
    Web sites, 46
Roper Starch, 79, 100
rotating images on Web sites, 52
roundtables or briefings online, 170
Rowsom, Michael, 318
R U Sure, 314

S
sales channel from Internet, 20–21
Sales.com, 267–268
sales force model, 312–313
sales organization impact from
        Internet marketing, 342–343
SAP, 11
SBC, 13, 250
sci (science) newsgroups newsgroups,
        95
Seagate Technology, 196, 261
search engines, 79–93. *See also*
        keywords
    <TITLE> tags, 85–86, 87
    About.com, 89–90, 91
    advertising on, 137, 142
    AltaVista, 79, 85–86, 87, 88,
        90–91
    Ask Jeeves, 91–92
    banner advertising on, 137
    competition research, 86–87
    coverage of Internet, 5, 79
    crawlers, 79, 85–86
    descriptions, 87, 88
    Direct Hit, 92
    directories, 82, 84, 142
    Excite, 85–86, 87, 88, 92
    flames, 80
    Google, 85–86, 87, 88, 92
    HotBot, 79, 85–86, 87, 92
    hyperlinks for, 80
    image maps caution, 80

intelligent agents (bots), 79, 80
links and rankings, 87
Lycos, 79, 86, 88, 92–93
meta refresh tags caution, 81
meta-tags, 76, 84, 86–87, 88
newsgroups, finding with, 95
NorthernLight, 85–86, 87, 88, 93
portals, 89
rankings, 82, 85, 86, 87, 88
registration with, 79–80, 85–86
resubmitting to, 81
revisiting schedule, 81, 84
site maps for, 80
spamming, 88
special characters and, 81
spiders, 79, 85–86
submitting to, 79–80, 85–86,
88–89
title changes and, 81, 84
use of, 79
Web site design tricks, 80–81
Yahoo!, 79, 82, 85–86, 87, 93
Searchenginewatch.com, 89, 90
"Secret Cat-and-Mouse Game Online,
A," 64
Secure Payment/SET, 322
security issue of selling online, 300,
322, 323
"self-service," 234–235
selling online (e-commerce), 299–327.
See also communities and
exchanges online; order
generation system; partnering
accessories, 307–308
auctions, 253–256, 310
brick-and-mortar companies and,
299, 302
catalogs, 309
customization for, 304, 325–326
Dash.com, 314
Dell Computer, 303–308
Dell Exchange, 308

DellHost, 307
Dell Learning Center, 308
Dell Premier Web pages, 306–307
Dell Software and Accessories,
307–308
exchange service, 308
growth of, 301–302, 303
hosting business, 307
infrastructure cost, 300–301
latest technology, 304
learning service, 308
mail-order model, 25, 309
malls (virtual), 310
mySimon, 313–314
order fulfillment, 214–215,
325–326
order processing, 306–307
price for performance, 304
privacy issue, 300
regulatory environment, 301
reseller model, 275, 276–277,
310–312
Respond.com, 314, 315
retail model, 308–310
R U Sure, 314
sales force model, 312–313
security issue, 300, 322, 323
service and support, 304
shareholder value, 304
shopping "bot," 313–314
storefronts, 306–307, 309, 316–317
telephony, 204, 220, 232–233, 312
Value-Added Resellers (VARs),
275, 277, 311
Web site for, 305–306
SeminarFinder, 176
Seminar Information, 176
SeminarPlanet, 176–177
seminars (online), 72, 167–168
SeminarSource, 177
senior management and Internet
marketing, 339–340

Sento Corporation, 109
serial e-mail, 111
servers for order generation systems, 320
service companies impact of Internet, 12–13
service providers for communities, 249–250
services
    for customer relationship management (CRM), 227–232
    for events online, 164–166, 181–182
    for fulfillment, 216–218
    for newsletters (e-mail), 113
    for promoting events online, 176
    for public relations, 145–146
services of communities, 265–266
Servicesoft, 227
shareholder value, 304
shelf space (unlimited), 348
shipping, 38, 318, 325
Shockwave technology, 131
Shop.org, 303
shopping "bot," 313–314
shopping cart capability, 317
Siebel Systems, 60, 67, 267–268
signature files for newsgroups, 97
Silverstein, Barry, xxv, xxvii, 158
Singer, Marc, 297
site maps for search engines, 80
skyscrapers and boxes, 126
Slashdot, 268–269
Small Office Home Office (SOHO), 210
SmartForce, 183, 308
smart links in banner advertising, 130
SmartPlanet, 183
Smith, Michelle Lanter, 223–224
soc (social issues) newsgroups, 95
software for events online, 165–166
software impact of Internet, 11

SOHO (Small Office Home Office), 210
"solution databases," 208, 244
SonyStyle.com, 311
spamlaws.com, 105
spamming
    e-mail, 99, 102, 104–105
    Internet marketing, 5
    keywords, 83
    search engines, 88
special characters and search engines, 81
SpeechWorks International, 33
speed of fulfillment, 186, 187–188, 190
spiders, 79, 85–86
Spidertop, 144
sponsorships
    communities, 267–269
    newsletters (e-mail), 114, 135, 140–142
    Web sites, 67–68, 79, 127
Sprint, 6
staff requirements for Internet marketing, 355–358
Stamps.com, 318
StarOffice, 10
"State of Online Retailing 4.0, The," 303
State of the Interactive/E-Commerce Marketing Industry, 329–330
Statmarket, 3
"stickiness" of Web sites, 54, 252
StickyAds, 144
storefronts (virtual)
    affiliate programs, 283–284
    selling online, 306–307, 309, 316–317
"strategic alliances," 275
streaming media, 163–164, 166
subject line in e-mail, 122
SubmitOrder, 194, 217

submitting to search engines, 79–80,
85–86, 88–89
success from integrating online and
offline marketing, 345–346
success stories for events, 172
suffixes for domain names, 49
Sundial.com, 288–289
Sun Microsystems, 10–11, 60, 206, 267
Sun-Netscape Alliance, 10
Superstials, 126
surveys (e-mail), 115–116, 222–224
Sweeney, Susan, 78
sweepstakes for advertising, 142–143
Sybase, 174, 237
Symantec, 237
"synchronized advertising," 359

T
talk (conversation) newsgroups, 95
targeted audiences, 331–332, 354
TargetMessaging, 117
Tarter, Jeffrey, 237
tax differences and global marketing,
38
taxes and order generation systems,
323–324
TCI, 6
TechCalendar, 177
TechRepublic, 258
TechTarget, 259
TechWeb, 256
teleconferencing, 165, 169–170
telemarketing for promoting events
online, 180
telephone for fulfillment, 189
telephony technology, 204, 220,
232–233, 312
television converging with Internet, 15
"tell a friend" theme, 121
Teradata CRM, 232
Terra Lycos, 93

Terra Networks, 252
testing
advertising, 135, 139, 140
affiliate programs, 282–283
banner ads, 135
communities, 273
events online, 169, 173, 175
Web Response Forms (WRFs), 75
text
e-mail, 123
newsletters, 113
thread of newsgroups, staying on, 96
Time Digital, 313
Time magazine, 14
Time Warner, xxvi, 12, 249
title (<TITLE>) tags, 85–86, 87
title changes and keywords, 81, 84
toll-free 800/888/877 telephone
numbers, 24–25
Topica, 95, 113
topic of newsgroups, keeping on, 96
trade advertising, 139
TradeOut, 255–256
trade shows, online, 146, 167
trade shows, traditional, 149–151
traditional
advertising, 140
fulfillment, 185–189
media, subordinate to Internet,
26–28
media and Web sites, 51
partnering, 275–279
promotions, 177
traffic generation, 60–64. *See also* link
strategies; Web sites; WRFs
(Web Response Forms)
advertising for, 131–132, 134
"alert services" for, 61
autoresponders for, 61
blocking Web site access, 64
cookies for, 61–62

databases for, 51, 62–63
e-mail for, 61, 123
interactivity for, 63–64
Java & JavaScript for, 63–64
multimedia for, 63–64
"My" pages for, 51, 62–63,
    236–237
"New for You" pages for, 63, 236
newsgroups for, 94
newsletters for, 61, 113, 114
one-to-one marketing for, 51,
    62–63, 348–349
personalization for, 51, 62–63
"remembering" visitors for, 51,
    62–63
traffic on Internet, 5
transformation of direct marketing,
    24–31
transitional marketing strategy,
    28–29, 328–363
translation tools, 35
Travelocity, 215
trend tracking for promoting events
    online, 176–177
trials online, 212–213
TSNN, 146, 177
turnkey programs for partnering,
    276–277

U
Unicast, 126
Uniform Resource Locators. *See* URLs
United Kingdom market, 34
University of Texas, 3
unsolicited (spamming) e-mail, 99,
    102, 104–105
unsubscribing (opt-out), 106
updating ease
    of advertising online, 139
    of fulfillment online, 207
    of Internet marketing, 347–348

updating timeliness of Web sites, 52
UPS, 9, 218, 317–318
upselling technique, 226–227
URLs (Uniform Resource Locators)
    for direct marketing, 26, 34–35
    for global marketing, 26, 34–35
    for partnering, 278
    for Web Response Forms (WRFs),
        70, 74
U.S. Congress, 16
usage statistics for e-mail, 100
USA Networks, 252
Usenet, 93
Usenet Info Center Launch Pad, 95
Usenet Volunteer Vote Takers (UVT),
    98
user groups as communities, 248–249
user's mailbox and e-mail, 104
users reached by Internet, 16–17
UUNET, 295–296
UVT (Usenet Volunteer Vote Takers),
    98

V
VA Linux Systems, 268
Value-Added Resellers (VARs), 275,
    277, 311
valued customer relationships, main-
    taining, 222–224
ValuePage, 143, 324
VARs (Value-Added Resellers), 275,
    277, 311
VentureDirect, 129
VeriSign, 289
VerticalNet, 262–263
vertical portals (vortals), 251
view-throughs, 140
viral marketing, 120–121
virtual vs. live seminars, 154–156
Voice Over IP (VoIP), 165, 232–233
vortals (vertical portals), 251

W

Wall Street Journal, The, 21, 64, 146, 170, 331, 360

Wall Street Journal Interactive Edition, The, 215

Washington Post, 268

Webcasts, 144, 164, 168

Web Center, 233

WebCollage, 296

WebConnect, 109, 129

WebCrawler, 85–86, 87, 88, 92

WebEx, 181–182

Web Host Industry Review, The, 307

Web hosting services for order generation systems, 320–321

Webmercials, 126

WebOS, 11

Web Response Forms. *See* WRFs

Web sites, 46–77. *See also* link strategies; search engines; traffic generation; Web sites effectiveness measurement

    advertising on, 51, 138

    Apple, 56

    banner ads on, 51

    Beyond.com, 57

    brochureware, 48

    buttons, 53–54

    channel partners and, 291–292

    Cisco Systems, 57

    content, high-value, 54

    copywriting, 50

    customer relationship management (CRM), 240

    database technology for, 51, 62–63

    Dell Computer, 57–58

    design tricks for search engines, 80–81

    "Do It Again" category of visitors, 56

    domain name suffixes, 49

    downloading times, 54, 55

    drop-down menus, 53

    Dynamic HTML (DHTML), 53

    errors, checking for, 53

    "eye candy," 47

    forms on, 42–43, 47, 49, 50, 69–71

    fulfillment, 194

    games caution, 55

    Hewlett-Packard, 58

    home pages, 49, 52

    IBM, 58

    Internet marketing, xxx

    intersponding and, 39–43

    lead generation and qualification, 47–56

    links for fulfillment, 189

    "Loitering" category of visitors, 56

    Macromedia, 58–59

    McAfee Associates, 59

    measurement capabilities of, 47

    Microsoft and Microsoft Network (MSN), 59

    navigation of, 41–42, 49, 53–54, 86

    needs of visitors and, 56

    newsletter subscription, 51

    offers on, 47, 49, 50–51, 55

    "on-site" banner ads, 51, 139

    Oracle Corporation, 59

    partnering, 278

    privacy policy on, 55

    promoting events online, 179

    promotional areas on, 47, 49, 50–51

    "remembering" visitors, 51, 62–63

    response areas on, 47, 49, 50

    response paths, 54–55

    response times, 54

    return on investment (ROI), 46

    rotating images, 52

    selling online, 305–306

Siebel Systems, 60
"stickiness," 54, 252
suffixes for domain names, 49
Sun Microsystems, 60
traditional media and, 51
updating timeliness, 52
Web Response Forms (WRFs) on, 47, 49, 50
"What's New" area on, 52
WorldCom, 60
Web sites effectiveness measurement, 64–75. *See also* Web sites; WRFs (Web Response Forms)
customer transition with "mini-sites," 67
form response analysis for, 65
hits, 64–65
interactions of visitors, tracking, 65
launching products with "mini-sites," 66
"mini-sites" for, 65–67
offer promotion with "mini-sites," 66
overview, 48, 52–55
sponsored sites for, 67–68, 79, 127
tools for, 65
WebTrends, 65
WebTV, 15
"What B2B Marketers Need to Know about Spam," 105
"What's New" area on Web sites, 52
white papers for public relations, 148
Wink Communications, 15
WIPO (World Intellectual Property Organization), 16
WIRED, 191
Wired Digital, 131
wireless Internet, 7
within-the-ad responses, 133–134, 326
word-of-mouth advertising, 220

Worldata, 129
WorldCom, 6, 60, 165, 233
WorldGate Communications, 15
World Intellectual Property Organization (WIPO), 16
World Trade Organization, 16
World Wide Web for global marketing, 34–35
WRFs (Web Response Forms), 69–71. *See also* Web sites effectiveness measurement
banner advertising termination point, 71–72, 127, 134
call to action, 70
construction basics, 72–75
copy for, 73
downloading instructions in, 73
filling-out, 73
fulfillment from, 72, 73, 193
headlines, 72
intersponding model and, 42–43
lead generation and qualification, 71–72, 74
"leaking leads," 71
link to corporate Web site at end, 73–74
offer in, 70, 73
private access from, 73
product information in, 73
responses, capturing, 73–74
seminar (online) campaigns and, 72
testing, 75
Uniform Resource Locators (URLs), 70, 74
Web sites and, 47, 49, 50

X
Xing Technology, 164
XML (eXtensible Markup Language), 206

Y
Yahoo!
    communities, 251, 252
    Fushion Marketing, 164
    Industry Marketplace, 264
    search engine, 79, 82, 85–86, 87,
        93
Yankee Group, The, 13, 20, 346

YesMail, 109

Z
Zaplets, 119
ZDnet, 5, 112, 126, 147, 259
ZDUniversity, 183
Ziff-Davis, 183, 259
Zoomerang, 116

Reader Feedback Sheet

Your comments and suggestions are very important in shaping future publications. Please email us at *moreinfo@maxpress.com* or photocopy this page, jot down your thoughts, and fax it to (850) 934-9981 or mail it to:

Maximum Press

Attn: Jim Hoskins

605 Silverthorn Road

Gulf Breeze, FL 32561

_____

_____

_____

_____

_____

_____

_____

_____

_____

_____

_____

_____

_____

_____

_____

_____

_____

_____

*101 Ways to Promote
Your Web Site,
Third Edition*
by Susan Sweeney, C.A.
488 pages
$29.95
ISBN: 1-885068-57-3

*Marketing
With E-Mail,
Second Edition*
by Shannon Kinnard
352 pages
$29.95
ISBN: 1-885068-51-4

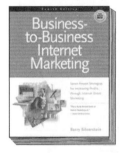

*Business-to-Business
Internet Marketing,
Fourth Edition*
by Barry Silverstein
528 pages
$29.95
ISBN: 1-885068-72-7

*Marketing on
the Internet,
Fifth Edition*
by Jan Zimmerman
512 pages
$34.95
ISBN: 1-885068-49-2

*Internet Marketing
for Information
Technology
Companies,
Second Edition*
by Barry Silverstein
464 pages
$29.95
ISBN: 1-885068-67-0

*The Business Guide to
Selling Through
Internet Auctions*
by Nancy Hix
608 pages
$29.95
ISBN: 1-885068-73-5

*Building Intranets
with Lotus Notes &
Domino 5.0,
Third Edition*
by Steve Krantz
320 pages
$39.95
ISBN: 1-885068-41-7

*Internet Marketing for
Less Than $500/Year,
Second Edition
by Marcia Yudkin*
352 pages
$29.95
ISBN: 1-885068-69-7

To purchase a Maximum Press book, visit your local bookstore
or call 1-800-989-6733 (US) or 1-850-934-4583 (International)
online ordering available at *www.maxpress.com*

101 Internet Businesses
You Can Start
From Home
by Susan Sweeney, C.A.
520 pages
$29.95
ISBN: 1-885068-59-X

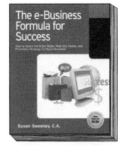

e-Business Formula
for Success
by Susan Sweeney, C.A.
360 pages
$34.95
ISBN: 1-885068-60-3

Exploring IBM
RS/6000 Computers,
Tenth Edition
by Jim Hoskins
and Doug Davies
440 pages
$39.95
ISBN: 1-885068-42-5

Exploring IBM @server
iSeries and AS/400
Computers,
Tenth Edition
by Jim Hoskins and
Roger Dimmick
560 pages
$39.95
ISBN: 1-885068-43-3

Exploring IBM @server
zSeries and
S/390 Servers,
Seventh Edition
by Jim Hoskins
and Bob Frank
432 pages
$59.95
ISBN: 1-885068-70-0

Exploring IBM
e-Business Software
by Casey Young
308 pages
$49.95
ISBN: 1-885068-58-1

Exploring IBM
@server xSeries
and PCs,
Eleventh Edition
by Jim Hoskins
and Bill Wilson
432 pages
$39.95
ISBN: 1-885068-39-5

Exploring IBM
Technology, Products
& Services,
Fourth Edition
edited by Jim Hoskins
256 pages
$54.95
ISBN: 1-885068-62-X

To purchase a Maximum Press book, visit your local bookstore
or call 1-800-989-6733 (US/Canada) or 1-850-934-4583 (International)
online ordering available at *www.maxpress.com*